BULGARIA UNDER COMMUNIST RULE

Bulgaria Under Communist Rule

J. F. BROWN

PRAEGER PUBLISHERS

New York • Washington • London

PRAEGER PUBLISHERS
111 Fourth Avenue, New York, N.Y. 10003, U.S.A.
5, Cromwell Place, London S.W.7, England
Published in the United States of America in 1970
by Praeger Publishers, Inc.

© 1970 by Praeger Publishers, Inc.

Library of Congress Catalog Card Number: 78–83329

Printed in the United States of America

Author's Preface

IN THIS BOOK I try to describe and analyze the main aspects of Communist rule in Bulgaria between 1953 and 1968. I have chosen to begin at 1953 for two reasons: first, because the death of Stalin marked the beginning of a process by which Bulgaria slowly and fitfully emerged from her Stalinist shell; and, second, because this period of Bulgarian history has received practically no intensive study in the West. The period from 1945 to 1953—and a bit beyond—has been most ably covered in the compendium "Bulgaria" edited by Professor L. A. D. Dellin and published in 1957. It has been described more generally by Professor Robert Lee Wolff in his excellent book *The Balkans in Our Time*; by Professor Hugh Seton-Watson in *The East European Revolution*; and by other writers. Particular aspects of this period also have been well covered —see, for example, the brilliant study of Traicho Kostov by Professor Adam Ulam in his *Titoism and the Cominform*. The Bulgarian Communist Party prior to its assumption of power has been described by Joseph Rothschild in his history of the Party up to 1936 and by Professor Nissan Oren in his study of the Party between 1934 and 1944. Professor Rothschild's is the best published study of the early history of any Eastern European Communist Party, and Professor Oren's work—still an unpublished Ph.D. dissertation at the time of writing—is a worthy complement to it. I have relied heavily on all these works—and on several others— for the first chapter of this book, which is really an introduction to the main subject. I have ended the book at 1968 simply because that was as late as I could go and still keep some kind of judgment

v

and perspective on the events discussed. One of the many tempta-
tions of writing contemporary history is to try to include everything that has happened right up to the moment the book finally
goes to press. I have avoided this temptation, hoping that the
analysis and predictions I have made will not be too quickly
shattered and that my study may be as complete and rounded
as any work of contemporary history can be.

The first eight chapters deal with the political and economic
development of Communist Bulgaria on a more or less chronological basis, bringing the situation up to 1968. Then follow four
chapters dealing with particular aspects of public life and policy
throughout the period of Communist rule. They cover education
and the problems of youth, agrarian policy, the cultural and intellectual scene, and foreign policy. These subjects lend themselves
readily to separate treatment and I considered it more convenient
not to include them in a chronological narrative. The last chapter
is a brief summing-up and judgment on the achievements and
failures of the Communist regime.

Bulgaria is the least noticed of all the Eastern European Communist states (including even Albania, which achieved fame, if
not fortune, in the early sixties). In some ways her obscurity has
been deserved; she has had little impact on the Eastern European
scene; her internal policy has led to no real developments in the
form or substance of Communist rule as such; and in Communist
ideological terms her rulers have added little to the "treasury of
Marxism-Leninism." In such a situation there is a danger that the
writer will strain every nerve to try to make his subject more interesting than it really is. This is another temptation I hope I have
avoided. But the following pages should show that Bulgaria between 1953 and 1968 was by no means an eventless continuum,
that this decade and a half was marked by periods of ferment,
political drama, and disruption, and that the period as a whole
was one of gigantic economic and social transformation. These
facts persuaded me that writing this book was an attempt worth
making.

I could not have written it without access to the archives of
Radio Free Europe in Munich, which were generously placed at
my disposal, nor could I have written it without the collaboration
of several of my Bulgarian colleagues there. For several years I
specialized in the study of Bulgarian affairs and received from
these colleagues nothing but the most wholehearted help. Many
parts of this book are based on Radio Free Europe analyses. Some

of these I wrote myself, others I helped to prepare; others were mainly the work of my co-workers. I wish particularly to thank Miss Rada Nikolaeva, who taught me to read Bulgarian and who prepared the material for the indices of this book. I also owe much to Kaloyan Kaloyanoff, a colleague of several years, for his generous help and encouragement. There are several others I would wish to name but the publicity would do their relatives in Bulgaria no good. Among other colleagues who can be named I wish to single out Michael Costello, Harry Trend, Henry Schaefer, and Paul Collins. I must add, however, that the views expressed in this book are my own, as are any errors that may disfigure it. I thank my secretary, Francis Le Towt, not only for typing the first draft of the manuscript but also for furthering the work in innumerable other ways. Edith Thorma excellently typed large parts of the final draft. To Ralph Walter, Director of Radio Free Europe, my thanks go for his encouragement and the general help that RFE has always given me.

The final touches to this study were put when I was a Senior Fellow at the Research Institute on Communist Affairs at Columbia University headed by Professor Zbigniew Brzezinski. At the Institute I wish especially to thank Mrs. Christine Dodson for her cheerful and resourceful help.

Finally, as ever, thanks to Margaret for her wisdom and patience and to Alison and Julie, to both of whom I dedicate this book, for just being there.

J. F. BROWN

New York City
June, 1969

Contents

BULGARIA UNDER COMMUNIST RULE

I

The Foundations of Communist Power

BULGARIA'S POSITION during World War II was a peculiar one. By her declaration of war against Britain and the United States in December, 1941, she placed herself squarely on Germany's side against the Western allies. But she never declared war on the Soviet Union. This was partly due to the shrewdness of Czar Boris, who hoped by diplomatic means to gain the maximum advantage out of the war without becoming directly involved in it, and partly to the government's awareness that a war with the Soviet Union would be distinctly unpopular with the majority of the Bulgarian population. Britain, on the other hand, had never been popular in Bulgaria—largely because her traditional Balkan policy had worked against what all Bulgarians considered the rightful claims of their country to territories denied them since independence in 1878. Britain was blamed for the fact that the Macedonian territories, now part of Yugoslavia and Greece, had not been incorporated into the new Bulgarian Kingdom. As for the United States, it was more popular but little known, and the declaration of war against her aroused little or no emotion.

At first it seemed that Bulgaria was doing very well out of her peculiar wartime position. Even before her declaration of war on the Western allies, she had recovered practically all of the territory she claimed had been wrongly denied her and for which she had suffered such losses in the Balkan Wars and in World War I. In August, 1940, she regained South Dobrudja, lost to Rumania in 1913, and by supporting Germany in her Balkan campaign in the spring of 1941 against Yugoslavia and Greece, she fulfilled her

3

irredentist demands for Macedonia and parts of Greek Thrace. The policy of Boris and his premier, Bogdan Filov, seemed to have paid off perfectly. All that was now needed was to sit tight and await the Axis victory against the Western allies and the Soviet Union which looked distinctly probable. In the meantime, Bulgaria was escaping the physical destruction of war. German troops were stationed in the country but they behaved themselves well. Economic conditions were good and most sections of the community were well off.

Not all Bulgarians, of course, shared the mood of general satisfaction. The pro-German alliance worried the leaders of those political parties opposed to the government, such as the Agrarians, the Democratic Party, and the Social Democrats. These leaders also strongly opposed the dictatorial nature of the Boris regime in domestic affairs. But these leaders, too, had been fully committed to the recovery of Bulgaria's "lost" territories and could not, therefore, wholeheartedly oppose a policy which had achieved precisely that. Moreover, representatives of these democratic parties continued to hold seats in the *Subranie*, the Bulgarian parliament; the Boris regime, though increasingly authoritarian, still kept at least a semblance of constitutional practice. These representatives of the "tolerated opposition," though reduced to ineffectiveness, could still air their views from time to time and were officially part of the political process. Total opposition, therefore, was practically confined to the Communists. But even had the Communist Party been strong numerically and organizationally it could have made little headway against the nationalist euphoria so marked in the early period of World War II.

As it was, the Bulgarian Communist Party was not strong either numerically or organizationally. An offshoot of the Bulgarian Social Democratic Party founded in 1891, the Party began to take definite shape in 1903 when the Social Democrats split into "broad" and "narrow" factions, the latter under Dimitur Blagoev, the "father" of Bulgarian Communism. It was this "narrow" faction—a counterpart to the Bolsheviks in Russia—which formed the nucleus of the Communist Party. In 1919 it left the Second (Socialist) International and took part in the forming of the Third (Communist) International in Moscow, assuming the name of the Bulgarian Communist Party (BCP).[1] As the oldest Communist Party in the Balkans and the Party that produced such in-

[1] See Joseph Rothschild, *The Communist Party of Bulgaria: Origins and Development, 1893–1936* (New York, 1959).

ternational giants as Blagoev, Vassil Kolarov and especially Georgi Dimitrov, the BCP enjoyed a great reputation in the Comintern and among leftist opinion generally. But this reputation abroad was hardly matched by any great success or political aptitude at home. Its following, in an overwhelmingly peasant country, was largely confined to intellectuals, some students, and certain groups among the small working class; before World War II it never exceeded a membership of 30,000.[2] For mass following it could not compete with the Bulgarian Agrarian Union, the party of the peasants. Its difficulties were compounded by constant interference in its affairs by the Comintern in Moscow, ineptitude and misjudgment on the part of its leaders at home, and fitful periods of rigorous persecution by the Bulgarian authorities. After a disastrously unsuccessful uprising in September, 1923, it resorted to acts of terrorism that culminated in the bloody failure to assassinate Czar Boris in the *Sveta Nedelia* cathedral in Sofia in 1925. After this disaster it faded for several years into almost complete insignificance. It revived again considerably in 1931–32 in popularity and organizational strength under the *Naroden Blok* regime, a type of popular-front experiment that proved to be shortlived. Later, persecuted by successive regimes that were becoming increasingly authoritarian, and weakened by "left sectarian" schisms that also rent many other Communist Parties during the same period, it again lapsed into almost complete ineffectiveness.

The Party During the War

In mid-1941, when the Germans attacked the Soviet Union, the Party had managed partly to recover from the blows of the thirties. In 1939 it had merged with the extreme left-wing Workers Party, which was also illegal. At the time of the German attack on the Soviet Union it claimed 10,600 organized members and a youth organization of 19,000.[3] Directing it from within Bulgaria itself was a Politburo of five which included three names later to become famous in Bulgarian history; Traicho Kostov, who was Party Secretary; Tsola Dragoicheva; and Anton Yugov. Directing it from Moscow, insofar as this could effectively be done, was a buro-in-exile composed of Dimitrov, Kolarov, Georgi Damyanov,

[2] L. A. D. Dellin (ed.), *Bulgaria* (New York, 1956), p. 112.

[3] Figures quoted by Nissan Oren, "The Bulgarian Communist Party, 1934–1944" (unpublished Ph.D. dissertation, Columbia University, 1960), p. 202.

Stanke Dimitrov, and the newly added Vulko Chervenkov. All except Stanke Dimitrov, killed while trying to land in Bulgaria in 1944, were also to play decisive roles in Communist Bulgaria.

After the German invasion of the Soviet Union, the Bulgarian Communists were formally committed to a policy of armed resistance, but this policy was never seriously implemented until after the Soviet victory at Stalingrad in 1943 and did not gain full momentum until Soviet troops entered Rumania and began to approach the Bulgarian border. There were several reasons for this. The Communists were held in considerable suspicion by the bulk of the population which, until late in the war, was relatively well off and untouched by the rigors of the conflict. In this situation, armed resistance could not get enough support to be effective, as it did in Yugoslavia. There was also the fact that Bulgaria was not fighting Russia; hence an important psychological spur to armed resistance was lacking. These two factors aroused much questioning among Communists themselves about the wisdom of armed resistance. Many Party members were content to settle for less extreme measures such as sabotage, strikes, and quiet infiltration of the Bulgarian armed forces, and to wait till the time was more suitable for armed struggle. Finally there was the alertness and power of the Bulgarian armed forces and particularly the security police, which ruthlessly hunted down Communists and their sympathizers.

Inevitably, after the Communist consolidation of power, attempts were made to magnify the size of the resistance effort during the war. At times the impression was given that the Bulgarian effort could almost be placed alongside that of Tito and the Yugoslav Partisans. But the most reliable expert on the subject estimates that "the grand total of the active Bulgarian resistance at its peak might well have been in the vicinity of 12,000."[4] In view of the odds against them these 12,000 performed heroically and, on occasions, effectively. Those operating close to the Yugoslav frontier were the most successful because they could cross the frontier and gain the respite of the "free zone" Tito's Partisans had established just inside Yugoslavia. The most effective Bulgarian Partisan commando was Slavcho Trunski, who led a detachment in this area; his postwar career will be dealt with later in this book. The officer commanding all resistance forces toward the end of the war was Dobri Terpeshev, also to figure prominently in later pages; his performance was subsequently to be ignored in

[4] Oren, *op. cit.*, p. 280.

official accounts of the resistance because of his fall from political grace after 1950.

The Communists' main *political* efforts during the war were directed toward creating a broad anti-fascist coalition composed of all factions opposed to the Boris regime. But they failed to persuade the leaders of the Agrarians, the Social Democrats, and the Democratic Party to cooperate with them and this was the main reason for their isolation. Their proposed instrument for a combination of anti-fascist forces was the Fatherland Front, essentially a revival of the popular front idea of the thirties. Georgi Dimitrov first proposed it from Moscow as early as the end of 1941 and the program of the Front was first broadcast over the Soviet-based "Hristo Botev" radio in the summer of 1942. It was a broad, vague document, designed to appeal to all Bulgarians of democratic inclinations, and was very self-effacing about the demands of the Communist Party. As has been said, the Communist efforts made no impression on the leaders of three main democratic parties. But, as the war continued, this disappointment began partly to be offset by the response from certain democratic leaders who, though less prestigious than the intransigent Nikola Mushanov (Democratic Party), Dimitur Gichev (Agrarians), and Hrustiu Pastukhov (Social Democrats), nevertheless did offer the prospect of some mass support. A section of the Social Democrats, led by Grigor Cheshmedzhiev and Dimitur Niekov, agreed to cooperate although they had no liking for the Communists as such. Some members of the *Zveno* (Link), that had carried out the 1934 coup that ended the *Naroden Blok* experiment, also declared their willingness. The most notable of these were Kimon Georgiev and the real power behind *Zveno*, Colonel Damyan Velchev, who still retained some influence in the army. The most important allies gained by the Communists, however, were the *Pladne*[5] Agrarians, a left-wing offshoot of the main Agrarians, who had cooperated with the Communists in the thirties. In the absence of Dr. G. M. Dimitrov (Gemeto), who was in exile during the war, the *Pladne* Agrarians were led by Nikola Petkov. The son of a Liberal premier assassinated in 1906 and the younger brother of an Agrarian leader assassinated in 1924, Petkov, though little known politically, had both an appealing name and personality. Though not pro-Communist, he admired the Soviet Union and the courage and verve of many Bulgarian Communists; he also strongly believed in a

[5] The name means *Noon*, the title of the group's newspaper.

democratic-Communist coalition. He was, therefore, ready to listen to Communist proposals.

In September, 1943, the Fatherland Front took organizational shape through the formation of its first National Committee. From then on the Communists had an instrument with which to work, and this proved increasingly viable as the war drew to its close and the victorious Soviet troops approached ever nearer. Though the Communists continued to seek the cooperation of outstanding personalities like Gichev and Mushanov, they had already accomplished the classic ploy of splitting the opposition, actual or potential. By successfully winning over the *Pladne* Agrarians and the Social Democrats of Cheshmedzhiev, they were weakening the unity of those democratic forces with which they would have to contend when the fascist government was overthrown.

It was during the twelve months between the formation of the National Committee of the Fatherland Front and the Communist led *coup d'état* of September 9, 1944, that armed resistance reached its peak. This coincided with the steady disintegration of the fascist regime in Bulgaria. Boris, who had been expected to steer Bulgaria out of the war, had died mysteriously in August, 1943, after a visit to Hitler. The regime was now completely dominated by Filov, who had become the effective leader of the three-man regency (created because the royal successor, Simeon II, was a minor). Filov and the new premier, Dobre Bozhilov, continued the regime's strongly pro-German policy and resolute persecution of Communists. But as Soviet troops rolled inexorably toward the Rumanian frontier, their policy carried less and less conviction.

The Communists, however, continued to press for cooperation with the "tolerated" opposition leaders like Gichev, Mushanov, and Pastukhov and, for a short time, even negotiated—abortively —with Premier Ivan Bagryanov, who replaced Bozhilov in the spring of 1944. In the light of what was to happen later it may seem odd that the Communists were so eager for the cooperation of these "bourgeois" leaders, especially since they already had the cooperation of certain non-Communist groups in the Fatherland Front. Their attitude can best be explained by their complete unawareness that the final victory and full power were so close at hand. The Soviet armies, though advancing swiftly, were expected to encounter stiff opposition on Rumanian soil; no one suspected that the Antonescu government there would be overthrown and that Rumania would then enter the war on the allied side. Moreover,

Bulgaria was "neutral" in the Russo-German conflict; hence, it was far from certain that Soviet troops would occupy Bulgaria and hand the Communists power on a silver platter. Indeed, since Bulgaria was formerly at war with the Western allies, it was expected that any new government in Bulgaria would have to deal with them rather than the Russians in a victor-vanquished relationship. The Western allies would certainly insist on an important place in any new government for men like Gichev, Mushanov, and Pastukhov.

Events soon proved that such caution was not necessary. Rumania capitulated on August 23, 1944; the Soviet Union not only refused to recognize Bulgaria's neutrality but declared war on the democratic government of Muraviev, who replaced Bagryanov at the beginning of September. On September 9, 1944—to become the most celebrated day in the Bulgarian Communist calendar— the Muraviev government itself was overthrown and the Fatherland Front government was installed.

The Fatherland Front Government

In the first Fatherland Front government that took power immediately after September 9, 1944, Communists were by no means conspicuous. In the Regency Council of three, there was only one Communist, Todor Pavlov, another name that will figure frequently in this study. Among the sixteen members of the Council of Ministers, headed by Kimon Georgiev of *Zveno*, there were only two Communists, one at the Ministry of the Interior, the other at the Ministry of Justice. It seemed that they were being modest indeed.

But, in terms of what the Communists saw as their main task immediately after September 9, they had the right amount of power in the right places. The first essential was to rout all sources of opposition in the country at large so as to secure their base of power. For this they needed control of the police and the courts: hence their insistence on holding the Ministries of the Interior and Justice. Anton Yugov, as Minister of the Interior, founded the "People's Militia" which, backed by the Red Army and a mushrooming security apparatus, terrorized the country by mass arrests. The "judicial" counterpart of the People's Militia were the "People's Courts" which condemned thousands of real or imagined enemies of the new order to death or to long periods of imprisonment. All the apprehended leaders of the wartime fascist governments—Filov, Bozhilov, and Bagryanov among many others —were executed. Some of the democratic politicians the Communists had been trying so assiduously to woo a little earlier—men like Gichev and Mushanov—received prison sentences. The blameless Muraviev received a life sentence. In the country as a whole the purges and trials ranged far and wide. The new regime officially admitted 2,138 death sentences and 1,940 long prison terms.[6] The number was certainly much larger both for death sentences and jail terms.

No one can condone these massacres: the Bulgarian Communists had the dubious distinction of making the bloodiest beginning of all the new regimes in Eastern Europe. At the same time, terror as an instrument of government had its precedents in Bulgaria. The White terror after the overthrow of the Agrarian leader Stambolisky in 1923, and after the abortive Communist rebellion in September of that year, was not much different in principle from what went on after September 9, 1944. Indeed, what probably made the new Red terror more atrocious than it might otherwise have been was the lust for vengeance nursed by many Communists. The older ones could remember 1923 and the persecution afterwards. Fresh in the memory of old and young alike were the wartime brutalities of the police and security services. There were many old scores to settle and most were settled without mercy. If many innocent people got in the way during the process, the new Bulgarian leaders were hardly squeamish enough to be concerned over them.

While this mass terror was proceeding, the Communists were completely reorganizing local government to their own advantage. This was done through the creation of Fatherland Front committees, dominated by the Party, and answerable to it rather than to the nominal government in Sofia. The director of this operation was Tsola Dragoicheva.

Once they had eliminated the mass of enemies of the new regime, real or imagined, the Communists set about removing all vestiges of independence from the Fatherland Front. The men they had induced to cooperate with them, like Petkov and Cheshmedzhiev, had political bases of their own and believed in genuine cooperation on a democratic basis. The Communists, therefore, began the second phase of their splitting tactics. Their main targets were the *Pladne* Agrarians, their only partners with anything like a following in the country. Dr. G. M. Dimitrov, who had re-

[6] Robert Lee Wolff, *The Balkans in Our Time* (New York, 1967), p. 293.

turned from wartime exile and was bent on a more independent policy for his party, had now resumed its leadership; he was forced to resign and subjected to such threats that he took refuge in the office of the American political representative in Sofia. He was later allowed to leave the country. Nikola Petkov, the wartime leader of *Pladne*, took over the leadership once again; he was also a deputy premier in the government. But Petkov also showed an intolerable independence and in August, 1945, he was removed in favor of Alexander Obbov, an old *Pladne* leader who was the kind of pliant tool the Communists wanted. Obbov was later succeeded by Georgi Traikov, who has figured prominently in the development of Communist rule in Bulgaria. The same treatment was accorded the Socialist, Cheshmedzhiev. He, and many of his colleagues were removed from their posts and Dimitur Neikov was left in charge of the rump Socialist group that was still prepared to cooperate. In the meantime a drastic purge had begun in the armed forces which culminated in the dismissal of Damyan Velchev from the post of Minister of War. Velchev had served the Communist cause well, but he was a man of character and had influence in the army in his own right. Therefore, he could not be trusted to control such an important instrument of power. He was luckier than most; at the end of 1946 he became Minister to Bern, where he passed his days quietly till his death in 1954.

The New Edifice

Georgi Dimitrov arrived from Moscow late in 1945 and found the domestic situation well in hand. His most important immediate task was to supervise the erection of a new political and constitutional edifice to reflect the rapid changes forced on the country. The monarchy was clearly anachronistic in the present situation. After a plebiscite held in September, 1946, it was abolished and Bulgaria was proclaimed a People's Republic. The plebiscite was, of course, conducted in a manner less than fair. Had it been held under free conditions, the end result—the declaration of a republic—might well have been the same, however, since the monarchy had suffered severe losses of prestige as a result of Bulgaria's disastrous alignments.

More significant were the elections for a Grand *Subranie*[7] to

[7] To be distinguished from an ordinary regular *Subranie*. A Grand *Subranie*, according to the Tirnovo Constitution of 1879, was necessary to change the Constitution.

formulate a new constitution for the republic. This took place in October, 1947, and, for the last time, a "tolerated opposition" was allowed to participate. This opposition was dominated by the Agrarians led by Nikola Petkov who, after his expulsion from the Fatherland Front, had gone over to open opposition to the Communists and was behaving with great courage in the face of increasing terror. Some Socialists, now led by Kosta Lulchev, and some independent liberals made up the opposition which united behind Petkov. The continued tolerance of an opposition in view of all the repressions that had taken place is perhaps puzzling. It can be explained only as a gesture to placate the American and British missions which had been in Bulgaria since 1945 and had done their best to mitigate the terror and the blatantly undemocratic practices the Communists had conducted. The new regime was also anxious to win diplomatic recognition, which Britain and the United States had not yet granted.

The results of the elections, held in an atmosphere of terror, were revealing. The Fatherland Front won, of course, but the opposition polled 1,300,000 votes—almost 30 per cent. This was not just a tribute to the courage of so many Bulgarian citizens; it is yet another point—this study will produce several more—undermining the widely held notion that the Bulgarian people welcomed the new Communist regime, its policy and its exclusively pro-Soviet orientation. If, in an election held under such conditions, some 30 per cent of the electorate rejected the Communists, then the Communists might well have found themselves in an embarrassing minority in a fair election, as the Hungarian Communists did in 1946.

That the Communists' toleration of the opposition was just a cynical tactic was shown by what happened after the elections. The new government, with Dimitrov himself as Premier, represented Bulgaria at the Paris Peace Treaty in February, 1947. This treaty, signed by all the former belligerents, recognized the new Bulgaria as a sovereign state, a fact to which all the signatories agreed. One day after the U.S. Senate had ratified the treaty, in June, 1947, Petkov was arrested. The story of his trial, his judicial murder, and his fantastic courage, though hardly relevant here, is an epic in itself.[8] The incident shocked the free world and brought shame on the Bulgarian government. But, at the same time, Petkov's high principles and enduring courage exemplified the forti-

[8] See, especially, Michael Padev, *Dimitrov Wastes No Bullets, Nikola Petkov: The Test Case* (London, 1948).

tude and decency of the Bulgarian nation. The Bulgarian people gained by his tragedy; the Bulgarian regime lost whatever sympathy it may have had.

The execution of Petkov marked the end of any effective opposition in Bulgaria. During 1948 the *Gleichschaltung* proceeded apace. The puppet Socialist Party was merged with the Communists, Lulchev was sentenced to a long prison term, and *Zveno* was disbanded. So was the free Agrarian Union. What remained was the Agrarian Union under Obbov and later under Traikov. This became the only political party in Bulgaria other than the Communist. But its complete subordination to the Communist Party was never in doubt. At the fifth BCP congress in December, 1948, Dimitrov had every reason to feel satisfied. The "progress" since 1945 had indeed been impressive.

The Dimitrov Constitution

Reflecting and legitimizing the new edifice that had been so hurriedly built was the "Dimitrov" constitution, approved by the Grand *Subranie* in December, 1947. It replaced the very liberal "Tirnovo" constitution of 1879 and was almost completely modeled on the Soviet "Stalin" constitution of 1936. (As originally presented to the *Subranie,* the new constitution contained many of the old "Tirnovo" principles. But this was quietly scrapped in favor of the virtual copy of the Soviet model that was eventually approved.)

The constitution proclaimed Bulgaria a "people's republic" with a "people's democratic" form of government.[9] It denied the principle of separation between legislative, executive, and judicial forms of government, declaring all power to be vested in the people, with universal suffrage for all over 18. It included provisions for the public ownership of the means of production but also sanctioned the existence of private property—here it differed from the Soviet model—provided this was not detrimental to the public interest. It gave the state *carte blanche* to nationalize whatever it wanted to. Social welfare was considered the sole responsibility of the state. In its provisions for the legislature the new constitution followed the Soviet model almost to the letter. The National Assembly (*Subranie*) was to be the supreme organ of state power

[9] For the full text, see Andrew Gyorgy, *Governments of Danubian Europe* (New York, 1949), p. 337.

and the only legislative organ of the Republic. It was to elect a Presidium, appoint the government, amend the constitution, decide on war and peace, approve the budget and state plans, grant amnesties and select judges of the Supreme Court as well as the State Prosecutor. It was to be elected for a term of four years on the basis of one representative to 30,000 inhabitants and was to hold ordinary sessions twice a year. The laws it passed were to be promulgated and published through the Presidium. The Presidium of the *Subranie* was formally to combine both legislative and executive authority, and was to be in permanent session. It was to be elected by the *Subranie* and to consist of 19 members, including a President, two vice-presidents and a secretary. The President of the Presidium soon came to be regarded as the titular head of state.

The government was described as the "supreme executive and administrative organ of the state." It was to consist of a President of the Council of Ministers (premier), any number of vice presidents (deputy premiers) and ministers as well as presidents of various commissions—such as Planning, State Control, etc.—holding ministerial rank. The government was to be responsible to the *Subranie* or, when this body was not in session, to the Presidium.

The constitution divided the country, for administrative purposes, into districts and communes, each run by a People's Council with a president at its head. The Council of Ministers in Sofia could annul any action taken by a local council, however.

In the judiciary, the "supreme judicial control over every kind and grade of court" was to be exercised by the Supreme Court, elected by the *Subranie* for a five year term. The courts generally were to comprise elected judges and lay assessors. The State Prosecutor was to be elected by the *Subranie* for a period of five years and was specially assigned to see to the punishment of crimes affecting the "state, national, and economic interests" of the Republic.

Like all Communist constitutions, the Bulgarian was impressive in that part dealing with the rights and obligations of citizens. A great many civil liberties, as well as economic and social rights, were explicitly guaranteed: equality before the law and equality of women; complete racial, national, and religious equality; special protection for working mothers and their children; the right (and duty) to work and to receive a free education. In addition, labor and social benefits, like social security and limited working hours, were specifically guaranteed. Freedom of speech, press and as-

sembly were assured, as was the freedom to form associations "provided they were not contrary to the State and public order."
Associations aimed at reversing the system begun on September 9,
1944 were expressly forbidden.[10]

Any worthwhile analysis of the Dimitrov constitution would
require a constitutional or legal specialist. All that is relevant here
is to try to estimate its impact on the state's development. Its administrative provisions proved, in the main, workable until the
economy, and especially industry, became complex enough to demand more flexibility and autonomy and less of the centralized
control which characterized them. The administrative-territorial
reorganization of 1959 (See Chapter 6) was the first serious
attempt to cope with a defect which, by them, was becoming
intolerable. The best features of the constitution, in both intent
and implementation, were its labor and social welfare provisions
and its passages on education. Though the record of "bourgeois"
Bulgaria in public welfare and education had been relatively good,
the social philosophy contained in this part of the constitution
(as in similar parts of all Communist constitutions) represented a
momentous advance. As for implementation, though this has been
less impressive than the intent, nonetheless many older Bulgarians
do concede that this is the one area where Communist rule has
brought benefit. To the young, however, who take such benefits
for granted, the Bulgarian welfare state means little or nothing.

The provisions guaranteeing civil liberties and political free-
doms arouse the greatest cynicism. These have never been fulfilled
in the Western sense of legality—nor, by the Communists' own
admission, were they fulfilled for long periods under their own
definition of socialist legality. In the constitution itself, these
guarantees were hedged with qualifications so broad as almost
to invite their abuse. And their abuse was made supremely easy
under a judicial system that was manifestly a part of the state's
security apparatus, where the presumption of guilt took precedence
over that of innocence.

Many educated Bulgarians—even those supporting the new
regime—must have contrasted this new document with the old
"Tirnovo" constitution it replaced. The "Tirnovo" constitution,
approved in 1879, was astonishingly progressive for its time and
remained a model for liberal constitutionalists for many years. It

[10] The foregoing summary of the most important points of the Dimitrov
constitution was based on the excellent treatment in Dellin, *op. cit.*, pp. 89–
101.

is easy, of course, to be cynical about this document—to say that it was more honored in the breach than the observance—but this would not be quite fair. Even in the grimmest days of Bulgaria's history as a newly independent state, the "Tirnovo" constitution remained an inspiration, a spur, and a yardstick by which the sometimes sordid political practices of the time could be judged. The greatest testimony to its abiding influence was the fact that the first (rejected) draft of the new Communist constitution in 1947 contained a surprising number of its principles and provisions.[11] Such prestige the "Dimitrov" constitution could never claim.

The Organization of Religion

Any discussion on the groundwork laid by the Communists during this period should include at least a brief discussion of their policy toward organized religion.

The Bulgarian people were overwhelmingly Eastern Orthodox in religion. At the 1934 census, 5,128,890 persons of a population of about six million were Orthodox (84.5 per cent).[12] The next largest group was Moslem (13.5 per cent), and the remainder were divided into insignificant numbers of Jews, Roman Catholics, Protestants, and Armenian Gregorians. When the medieval Bulgarian kingdoms were at their most powerful, the Bulgarian Church was a patriarchate headed by a Bulgarian Primate. After the Turkish conquest it lost its independent status and, under the Ottoman *millet* system of administration, became part of the Orthodox *millet* headed by the Patriarchate of Constantinople. As such, it was largely run by Greek priests, with Greek as the recognized liturgical language.

Bulgarian Orthodox priests played a notable part in the beginning of the independence movement in the nineteenth century and an autonomous Bulgarian Church came to be regarded as an essential demand of the independence struggle. In 1870 the Turkish government permitted the establishment of an autocephalous Bulgarian Orthodox Church, known as an Exarchate. The area covered by this Exarchate included not only present-day Bulgaria

---

[11] On the "Tirnovo" constitution and its history, see Cyril E. Black, *The Establishment of Constitutional Government in Bulgaria* (Princeton, 1944).

[12] Dellin, *op. cit.*, p. 182.

but most of Macedonia and Thrace as well, a fact unquestionably strengthening the later Bulgarian claim to these territories. In 1872 the first Exarch of the new Church was elected but the Patriarchate of Constantinople refused to recognize the new Church. The Bulgarian Church was, therefore, considered schismatic until 1945 when Constantinople agreed to accept the new Exarch, Stefan.

The Bulgarian Church was a state church and its clergy were state officials paid by the state. It was never, therefore, the alternative center of power to the state that the Roman Catholic Church was in countries like Poland, Hungary, and even Czechoslovakia. Hence it was easier for the Communists to subdue it and induce it to cooperate. But this was not done without severe persecution in the first years after 1945. Some church leaders were executed and imprisoned and many priests were either imprisoned or banished from their parishes. Even the Exarch, Stefan, originally friendly to the new order, was found too independent and banished to a monastery in 1948.

But the Bulgarian Communists, though despising religion and rigorously persecuting independent-minded members of the clergy, have seen the value of the Orthodox Church as a symbol of Bulgarian national unity. It was they who encouraged the healing of the schism with Constantinople and approved the appointment of Stefan as Exarch in 1945; a few years later, in 1951, they encouraged the elevation of the Exarchate to a Patriarchate, a status the Bulgarian Church had not enjoyed for 600 years. In 1953 Metropolitan Kiril of Plovdiv was elected Bulgarian Patriarch. Since then, Kiril has collaborated closely with the Communist regime but has sought to preserve as much of the dignity of the Church as possible in very difficult circumstances. In the 1960's he has become known as a quiet but persistent advocate of closer collaboration between the Orthodox and Roman Catholic Churches, and of Christian unity in general.

But it was not only as a propaganda symbol of national unity that the Communists supported the international claims of the Bulgarian Church. Their action was also one facet of the exclusively pro-Soviet orientation of their foreign policy. By the creation of a Bulgarian Patriarchate, the Russian Patriarchate (long an instrument of Czarist and then of Soviet foreign policy) was strengthened in its rivalry with the declining Constantinople Patriarchate for effective primacy over all Orthodox Christians. Without pressure from the Russian Church it is very doubtful whether Constantinople would have officially recognized the Bulgarian Patriarchate. The Bulgarian Church, like the Bulgarian state, became a client of its counterpart in Moscow.

Thus, Communist policy toward the Church in Bulgaria has been to increase its standing and prestige abroad while breaking any semblance of its independence at home. By and large, this policy has been impressively successful.

The Economic Groundwork

Nationalization, which was introduced comprehensively in all the Eastern European states after 1945, was nothing new for Bulgaria. Ever since independence in 1878 the railroads, port facilities, and most of the mines had been under state control. Beginning at the end of 1947 and continuing through the following year, this state control was extended to all important branches of industry, banks and insurance companies, practically all foreign and some domestic trade concerns, and large urban buildings. In terms of gross output of industry, the share of the nationalized sector in 1948 came to 85 per cent. But in that year the state sector only accounted for about 39 per cent of the national income—45 per cent if one includes the agricultural cooperatives.[13] The discrepancy is explained, of course, by the fact that Bulgaria was still overwhelmingly an agrarian country and agricultural collectivization had not yet been extensively introduced.

In 1947, before the extreme nationalization campaign had actually begun, the Fatherland Front government launched a Two-Year Plan of economic reconstruction aimed at making up for the damage of wartime and considerably surpassing the industrial production levels of 1939. Actually Bulgaria had suffered very little economic damage in the war compared with Yugoslavia and Greece, and even Rumania. Allied air raids from 1943 onwards had done considerable damage but had in no way crippled the economy and there had been no real fighting on Bulgarian soil. Bulgaria did have to pay the costs of stationing Soviet troops on her territory until 1947 but that was just about the only financial payment she ever did make for her part in the war. The peace treaty of 1947 fixed her war reparations to Yugoslavia at $25 million and to Greece at $50 million. The Yugoslavs—before Tito's break with Stalin—graciously remitted their $25 million; Bulgaria's refusal to pay the debt to Greece bedeviled relations

[13] Dellin, *op. cit.*, pp. 268–69.

between the two countries for almost twenty years after hostilities had ended.

The Two-Year Plan, which the regime claimed in 1948 had been overfulfilled by 6 per cent, already showed the direction the Bulgarian economy was to take in the years ahead. The main concentration was, of course, on electrification and heavy industry. The industrial city of Dimitrovgrad in the Maritsa valley, with huge cement and chemical plants, was planned, as was a large hydroelectric dam near Kazanlik in the Tundja valley. Industry and mining were scheduled to receive 45 per cent of the total amount invested, while agriculture was to make do with a skimpy 6 per cent.

The First Five-Year Plan (1949–53) was a much more elaborate, ambitious affair. As approved by the Fifth Party Congress in December, 1948, the gross value of industrial output was to increase by 119 per cent compared to 1948, or more than four times the pre-war level. Out of this increase, Sector "A" (heavy industry) was to increase by 220 per cent and Sector "B" (light and consumer industries) only by 75 per cent. Within heavy industry itself, the lion's share of investments went to coal, iron, steel, electricity, and machine tools. Since heavy industry in Bulgaria had hardly existed before the war, the astronomic percentage increase planned for some branches meant very little.[14] They were, however an earnest of the regime's intentions to transform Bulgaria as rapidly as possible. The ratio between the value of heavy and light industry in 1939 had been 24:76; in 1948 it was 30:70; in 1953 it was to be 45:55. Under such planning the standard of living, despite the lip-service constantly paid to its improvement, was grossly neglected. Agriculture, however, received greater attention than in the two-year reconstruction plan: its share of total investments over the five-year period was to be 17.4 per cent.

As usual, during the implementation of the plan there were many deviations from its original stipulations. Agriculture, for example, fared less well than had been promised in the allocation of investments, receiving only 13.4 per cent of the total between 1949 and 1952 against the 17.4 per cent planned; the total gross investment fell considerably short of what had been projected. The plan as a whole was eventually declared fulfilled by the end of 1952, i.e., one year ahead of schedule. However, the methods of calculation used and the massive manipulation of the resulting statistics (to be referred to again in the course of this study) were

14 Dellin, *op. cit.*, p. 270.

such that no real assessment of this claim can be made. But the regime's own figures make it clear that only the overall industrial target had been fulfilled by the end of 1952 and even this was not in the proportions specified in the original plan. In agriculture the performance fell considerably below what had been planned.[15]

The Destruction of the Home Communists

By 1949 the stage had been set for that trial of strength between "home" and the Soviet trained "Muscovite" Communists which became a feature of nearly all the Eastern European states in the early years after the imposition of Communist rule. A power struggle between these two factions might well have occurred in most of these states regardless of the Tito-Stalin rupture in 1948, but that event accelerated the struggle and "Titoism" provided a convenient issue for the Muscovites to use against their opponents. There was hardly any real struggle: Gomulka, Rajk, and Kostov were virtually powerless against the forces in Moscow that were bent on their destruction.

After the war, Traicho Kostov emerged as the most outstanding of the home Communists in the BCP. Indeed, in some respects, he was the most powerful man in the country. Dimitrov and Kolarov enjoyed far more prestige but, for a quarter of a century, had had relatively little contact with Bulgarian affairs. Kostov was virtually in charge of the economic recovery and expansion of Bulgaria and the establishment of the socialist structure of the economy. His earlier career had been similar to that of many older Bulgarian Communist leaders. Though a railway worker's son, he had studied law at Sofia University and had then become a revolutionary, suffering all the privations of this hazardous profession. He had a crippled back incurred from jumping through a window to escape the rigors of one of his many police interrogations. Kostov was an ardent Communist with a streak of toughness that made him both a ruthless official and a heroically tenacious opponent under pressure of any kind.

The full story of his humiliation, trial, and execution is not relevant to the purpose of this study and has, in any case, been fully told elsewhere.[16] In March, 1949, he was accused at a Central Com-

15 Dellin, *op. cit.*, p. 274.
16 See especially Adam Ulam, *Titoism and the Cominform* (Cambridge, Mass., 1952).

mittee meeting of being nationalist and anti-Soviet, and was dismissed from the Politburo and his posts as deputy premier and chairman of the Economic and Financial Commission. If one accepts the Stalinist definitions of "nationalist" and "anti-Soviet," there was indeed some truth in these charges, since Kostov had evidently objected to some economic agreements with the Soviet Union which he considered unfair to Bulgaria. Thus the accusation of Titoism crystallized against him (though Tito actually held a strong personal loathing for Kostov), and this was followed by the inevitable concomitant accusations that he had been an economic saboteur, a British spy, an agent of the royalist police, and so on. He was tried and executed in December, 1949, after a resolute defense in which he refused to admit some of the charges against him.

Even without the convenient issue of Titoism, a decisive power struggle within the BCP could not have been postponed much longer. Dimitrov was already sixty-three when he returned to Bulgaria in 1945, a tired, ravaged hero. Kolarov was sixty-eight, and in very poor health. The problem of succession was therefore a pressing one. None of the other returning Muscovites had anything resembling the prestige of Dimitrov and Kolarov, and so, from the standpoint of authority, stature, and experience, the leadership of the Party would logically pass to one of the home Communists. Kostov was the natural choice but Yugov and Terpeshev, also home Communists, had a stronger claim than any of the Muscovites. Clearly the prospect of the home Communists dominating any future regime was an impossible one for Stalin to tolerate, particularly in view of the break with Yugoslavia and Kostov's personality and independent spirit. Therefore, a new Muscovite champion had to be found and he soon emerged in the person of Vulko Chervenkov.

Chervenkov will play a most important part in the study that follows and his personality and abilities will be analyzed in the course of it. What is important to note here, however, is that in the early postwar period very few people imagined he would achieve power. He had been in the Soviet Union since 1925 but had not been prominent among the Bulgarian exiles there and was little known in Bulgaria itself (he had made broadcasts to his native land over the Soviet-sponsored "Hristo Botev" radio, but under an assumed name). He returned to Bulgaria only in 1946 to become the Chairman of the Committee on Science, Art, and Culture, a post that hardly seemed the stepping-stone to supreme political power. But he had three things on his side: first, he did have brains, personality, and ruthlessness; second, he had married Georgi Dimitrov's sister; third—and most important—he was trusted by the Soviets, who had evidently picked him as the successor to Dimitrov and Kolarov.

His turn was to come soon. Dimitrov went to Moscow in January, 1949, and died there the following July (he had clearly outlived his usefulness to Moscow and this, together with the terror-ridden atmosphere at Stalin's court, led to speculation over the nature and cause of his death). Kolarov died soon after Dimitrov, in January, 1950. By then it was clear that Chervenkov was Moscow's nominee and that the political power of the home Communists was fast declining. Yugov lost his post as Minister of the Interior in 1948 and this was only his first step down from political prominence. Others followed him, including Terpeshev and Tsola Dragoicheva. By 1950 Chervenkov was both Premier and Secretary-General of the Bulgarian Communist Party, a meteoric rise for a man little known five years before. He quickly set about further humiliating the older home Communists and removing practically all of them from key posts in Party and government. He replaced them either by Muscovites loyal to him (such as Ruben Levy-Avramov, Karlo Lukanov, and General Petur Panchevski) or by members of the younger generation of home Communists (like Georgi Chankov, Georgi Tsankov, and Todor Zhikov). His policy was the sovietization of Bulgaria. Both the men he chose and the policy he followed will be discussed extensively in the following pages.

2

Stalin's Death and the New Course in Politics

STALIN'S DEATH on March 6, 1953, was officially greeted in Bulgaria by five minutes of silence, followed by the blowing of all sirens and the firing of cannon salutes. As a more permanent memorial to the Soviet leader, who probably received more official reverence in Bulgaria than in any other satellite, the Central Committee and the Ministerial Council ordered the erection of a huge statue of Stalin in the center of Sofia.

Then Bulgaria—both the regime and the people—waited. For the Bulgarian leaders, now even more than in Stalin's lifetime, Moscow was the focal point of their existence. The power struggle going on there clearly would affect their future, and none realized this better than Chervenkov himself. More completely than any other Eastern European leader, Chervenkov had modelled his style and scope of government on Stalin and none, except perhaps Bierut in Poland, owed his leading position to Stalin in quite the same degree. Chervenkov was born in 1900, the son of a noncommissioned officer in the Bulgarian Army. He had received a good general education, graduating from a Sofia gymnasium in 1919. Throughout his later student career he was active in political agitation against Bulgaria's participation in World War I. In 1919 he joined the Bulgarian Communist Party, but was still a relatively unknown member when he was forced to go to the Soviet Union after participating in the Sveta Nedelia bomb plot against Czar Boris in 1925. He attended the Marx-Engels Institute in Moscow and apparently also lectured there after graduation. There was no doubt that Chervenkov fully understood Communist ideology and, though lacking the intellectual stature of a man like Kolarov, was generally recognized by exile Bulgarians as a competent theoretician and a man of high intelligence.

Of towering physique and coarse, unprepossessing appearance, he was unpopular among his colleagues for his arrogance and sarcasm. Though he helped himself politically by marrying Dimitrov's sister, Elena, there is no reliable evidence to suggest that the two men were close friends. It is not difficult to see why Chervenkov appealed to the Soviets. He was young, vigorous and intelligent and, after twenty years of Soviet experience, he was thoroughly indoctrinated in the Stalinist ethos. He was a devoted Stalinist and was considered completely dependable. He could be relied on to be thoroughly dictatorial in Bulgaria but obedient and pliant to Moscow.

Chervenkov did assume dictatorial powers in Bulgaria. He not only combined the posts of Premier and Secretary-General of the Party but sought to dominate practically every aspect of public affairs, more so than any of his satellite counterparts. In the other Eastern European states—even in Yugoslavia, despite Tito's dominance—there was a rough division of labor even though one man was the recognized leader. Thus in Hungary, Rakosi was leader, but Gero handled economics and Revai culture and ideology. In Rumania there was a very uneasy division between the home Communist, Gheorghiu-Dej, and the Muscovites, Pauker and Luca. In Poland Hilary Minc was the economic dictator under Bierut and in Czechoslovakia the ailing Gottwald was incapable of wielding complete power. But in Bulgaria (with the possible exception of the military, where the Soviet-trained Georgi Damyanov and Ivan Mihailov became solidly entrenched), Chervenkov allowed no rivalry. Chervenkov's imitation of Stalin was particularly marked in his dominance of the cultural and ideological spheres. Here, his years of study at the Marx-Engels Institute in Moscow and his genuine interest in Bulgarian and Russian literature made him respected almost as much as his power made him feared.

Now his model and guarantor had suddenly left the scene. Chervenkov knew that, despite the mystic awe in which Stalin had been held, the Soviet Union was facing a power struggle and long-overdue policy changes were inevitable. Nor could Bulgaria be insulated against these changes even though some Stalinist policies, notably in the economic sphere, were still functional in undeveloped Bulgaria long after they had become obstacles to progress in the Soviet Union and the more advanced Eastern European states.

Understandably, Chervenkov's most immediate concern was for his own position. It must have been galling for a man of his dictatorial nature to see his supreme power threatened so soon after he had consolidated it. He had been both Premier and Secretary-General for less than three years; now Stalin's death would certainly accelerate the trend away from one-man rule towards collectivity, which had been signaled as early as the 19th CPSU congress in 1952. His actual position and influence were safe for the moment, since the new Soviet leadership would prefer stability in the satellites during the delicate period of transition. Nonetheless, even the theoretical sharing of power contained the seeds of danger and this Chervenkov knew. Moreover, though his power was virtually unchallenged after the decimation of the Kostovites, he had still been unable to eliminate men like Yugov and Dobri Terpeshev. Yugov, particularly, though humiliated in 1950, remained a Minister and a Politburo member, a possible rallying point for disaffection and enough of an opportunist to use any new trend for his own advantage.

As for the backbone of the regime, the Party apparatchiks only recently installed in their posts, the mood was apparently one of nervousness. Unofficial reports from Bulgaria at that time speak of relaxation and a greater permissiveness on the part of officials, almost an attempt to court favor with those they were governing. This was only natural. For many members of the new regime, the traumatic shock of Stalin's death would stir fears about the very survival of that regime and of the posts and privileges it had given them. The sullen passivity of the population could change into open hostility; hence the uneasiness of the country's new ruling class.

As for the population, its mood seems to have been one of both tense expectation and a certain relief. That there was a greater spirit of confidence in the country was shown by one foreign correspondent's report that many people seemed less afraid of contact with foreigners.[1] But the most notable example of the popular mood was the riot and strike of several hundred tobacco workers in Plovdiv in May over new regulations of work involving greater effort for an incommensurate reward. This certainly was a small affair compared with the massive demonstrations in East Germany and the riots in Pilsen that were soon to follow. But it was the first recorded evidence of popular resistance after the death of Stalin and, along with the earlier sporadic riots against collectivization

[1] *Neue Zuercher Zeitung*, April 27, 1953.

in 1948 and 1950, should serve to counterbalance the widespread assumption that the Bulgarian people passively accepted the imposition of their Communist system.[2]

This incident in Plovdiv had a by-product of some political importance. The leader sent from Sofia to deal with the strikers was none other than Anton Yugov. Though born in Greek Macedonia, Yugov had "adopted" Plovdiv as his Bulgarian home and had been a tobacco worker there himself; it not only became his parliamentary constituency after 1945 but his local power base. He was therefore the right man to send in many respects, but still a significant choice in view of his previous disgrace. It was both a sign of the regime's need of him and a first-class opportunity to re-establish himself politically. He seized it with both hands, promising the cheering workers a redress of their grievances, and returned in triumph to Sofia, once more a force to be reckoned with. Yugov's performance at Plovdiv was evidence of his effectiveness and skill as a politician. As Minister of the Interior in the bloody days of the Communist takeover, he had been unsurpassed throughout Eastern Europe for ruthlessness and brutality. Yet at Plovdiv he showed both courage and a disarming personality as well as the ability to grasp political opportunities. Whether the outcome of the Plovdiv strike was as happy for the workers as it was for him is doubtful. Yugoslav sources reported that eight ringleaders were subsequently sentenced to death,[3] a fact not confirmed by other more objective sources. It seems likely, however, that reprisals were indeed taken against the leading "trouble-makers."

The Plovdiv strike was the best Bulgarian example of the restlessness that sprang up throughout Eastern Europe immediately after Stalin's death. The reforms instituted by the new leaders in Moscow were motivated less by any restlessness in the Soviet Union than by the realization that the past system had become technically unviable. A distinguished Czechoslovak economist has since argued that this was also almost the sole reason for the "new course" in some of the Eastern European states after March, 1953. He claims that—at least in the more industrially advanced of these states—the scaling down of economic targets was made necessary solely by the workings of the economic cycle and not by any political need to respond to expressions of mass discontent.[4] Though this argument has much substance, it is too dogmatic even

---

[2] For a report on the Plovdiv strike, see *The Manchester Guardian*, July 6, 1953.
[3] Radio Belgrade, July 14, 1953.
[4] Josef Goldmann, *Planovane Hospodarstvi* (Prague), September, 1964.

when applied to the author's own Czechoslovakia. It is, therefore, much more dogmatic when applied to Bulgaria. The embryonic Bulgarian industry[5] was then (as it still is today) in a period of boom, and economic cycles were irrelevant. The main issue in Bulgaria was popular discontent in both agriculture and industry; the grievances were chiefly expressed in economic terms, but (in contrast to the protests in the Soviet Union) they had clear political overtones. Thus, the impetus for the new course certainly came from Moscow, but the situation to which it was applied in Bulgaria and in other Eastern European states, where Communist governments were so new, differed markedly from that in the Soviet Union, where the Communist system was nearly forty years old.

The Scope of the New Course

The first important sign of the new course in Bulgaria appeared almost immediately after Stalin's death: it was the relaxation of police terror. This is a process impossible to document, but the testimony of both visitors and citizens during that period confirmed the greater permissiveness in Bulgarian society as a whole. The secret police were still there, but their presence was felt less. Officials became more "human," citizens were encouraged to bring their grievances to the notice of the authorities; even such enemies-by-definition as kulaks and small landholders ("private peasants") were left alone more than they had been for the previous five years. It became a little easier to travel abroad and the government even permitted a trickle of emigration. The Party press began to urge officials to show more concern for the welfare of the masses and to work for greater participation in public affairs. Anti-state attitudes still had to be fought ruthlessly but greater care was necessary in ascertaining who the real enemies were.[6] In this campaign Cervenkov himself played a leading role and set a good example. He became more accessible to the public and the belief began to get around that if one could only get to Chervenkov then justice would be done. In various speeches, Bulgaria's "little Stalin" sought to change his image by cautioning against lack of discrimination in persecuting enemies and urging the application of what later be-

---

[5] It was only in August, 1953, that Bulgaria began producing its own steel, by the commissioning of the Lenin Metallurgical Plant at Dimitrovo (Pernik); Radio Sofia, August 8, 1953.

[6] See, for example, *Rabotnichesko Delo* (Sofia), July 16, 1953.

came known as "socialist legality."[7] Perhaps the most important symbol of these attempts to instill a new atmosphere was the amnesty for political prisoners which took effect on September 9, 1953, the ninth anniversary of Bulgaria's liberation. The number affected has never been made known but it was believed to be considerable; this amnesty apparently had a good effect on the population.

In the economic sphere the new course was introduced by degrees, in a number of steps that amounted to a considerable modification of previous policy. In August a decree of the Party Central Committee and the Ministerial Council authorized a reduction in the price of a large number of goods. The most important decreases affected meat, milk, and dairy products, the average reduction being in the range of 8 per cent. It was a "genuine" measure in that the goods affected included many consumed daily in every household. It was not mainly confined, as were many later price reductions in Bulgaria and the rest of Eastern Europe, to articles not in general use that had proved unsaleable.

In his speech commemorating the September 9 liberation anniversary, Chervenkov announced more concessions. This was the speech that confirmed the new course as the most important new plank in regime policy.[8] Most of the material concessions announced by Chervenkov went to the farmers. This was understandable, if only because the vast majority of the Bulgarian work force was still engaged in agriculture.[9] But it was also necessary, because progress in agriculture had been painfully slow, especially when compared with the spectacular quantitative increases in industrial production since 1948.[10] Chervenkov announced a reduction of between 10 and 50 per cent in compulsory deliveries from the collectivized sectors; the availability of credits for the collectives on better terms than before; and the cancellation of some debts which the collectives owed because of unpaid taxes. Other concessions were granted but these—especially the cuts in compulsory deliveries—were the most important and brought considerable relief to the collective farms. But no concessions whatever were granted to the private farmers who, according to officials, still cultivated

[7] See, for example, his speech on the eve of the liberation anniversary of September 9, the "new course speech"; *Rabotnichesko Delo*, September 9, 1953.

[8] *Ibid.*

[9] As late as 1959 it was estimated that agriculture provided some 70 per cent of total employment. See *U.N. Economic Survey of Europe, 1960* (Geneva, 1961), chap. 6, p. 22.

[10] *Ibid.*, chap. 6, p. 20.

nearly 40 per cent of the arable land at the beginning of the year, an estimate probably too conservative.[11] In fact a decree late in December, 1953, actually increased the grain delivery quotas for the private peasants. Clearly the aim was to make discrimination in favor of the collectivized peasant so obvious as to force the private peasants into the collectives.

The regime's determination to woo the peasants and win them over for collectivization was shown by a propaganda gambit that was used with increasing frequency after 1953. Former leaders of the Bulgarian Agrarian Union were sent out to try to persuade the peasants of the merits of collectivization and to convince them that the regime's agricultural policy was in the great tradition of the Agrarians established by Alexander Stambolisky. The fact that Stambolisky had been a bitter enemy of the Communists until his overthrow and murder in 1923 was now conveniently forgotten. The regime managed to persuade or coerce the great leader's son, Assen, to appear on its platforms; later he was joined by men like Assen Pavlov, a former follower of Nikola Petkov, and Vergil Dimov. Perhaps the biggest showpiece of all in this propaganda parade, Dimov had been a close friend of Dimitur Gichev, the Agrarian leader jailed in 1945, and was Minister of the Interior in the Muraviev government immediately before the Fatherland Front coup on September 9, 1944. Another gesture was the trial in September, 1954, of a number of former officers, including General Ivan Vulkov, Minister of War in 1923, for the murder of Stambolisky thirty-one years before. Vulkov and six others were sentenced to death, although this was later commuted to twenty years' imprisonment.[12]

These moves were a confession of the regime's failure to attract the peasants and induce them to accept collectivization gracefully. They also illustrated the ineffectiveness of the puppet Agrarian Party, led first by Alexander Obbov and later by George Traikov. In fact, Chervenkov always treated this party with contempt and was later to be criticized for it when he was finally disgraced in 1962.

Though less ostentatiously courted, Bulgaria's small but growing working class was not entirely forgotten in the concessions that were granted during this period. They had certainly suffered many hardships in trying, as Dimitrov had put it in 1948, to achieve in 10 to 20 years what other countries had achieved in a century.

[11] See Robert Lee Wolff, *The Balkans In Our Time* (Cambridge, Mass., 1956), p. 530.

[12] *Otechestven Front* (Sofia), September 30, 1954.

Conditions in some of the rapidly-developing manufacturing industries were tolerable at best, but in some of the extractive industries they were evidently unbearable. This caused a great amount of labor turnover. An extreme but illustrative example occurred at the Dimitrovo (Pernik) coal mine: at the beginning of 1952, 11,000 workers were employed there; during the course of the year, 11,000 left.[13] The regime's response to this situation before Stalin's death was to issue a decree (in February, 1953) imposing severe penalties for the violation of work contracts. The great unpopularity of this measure led to its abrogation the following November as part of the new course.

A crumb of comfort was also given to clerical workers in government ministries and public offices. A decree of the Ministerial Council, published on October 3, 1953, forbade the widespread practice of forcing personnel to do overtime. This measure was announced as a relief to the office workers "in order to create favorable conditions for an upswing of the political and cultural level of state employees, and to make it possible for them to give more time to their families and the education of their children."

A more significant sign of a change in the regime's doctrinaire attitude was a government order at the beginning of February, 1954, moderating the previously repressive policy toward private artisans and traders. No statistics are available to document the decrease in the numbers of private entrepreneurs, but in view of the prohibitive taxes levied upon them and the refusal of the authorities to give them any help, it must have been substantial by 1954. Now the authorities realized that private artisans and traders could supply much-needed services, and thus help to alleviate some of the minor frustrations the population had been suffering for the last few years. Accordingly, these entrepreneurs' taxes were slightly reduced and state factories were ordered to ease the supply of necessary materials and to give them assistance where possible.

The Sixth Bulgarian Party Congress: February–March, 1954

The Sixth Bulgarian Party Congress began on February 25, 1954, almost a year after the death of Stalin. It had been a year of varied improvement in Bulgaria. The piecemeal measures cited above were small, but in the climate of the period they were not insignifi-

[13] Message from Chervenkov to Party, State, and Economic Officials, January 13, 1953; *Rabotnichesko Delo*, January 14, 1953.

cant; they were the first rays of light many Bulgarians had seen
for almost a decade. Above all, the pall of fear, the chief characteristic of Stalinism in both the Soviet Union and her satellites, had
lifted considerably.

But apart from the recession of terror, none of these improvements signaled any basic change or genuine program of reform.
Bulgaria was not alone in this respect in Eastern Europe. Only in
Hungary, where Rakosi had to give up the premiership to Imre
Nagy (who turned out to have a completely different policy),
were the changes of real political importance. In Czechoslovakia,
the timely death of Klement Gottwald did lead to a reshuffle at
the top; but the new Party leader, Antonin Novotny, moderated
the political course rather than changing it in any basic way. In
Bulgaria, however, as in neighboring Rumania, power had remained, and was to remain, in the hands of essentially the same
people.

In December, 1953, the government avoided an opportunity to
give the government a new look. Elections to the Subranie were
hold that month; they were of the usual Communist pattern and
had the usual Communist result, although the atmosphere in
which they were held was more relaxed than before. The previous
government automatically resigned but the new one showed only
one change: Deputy Premier Karlo Lukanov disappeared from
the lists. Even this, however, was of no real significance since
Lukanov was soon sent to Moscow as Ambassador on the death
of Stella Blagoeva, the daughter of the founder of the BCP, in
February, 1954. Lukanov had spent many years in Moscow in the
inter-war period and, after the war, had owed his preferment to
Chervenkov. His mission in Moscow was an important one: to
keep his master informed of the activities and intentions of the
new team in the Kremlin.

Chervenkov retained the premiership in the new government of
December, 1953. In retrospect, this seems a clear indication that he
planned to give up the Party leadership at the forthcoming congress. Obviously, all the satellites had to follow the collegial trend
toward separation of Party and state posts that had just been
established in the Soviet Union. This had already happened in
Hungary and Czechoslovakia and was to happen in Poland and
Rumania in the course of 1954. Still, it surprised many observers
when it occurred at the Bulgarian congress, and it led to the inevitable crop of rumors that Chervenkov was on his way out, that
after the death of Stalin and the execution of Beria in December,

1953, he could not survive. It was, however, simply a game of musical chairs to the tune played by the Soviet Union.

Just why Chervenkov retained the Premier's post rather than that of the Secretary-General of the Party is difficult to explain. He was not alone in this, for Rumania's Gheorghiu-Dej made the same choice later in the year and the Party leadership went to Gheorghe Apostol. But in 1955 Gheorghiu-Dej reassumed the Party leadership and shed the premiership. Again in retrospect, the slow political demise of Chervenkov—the end came only in 1962—can be seen to have begun with this action. No matter how powerful he remained, he began slowly to lose the power of patronage, the control over the *nomenklatura,* invested in the leadership of the Party. He must have realized the danger but evidently considered the chance worth taking. He may have been influenced by events in Moscow where Malenkov, who looked to be Stalin's heir, had taken the Premier's post, while the apparently less significant Khrushchev was First Secretary. Chervenkov probably also felt confident that he could choose a safe and malleable new First Party Secretary. The reasons may have seemed shrewd at the time, but later the miscalculation, particularly over the course of developments in Moscow, became clear.

The man who became First Party Secretary (the old title of Secretary-General was abolished, as it was in the Soviet Union and elsewhere in the Communist world) certainly seemed to present no problems. Todor Zhivkov was then forty-two years old, the youngest man ever to have become the leader of a ruling Communist Party. Of poor peasant stock and little formal education, he had become a printer by trade and joined the underground Young Communist League in 1928; subsequently, in the Party itself, he had made his way up through the Sofia District Party Committee. During the war he established a quietly meritorious record as a Communist Partisan. He only became a full member of the Party Central Committee at the Fifth Congress in 1948. But he rose rapidly thereafter, becoming especially powerful in Sofia. In 1948 and 1949 he was simultaneously First Secretary of the Sofia City Party Committee, President of the Sofia City Party Committee of the Fatherland Front and President of the Sofia City People's Council. In 1950 he became a Secretary of the Party Central Committee and a candidate member of the Politburo and in the next year a full member of the Politburo.[14]

[14] His early career closely resembled that of Antonin Novotny in Czechoslovakia. For Novotny, see J. F. Brown, *The New Eastern Europe: The Khrushchev Era and After* (New York, 1966), p. 259.

Despite his rapid ascent, Zhivkov had never been considered leadership material. Of the rising young men he was considered a poor second to Georgi Chankov, head of the State Planning Commission and the brightest member of Chervenkov's "kindergarten." In fact, it may have been precisely because of his lack of personality that he was favored by Chervenkov and accepted without opposition in the Party at large. Judging by the very inactive part Zhivkov was to play for the next two years, Chervenkov's judgment of both man and situation seemed correct. The clearest example of the minor role Zhivkov played was that, though nominally Party leader, he was not included in the Bulgarian delegation to the Twentieth CPSU Congress in February, 1956. But Zhivkov was slowly but steadily to gain in stature, authority and ability as a Party politician; and this, together with developments in the Soviet Union and intra-bloc politics, eventually caused Chervenkov's undoing.

But even at the Sixth Congress, master of the situation though he still seemed, Chervenkov could not have been fully satisfied. The fact that Zhivkov was a home Communist and a partisan implied a rehabilitation of the group which Chervenkov had driven from power in 1949 and 1950. Other elections at the congress confirmed this. Dobri Terpeshev, one of the most prominent (and popular) home Communists after 1945, who had gone into oblivion after the fall of Kostov, was elected to the Central Committee. So was Slavcho Trunski, a partisan general who had maintained contact with Tito's partisans in the war. He too had virtually disappeared after 1949; now he was back as a Central Committee candidate.

The election of these men (and others, including the former head of the army's political administration, Boyan Bulgaranov, and the former Minister of Education, Kiril Dramaliev, who had also suffered from Chervenkov's rise), was important politically and psychologically.[15] True, it should not be magnified. Only a handful of the 97 full and candidate members of the new Central Committee could be counted as old enemies of Chervenkov. But, of these 97, 40 were new and the vast majority of these were not part of Chervenkov's patrimony. In fact, it was out of this Central Committee that Zhivkov was to form his own group. Men like Diko Dikov, Stanko Todorov, Boris Velchev, Pencho Kubadinski,

[15] None of these men, though eclipsed after Kostov's execution, lost their Party positions, but these positions became only nominal. Their re-election at the Sixth Congress meant full rehabilitation and a return to public life.

and Tano Tsolov became the core of this group and a few years later were rewarded handsomely.

Most disturbing of all to Chervenkov, however, was the dramatic revival of Yugov. From being close to physical elimination after the fall of Kostov, he had come now to be second in importance only to Chervenkov. It was he who benefited, more than any other man in Bulgaria, from the death of Stalin. At the Sixth Party Congress his Politburo status was confirmed and the following September he became first deputy premier. His handling of the Plovdiv tobacco riot had increased his prestige and, at least initially, he was the natural rallying point for all those older home Communists and the remnants of the Kostovites who were coming back to positions of authority.

Another interesting re-emergence was that of Dimitur Ganev. After a colorful career in prewar South Dobruja, then part of Rumania,[16] Ganev had been very prominent in the new regime after 1945 as a member of the Politburo and Minister of Foreign Trade from 1948 to 1952. But he, too, was caught up in the waves of recrimination that followed the Kostov trial and was publicly humiliated in 1950. In 1952 he was sent into exile as Ambassador to Prague. At the Sixth Congress, however, he made his comeback. Though not re-elected to the Politburo (he had nominally retained his membership), he became a Central Committee secretary. Ganev was to return to the Politburo in 1957 and become titular head of state a year later, on the death of Georgi Damyanov. Upon his re-emergence in 1954, some of the older home Communists who disliked Yugov began looking to him as their natural leader.

The New Politburo: The Influence of the Military

A few facts, figures, and comments on the new Politburo elected at the Sixth Congress, and on the Party membership as revealed in Chervenkov's report, illustrate some of the important developments in the previous few years. The new Politburo consisted of the following members: Georgi Chankov, Vulko Chervenkov, Georgi Damyanov, Rayko Damyanov, Ivan Mihailov, Encho Stay-

[16] During this stage of his career, Ganev joined the Rumanian Communist Party; he became member of both the Central Committee and the Secretariat of that Party in 1934. After the Treaty of Craiova in 1940, which handed South Dobruja back to Bulgaria, he reassumed his membership in the BCP.

kov, Georgi Tsankov, Anton Yugov, Todor Zhivkov; candidate members were Petur Panchevski and Todor Prahov.

Of the nine full members, three were Muscovites par excellence (Chervenkov, Georgi Damyanov, and Ivan Mihailov); another, Raiko Damyanov, had spent several years in the Soviet Union before the war and can be considered a Muscovite. The other five were home Communists but three of these (Chankov, Tsankov, and Zhivkov) were of the younger, "post-Kostov" variety and were protégés of Chervenkov. Only Yugov and Encho Staikov, a new member, were home Communists of the older generation. The other new member besides Staikov was the Muscovite, Mihailov; thus symmetry was preserved as it was in the case of the candidate-members with Prahov, the home Communist, and Panchevski, the Muscovite.

One of the most striking features about this new Politburo was the strength of military representation in it; and, despite the recovery of ground by the home Communists mentioned above, this representation was entirely Muscovite. Georgi Damyanov, Mihailov, and Pancheski had all been officers in the Red Army and were all Soviet citizens. Damyanov, the senior of the three, had been Chairman of the Presidium of the National Assembly (titular head of state) since 1950 and would probably have warranted Politburo status on that account alone. But he was also considered to have excellent contacts in the Soviet general staff and had been the man mainly responsible for reorganizing the Bulgarian Army on Soviet lines after the war.

Ivan Mihailov had returned to Bulgaria in 1945 with the Red Army and had been transferred to the Bulgarian Army with the rank of major-general. He too had helped direct the reorganization of the Bulgarian Army and in 1950 had been appointed deputy minister of national defense and a deputy premier. The fact that he was made a deputy premier while still only the deputy head of a government department attests to Mihailov's sphere of responsibility being broader than the purely military, and his election to the Politburo in 1954 only strengthened that impression. Indeed, throughout almost the entire history of the Communist regime in Bulgaria, Mihailov seems to have had a special status. Though his first task was to provide a dependable link between the Bulgarian Army and the Red Army, he seems later to have represented for Moscow an element of continuity and stability. Within the Bulgarian regime itself, he was always rigidly faithful to the Soviet alliance, and his Moscow connections inevitably gave him increased prestige and authority. But his own ability and personality certainly added to his influence. Never associated closely with any Party faction, in fact always seeming "above the battle," he has shown great political longevity, and as late as 1968 still remained a full Politburo member and a deputy premier. His background, career, and special status display striking similarities with those of General Emil Bodnaras in Rumania.

General Petur Panchevski is a more straightforward and less interesting character. He spent nearly twenty years as a Soviet officer and when he returned to Bulgaria in 1945 was said to have spoken only a very poor Bulgarian. A competent soldier and good organizer, he became Minister of National Defense in 1950 when Damyanov was elevated to the state presidency. In the military hierarchy he was, therefore, Mihailov's superior; but he clearly carried less political weight in both the government and the Party.

It is not easy to account for this increase of military influence in the top party leadership. The foreign policy of the Soviet camp since the death of Stalin had been marked, not by an increased bellicosity, but by an apparent desire for a diplomatic arrangement with the West. This policy was dictated by Moscow, but all the satellites had their roles and Bulgaria was expected to improve her relations with Yugoslavia and Greece. Perhaps the new Soviet leadership, resenting Chervenkov (as it resented Rakosi in Hungary) and yet wishing to ensure control over a strategically important ally, opted for the strongest and most important element in Bulgaria, the army. Then, too, there were no Soviet armies in Bulgaria; therefore, the more Soviet-trained generals there were in her regime, the safer the situation would be during this period of uncertainty and change.

However, there may have been a more profound reason. Ever since the liberation from Turkey, the Bulgarian military had played an important part in the nation's politics—a part that was often dominant and sometimes unconstructive. This was due both to the honor in which the army was generally held by the public and the fact that, in the all-too-frequent periods of political upheaval, the military had represented both stability and continuity. The post-war situation, of course, was different in many respects. The old officer corps—which, despite its many political faults, had been nothing if not patriotic—was gone. The commanders of the new corps included many men who owed allegiance to Moscow rather than Sofia. Still, an institutional tradition need not depend for its survival on those who man the institutions at any particular time and it is quite possible that this military prominence in the top echelons of the party simply represented the old tradition, carried over into the new Bulgaria. Later in the course of the Communist regime, when most of the Soviet-trained generals had been replaced by old partisans, the pattern was largely the same.

In view of these speculations, a remark made by Chervenkov in his report to the Sixth Party Congress is particularly interesting. While urging continued vigilance against the real internal enemies of the regime, Chervenkov cautioned against suspicion of everyone who was not a member of a progressive organization. "It is also a fault," he continued, "to consider as members of the enemy camp all those officers of the Bulgarian Czarist Army who were discharged after September 9, 1944."[17]

Many of these officers had been executed during the terror between 1945 and 1948, and many of those who survived had been imprisoned or sent to labor camps. Those lucky enough to escape the rigors of Communist justice were faced with poverty and victimization. After Stalin's death the situation moderated, and some imprisoned officers were released in the amnesty of September, 1953. However, Chervenkov's remark indicated that the condition of many was still deplorable. It probably reflected as well the resentment that many Bulgarians, particularly the older generation, felt over the way the officer class had been treated. But it was also a political thrust by Chervenkov against the Muscovite military group in the regime, since this group, led by Damyanov, Mihailov, and Panchevski, had been responsible for the brutal purge of the old officers. And it was this group—and Chervenkov must have resented them bitterly—whose connections with Moscow had proved stronger and more permanent than his own, because they were not dependent on a single, mortal man, but on an institution: the Red Army.

Party Membership in 1954

Chervenkov announced at the congress that the total membership of the Party was 455,251; this included 366,142 full members and 87,109 candidates. At the Fifth Party Congress in 1948, the total membership had been about 496,000. The difference of over 40,000 was due to the great purges of the Kostovites, real and

[17] *Rabotnichesko Delo*, February 26, 1954.

suspected, between 1948 and 1950 and a rooting out of undesirables who had joined the Party for opportunistic reasons after the liberation.

It also emerged at the congress that there had been an important shift in the social composition of the Party since 1948. The proportion of peasants dropped considerably and that of workers increased. In 1948 the number of peasants was 207,409, or 44.74 per cent of total membership; by 1954 this number had dropped to 180,998, or 39.76 per cent of the total. The number of workers had risen from 122,896 (26.5 per cent) in 1948 to 155,081 (34.06 per cent) in 1954.[18] The increase in the number of workers was mainly a reflection of the growing industrialization of Bulgaria. The drop in the number of peasants, however, was probably due mainly to purges of "kulaks" and other unreliable elements. Some genuine kulaks may well have joined the Party in the early post-liberation period to escape persecution. But one may assume that many of those expelled had been branded as kulaks simply because of their resistance to collectivization. These statistics would seem to disprove the sweeping generalization that the Bulgarian peasants not only did not resist collectivization, but readily accepted it.

[18] For a fuller tabulation see Dellin (ed.), *op. cit.*, p. 130.

3

The Economic Policy of the New Course, 1953-57

ON JANUARY 27, 1954, the Sofia press published the economic directives for the new 1953-57 Five-Year Plan.[1] These directives were then presented to the Sixth Congress by Georgi Chankov, the chairman of the State Planning Committee.

Briefly, the directives were these: the total volume of capital investments was to be roughly doubled compared with the provisions of the previous (first) Five-Year Plan of 1949-53. As for planned investments in the various branches of the economy, those for agriculture and forestry were to increase over 2.3 times; for industry, over twofold; for coal production, by five times; for electrification, by 90 per cent; for the light and food industries, over 2.2 times; for transportation and communications, about 30 per cent; for education, culture, health, and communal needs, 2.7 times; and for house construction, 3.7 times.

The planned target for gross industrial production was an increase of some 60 per cent by 1957 over 1952, at 1952 prices. Electric power was to be doubled over the same period: lignite coal production was to be increased 2.7 times, brown coal by 60 per cent, black coal 2.5 times, and anthracite by 100 per cent. The production of ferrous metallurgy was to be built up by putting into operation a new lead and zinc plant; by enlarging the Lenin metallurgical plant at Dimitrovo, opened the previous August; and by the construction of a copper plant at Medet, near Sofia, to be completed in 1958. To support these industries, the production of

[1] *Vecherni Novini* (Sofia), January 27, 1954.

39

iron ore was to increase 2.9 times, copper ore 3.4 times, lead concentrate by 41 per cent, zinc concentrate by 90 per cent, and copper concentrate 3.6 times—all in comparison with 1952.

Production in the machine construction industry was to increase 78 per cent by 1957, in the chemical industry by 90 per cent, in construction materials by 82 per cent and in the timber processing industry by 47 per cent. "Decisive improvements in the variety and quality of [consumer] goods for broad consumption" were planned, as were improvements in internal trade, the standard of living of the workers, health preservation, education, and culture. In agriculture, the production of crops and livestock was to increase by 66 per cent over the 1952 level.

It was clear from these directives that the hard-pressed Bulgarian citizen could expect some relief from the trials he had undergone between 1948 and 1952. The investment outlays on agriculture, light industry, and particularly on housing all pointed to a deliberate effort by the regime to raise the depressed standard of living. The 3.7-fold increase in capital investment for housing, for example, was accompanied by sensible provisions for the granting of credits by the Bulgarian Investment Bank for the building of cooperative and individual houses for workers, state employees, and collective farm members. The loans could go up to 40,000 leva with repayment over 25 years, provided the borrower had at least 30 per cent of the required credit invested in private funds in the investment bank.

The reasons for these gestures to the public were both political and economic. Clearly, after five years of the most rigorously applied Stalinism the discontented public had to be appeased. After all, everybody was doing it, from the Poles to the Albanians, following the example set by Moscow. And the upheavals in East Germany, the riots in Czechoslovakia, and the rumblings in Bulgaria itself had added particular urgency to the need for concessions. Moreover, the Bulgarian economy showed signs of a need for stabilization and relaxation after the excesses of the previous five years. In Chapter 2, the argument of the Czechoslovak economist, Dr. Josef Goldmann, that the scaling down of industrial plans after Stalin's death was due solely to the workings of the economic cycle and was not prompted by political considerations of mass discontent,[2] was dismissed as having little application to Bulgaria. But, while maintaining that the concessions after 1953 were mainly motivated by political considerations, it must be ad-

[2] *Planovane Hospodarstvi* (Prague), September, 1964.

mitted that even the undeveloped Bulgarian economy had been overstrained and had become considerably unbalanced.

The aims of the First Bulgarian Five-Year Plan (1949–53) had been to raise accumulation to 25–30 per cent of national income[3] and to attain a huge increase in heavy industrial output. It will be recalled that the plan required an increase in gross output over the five year period of 220 per cent in capital goods (sector "A") and 75 per cent in consumer goods (sector "B"). These industrial targets were considerably surpassed, on paper at least,[4] and the plan was wound up. There can be no doubt that the quantitative advances were very impressive indeed. The gross output of capital goods increased by 253 per cent; generated electricity increased by 194 per cent; fuels by 88 per cent; ferrous metallurgy by 1,200 per cent; non-ferrous metallurgy by 271 per cent; metal-using industries by 381 per cent; and so on. Some of the increases for consumer goods were also very high: leather and footwear by 239 per cent; textiles and clothing by 176 per cent; and food processing by 132 per cent. Georgi Dimitrov had said at the Fifth Party Congress in December, 1948, that "Bulgaria [is] to catch up in what she has missed in the past, and to achieve in ten to twenty years what other countries have achieved in a century."[5] Taking these figures at their face value, his slogan did not seem to utopian.

But the successes concealed some organic problems within the economy. These problems were similar to those afflicting the other Eastern European economies, although their effects were less serious in Bulgaria than in the more advanced nations, such as Czechoslovakia and East Germany.

The Achilles' heel of the Bulgarian Communist economy has always been agriculture and at no time was this more apparent than in the first planning period. In terms of total fixed investments, agriculture had not been quite as neglected as in some other Communist states.[6] But in Bulgaria it was definitely treated as the

---

[3] In Communist states, national income is defined as net commodity output *plus* productive services.

[4] For an expert—and tactful—discussion of the difficulties involved in assessing the real worth of Bulgarian economic statistics during this period, see *U.N. Economic Survey of Europe*, 1960 (Geneva, 1961), chap. 6, sections 6 and 8.

[5] G. M. Dimitrov, "Political Report to the Fifth Congress of the Bulgarian Communist Party" (Sofia), 1948.

[6] The average annual percentage of gross fixed investment between 1949–53 has been 15.3 for agriculture and forestry: *U.N. Economic Survey of Europe*, 1960, chap. 6, p. 30.

poor relation of heavy industry and considered one of the main sources for the accumulation of means for capital investments. Production all but stagnated and, in three years out of the five, gross output was below the 1948 level. Only excellent harvests in 1951 and 1953 prevented disaster and enabled the regime to claim a 17 per cent increase in gross output over the whole period.

There were many reasons for this failure—natural, technical, economic, and political. In the first place, the weather had been poor during three of the five years and this, of course, loomed large in the official excuses. (When a good harvest occurs in the Communist states, it is credited to the regime's "brilliant" agricultural policy; a bad harvest is blamed on the weather.) Also, in the early phases of collectivization much of the investment was concentrated on providing the necessary facilities for the collectives—stables, barns, administrative buildings and services, machine tractor stations—rather than on improving production as such. Moreover, investments designed for sensible and productive projects such as irrigation systems and land amelioration were often wasted because of incompetence or inadequate technical knowledge.

A more serious problem was that the peasants themselves— whether already collectivized or still private—were given far from adequate incentives. That material incentives were too low throughout the 1948–56 period was later admitted by the Party itself at the April plenum of 1956.[7] In view of the improvements that took place between 1953 and 1957, the situation during the First Five-Year Plan must have been very bad indeed. The price and procurement systems certainly taxed the peasant hard, and the compulsory deliveries (which, though progressively reduced, were not finally abolished till 1959) discouraged the growth of livestock and led to much slaughtering, since the levies were based on the number of livestock owned.

In any case the amount of fodder available was not sufficient to maintain, let alone increase, the number of livestock. As for farm prices and incomes, government statistics have been significantly reticent about the early period of the First Five-Year Plan. Only when prices began to be increased from about 1952 onwards were statistics given. As for incomes in the collectives, these were based on the Soviet *trudoden* (labor-day) system and they fluctuated with the weather and the harvests. In the good harvest

[7] *Rabotnichesko Delo* (Sofia), June 11, 1956.

years of 1951 and 1953, the average labor-day payment stood at 14 and 10.4 leva (in cash and kind) and the total annual income at 2,590 and 1,963 leva respectively. In 1952, when the harvest was relatively poor, the average labor-day payment was 8.7 leva and the total income for the year 1,370 leva.[8] It can be said, of course, that the peasants fed themselves from their private holdings if they remained uncollectivized or from their private plots if they were in collectives. But these incomes were very low (as was later admitted) and, even if they had been considerably higher, the great scarcity of consumer goods and building materials would have deprived the peasants of virtually all incentive. It is not possible to give a safe comparison between peasant and worker incomes during this period but, in the cities, industrial employment rose rapidly and the nominal wages of workers increased considerably. Nonetheless the failures in agriculture led to a decline in the per capita consumption of goods between 1948 and 1952.[9] This, combined with the very small increase in the availability of non-food consumption goods, led to serious strain in the consumers' market and in 1952 the regime was compelled, like most others in Eastern Europe at this time, to introduce a currency reform. (The reform followed the advice of resident Soviet experts, who abounded in all walks of Bulgarian public life at the time.) All cash holdings had to be exchanged at the rate of one new leva for 100 old leva, while the exchange rate for prices and wages was at three new leva for 100 old. At the same time consumer rationing was abolished, but new, increased prices were fixed in the range between the old rationed price and the free market price. The abolition of rationing had little immediate effect, since food supplies were scarce, and it was a sad commentary on the government's solicitude for its subjects that, during the period of the First Five-Year Plan, exports of agricultural products doubled in volume while imports of foodstuffs were reduced.

In the investment sector as in the consumers' market, there were considerable strains. This was due to an extraordinarily rapid rise in total accumulation up to 1953, when it reached its peak. It rose from 3.9 billion leva (at 1952 prices) in 1948 to 7.1 billion in

[8] *U.N. Economic Survey of Europe, 1960*, chap. 6, p. 34.

[9] *Ibid.*, p. 39. For an excellent general essay on Eastern European agricultural policies and problems during this period, see L. A. D. Dellin, "Agriculture and the Peasant," in Stephen Fischer-Galati (ed.), *Eastern Europe in the Sixties* (New York, 1963).

1951 and then to 8.2 billion in 1953. This resulted in the nation's resources being spread too thin on huge industrial projects that would not begin to pay off for several years. The result was a very slow increase in the value of fixed assets by 1953. Clearly, there was a need for retrenchment, a relaxation of the investment boom and a concentration on completing projects already started rather than on starting new ones.

Thus, for these economic reasons as well as those of a more pressing political nature, the Second Five-Year Plan was a much more modest effort, particularly where investments were concerned. In fact, net fixed investment was practically stabilized at the 1954 level and there was no sharp rise until 1958. There was also a greater stress, as mentioned earlier, on agriculture and various other areas that would raise the general standard of living (these, in investment statistics, are usually lumped together under the heading "Cultural and Social Allocations"). The following table shows the percentage distribution of limited capital investments in the main sectors during the period 1952–57:[10]

	1952	1953	1954	1955	1956	1957
Industry	48.1	51.5	53.6	53.2	53.4	62.0
Rural economy	9.1	7.4	11.0	15.0	15.0	10.5
Transport	16.0	17.7	12.1	10.1	10.0	10.4
Cultural and social allocations	10.1	10.9	15.8	15.9	16.3	11.9
Miscellaneous (Admin., trade and procurement, construction, etc.)	16.7	12.7	7.5	5.8	5.3	5.2

These figures show that, although industry continued to receive the lion's share of investments, the rural economy and cultural and social allocations showed very big increases, especially in 1955 and 1956. Whereas in 1952 these two sectors had only 19.2 per cent of total investments, in 1956 they received 31.3 per cent.

Light industry, however, continued to receive relatively short shrift in the investments allocated to industry as a whole. The following figures show the proportionate stress given to heavy indus-

10 *Planovo Stopanstvo* (Sofia), No. 2, 1957.

try (Sector "A") and light industry (Sector "B") between 1952 and 1957:[11]

	1952	1953	1954	1955	1956	1957
Heavy industry	87.1	86.0	86.9	89.8	90.4	88.1
Light industry	12.9	14.0	13.1	10.2	9.6	11.9

This neglect of Sector "B" was later admitted by First Secretary Zhivkov at the Seventh BCP Congress in June, 1958. Light industry, said Zhivkov, was lagging behind the "quickly growing needs of the country" and "serious attention" would have to be paid to the development of the light and consumer goods industries.[12]

Still another pointer to a general rise in the standard of living during this period is contained in the statistics for the distribution of national expenditure.[13]

	1952	1953	1954	1955	1956	1957	1958
National income	24.4	29.3	28.8	31.6	33.0	37.3	40.9
Accumulation rate	6.5	8.2	5.4	5.2	4.6	6.9	6.6
Consumption							
Personal	16.4	19.3	21.5	24.2	26.0	28.0	31.6
Collective	1.5	1.8	1.9	2.2	2.4	2.4	2.7
Total	17.9	21.1	23.4	26.4	28.4	30.4	34.3

These figures (in billions of leva at 1952 prices) show that the rate of accumulation dropped sharply from 1954 onwards, reaching its sharpest decline in 1956, when it fell to just under 14 per cent of the national income. (From 1951–53, it had been about 28 per cent; the year 1956, it should be recalled, was the year of the Twentieth CPSU Congress and the Bulgarian April plenum which saw the demotion of Chervenkov from the premiership and a temporary acceleration of the new course.)

It is true, of course, that these percentage figures for accumulation and consumption are not an accurate guide to the development of the standard of living, but the proportions changed so greatly from 1954 that they indicate a definite trend toward improvement. And these indications are borne out by statistics pre-

[11] *Ibid.*
[12] *Trud* (Sofia), June 3, 1958.
[13] U.N. *Economic Survey of Europe, 1960*, chap. 6, p. 21.

pared by the Secretariat of the United Nations Economic Commission for Europe. The U.N. economists estimate that real wages rose in Bulgaria by 75 per cent between 1952 and 1958 and that the average labor-day payment on collective farms in 1958 was 35 per cent higher than in 1951, 2.5 times that of 1952 and nearly 80 per cent higher than in 1953. There were also considerable increases in pensions and other social security benefits, and collective farm members were brought within the pensions scheme in 1957. These benefits, along with an increase in the lowest wages and salaries, were a consequence of the April plenum in 1956. As for the consumption of foodstuffs, the pattern had definitely improved by 1957. For example, the annual per capita consumption of meat and meat products in 1953 was 19.3 kilograms, in 1957 it was 28.6; in 1953, the average Bulgarian ate 74 eggs; in 1957, he ate 98. The figures for fruit were 59.3 kgs in 1953 and 90.3 in 1957; for vegetables, 64.8 and 88.3 respectively. However, it should be noted that, though the Bulgarian diet was better balanced in 1957 than before the war, the per capita consumption of an important food like milk had been much higher in the 1930's. Bulgarians generally ate much better before the war than they did after it, at least until about 1954.[14]

During this period there was also a considerable increase in the rate of house-building. Taking the whole decade between 1948 and 1958, housing standards in terms of floor space per capita rose by some 15 per cent, and this figure becomes even more respectable when the 8 per cent increase in the population during this period is taken into account. This did not mean that the growing housing problem was being solved, particularly in the cities where the situation was made acute by the influx from the countryside due to industrialization and mechanization. Indeed, early in 1955 a temporary halt was made in the issuance of residence permits for newcomers in the cities of Sofia, Plovdiv, Burgas, Varna (Stalin), and Russe.[15] But there was a decisive improvement in the villages, and one of the strongest impressions which travelers in the Balkans bring back is of the prosperous appearance of the Bulgarian countryside; in fact, it appears more prosperous than that of any other country in the region, socialist or capitalist.

This period also saw striking increases in medical facilities and

[14] *U.N. Economic Survey of Europe*, 1960, chap. 6, p. 39.
[15] *Izvestia na Presidiuma na Narodnoto Subranie* (Sofia), March 18, 1955.

educational opportunities, as can be seen from the following percentage figure:[16]

	1939	1948	1952	1958
Medical facilities (per thousand population)				
Doctors	0.50	0.66	0.87	1.33
Hospital beds	1.69	2.58	3.90	4.87
Students (per thousand population)				
University	1.8	—	4.8	5.5
Secondary	13.6	25.2	24.1	27.8
Teachers (per thousand pupils)				
Primary	29.1	35.8	38.5	41.9
Secondary	40.0	40.0	44.3	53.4

The improvement in medical facilities is generally considered one of the most notable achievements of the Communist regime in Bulgaria, even by staunch anti-Communists. Indeed, by the beginning of the 1960's the supply of doctors and dentists was beginning to exceed the demand and a number of members of both professions had to seek work elsewhere, in East Germany and Sweden. As to education, the figures are impressive but it should be remembered that pre-Communist Bulgaria had a good record for literacy and educational opportunity and that, since the Communist takeover, the standard of educational attainment has dropped in many subjects. However, this phenomenon is not confined to Bulgaria or the Communist world.

Main Economic Changes Up to 1957

By 1957, Bulgaria had become an industrial/agrarian country. In 1939, the ratio between agriculture and industry in terms of contribution to the national income had been 75.2 to 24.8 in favor of agriculture; already by 1956 this had swung to 67.5 to 32.5 in favor of industry.[17] In 1957, Bulgarian industrial production was about eight times what it was in 1939;[18] industry contributed 52.5 billion leva to the net national income as against 19 billion in 1948. Agriculture and forestry combined had contributed 23.9 billion in

[16] *U.N. Economic Survey of Europe*, 1960, chap. 6, p. 40.
[17] *Rabotnichesko Delo*, October 9, 1957.
[18] Zhivkov's report to Seventh Party Congress. *Trud*, June 3, 1958.

1948 and by 1957 had only increased its contribution to 25.5 billion.[19] In 1934, the population of Sofia had been 287,000; by 1954 it was about 600,000.

By 1958, the number of workers in state and cooperative industry and handicrafts had reached 589,000 as against 262,000 ten years earlier. From 1948 to 1956 (the last year for which official figures were given) the total number of those employed in the private handicraft sector dropped from 81,000 to 45,000.[20] Total non-agricultural employment more than doubled in the decade 1948–58 from 710,000 to 1,460,000. Despite these great changes brought about by the rapid pace of industrialization, it was officially stated that agriculture still provided some 70 per cent of the total employment.[21]

Among the major Bulgarian industries, textile and clothing plants still employed the largest number of workers, followed by another light industry, that of food processing. This may seem paradoxical in view of the relatively low share of capital investment allocated to Sector "B." But these two industries were "traditional" in Bulgaria, being well established before the Communists came to power. Equally important, it was these two industries, especially clothing and textiles, which absorbed many workers from the small private workshops when these were taken over by the state. The state enterprises in electricity, fuels, metallurgy, and chemicals absorbed few workers from the private sector. Hence the shift in emphasis toward these heavy industries was greater during the period under review than might be gathered from the volume of manpower employed. Similarly the figures for output (net or gross) of the consumer goods industries give a misleading picture since, during the 1950's, small-scale farm and household industry began to be recorded in official statistics for the first time. Moreover, in these industries there was also an increasing duplication of inputs "due solely to a rising degree of processing of farm produce and the 'industrialization' of a considerable volume of former cottage or farm activity—cattle slaughtering, dairying, distilling, baking"[22]— that had not previously been recorded as industrial output.

[19] *U.N. Economic Survey of Europe*, 1960, chap. 6, p. 19; at 1939 prices.
[20] *Ibid.*, p. 23.
[21] *Ibid.*, p. 22. For 1957, Zhivkov gave the number of "able-bodied persons engaged in work in the public sector of the cooperative farms" as 1,656,000. If these figures are correct, the extra percentage would be made up by workers in the State Farms, MTS, private farms, etc.
[22] *Ibid.*, p. 25.

Thus, the output of consumer goods was still given in 1958 as 54.5 per cent of the total against 63.3 per cent in 1948. The output of capital goods had risen from 5.5 to 9.4 per cent of the total, and that of intermediate goods from 31.1 to 36.1 per cent.[23] These figures, however, should be seen in the light of the reservations made above.

The most rapidly expanding industries between 1953 and 1957, in terms of gross output and number of employed, were metallurgy, chemicals, metal working (here, too, there had been some absorption of private artisans), and the generation of electricity. Faithfully abiding by the importance Lenin had given to electrification, the Bulgarian Communists had made this their biggest single preoccupation in the economic field. During the period 1949–51, over one-third of all centrally planned industrial investment was devoted to electrification and, between 1949 and 1958, the fuel and power sector as a whole received almost 40 per cent of central industrial investments. By 1958, electricity generation had increased 5.5 times over its 1948 level. During the same period, coal production increased 3.5 times, but, because of the unsuitability of Bulgarian coal for coking, ever-increasing quantities of coking coal had to be imported, mainly from the Soviet Union.

The metallurgical industries were the second most favored branch in terms of allocations of investments. The most spectacular result of this policy was the appearance of a Bulgarian iron and steel industry of some dimensions. It was still small and, by 1958, the whole ferrous metallurgical industry only accounted for 1.2 per cent of total industrial output but—to give an idea of what it had developed from—its output increased by 5,457 per cent between 1948 and 1958. After 1958 it was to be expanded greatly by the construction of the gigantic combine at Kremikovtsi, near Sofia.

Less spectacular was the expansion of non-ferrous metallurgy. Bulgaria has always been relatively well-endowed in such profitable metals as lead, zinc, and copper, and their swift exploitation was a highly sensible policy on the part of the regime, leading to a growth in exports.

The metal-using industries also expanded quickly and by 1958 they employed almost as many workers as the food-processing industry. Bulgaria now produced such complex items as railway rolling stock, a variety of internal combustion engines, and elec-

[23] *Ibid.*, p. 24.

trical equipment, as well as textile machinery, food- and tobacco-processing machinery, agricultural implements, and radios. But most of this production was highly uneconomical, since the individual products were produced in far too small quantities and the quality of most of the products was very poor. Later, the need for greater specialization (in many cases in the context of Comecon cooperation) and modernization was realized.

The chemical industry—again, in many branches, virtually a new industry for Bulgaria—was given great emphasis by the regime from 1950 to 1954, when it received 12 per cent of the total centrally planned industrial investments. It was much less favorably treated for the next four years, a fact reflected in its much smaller rate of output increase. Up to 1958, the production emphasis was on basic chemicals and fertilizers. Such basic chemicals as caustic and calcined soda were largely exported. However, the nitrogenous and phosphoric fertilizers were used in domestic agriculture where they were badly needed, but production was insufficient and large supplies still had to be imported.

Obviously, these important changes in Bulgaria's industrial structure were bound to be reflected in the commodity composition of her foreign trade. Before discussing this, however, it is worth noting the most striking change of all in Bulgaria's foreign trade after World War II: its drastic reorientation toward the Soviet Union. Germany and Austria had accounted for over half the prewar foreign trade of Bulgaria; now the U.S.S.R. accounted for almost exactly the same share: in 1958, she took 53.8 per cent of Bulgaria's exports and supplied her with 52.7 per cent of her imports. Other Communist states, including those in Asia, took another 31.3 per cent of her exports in that year and supplied her with 22.4 per cent of her imports.[24]

Bulgaria's traditional exports had been tobacco, foodstuffs, and very little else. As late as 1948, these commodities, together with a small amount of metal and ores, constituted 88 per cent of her exports. Later, a considerable export in textiles and fabrics grew up and there was a significant increase in the volume of processed products exported.

The rise of industrialization was also reflected in the foreign trade structure: by 1958, engineering products accounted for almost 10 per cent of exports. But at this comparatively early date in Bulgaria's postwar industrialization, it was imports rather than

[24] *Ibid.*, p. 36.

exports that reflected the great changes taking place in the economy. Imports of industrial equipment quadrupled between 1948 and 1958 and, despite the establishment of a domestic iron and steel industry, Bulgaria still had to import 60 per cent of the steel she used and even 40 per cent of all her textile materials. She was almost completely dependent on imports for her coke and oil products. Machinery and equipment, fuels, and raw materials still accounted for 85 per cent of her imports.[25] Bulgarian economic policy after 1958 was largely designed to make the country less dependent on outside supplies of many of these commodities. During the period up to 1958, the terms of trade were strongly against her, as it was against all exporters of primary products. Therefore, the main reason that the standard of living had to be kept low, in spite of the real improvements after 1954, was the need to export as much as possible in order to pay for the huge volume of imports for industrialization.

Inevitably the regime had to look for foreign credits, which came predominantly from the Soviet Union. Between 1947 and 1951, Bulgaria received loans amounting to $237,000,000 (at 2 to 3 per cent interest) and, between 1955 and 1958, another $213,000,000. In the sixties, the dependence on the Soviet Union increased further, with more huge loans in 1961 and 1966. Bulgaria's economic dependence on the Soviet Union has had a great bearing on both her foreign and domestic policy.

Of all the changes which took place in the Bulgarian economy in the fifties, however, none was so spectacular or fundamental as the collectivization of agriculture. Its effect on agricultural production was disappointingly slight: the average annual net increase in production was 2.4 per cent.[26] But it changed the face of the country. From a patchwork quilt of dwarf peasant holdings, the Bulgarian countryside was, by the end of the fifties, dominated by about 975 huge collective farms of an average size of 4,500 hectares, the biggest in Eastern Europe. Even more important than the visible change was the deliberate destruction of the old peasant society with its traditional values. These values, and especially the peasant's feeling—no matter how illusory—of being master of his own destiny, had always been recognized by the Communists as one of their greatest obstacles. Hence, collectivization was not simply an economic move to make agriculture more efficient (which was badly needed) or even to facilitate the industrialization

[25] *Ibid.*, p. 36.
[26] *Novo Vreme* (Sofia), March, 1959, p. 23.

of the country. It was designed to destroy a civilization considered totally incompatible with the new one the Communists wished to build. In this aim the Communist authorities have achieved much success, although the attention which the collectivized peasants have lavished on their private plots (See Chapter 9), attests to the persistence of the ownership instinct. As yet, however, no real urban civilization has had time to grow in place of the old. This, of course, is a very long-term process, and many of the social problems which Bulgaria and other Eastern European countries have had to face over the last twenty years have been due to the hiatus which the destruction of the old civilization has left.

4

The April Plenum: Its Effects on Bulgarian Politics

THE FACT THAT Chervenkov had nominally relinquished the post
of Party leader at the Sixth BCP Congress in March, 1954, made
little apparent difference to the process of decision-making. Chervenkov continued to be the number one leader, a fact later admitted at the April plenum in 1956 when he lost the premiership.
The potential danger for him in choosing to give up the Party
leadership has already been mentioned in Chapter 2: Zhivkov
was given the chance to build a patrimony of his own and the re-
surgent Yugov was clearly becoming more powerful than he had
ever been. But to the Party rank and file and to the public at large,
the situation seemed very much as before.

But though the Party's power seemed undisturbed, the *manner*
of its wielding was visibly different. The changes that had been
emerging since the death of Stalin now became clearer. In the
first place Chervenkov, at least in public, seemed at pains to adapt
himself to the new collegiality now so evident in the Moscow
leadership. A correspondent of the *Neue Zuercher Zeitung* who
visited Bulgaria in May, 1954, wrote at some length about this
change in style. At public meetings, the customary rhythmic
chanting of the name "Chervenkov" was dropped; now only the
dead Dimitrov was singled out for individual praise. At the May
Day celebration in 1954, Chervenkov stood among the other mem-

bers of the Politburo, demonstrating the new-found enthusiasm for the principle of collective leadership.[1]

But this was not the only change. The internal relaxation, begun shortly after Stalin's death, was continued and broadened. Several labor camps were closed and the prisoners either released outright or brought before the courts so that their cases could at last be heard. The redress of ordinary citizens' grievances was accelerated and Chervenkov himself—as mentioned in Chapter 2—became more and more accessible to the public; indeed, he began to be known as a man who could get things done for the individual. Thus a man who earlier had been hated and feared began to acquire something of a reputation as a tribune of the plebs and it was this, together with the opinion that he was pushed out of office by the Soviets and the Yugoslavs, which was to bring Chervenkov considerable popular sympathy after April, 1956.

This internal political relaxation, and the relief and greater public confidence it brought, was accompanied by an improvement in economic standards which were a reflection of the more balanced economic policy discussed in Chapter 3. Most visitors to Bulgaria during this period, as well as most refugees from it, attested to the greater supply of fruit, vegetables, and other foodstuffs in the shops and to the small but perceptible rise in real incomes. In the countryside, the suspension of the collectivization drive, temporary though it was, also improved morale, as did measures to promote material incentives on the collectives themselves.

Soviet policy toward Bulgaria also helped to produce a better atmosphere. Bulgarians—a far-from-quixotic people—generally regarded the close alliance of their country with the Soviet Union after World War II as inevitable. Almost all of them undoubtedly deplored the subservience to the Soviets, and judicial crimes like the Muscovites' murder of Kostov aroused universal indignation. But Bulgarians were preoccupied with their daily affairs and, unless the Soviet presence impinged on them directly, they were probably not unduly concerned about foreign policy during this period.

Two aspects of the Soviet connection, however, certainly did affront their dignity. The first was the presence in Bulgaria of a small army of Soviet experts, advisers, technicians, and burocrats, all of whom were living comfortably at a time when the Bulgarian

[1] *Neue Zuercher Zeitung*, June 6, 1954.

standard of living was very low and the personal freedom of ordinary citizens was sharply limited. The Soviet experts are said to have received from the Bulgarian treasury salaries four times higher than those of their Bulgarian equivalents.[2]

The second ever-present irritation was the blatant Soviet economic exploitation of Bulgaria. The controversy over the extent and continuance of Soviet economic exploitation of the Eastern European countries has occupied professional economists for many years. Against the admitted fact that the Soviet Union sells many of her raw materials to these countries at higher prices than to others and pays less for many of her imports from them than do other states importing the same products, there is the counter-argument that the Soviet Union provides a long-term guaranteed market for many Eastern European products which could not be sold elsewhere in anything like the same volume. Moreover, large Soviet credits, it is pointed out, have enabled these countries to industrialize. But whatever the merits of these arguments over the last ten years or so, it is generally agreed that, during the Stalinist period, the Eastern European states—particularly Bulgaria and Rumania—were exploited as seldom before in their history.

It was these two aspects of the alliance which the Soviet and Bulgarian governments now set out to mitigate. The number of Soviet experts was gradually reduced as trained Bulgarian cadres were able to take their places, and those remaining had their salaries considerably reduced and some of their privileges restricted in 1954 and 1955. The behavior and tact of these experts were also said to have noticeably improved.

In the area of economic relations, the Soviets agreed to remove the most conspicuous instruments of exploitation. These were the five joint Bulgarian-Soviet companies that had been set up after September 9, 1944—the Bulgarian equivalents of the more notorious Sovroms in Rumania. The five were: Savetsko-Bulgarsko Gorno Obshetestvo, a mining company exploiting uranium deposits near Sofia, the produce of which was sent straight to the Soviet Union; the Gorubso mining company, exploiting the lead and zinc mines in the Rhodope basin; the Sovbolstroi building company, formed mainly out of former German building companies whose assets were given to the Soviets by the 1947 peace treaty with Bulgaria; the Tabso civil aviation company, Bulgaria's

[2] Robert Lee Wolff, *The Balkans in Our Time* (Cambridge, Mass., 1956), p. 482.

only airline; and Korbso (former Koralovag), a former German ship construction and repair company in Stalin (Varna).[3]

Adopting the same policy as it had toward the Sovroms in Rumania, the Soviet government sold its own shares in these companies back to the Bulgarians. In October, 1954, the shares of Korbso, Tabso, and Sovbolstroi were sold back[4] and in November, 1955, those of Gorubso.[5] The uranium project was, of course, the most valuable to the Soviets and it is not surprising that they retained their share in that the longest, as they did in its Rumanian equivalent, Sovrom Quartz. It was unofficially reported that this was only restored in the course of 1956. The Soviets sold their shares for a total price of 650 million leva ($96,000), to be paid over ten years.

During this same period, another important gesture was being made. Traicho Kostov's real or alleged supporters, who had been persecuted in 1950 in the aftermath of his trial, were gradually being released from prison. The unofficial rehabilitation of this group had, of course, been heralded by the Sixth Party Congress, which saw the political return of Terpeshev and Bulgaranov and —most striking of all—of General Slavcho Trunski, who had been imprisoned in 1951.[6] The emergence of Yugov as effective number two of the regime was perhaps, however, the most important vindication of the home Communist group. It is impossible to tell how many Kostovites were released under this new policy of clemency, partly because it was never clear how many were originally imprisoned in regime jails and detention camps. Some unofficial reports estimate that up to 10,000 political prisoners were released between the Sixth Party Congress and December, 1955.[7] But most of these were not Kostovites; they were either Agrarians or "bourgeois" anti-Communists arrested in the terror between 1945 and 1948. The most prominent Kostovite released during this

[3] L. A. D. Dellin (ed.), *Bulgaria* (New York, 1956), p. 356.

[4] *Izvestia* (Moscow), October 11, 1954; *Rabotnichesko Delo* (Sofia), October 12, 1954.

[5] *Rabotnichesko Delo*, November 26, 1955.

[6] In the course of 1954, Trunski was made commandant of the Military Academy in Sofia. Before his imprisonment he had been commander of the Third Bulgarian Army Corps.

[7] Reuters reported from Belgrade on November 21, 1955, that 400 political prisoners had been released under an amnesty, the most prominent of whom was Boris Bumbarov, a former leader of the *Pladne* group of Agrarians. Bumbarov later appeared on regime platforms urging the peasants to cooperate with collectivization.

period was the former Politburo member and Finance Minister Petko Kunin, arrested in 1949 and sentenced to life imprisonment the following year.[8] At the Eighth Party Congress in 1962, Kunin was re-elected to the Party Central Committee and became one of the most ardent proponents of economic reform.[9] It was also unofficially reported that Kostov's widow had been given a state pension early in 1955.

These gestures to the Kostovites, coupled with the release of Agrarians and others, added to the feeling of popular relief which the new course had engendered. Another gesture with both internal and external ramifications was the release, in July 1955, of all those connected with the Shipkov case. Mihail Shipkov was an employee of the American Legation in Sofia at the time of the Kostov trial. The American Minister, Donald R. Heath, had been "implicated" in the case since one of the accusations against Kostov was that he had spied for the United States. After refusing the demand for Mr. Heath's recall, Washington broke off diplomatic relations with Bulgaria in February, 1950. Shipkov and another employee of the Legation, together with three others, were indicted for espionage and sabotage. Shipkov, who had been granted asylum in the American Legation, tried to leave the country, but was arrested. After showing great fortitude in the face of the worst kind of torture and brutality, he was finally sentenced to fifteen years' imprisonment.

The release in 1955 of all those imprisoned in this case was a by-product of the Kostovite rehabilitations, but it was mainly a move to refurbish Bulgaria's tarnished international image. It also coincided exactly with the Geneva summit conference, the high-water mark of the strenuous efforts toward "peaceful coexistence" which Moscow, and hence her allies, had been making since the death of Stalin. Bulgaria's response to the new policy from Moscow was reflected mainly in efforts to improve relations with Yugoslavia and Greece. But during this period, Bulgaria was particularly eager to gain admittance to the United Nations, and the release of Shipkov should be seen mainly in this light. Indeed, the general release of political prisoners and the whole internal relaxation may have been motivated partly by the wish to escape Bulgaria's international ostracism. If so, it succeeded; Bulgaria, along with Albania, Rumania, and Hungary, was admitted to the U.N. in

[8] Wolff, *op. cit.*, p. 481. Kunin was earlier thought to have committed suicide in his cell.
[9] See Chapter 7.

December, 1955. The resumption of diplomatic relations with Washington, however, was only to come in 1959.

Impact of Soviet Changes

If internal developments in 1955 were influenced to some extent by changes in relations between East and West, they were to be far more influenced in the coming months by changes in Eastern Europe itself. In the early part of 1955, two important changes occurred that might at first have seemed to presage a return to a harder line, not only in Bulgaria but throughout the Communist bloc. The first was the dismissal of Malenkov as Soviet Premier in February. That Malenkov had been losing ground in the power struggle with First Secretary Nikita Khrushchev certainly had been evident for some time to assiduous Kremlin-watchers like the Bulgarian leaders. The focal point of the struggle was the question of the priority of heavy industry; this was made public by the remarkable differences of opinion on the subject shown by the government organ, *Izvestia*, and the Party paper, *Pravda*, in December, 1954.[10] Malenkov's dismissal was followed by that of Hungary's Premier Imre Nagy in April, 1955. Thus, within two months, the chief Soviet proponent of the economic new course had gone as well as the man who, more than any other Communist bloc leader, had sought to give revolutionary *political* substance to the new course.

The impact of these events on Bulgaria, however, turned out to be relatively slight. Khrushchev's neo-Stalinism was confined solely to industry; on almost all other matters he was to reveal himself as the great reformer. And it was his reformism, not his neo-Stalinist position on industry (later to be abandoned), which was to have a real impact on the satellites. The Bulgarian press, like its counterparts elsewhere, naturally supported the Soviet's renewed emphasis on heavy industry; but in Bulgaria as in the other satellite states, the new program led to no real change in economic policy.[11] In Bulgaria, it is true, the overwhelming preponderance of industrial investments had gone to Sector "A" even in the new course,[12] but the defeat of Malenkov led to no cutback in the

[10] See Zbigniew K. Brzezinski: *The Soviet Bloc: Unity and Conflict* (Cambridge, Mass., 1960), p. 156.

[11] See E. Taborsky, "The 'Old' and the 'New' Course in Satellite Economy," in *Journal of Central European Affairs*, January, 1958.

[12] See Chapter 3.

planned allocations to agriculture or social and cultural construction. Nor did it lead immediately to a re-acceleration of the collectivization campaign. This, however, was to get underway after the autumn harvest. In a speech at the end of December, Chervenkov stated that "most probably the time is not far off when the collectivization of the Bulgarian village economy will be completed."[13] This was an expression of intent, which resulted in a 15 per cent increase in the collectivized area in 1956.[14]

The change that *did* have the most far-reaching repercussions on all the Eastern European states was the Soviet *rapprochement* with Yugoslavia. From the very beginning of his ascendency in the Soviet Union, Khrushchev set himself the task of fence-mending in the socialist camp. The fact that he was later to preside over the partial disintegration of the camp should not obscure the wisdom of his early awareness that the Stalinist system of intra-bloc relations needed overhauling.[15] In 1954, he and Malenkov had visited China in an effort to put Sino-Soviet relations on a more equitable and viable footing. The following year it was time to try with Yugoslavia; hence the dramatic visit of Khrushchev and the new Soviet Premier, Bulganin, to Belgrade in May.

The Soviets found Tito in an understandably self-confident mood, interpreting Khrushchev's move as a complete vindication of all he had stood for. Toward the new Soviet leaders the Yugoslavs were firm but conciliatory. Toward some of the old satellite leaders, who had opposed Belgrade implacably for five years between the break with Moscow and Stalin's death, they were not prepared to be so forgiving. Tito's three principal Eastern European enemies were Matyas Rakosi, Chervenkov, and Enver Hoxha in Albania. (His antipathy toward Gheorghiu-Dej, also a "Stalinist" leader of a neighboring country, was markedly less evident, probably because Rumania's attacks on Belgrade had been relatively moderate.) Two of these opponents, Rakosi and Chervenkov, were to fall during the next year; Hoxha barely managed to survive a plot against him in April, 1956.[16]

Tito never openly criticized Chervenkov as he did Rakosi,[17] but

---

[13] *Rabotnichesko Delo*, December 22, 1955.

[14] See Chapter 9.

[15] Khrushchev's conception of what the new socialist camp or commonwealth should be like was contained in an editorial in *Kommunist* (Moscow), No. 14, 1955.

[16] See William E. Griffith, *Albania and the Sino-Soviet Rift* (Cambridge, Mass., 1963), pp. 24–25.

[17] See his speech at Karlovac, July 27, 1955; *Borba* (Belgrade), July 28, 1955.

his enmity for him was no secret and criticisms of Bulgarian policy were frequent in the Yugoslav press. Chervenkov was well aware of all this, and he and the many anti-Tito Stalinists still in power in Sofia must have viewed this new development with the greatest apprehension. On his way back from Belgrade, Khrushchev paid a one-day visit to Sofia. He then went to Bucharest, where he met with the Rumanian leaders, Rakosi and his new Premier, Andras Hegedus, and the Czechoslovak Party leaders, Novotny and Hendrych. The aim was to brief the satellite leaders on the change in policy toward Yugoslavia and on the results of the talks with Tito.

After Khrushchev's one-day visit to Sofia, a brief communiqué was issued, stating that international questions had been discussed and complete unanimity had prevailed. But Sofia was evidently not deceived by such blandness, and from then until Chervenkov was finally demoted the following April, it was generally expected that he would have to go. Indeed, when he temporarily retired from public life in August and September, 1955 because of illness (he had long been a victim of elephantiasis), it was widely rumored that his fall was imminent.[18]

Bulgarian opinion probably magnified the part that Tito played in Chervenkov's fall. It fitted in all too well with the Bulgarian image of Yugoslavia as traditionally a hostile and generally successful conspirator against their country. The theory also has an admirable neatness and the "plot" had a triumphant finale (for the Yugoslavs), with Moshe Pijade and a Yugoslav parliamentary delegation watching the April, 1956, session of the Subranie in Sofia that confirmed Chervenkov's dismissal—a veritable Yugoslav Shylock coming to collect his pound of flesh. The Yugoslavs were jubilant when Chervenkov fell and, with their cheerful blend of conceit and parochialism, willingly claimed the lion's share of the credit. But, though Yugoslav influence was certainly an important factor, there was more to it than that. Chervenkov's fall (and, even more clearly, that of Rakosi in Hungary) reflected the changes in Soviet policy and prejudices, and in the internal situation as well.

If Khrushchev had wanted to keep Chervenkov (or Rakosi) he would hardly have surrendered to Tito's wishes, despite his wish to appease the Yugoslavs. Had he wished to protect him, he might have pointed out to Tito that Chervenkov, despite his black record against Yugoslavia, could be made to change his policy toward Belgrade and had in fact begun to do so. This was indeed

[18] See, for example, Reuters (Vienna), September 23, 1955.

true. The image of Chervenkov as a blood-red incorruptible, refusing to sacrifice his Stalinist principles regardless of what happened in Moscow, will not stand examination as far as either domestic or foreign policy was concerned. He *had* shown himself ready to improve relations with Yugoslavia. As early as September, 1953, he had made Liuben Angelov, an important deputy foreign minister, Ambassador to Belgrade, as an earnest of his good intentions. In several speeches, most notably at the Sixth BCP Congress in March, 1954, and later at the Twentieth CPSU Congress itself, he had stressed the need for *rapprochement*.

The fact was that Khrushchev's policy coincided with Tito's prejudices. The new Soviet leader, impressed with the need for reform, cannot have looked favorably on the many satraps in the satellite states who owed their positions to Stalin and would hardly be genuine cooperators in any new policy. Khrushchev evidently considered some of these men to be unrepresentative of the people they were trying to govern, and hence incapable of achieving the consensus necessary to govern effectively. During this period, the doctrine of satellite autonomy in internal affairs was still something for the future, despite the *rapprochement* with Tito. Internal autonomy was not fully accepted until after the Polish October and the Hungarian Revolution in 1956. Therefore, the internal policy of the Soviet Union, whether retrograde or reformist, was the firm guide for policy in the Eastern European states also. Despite the new course, followed in varying degrees by all these states, Khrushchev could hardly have believed that this represented a genuine change of heart in several of the countries concerned.

Even more important were considerations arising from the struggle for power that was shaping up in Moscow as early as 1955, principally between Khrushchev and Molotov. This was to be the decisive round of the post-Stalin power struggle which had begun with the dismissal and execution of Beria and had continued with the demotion of Malenkov. Khrushchev may well have felt that, in such a struggle, most of the Eastern European leaders would side with the old, safe Molotov clique rather than with the new and unpredictable situation he represented. Hence the need to guard his flank before the coming showdown,[19] and hence also the

---

[19] There is some evidence to suggest that the Stalinist factions in Eastern Europe not only sympathized with Molotov but expected him to win the power struggle. A former member of the Harich group in East Germany, Manfred Hertwig, who later escaped to the West, reported that during his

inference that, even at this early date, Eastern European politics could have a bearing on Soviet politics.

The implication of this argument, of course, is that Khrushchev would have liked to have a clean sweep of all those Eastern European leaders too long in power to be trusted. This can neither be proved or disproved, but it does not seem too far-fetched a supposition. Chervenkov, after all, was ousted in April, 1956, and Rakosi the following July. Bierut died in March, 1956, so this problem solved itself. Where the case seems to break is with Gheorghiu-Dej in Rumania and Ulbricht in the German Democratic Republic (G.D.R.). Gheorghiu-Dej, however, did not attain real power in his country until May, 1952, with the purge of the Muscovites, Ana Pauker and Vasil Luca. His loyalty, moreover, was not, as Pauker's and Luca's had been, to the pre-Khrushchev ruling group and the Stalinist ethos in the Soviet Union. Even so, Professor Fischer-Galati has argued that Khrushchev did, in fact, try to unseat Gheorghiu-Dej in 1955 and 1956 and failed only because of Dej's skill and his strong support in the Rumanian Party.[20] Ulbricht, for his part, never enjoyed good relations with Khruschev despite his skillful adaptation to the changes in Moscow and it is quite possible that—but for the events of October and November, 1956 in Hungary and Poland, which pointed to the need for stability—a successor would have been found for him also. Enver Hoxha in Albania may have been left to the Yugoslavs, just as Stalin had been prepared to leave him; an unsuccessful attempt was made to unseat Hoxha in April, 1956. Novotny of Czechoslovakia had been First Party Secretary only since March, 1953, and as one of the newer generation of apparatchik leaders quickly gained the confidence of Khrushchev and was never to lose it.

However, the fact that Chervenkov was on Khrushchev's demolition list as well as Tito's does not fully explain the relative ease with which he was ousted. Without denying the paramount influence the Soviet Union still had in Eastern Europe in 1956, it seems

---

interrogation in early 1957, the G.D.R. attorney-general Melsheimer told him: "You seem to have bet on Khrushchev, and then you discovered too late that the man of the future is Molotov." *Unteilbares Deutschland*, No. 4, 1960, quoted by Evelyn Anderson in Walter Laquer and Leopold Labedz (eds.), *Polycentrism, the New Factor in International Communism* (New York, 1962), p. 94, footnote 4.

[20] Stephen Fischer-Galati: *The New Rumania: From People's Democracy to Socialist Republic* (Cambridge, Mass., 1967), pp. 44–77.

too simplistic to accept fully the notion that the Kremlin simply had to give the signal for heads to roll. If Khrushchev did try to get rid of Gheorghiu-Dej he failed, and Ulbricht survived to become a seemingly permanent figure on the Eastern European landscape. With all their power, and with Soviet blessing, the Yugoslavs could not dispose of Hoxha. Part of the reason may have been that powerful sections of the Soviet leadership still supported these Stalinists and successfully thwarted Khrushchev. But part of the reason also lay in the situation in each Party, its stability, and the strength of the leader concerned.

The April Plenum and the Demotion of Chervenkov

Within the Bulgarian Party, Chervenkov certainly remained the strongest single personality and, for some time after he lost the premiership, still had great influence and commanded the allegiance of most of the rank and file. But since the death of Stalin he had not been omnipotent. He was a Muscovite who had come to power over the dead body of the leader of Bulgaria's home Communists and had used his power to humiliate the members of that very powerful faction. The unpopularity of his policy had been matched by that of his person: arrogant and mistrustful, he had none of the personal attractiveness that, at times, was the saving grace of a tyrant like Gottwald or Bierut.[21] When Stalin died, therefore, the main plank of his support was removed. Disgraced figures like Yugov, Terpeshev, Trunski, and Bulgaranov reappeared with full vigor, representing the comeback of the older generation of home Communists. This group not only resented Chervenkov but also thirsted for the power so long denied them. At the Sixth Party Congress in March, 1954, Chervenkov had been replaced as Party Secretary by Todor Zhivkov, one of his "kindergarten" and seemingly a safe choice. But Zhivkov, a home Communist of the younger generation, slowly became a rallying point for a large group of younger Communists of similar background. Given the inclination of the Soviet Party leader, this group would not break a lance for Chervenkov, while the older group would positively relish his downfall.

[21] Party gossip in Sofia always maintained that there was a strong personal antipathy between Khrushchev and Chervenkov and that this played a role in the latter's downfall. All that can safely be said is that Khrushchev's antipathy sounds plausible and it certainly did not help Chervenkov—or Rakosi.

Thus Khrushchev's policy, Tito's enmity, and the situation within the Bulgarian Party all contributed to Chervenkov's fall. It was occasioned, of course, by the Twentieth CPSU Congress in February, 1956. The Bulgarian delegation to the congress was curious in that it did not include the First Party Secretary, Zhivkov. This presumably was a reflection of Zhivkov's real lack of seniority; all the same it was an astonishing and unprecedented omission. Chervenkov led the delegation and its other members were Yugov, Ganev, and Todor Zvezdov. The inclusion of Yugov and Ganev fully confirmed the revival of their importance after 1954; because of his previous treatment of them, neither was a man whom Chervenkov could trust. Zvezdov, a candidate member of the Central Committee, was by far the most junior of the delegation, but his inclusion was interesting because he was one of Yugov's men—First Party Secretary in Yugov's power stronghold at Plovdiv. Six years later, when Yugov ended his career in disgrace, Zvezdov, still in Plovdiv, also went into oblivion.

The Bulgarian delegation, like all the other foreign delegations and the vast majority of the delegates from the CPSU, came to the Twentieth Congress with no idea of what was in store. Khrushchev's opening speech on February 14 contained nothing sensational. Thus the unknowing Chervenkov could make a confident speech in which he stressed, for the benefit of his host, the growing *rapprochement* between Bulgaria and Yugoslavia. He also strongly emphasized the merits of agricultural collectivization which had resumed in earnest in Bulgaria.[22] With unconscious irony, he assured his audience that the BCP was "enchanted by the Leninist style of work of the present congress."[23]

Khrushchev's bombshell, for which Mikoyan lit the fuse, was given before a select audience of the CPSU on the night of February 24–25. Under the guise of an attack on the cult of personality, which had been under intermittent fire since Stalin's death, he delivered his famous secret speech vilifying the old dictator and some of his misdeeds. All, that is, committed inside the Soviet Union; one of the great omissions of the secret speech was any condemnation of Stalin's policies in Eastern Europe. It was a speech for domestic consumption and primarily for domestic purposes, although the intention to destroy the myth of Stalin's in-

[22] *Zemedelsko Zname* (Sofia), of March 1, 1956 announced that 25,000 new farmers had entered the cooperative fold in the first two months of 1956.
[23] *Rabotnichesko Delo*, February 18, 1956.

fallibility, thereby shattering the Stalinist system, obviously had implications for Eastern Europe also. No foreign delegates were admitted to this special session, but by the time they left Moscow most of them—certainly the Bulgarians—knew the gist of it and guessed its implications for them.

What took place in the corridors of power in Sofia during the whole of March—between the end of the Twentieth Congress and the beginning of the Bulgarian Central Committee plenum on April 2—is unfortunately not known, although expectancy in the capital was great and rumor rife. The press gave no hint of the attack against Stalin. On March 20, *Borba* gave the first extensive Eastern European summary of Khrushchev's speech. This was closely followed by an article on March 23 in the Polish Party daily, *Trybuna Ludu*, by Roman Werfel, who reported the attack on Stalin under the title, "Letter to a Comrade." But neither in Bulgaria nor Rumania was any such information published. Still, the contents of the *Borba* article must have trickled through to some Party members and the mood of expectancy in Sofia was heightened by the publication in *Rabotnichesko Delo* of March 25 of an article entitled "The Creative Character of Marxism-Leninism." Though not attacking Stalin directly, the article called for a complete elimination of the cult of personality. Bulgarians with memories certainly remembered that articles like this had been published on the eve of the Sixth BCP Congress in 1954 which had cost Chervenkov his Party leadership.[24] On March 29, the main Sofia dailies reprinted an editorial from the previous day's *Pravda* entitled, "Why is the Cult of Personality Alien to Marxism-Leninism?" and, on March 31, *Rabotnichesko Delo* again attacked the cult, but not Stalin, in an editorial "On the Role of the Person in History." Obviously, all this was a build-up for something, and many citizens of Sofia must have suspected what it was.

Their suspicions were confirmed to the wildest possible degree by the arrival in Sofia on April 5 of the Yugoslav delegation headed by Pijade, President of the Yugoslav National Assembly. Pijade actually arrived three days after the plenum of the Bulgarian Central Committee had begun, although there had been no official

---

[24] For example, *Rabotnichesko Delo*, February 12, 1954: "The cult of personality leads to a minimization of the role of the Party and its leading organs, and freezes the personal initiative and activity of Party organizations and members."

word of its convocation.[25] On April 8, however, the suspense was relieved by a Radio Sofia broadcast stating that a plenum of the Central Committee had been held from April 2–6 and giving the text of the resolution "unanimously" approved by the plenum.[26] This resolution had been preceded by "extensive discussions" (these were not published) and the plenum had been opened by First Party Secretary Zhivkov, who had elaborated on the Twentieth CPSU Congress (which he had not attended) and the lessons to be drawn from it.

The resolution treated Stalin with the greatest caution. The Central Committee plenum, it said, acknowledged the importance of the decisions reached at the Twentieth CPSU Congress for the application of Leninist norms in Party life, for collective leadership, and for the development of intra-Party democracy. It also acknowledged the great contribution of the congress to the "unrelenting fight against the remnants of the cult of personality which spread during the last years of Stalin, belittling the importance of the Party, the working classes, and collective leadership." The lessons of the Twentieth Congress, as applied to Bulgarian conditions, would have to serve as the basis for all work by the Bulgarian Party.

On Chervenkov, the resolution was more precise and, though not explicit, it left no doubt about his imminent demotion. The plenum considered that the efforts of the BCP to construct socialism would have had better results but for the personality cult and its non-Marxist methods. These methods had been allowed to grow considerably in the Party and the whole of Bulgarian public life. The "cult of comrade Vulko Chervenkov" had considerably altered the Party's "traditional and tried methods of work," its internal democracy, and its collective leadership. This had resulted in a "sometimes one-sided settlement" of questions and had harmful repercussions in the organizational, ideological, and economic apparatus of Party and state. The plenum had worked out measures to eliminate the personality cult and the harmful measures connected with it.

The resolution also announced that the number of Central

[25] The confusion at the time is shown in Reuters and AP reports from Vienna, quoting "usually reliable sources," stating on April 3 that a plenum had been held from March 31 to April 2. They probably meant meetings of the Politburo which must have been in almost constant session during those days.
[26] The Resolution was published by *Rabotnichesko Delo* on April 8, 1956.

Committee secretaries had been increased to five. To the very small Secretariat of three (Zhivkov, Ganev, and Boris Taskov) the names of Encho Staikov and Boyan Bulgaranov were now added. Staikov, then 54, was a home Communist, a journalist by profession who, before the war, had been editor of the illegal Party paper *Rabotnicheski Vestnik*, suffering long periods of imprisonment for his devotion to the cause. Elected to the Central Committee in 1948, he was a member of the Secretariat from 1952 to 1954. At the Sixth Party Congress he moved out of the Secretariat but was elected to the Politburo. His speciality was agitation and propaganda and his appointment may be explained by the need to strengthen these areas as a result of the Twentieth CPSU Congress and as a counterweight to Chervenkov. Bulgaranov's election was another gesture to all those who had suffered as Kostovites. A political general who had been discharged from the army in 1949, Bulgaranov was rehabilitated in 1953 and made a partial comeback as deputy Minister of State Supply and the Food Industry. At the Sixth Congress in 1954, he was elected to the Central Committee. He was already 60 in 1954 but was to enjoy a surprisingly long political career thereafter.

About Kostov, the resolution said nothing specific. But he was obviously the subject of a passage stating that the plenum deemed it necessary to take measures to strengthen socialist legality, to punish most severely any distortions of it, and to reinforce the judiciary's control over the application and execution of justice. In an address to the Sofia City Party *actif* on April 11, Zhivkov admitted that, because of infractions of socialist legality, "innocent comrades were accused and unjustly punished." This had been the case in Kostov's trial and some subsequent trials, he admitted. The sentences in all of these trials had now been annulled and the victims who were still in custody were to be set free. A Central Committee commission was to be established to reappraise all the material available on those trials in order to "rehabilitate before the Party and the people" all Communists who had been innocently sentenced.[27]

In this speech, which was in many ways more revealing than the Plenum resolution, Zhivkov made it clear that there had been opposition to the disclosures about Stalin or, at least, great confusion. Some comrades, "lacking correct information," wrongly considered that, by criticizing the cult of Stalin's personality, Stalin's work as a whole was being repudiated, "including his

[27] *Rabotnichesko Delo*, April 12, 1956.

undoubted services to the CPSU, the peoples of the U.S.S.R., and international Communism." The present task, said Zhivkov, was to conduct a Marxist-Leninist analysis of the historical facts in order to determine Stalin's rightful place in the history of the CPSU, as well as to expose the negative aspects of his work. Again the treatment of Stalin was cautious: compare this kid-glove approach with a Polish broadcast description of the dead dictator as "monstrously and pathologically suspicious."[28]

On Chervenkov, Zhivkov expanded somewhat on the plenum resolution. After his election as Secretary-General of the BCP (November 11, 1950), Chervenkov had been unjustly credited (Zhivkov did not say by whom) with practically everything: the victory of September 9 (1944, when Chervenkov was still in Moscow), the bolshevization of Bulgaria, the whole success in socialist construction; in short, *all* the successes of both Party and state. Chervenkov had placed himself above the Central Committee and this had led to a disparaging of the role of the Party itself.[29]

Zhivkov's address to the Sofia *actif* was part of a huge campaign of propaganda and explanation which followed the April plenum. Press and radio were saturated with comment (but with very little information of what actually went on at the plenum) and Politburo and Secretariat members spoke at meetings in all the important centers of Bulgaria. They said very little, but it was noticeable that Chervenkov was most sharply attacked by Yugov, the man who had suffered under him and who was to supersede him. Thus Yugov, speaking on his home-ground at Plovdiv, charged that Chervenkov's "wrong conceptions . . . and harmful methods of work created conditions for violations of socialist legality, impeded initiative, criticism, and self-criticism and negatively affected the education of Party cadres."[30] The relish was obvious.

On April 17, the National Assembly met (with Pijade in the distinguished visitors' gallery), "unanimously" accepted the resignation of Chervenkov as Premier and, in like manner, elected Yugov in his place. Thus the man who must have been close to liquidation in 1950 was now head of the government. Chervenkov was elected one of his deputy premiers. Other important changes were made at the same time. Georgi Chankov was promoted from deputy premier to first deputy premier, retaining his presidency of

[28] Radio Warsaw, April 8, 1956.
[29] *Rabotnichesko Delo*, April 12, 1956.
[30] *Rabotnichesko Delo*, April 16, 1956.

the State Planning Commission. This was probably more of a consolation prize than anything else for the ambitious Chankov. The most able and dynamic of the younger home Communists, Chankov might have expected the Party leadership in 1954 when Chervenkov stepped down. Instead the colorless and plodding Zhivkov was chosen, probably because he was "safer." Now Yugov had been preferred for the premiership. As events were to show, Chankov's impatience and ambition were soon to exceed permissive limits. Also promoted from deputy to first deputy premier was Georgi Traikov, leader of the puppet Agrarian Party. This was recognition neither of Traikov's limited abilities nor of his even more limited importance. It was essentially another attempt to court peasant opinion. It was not to be the last political shift from which Traikov was to benefit. He was later to become head of state, a symbol of the elevation of the collectivized peasantry. In addition to Chervenkov, one other new deputy premier was appointed. He was Karlo Lukanov, brought back from the embassy in Moscow where he had served since 1954. He had previously been a deputy premier and a President of the State Planning Commission. Now, in addition to his deputy premiership, he was made President of the newly created Commission for Labor and Labor Remuneration. In a matter of weeks, however, Lukanov became Foreign Minister on the death of Mincho Neichev.

Ferment After the Plenum

Such, essentially, was the April plenum and its immediate consequence—the resignation of Chervenkov. Khrushchev and Tito had their way. But apart from this, the strong impression left by April events was that neither Stalin nor Chervenkov came out of them too badly. Stalin's reputation was tarnished but by no means shattered and Chervenkov, though holding neither of the two offices he once united, was still very much a power in the land. He was a member of the Politburo and a deputy premier,[31] and (through his support in the middle and lower levels of the Party) still probably the strongest single figure in Bulgaria. Developments over the next two years were also to work in his favor. The unbridled course which destalinization ran in Hungary and Poland,

[31] It was perhaps no coincidence that the other new deputy premier, Lukanov, was a former Muscovite and a strong Chervenkov man. The third deputy premier, Raiko Damyanov, was also a Muscovite.

and even its comparatively mild impact in Bulgaria itself, caused a frightened reaction,[32] and forced the new regime to depend on Chervenkov's ability and authority to help restore "stability." But he had lost two vital bases of support: the sponsorship of Moscow, where Khrushchev, in spite of Stalinist hopes for his overthrow, was subsequently to consolidate his position, and the power of patronage at home, now in the hands of Zhivkov and Yugov. Without these, any recovery of his influence was bound to be only temporary.

As for the population, its reaction to the personal changes seems to have been one of cynicism. As mentioned earlier, Chervenkov was believed to have been pushed out mainly by Tito, and was considered the victim of a Yugoslav-Russian conspiracy. This produced a degree of sympathy for Chervenkov that he had never had before and hardly deserved. The cynicism was compounded by the general unpopularity of his successor. Yugov was a Communist in politics and a dandy in personal habits in a nation which did not have much time for either. But his blackest mark was his record as Minister of the Interior during the Red terror between 1945 and 1948. Yugov was the hatchet man during this period and won a grim renown for his ruthless efficiency and zeal. Later there was much popular sympathy for the Kostovites but little for Yugov who, though humiliated, was never persecuted and soon managed to wriggle his way back with an ease that must have looked suspicious. He was not a coward and was certainly no fool; he knew the Bulgarian proletariat and among his own tobacco workers perhaps still enjoyed some popularity. In brief encounters he was nothing if not plausible and, as Premier, was to charm more than one Western ambassador. But among the population as a whole he enjoyed little respect.

One result of the April plenum that all sections of the community did appreciate was the change of mood. The greater sense of personal freedom and confidence which had been growing since the death of Stalin now became far more manifest. There were rumors both from within the country and from Yugoslav sources that a number of secret policemen had been arrested after the April session of the National Assembly for persecuting innocent persons. These could not be confirmed but it seems at least likely

[32] See, for example, Yugov's statement when in Moscow in February 1957: "If they call us Stalinists because we are hard and irreconcilable in the face of opportunism and revisionism, then we feel honored in accepting the reproach." *Rabotnichesko Delo*, February 19, 1957.

that some security personnel were dismissed. At any rate, the very fact that such rumors could circulate at all was evidence of a change in popular attitudes.

Many spheres of regime-controlled activity showed greater permissiveness and relaxation. The most important was the Party itself. At Party meetings on various levels all over the country, held to study the lessons of the Twentieth CPSU Congress and the April plenum, previous mistakes were analyzed, criticisms were freely leveled at officials high and low, and the self-criticisms that followed were sometimes masochistic in their intensity. For a few months in Bulgaria, inner Party democracy really meant something.

It was not surprising that this mood was reflected in literature and the press. Developments in literature will be discussed in a separate chapter; as for the press, many examples could be given to show that it was at last becoming remotely readable. The efforts of Vladimir Topencharov, president of the Bulgarian Union of Journalists and editor of the Fatherland Front paper, *Otechestven Front*, are particularly worthy of note, since he was the journalist who spearheaded the move for greater democratization. Writing one day after the demotion of Chervenkov, Topencharov accused the Party and its leaders of estranging themselves from the ordinary masses.[33] He repeated these attacks with great force several times and *Otechestven Front* during this period became a powerful organ for reformist opinion. It was nothing like the audacious freedom of the press in Poland or Hungary, but for Bulgaria, this was Spring and many took advantage of it while they could.

The Braking Process

Indeed, the atmosphere, reflected and generated by men like Topencharov, was soon considered dangerously heady by the Party leaders, who saw that a brake must be put on the process they themselves had begun. In a definitive editorial on May 20 entitled "Against Petty Bourgeois Slap-Happiness," the Party daily, *Rabotnichesko Delo*, attacked Topencharov personally. His ideas, it charged, indicated a "hidden desire to see the BCP's role discontinued and have the country run by the press." Similar ideas were criticized as "anti-Party" and "anarchic," having nothing in

[33] *Otechestven Front* (Sofia), April 18, 1956.

common with the interests of either the Party or the people. End-ing on an atavistic note, the Party daily described the main duty of the press as being the "clarification of correct Party and govern-ment policy and the influencing of the labor force for the attain-ment of these policies."

The ferment in the press did not subside immediately after this warning and, as will be seen, the ferment in literature continued throughout 1957. But the *Rabotnichesko Delo* article quoted above was a clear sign that the regime would not allow the discus-sion to go too far and it was subsequently to show that it was easily the master of a situation which, in fact, never really threatened to get out of hand. The regime's main concern was to prevent the spirit of democratization within the Party from spread-ing to the nation as a whole. It was this reluctance that roused the ire of the Yugoslavs who, between the April plenum and Zhivkov's visit to Belgrade in October, kept up a steady fire on developments in Sofia.[34] In September, they magisterially judged Bulgaria last in the Eastern European destalinization race and criticized the Central Committee for obstructing genuine democratization.[35]

The Bulgarian regime safely negotiated the dangerous period be-tween the Poznan riots in late June, 1956, and the end of the Hungarian Revolution mainly for three reasons. Bulgarian society had not suffered the same political and economic strains which the Stalinist system imposed on countries like Poland and Hun-gary; hence popular frustration and antipathy toward the regime was less. Hatred of the Soviet Union was much less than in Poland and Hungary. Finally, the Bulgarian Party, unlike the Polish and Hungarian but like the Czechoslovak, East German and Ru-manian, avoided catastrophic splits during this relatively short period of tension.

On the last point, the Bulgarian Party was lucky. It had already begun to rehabilitate the Kostovites and restore to positions of authority the older generation of home Communists. The Party's ugly wound, therefore, though not completely healed, was less open than before. Chervenkov, the object of so much Party grievance, no longer held either the Party leadership or the pre-miership. In September, just a few weeks before the explosions in Poland and Hungary, the Party hastened to give more reality to the

[34] They were particularly irked and disappointed that Chervenkov still re-tained so much influence; see, for example, *Politika* (Belgrade), April 24, 1956; and *Nova Makedonja* (Skoplje), April 24, 1956.
[35] Radio Zagreb, September 1, 1956.

Kostovite rehabilitations. The commission to investigate the Kostov trials, set up at the April plenum under the chairmanship of Dimitur Ganev, reported to a Central Committee plenum held on September 7. It found that the sentences in these trials had been unjust and restored Party membership to all but two of the minor victims, these two being excluded on the grounds of their complete unsuitability for Party membership. At the same plenum, Zhivkov, now far more in the public eye, gave a long speech in which he repeated the promises of the April plenum: more Party democracy, independent judiciary, and greater control over the police. To this list of prime intentions he added another: the elevating of the National Assembly (Subranie) to the highest organ of people's government, a promise to be made many times after 1956. At the same time, however, the plenum resolution, with men like Topencharov in mind, warned against using the Twentieth Congress as a pretext to disparage socialist achievements and "strike at the prestige of the Central Committee."[36]

Although the situation remained calm, Bulgaria cannot have been entirely excluded from Moscow's general concern over Eastern Europe in this period. In July, Yugov, Chankov, Mihailov, and Tsankov visited the Crimea for talks with Mikoyan and Suslov. It was an important delegation: Yugov and Chankov were probably the two most powerful men in the government if one excludes Chervenkov, who was hardly acceptable to the Soviets. Mihailov, the most powerful influence in the armed forces, was Soviet-trained and trustworthy. Tsankov, the Minister of the Interior, controlled the first line of defense—the police and militia—against domestic turmoil. Whether trouble of any kind did break out during this period has never been adequately confirmed. A Western report of demonstrations in Plovdiv and Sofia in July was denied.[37] Rumor, of course, was rife during this period and it is possible there was tension at certain times and places but, for the reasons given above, it was never serious enough to lead to major disturbances.

Besides the political health of Bulgaria, another subject almost certainly discussed between the Soviet and Bulgarian leaders in the Crimea was Sofia's relations with Belgrade. It cannot have pleased the Soviet leaders that these relations were at such a low ebb. One important reason for the September Central Committee plenum,

[36] Radio Sofia, September 19, 1956.

[37] Agence France Presse, July 26, 1956. For denials see Reuters, July 28, and *Rabotnichesko Delo*, August 4, 1956.

where Zhivkov announced the full Kostovite rehabilitations and re-emphasized measures for democratization, may well have been the desire to placate Tito.[38] At any rate, at the end of September Zhivkov joined the list of ostensibly repentant Eastern European leaders traveling to Belgrade. Heading a parliamentary delegation, Zhivkov was accompanied by Chankov and several others. He arrived in Yugoslavia on September 22 and had to stay there till October 7 to be able to see Tito, who was in the Soviet Union for the greater part of the Bulgarian delegation's stay. Their talks with Yugoslav leaders, most notably Rankovic and Pijade, went cordially enough but the communiqué issued at the end of their talks lacked any degree of warmth. It implied that big differences still existed between the two Parties but that these should not prevent increased cooperation.[39] At a press conference in Belgrade, Zhivkov actually mentioned differences "in form and practice in socialist construction." It was "natural that some Yugoslav forms . . . should differ from Bulgarian forms."[40] These remarks were widely covered in the Yugoslav press but ignored in the Bulgarian press. Generally, Bulgarian media tried to present the visit as a great success.[41] The Yugoslav judgment was much cooler: Belgrade stressed the present differences rather than the agreement on future cooperation.[42]

The Revolution in Hungary

Zhivkov's party returned to Bulgaria on the eve of the dramatic upheavals in Poland and Hungary. Bulgarian attention—like that of the rest of the world—was riveted on these events. The regime watched them with nervousness and apprehension. The army was placed in a state of alert and extra security precautions taken. Again, because of conflicting and often absurdly exaggerated rumors, it is impossible to give an accurate picture of the situation between October 20 and November 4. Perhaps the most informative and balanced report on the mood at the height of the Hun-

[38] Mikoyan visited Belgrade at the end of July and on his return stopped over in both Sofia and Bucharest to inform his hosts about the Yugoslav situation.

[39] *Tanjug* (Belgrade), October 7, 1956.

[40] *Ibid.*

[41] See, for example, *Rabotnichesko Delo*, October 9, 1956, and *Otechestven Front*, October 10, 1956.

[42] Radio Belgrade, October 11, 1956.

garian tragedy was given by Reuters news agency from Vienna on October 9. Based on interviews with Bulgarian sources, its report said:

> People expressed sympathy with the Hungarians and added that it was obvious that most people in Sofia were well informed through listening to the Western radio broadcasts, and did not hide the fact. The Bulgarian people were excitedly discussing events in Poland and Hungary and often criticized the Bulgarian press, which gave only the official Communist line. Notices of Russian revolution celebrations (i.e., the October revolution—ed.) were torn down or scribbled on in the factories near Sofia, but no demonstrations against the U.S.S.R. were reported. Despite these signs of tension, however, the reports said, there have been no disturbances on a large scale.

Another source described the mood as "a sad resignation resembling fatalism, combined with admiration (for the Poles and Hungarians) and perhaps envy." The ordinary Bulgarians had hoped for a miracle but, as they so rightly realized, "they had no Gomulka."[43]

The "official Communist line," to which the Reuters report referred, was never more apparent than during the October–November days. The Hungarian revolution was a reactionary-fascist plot aided and abetted by imperialism and the "atrocities" of the rebels were painted in the most lurid colors. On October 28, Radio Sofia described the revolt as almost over. The installation of the Kadar government by Soviet troops was greeted with enthusiasm but Kadar's conciliatory program was completely ignored. The Bulgarian attitude toward Poland's liberalization was downright hostile at first and various Soviet attacks on Polish developments received full play.[44] Later, when the worst fears of the orthodox proved to have been groundless, the tone mellowed. Finally, when the Hungarian drama was over, the whole propaganda machinery of the regime went into action to give it its "correct interpretation." Besides the press and radio campaigns, agitprop meetings were held throughout the country. The speakers apparently were not challenged; it was a great mechanical success.

One result of the Hungarian Revolution was the collapse of the *rapprochement* with Yugoslavia. This was a serious embarrassment for Khrushchev, not least in his own struggle for supreme

---

[43] *The Times* (London), November 3, 1956.

[44] For example, Radio Sofia on October 20 broadcast the *Pravda* article of the previous day entitled "Anti-Socialist Articles in the Pages of the Polish Press."

power in Moscow, but was hardly seen as a tragedy by the Bulgarian Party, especially the dogmatist forces grouped around Chervenkov. On November 11, Tito made his Pula speech in which he regretted that Moscow had not lived up to the principles of equality between socialist states and of separate roads to socialism—principles that he and Khrushchev had agreed were applicable to *all* states. He condemned the first Soviet intervention in Hungary but gave qualified support to the second. Tito was trying to maintain the very satisfactory relationship just established with Khrushchev without sacrificing the principles on which he considered that relationship to be based.[45] The Bulgarian reaction to this speech was cautious and closely followed the Soviet line. The main Sofia dailies, for example, carried the November 23 *Pravda* article, "For a Further Consolidation of the Socialist Forces on the Basis of Marxist-Leninist Principles," which mildly attacked Tito. In general, one could detect in the Bulgarian press a sense of relief at the rebuff for the Titoist heresy and pleasure that orthodoxy, "the path of basic conformity," had been vindicated.[46] Later a note of aggressiveness became apparent and as early as 1957, the Bulgarians picked out Mjalko Todorovic (later to emerge as an outstanding reformer) as a dangerous ideologist for his attempts to revise the role of the Party in society.[47]

In short, the Bulgarian leadership, regardless of the different shades of opinion within it, was relieved over Moscow's cooling of relations with Tito. The reason for this relief lies in the situation which the tumultuous events of 1956 had caused within the Party. The Twentieth CPSU Congress, the April plenum, the dismissal of Chervenkov, the Soviet-Yugoslav *rapprochement*, and October in both Hungary and Poland—all these events had left their mark. True, no revolutionary situation was created, but the unsettling effect was obvious. The ferment was most apparent in the cultural field (this is discussed in Chapter 11). But within the Party itself, although there were no serious splits during the crisis period of 1956, there were rumblings of discontent which a nervous leadership could not take in its stride. As early as May, 1956, Generals Yonko Panov and Boris Kopchev had been dismissed from their posts as deputy ministers of defense, reportedly for their too-violent criticisms of Chervenkov and their demand that he be demoted more comprehensively. Older home Com-

---

[45] Brzezinski, *op. cit.*, pp. 229–34.
[46] See, for example, *Trud* (Sofia), November 24, 1956.
[47] Radio Sofia, March 14, 1957.

munists, like Dobri Terpeshev and Tsola Dragoicheva, were also reported thoroughly dissatisfied with the results of the April plenum. It was later officially admitted that various Party organizations, notably that of Sofia, had incorrectly interpreted the results of the Twentieth CPSU Congress and the April plenum and had been criticized for "some wrong statements and actions, and for displaying doubts about the correctness of Party policy, the foundation of Bulgaria's unshakeable friendship with the Soviet Union, and the Bulgarian people's democratic system." Such difficulties for the party were multiplied by the Hungarian Revolution.[48]

As late as June, 1957, such defects and dangerous tendencies were still being criticized. The April plenum had caused "poorly oriented and unstable Party members" to show "petty bourgeois hesitations and moods." As a result, careerist and opportunist elements had penetrated provincial organizations, "compromised honest Communists," and completely broken the unity of some organizations.[49]

This atmosphere, in combination with the restive mood of the general population, made the timid leadership welcome the renewed respect for orthodoxy that prevailed in the international Communist movement toward the end of 1956. Once the ferment abroad had died down, the ferment at home could be tackled more effectively. In this situation the conservative critics prospered and the conservative forces rallied, none more so than Chervenkov himself. From the beginning of 1957 to the end of 1958, Chervenkov seemed to have recovered much of the influence lost in 1956. In February, 1957, after ten months of virtual seclusion from the public, he was appointed Minister of Education and Culture in an extensive cabinet reshuffle. This move was evidently an attempt to use his authority and knowledge to crush the cultural ferment which had grown since the April plenum. In the same month, he accompanied Zhivkov, Yugov, Chankov, and Raiko Damyanov in the top-level delegation to Moscow for government and Party talks with the Soviet leaders. The inclusion of his controversial person in the delegation must have been cleared by Moscow beforehand; his acceptance not only showed the chastened mood of Khrushchev about Eastern Europe generally but his reacceptance of Chervenkov as a stabilizing force in Bulgaria. The Bulgarians had wide-ranging talks with the Soviet

[48] See speech by Nacho Papazov to Sofia Party organization, *Vecherni Novini* (Sofia), April 8, 1957.
[49] *Rabotnichesko Delo*, June 15, 1957.

leaders on international economic and Party questions and a series of important economic agreements. On the delegation's return to Bulgarian soil, at Russe on the Danube, it was Chervenkov, rather than Zhivkov or Yugov, who addressed a large meeting. The significance of this must have been readily understood by his audience and the country as a whole.

The Purges of 1957

Bulgaria's leaders had decided that, for order to be restored within the Party and in public life, it was necessary to root out those elements that were disturbing it. They chose this conservative policy rather than try to remove the basic cause of the dissension, which was the failure to press ahead with the reforms the April plenum had seemed to promise. The official complaints mentioned above indicated that a purge was in the offing. That a quiet but fairly extensive purge took place in the middle and lower apparatus during the spring and summer of 1957 can be surmised from fragmentary official reports and a whole series of rumors. But this was not enough: examples had to be made of higher officials whom the leadership found difficult. The inspiration for these top-level dismissals was the Soviet purge of Molotov, Malenkov, Kaganovich, and Shepilov in July; the Bulgarian victims were Chankov, Terpeshev, and Panov. They were purged at a Central Committee plenum held on July 11 and 12. Chankov lost both his Politburo and Central Committee posts and, immediately afterwards, his first deputy premiership. Terpeshev and Panov, who now held no government posts, lost their Central Committee memberships.

Dobri Terpeshev was one of the best-known and best-liked of the older home Communists. Colorful and amiable, he was the classic type of working-class revolutionary. He had been active in the 1918 and 1923 rebellions and subsequent underground work, and was one of the leaders of the Communist partisans during World War II. After the September 9 liberation he entered the Politburo but was not re-elected in 1948. His other positions had included Chairman of the Supreme Economic Council, Minister of Labor and Social Welfare and, for a brief period, Ambassador to Bucharest. In 1950 he was demoted in the wake of the Kostov trial and, though restored to favor during the new course, never regained his former prominence. This may have been because of age, but more probably resulted from the cheerful ineptitude he had demonstrated in the posts he had held. A genuine character, Terpeshev was a good example of the old revolutionary Communist for whom the transition from barricade to executive desk proved impossible.

Yonko Panov, a more consequential man whom people took seriously, had been notable in the pre-war underground Party for his strongly militant views and had become a general with the Communist partisans. A member of the Central Committee since 1952, he was appointed a deputy minister of defense in September, 1954, and lost his post in May, 1956, apparently because he did not think the April plenum had gone far enough.

Chankov was easily the most important of the three; in fact, he had been one of the most powerful men in Bulgaria. The question why he was purged and whether he really had anything in common with the other two is difficult to answer. Terpeshev and Panov were, after all, Communists of the older generation. They had become known as strong opponents of Chervenkov and as advocates of a more reformist course at home and less dependence on the Soviet Union abroad. It is doubtful, however, that either now aspired for positions in the top Party leadership. Chankov's political profile was far less clear. His previous record had suggested an able, tough apparatchik hardly disposed toward a faster pace of reform than that implemented since 1954.

The official criticisms of Chankov after his demotion often seem contradictory. Like most fallen idols, he was accused of practically everything. But the fullest criticism of him appeared in the Central Committee monthly, *Novo Vreme*. Chankov, "guided by unhealthy ambitions for primacy in the Party and country," had, it implied, "become the center of attempts to refute the Party line and to generalize individual errors and thus denigrate our regime." He had tried to change "the composition of the Politburo and the Central Committee" after the April plenum. He had "increasingly displayed disagreement" with the decisions of that plenum and had tried to thwart its decisions, particularly those connected with raising the standard of living—the increase of low wages and salaries, pensions, and family allowances and the improvement in the standard of living in agriculture.[50] These accusations constitute two conflicting changes: that Chankov was a leader in factional activity which, the regime had strongly implied previously, was essentially revisionist; and, secondly, that he acted

[50] *Novo Vreme* (Sofia), August, 1957.

like a Stalinist in opposing moves designed to increase the welfare of the people. This second accusation smacks of demagogy. The probable truth is that Chankov—always ambitious, and disappointed over his failure to get either the Party leadership or the premiership in the changes since 1954—became disaffected and did try to capitalize on the discontent and confusion in both Party and society after the April plenum.

How far he identified himself with Panov and Chervenkov is hard to say. It is worth noting that, in the similar purges carried out at the time in the Soviet Union and Rumania, an ill-assorted group found themselves bunched together. Malenkov and Shepilov, for example, made strange bedfellows with Molotov and Kaganovich, while in Rumania, the Stalinist Josif Chisinevschi was purged along with the reformist Miron Constantinescu. Whatever the reasons for the Moscow purge, it presented both Bulgarian and Rumanian leaderships with a chance to get rid of various threats and nuisances and to tar them with the same brush. The departure of Chankov was an important step on Todor Zhivkov's road to supreme power. It meant the elimination of a contemporary, a "natural rival" and a man more intelligent and forceful than himself. Later, in 1961, more was heard of the persistent Panov and Terpeshev, but Chankov disappeared from Bulgarian politics. In 1966 he became ambassador to Brazil, perhaps an act of precaution on the part of Zhivkov but a move that was hardly noticed in Bulgarian politics.

The purge of Bulgaria's own anti-Party group was followed by a considerable reshuffle in the top Party bodies. Three new full members of the Politburo were elected at the September plenum in 1957: Ganev, Taskov, and Bulgaranov. All three were veteran home Communists and two, Ganev and Bulgaranov, had been in disgrace after the fall of Kostov. None, therefore, could be considered a Chervenkov man, a fact worth noting since, though Chervenkov's influence had certainly revived, this was not being reflected in the key field of personnel changes. The two new candidate-members of the Politburo were Dimitur Dimov and Mladen Stoyanov. Dimov had been elected a candidate member in 1945 but lost this status at the 1948 congress. In April, 1955, he had been appointed Ambassador to Peking. Stoyanov was a dried-up veteran from the early days of the BCP who had spent long years in the Soviet Union.

More significant in terms of the future interplay of powers were the changes in the Secretariat and some of the new additions to the Central Committee. Taskov and Encho Staikov moved out and were replaced by Dancho Dimitrov and Stanko Todorov, two supporters of Zhivkov. Three of the new full Central Committee members, Mitko Grigorov, Pencho Kubadinski, and Tano Tsolov were also Zhivkov appointees. In a short time all three were to move up to the Secretariat and then the Politburo. The power of patronage, which a First Party Secretary always dispenses, was beginning to tell. On the other side, however, the reappearance of Todor Pavlov in the Central Committee must be recorded. A rigidly orthodox Stalinist philosopher, Pavlov had been chairman of the Bulgarian Academy of Sciences since 1949; he was a man who, if the "spirit" of the April plenum had been applied consistently in the sphere of education and culture, would have been ripe for retirement rather than promotion. But Chervenkov had been made Minister of Education and Culture the previous February to crush the cultural ferment. Pavlov was his ally in this task and hence was given a Party status more worthy of the importance of his mission.

To summarize the April plenum and its aftermath, one can say that Bulgarian politics in this period presented a case of arrested growth. Bulgaria was undeniably a much better place in which to live in 1957 than it had been in 1953 and the April plenum certainly played a big part in this process. But it was hardly the turning point in Bulgarian Communist history which the regime, anxious to create its myths, later made it out to be. The ferment in Eastern Europe which followed the Twentieth CPSU Congress and led to the Hungarian Revolution, and the relatively mild ferment in Bulgaria itself, so alarmed the timid Bulgarian leadership that it made strong and generally successful efforts to avoid the consequences of the April plenum. In retrospect, therefore, that plenum seems more the culmination of the progress since 1953 than the beginning of a new era after 1956. After a brief period of euphoria, Chervenkov's influence revived, the cultural ferment was submerged, and later, in 1958, the "great leap forward" in the economy began—an effort that was hardly conducive to a continuing relaxation of public life. Later, after the Twenty-Second CPSU Congress and Khrushchev's second bout of de-Stalinization, a new wave of relaxation began that had a considerable impact on Bulgarian life. But to argue that this later development was a logical consequence of the April plenum is to ignore what happened in

between, and to assume that the death of the cult of personality
—which did occur at the April plenum—was the only essential
ingredient for greater democratization. It may have been the essential *foundation,* but in Bulgaria that foundation was not consistently built on. Indeed, it was only resumed in earnest at the end
of 1961, over five years after the April plenum, when another lurch
toward democratization was made.

5

The Great Leap Forward: Its Course and Effects

THE TWO YEARS from the beginning of 1959 to the end of 1960 were probably the most spectacular in Bulgarian Communist history. This was the period of the "great leap forward," a movement which, though economic in nature, had ramifications for all important aspects of Bulgarian life.

The announcement of the "great leap forward" was as sudden as it was unexpected. The Seventh BCP Congress in June, 1958, approved the Third Five-Year Plan for the development of the economy. Its main outlines were as follows: Total industrial production was to increase 62 per cent by the end of 1962 as compared with 1957; of this, the value of heavy industrial output was to increase by 77 per cent and of light industrial production by 50 per cent. The gross value of agricultural production was to increase 35 per cent over the same period. The planned average annual growth rate for the national income was to be 8 per cent.[1] This was essentially a moderate plan compared with previous economic programs; its guiding concept was that industrial branches should be developed only when favorable natural conditions and resources existed, or when such branches were absolutely necessary for the national economy.[2] This concept led to greater stress being placed on the light and food industries than ever be-

[1] *Trud* (Sofia), June 3, 1958.
[2] See Yugov's speech at the Seventh Congress: *Rabotnichesko Delo* (Sofia), June 5, 1958.

fore, although preference was still given to heavy industry. In 1959, taking capital investments in industry as a whole, Sector "A" was planned to receive 69.5 per cent and Sector "B" 30.5 per cent. In no previous year had Sector "B" received more than 15 per cent.

Just as it seemed that the government and the nation were settling down to the implementation of this plan, a "nationwide" movement began in October, 1958, to fulfill it before the scheduled time, "in three to four years." The final expression of this movement was summed up in the Zhivkov Theses, published in the press in January, 1959, after their approval by the Central Committee.[3] The theses referred to "new tempos and scales of production" during the period 1959–1962–1965. Planning cycles were now no longer to be five years, but seven, in accordance with the new Soviet plan scheduled for approval at the Twenty-First CPSU Congress to be held in February, 1959. The theses provided for the total volume of industrial production in 1962 to be increased twofold and in 1965 by about three to four times compared with 1957. In agriculture, the theses demanded that the value of production be twice as much in 1959 as in 1958 and three times as much in 1960 as in 1958.

These few, dry figures give no idea of the excitement generated by the "nation-wide movement." The "great leap forward"—the press openly adopted this "Chinese" title—was the subject of numerous mass meetings throughout the length and breadth of the country. The regime's agitprop officials worked overtime to stimulate popular enthusiasm and the nation was plunged into the kind of uproar it had not experienced since the turbulent days after 1945. So that all would understand what was afoot, the regime propositions were put in simple form. The following Fatherland Front appeal was typical:

> What is the meaning of the slogan, "The Five-Year Plan in Three to Four Years"? It means to struggle for the fulfillment of the Five-Year Plan, in terms of the planned volume of production and national income, in three to four years instead of in five. In other words, in industry, transport, building, and trade, to produce the stipulated national income of the Five-Year Plan in four years; the rural economy in 1959 should produce about twice as much as in this year (1958—ed.) and three times as much in 1960.[4]

[3] *Rabotnichesko Delo*, January 20, 1959.
[4] *Otechestven Front* (Sofia), December 26, 1958.

It should be noted that what was meant here, and Zhivkov confirmed this,[5] was not the doubling and the tripling of *the rates of growth* but of the actual *value of the volume of production.* It is an important distinction because when the "great leap forward" was wound up at the end of 1960, the regime sought to justify itself by referring to rates of growth rather than volume of production.

Reasons for the "Great Leap Forward"

What prompted this "Bulgarian leap in the dark," as the London *Economist* so aptly described it?[6] The reasons were both economic and political.

The soundest economic reason for stepping up the pace of expansion was the fact that the economy, in spite of the great quantitative strides it had made, was still not working to full capacity. This had shown itself most clearly in Bulgaria's unemployment problem, a highly embarrassing reality in view of the socialist theory that this phenomenon was solely a product of capitalism. Whatever euphemisms the government might resort to, it has been estimated that there were at least 350,000 out of work in 1957 and 1958.[7] This unemployment resulted from labor displacement in the countryside due to collectivization and mechanization, the subsequent failure of industry to absorb those displaced, and the large reduction of the working force in private handicrafts and artisanry. Subsidiary reasons were the periodic reductions in the number of state employees and in the armed forces.

A number of remedial measures had already been carried out before 1958. These had included civilian replacement of military labor on various projects, the specific creation of new jobs in the annual economic plans,[8] and an agreement to process raw cotton from the Soviet Union for reshipment back to that country. The most interesting measure was the agreement to send 10,000 young people to the Soviet Union to do mainly agricultural work in 1957. This was probably the first experiment in labor migration in Eastern Europe. It foreshadowed agreements in 1967 between

[5] *Rabotnichesko Delo,* November 14, 1958.
[6] *The Economist* (London), January 3, 1959.
[7] See Radio Free Europe, "Report on Bulgaria: Background and Current Situation" (Munich), October, 1959, p. 47 and p. 50, footnote 2.
[8] For example, the 1957 plan envisaged the creation of 31,000 new jobs.

Hungary and the G.D.R. for the migration of Hungarian workers on contract to East German factories, and agreements between Bulgaria and the Soviet Union for the migration, also on contract, of several thousand Bulgarian forestry workers to northern Russia in 1967. But these measures checked rather than solved the problem. In 1959, however, the Zhivkov Theses foresaw 140,000 new jobs by the end of the year and 400,000 by the end of 1962.[9] This was expected to solve the problem—and it largely did, giving the "great leap forward" one of its few complete successes.

Not only was the economy not operating to capacity, it was still badly balanced. Despite the policy of redress after 1953, the continued preferential stress on heavy industry had caused rural production to lag still further behind. Whereas the annual average increase of industrial production between 1948 and 1958 was about 16 per cent, that of rural production had only been 2.4 per cent.[10] This would explain the seemingly astronomic targets in agriculture; they were a whirlwind effort to make up in three years the ground that had been lost in ten.

But this increased attention to agriculture and the food industry generally was not solely prompted by the need to balance Bulgaria's economy. It was also the result of Bulgaria's increased Comecon obligations in this sphere. Bulgaria had been a founder-member of the Council for Mutual Economic Assistance since it was founded in 1949. But as long as the organization had existed virtually on paper only, Bulgaria, like the other members, had concentrated on building up an economy on autarchic principles. After 1956, however, the Soviet leadership under Khrushchev began to see the possibilities of Comecon as an instrument of both economic rationalization and political coordination. As early as April, 1957, in a four-sided agreement signed with the Soviet Union, Czechoslovakia, and the German Democratic Republic, Bulgaria agreed to step up considerably her exports of natural and processed agricultural produce to these countries. (These three countries accounted for nearly three-quarters of Bulgaria's total exports in 1959 and over 67 per cent of her imports.) This agreement was extended at the twelfth session of the Comecon Council of Sofia in December, 1959. It was then planned that Bulgarian exports of fresh and canned fruit and vegetables to the member countries of Comecon should be double in 1965 what they were in 1958.[11]

In order to be able to meet these obligations, Bulgaria had to cut

9 *Trud*, March 27, 1959.
10 *Novo Vreme* (Sofia), March, 1959, p. 23.
11 *Rabotnichesko Delo*, December 17, 1959.

back production of such traditional commodities as wheat and cotton, but the Soviet Union agreed to make up these deficiencies.[12] Clearly, therefore, these agreements constituted an extra incentive for a leap forward in agriculture, especially in fruit and vegetables. In 1958, for example, 75 per cent more grapes were produced than in 1957 and 80 per cent more were planned in 1959 than had been produced in 1958.[13] In 1959, the volume of capital investments allocated to agriculture was almost double the volume allocated the previous year—807.9 million leva against 412 million.

In addition to these obligations to her socialist allies, the Bulgarian government was interested in developing trade with the Western countries and agricultural produce was, and still is, the only Bulgarian export readily acceptable in Western markets. As early as 1959, 8.2 per cent of Bulgaria's total imports came from the Federal Republic of Germany and these imports could be paid for only through increased exports of fruit and vegetables. This was a relatively small consideration, of course, but it may have played its part in forming the final resolve.

Influence of China

One of the most intriguing questions of the whole "great leap forward" episode was the extent to which it was influenced by events in China. Clearly the name itself—"great leap forward"—was borrowed from China, as was the spirit and fervor of the campaign that accompanied it. Nor is this the only evidence suggesting a fascination with the dazzling militancy of Peking. In October–November 1958, a parliamentary delegation led by Chervenkov visited China, had talks with Mao Tse-tung and other leaders and saw the new Chinese revolution at first hand. Chervenkov returned on November 6; eight days later, Zhivkov announced, in the context of mass economic mobilization, that Party and government employees were to do practical work for thirty to forty days a year —a practice borrowed directly from Peking.[14] Towards the end of November, it was announced that most of Bulgaria's collective farms had now been merged into about 1000 huge farms of 4,200 hectares each.[15] During this time there was a remarkably increased coverage of Chinese events in the press and Zhivkov himself stoutly

---

[12] *Ibid.*, March 12, 1957.
[13] *Otechestven Front*, March 13, 1959.
[14] Radio Sofia, November 14, 1958.
[15] *Ibid.*, November 22, 1958.

defended the principle of "leaps forward" in the building of so-
cialism (he did not, however, say Communism) in a speech to the
Central Committee in November.[16] The enthusiasm of the lower
Party ranks was shown by a remarkable report in *Rabotnichesko
Delo* on December 7, 1958, that the whole of Botevgrad county,
northeast of Sofia, had been turned into one huge collective farm.
Although not expressly stated, the implication was that this was
Bulgaria's first commune, it seemed that local zealots in Botevgrad
itself openly called it such. The very next day *Rabotnichesko Delo*
had to repudiate this report, adding darkly that the editor responsible for printing it would be "punished." On December 16, a
Radio Sofia commentary expressly denied that "Chinese methods"
were being adopted and reaffirmed that the BCP learned "primarily from the Soviet Union." The Chinese themselves, under
Soviet pressure, retreated on the ideological significance of the
communes at the December plenum of their Party. The question
for Bulgaria was conclusively settled by Chervenkov himself in an
article in January, 1959, stating that it was "completely wrong" to
think the communes marked the transition from socialism to Communism and arguing that the Chinese communes were a "form of
socialist construction" being carried out with the "aid of the
U.S.S.R. and the whole socialist camp."[17] As the Soviets inter-
vened with the Chinese, it is probable that they also expressed their
concern to the Bulgarians. The fact that Chervenkov wrote the
final repudiation does not necessarily remove the suspicion that
he was the one originally most enamored of the Chinese example.
Indeed, it would not be untypical of Communist practice if he
were forced to write the article precisely because he had been the
one most guilty of succumbing to the ideas he was now repu-
diating.

This brief episode has been worth recounting in some detail
because—leaving Albania aside—it was the only period in any
Eastern European country when the Chinese heresy seemed to be
taking hold. There have, of course, been splinter groups in other
Eastern European states with pro-Chinese sympathies, the Mijal
group in Poland being the best example.[18] It is also likely that

16 *Rabotnichesko Delo*, November 15, 1958.

17 *Rabotnichesko Delo*, January 15, 1959.

18 Kazimierz Mijal, a prominent member of the Bierut regime in Poland
and a hard-core Stalinist who had never reconciled himself to Gomulka's
rule, escaped to Albania in February, 1966. He wrote broadcasts for Radio
Tirana's Polish service and formed a "true" Polish Communist Party in exile.

larger groups in the Eastern Europe Parties—older Stalinists dis-
trustful of Khrushchev's reformism—have had suppressed sympathies with Peking. But none of this has come to the surface as
it did in Bulgaria at the end of 1958.

Nor, when the episode ended, was Bulgaria's preoccupation with
China completely over, although no such clear-cut examples were
to follow. The discredited dogmatists in the Bulgarian Party, the
followers of Chervenkov and later of Yugov, were often referred
to in Bulgaria simply as "the Chinese." In 1965, Zhivkov, in giving
details about the April conspiracy aimed at unseating him,[19]
branded the conspirators as followers of the Chinese line. In the
following year, when the Chinese cultural revolution reached its
height, the Bulgarian press and radio went to far greater lengths
than any other in Eastern Europe to repudiate it, making a particular effort to show why it was unsuitable for Bulgarian conditions.

Why this preoccupation? Why did the events in China seem
to have a greater impact in Bulgaria than in any other state except
Albania? Without coming to any firm conclusions, a few guesses
can be made. In the first place, the romantic tradition in the
Bulgarian Party had always been strong and with it, the tendency
to resort to violent, extreme measures in order to achieve a purpose. The abortive September uprising in 1923, the bombing of
the Sveta Nedelia cathedral in Sofia in 1923 in the unsuccessful
attempt to kill Czar Boris, the persistent "left sectarianism" in the
Party in the early thirties, the violent consolidation of power after
World War II—these examples show a predilection for dramatic
short-cuts that the Chinese Communists had now made their own.
There was also the presence in the Party of a very large Stalinist
or conservative faction, which remained in positions of political,
economic, and cultural importance even after its leaders, notably
Chervenkov, had first been demoted and later disgraced. Finally,
and most basically, Bulgaria was—and is—one of the most underdeveloped countries in Europe. Its Communist leaders were aware
of this situation and at the same time, were products of it. They
were conscious of Bulgaria's need to catch up quickly (and even
in the most pro-Soviet of them, there was an element of nationalism here) and probably watched with emulative sympathy the
massive efforts of China to do precisely the same. Hence the "great
leap forward" as official policy; hence also the evident desire of
some Bulgarian Communists to go much further in copying Chi-

[19] See Chapter 8.

nese methods. Even in the cultural policy as late as 1967, there were signs that this sentiment, or instinct, was not dead. Though the Chinese cultural revolution—in all its ramifications—was specifically repudiated, the reorganization of the Committee for Culture and Art (discussed in Chapter 11), the holding of the Congress for Culture, and the huge ideological offensive these moves implied—all had elements of the Chinese spirit about them that no other Eastern European regime has ever introduced in its cultural policy.

Strains in the Party

The political strains attendant on the "great leap forward" would have taxed the unity of even the most stable, strongly-led Communist Party. Since the April plenum of 1956, which had demoted Chervenkov, the Bulgarian Party was anything but stable. The purge of Chankov, Panov, and Terpeshev in July, 1957, had revealed the inner tensions. Under the iron rule of Chervenkov, a certain glacial unity had been imposed, but now the situation was fluid. Several factions emerged and, if they were not always contending for supreme power, they were all seeking influence over Party and government policy. The "great leap forward" added greatly to this tension and it was not long before it claimed its first important victim.

The apparent calm prevailing since the purge of Chankov, Terpeshev, and Panov in 1957 was rudely broken early in 1959 by the abrupt dismissal of Boris Taskov, first from his governmental post of Minister of Trade in March and then from his Politburo and Central Committee positions at a Central Committee plenum in April. The reasons given for Taskov's dismissal from the Ministry of Trade was that he was "unable to cope with the tasks entrusted to him";[20] but another reason, or "one of the main reasons," was divulged only after his dismissal from his Party posts in April. This appeared in an extraordinary article in the June issue of the Central Committee monthly *Partien Zhivot* and in an article in the June issue of *Novo Vreme* which was still more remarkable in its frankness. Taskov, a habitually outspoken man, had apparently cast doubt on the realism of the government's economic targets and especially on the directive that the Five-Year Plan was to be fulfilled in three or four years. He was mentioned by name

[20] Radio Sofia, March 14, 1959.

as one who had doubted the feasibility of the plans; this, according to *Novo Vreme*, was "one of main reasons" why he fell.

Although the humiliation of a Politburo member is by no means an insignificant matter, the real interest in the case lies not so much in the fate of Taskov but in the fact that support for him over the question of economic targets was considerable.

The rumblings had obviously been gathering volume for some time. As early as November 11, 1958, Zhivkov, at a Central Committee meeting, branded as "Enemy Number One" anyone who cast doubt on the possibility of fulfilling the Five-Year Plan in a shorter time.[21] Two months later he denounced the "lack of faith" in the Party's policy on the part of some members, warning that it could seriously undermine the prompt fulfillment of the economic plans. At the April plenum that saw the dismissal of Taskov, Zhivkov warned that the decisions and directives of the Central Committee were law for all Party members and organizations.[22] This admonition was necessary, he said, "because some of our comrades, who have a wrong attitude toward the question of collective leadership of the Party, think the Party will not have sufficient strength to put in his place anyone who attempts to undermine Party unity or who whispers against the Party line or leadership."[23] The BCP could not tolerate demonstrations of indiscipline and petty bourgeois laxity; any attempt to bypass the Central Committee, to create other centers of authority, to take important decisions without the knowledge of the Central Committee or contrary to its own decisions, or to conduct an individual policy, would be severely dealt with, Zhivkov said. His strictures were subsequently repeated by other leaders in Party meetings throughout the country.

The articles in the June issue of *Partien Zhivot* and *Novo Vreme* summed up and amplified these strictures, although their tone, especially that of *Novo Vreme*, was rather more threatening. *Novo Vreme* repeated Zhivkov's November threat to those who "whispered against the Party line" and bewailed the fact that old and tried revolutionaries who had surmounted many a hurdle in the past were now allowing themselves to be overcome by the magnitude of the tasks facing the Party. Both journals admitted the widespread nature of the "wavering," with *Partien Zhivot* stating that there were "people in the central posts and in the basic organizations" who continued in their "lack of trust and waverings." *Novo*

[21] *Rabotnichesko Delo*, November 12, 1958.
[22] Radio Sofia, January 19, 1959.
[23] *Ibid.*, April 21, 1959.

V*reme* warned that anyone who attempted to "bypass" the Central Committee would meet "crushing opposition."

In the excitement generated by these revelations it was not possible to discern the extent of serious active opposition within the Party, as opposed to negative waverings. It was clear, however, that Taskov was by no means alone in his discontent but that his views were shared by many at all levels. *Novo Vreme* warned against any attempts to create new centers or "sub-centers," against "taking important decisions without the knowledge of the Central Committee," and against "conducting some sort of individual policy." These were severe warnings and carried serious implications. They hardly seemed a reflection on Taskov's behavior since, though important and outspoken, he was hardly the man to conduct "some sort of individual policy." After the Eighth Party Congress in 1962, these warnings of three years before became more understandable. Prominent in the torrent of abuse that accompanied the fall of Premier Yugov were charges that he had disapproved of and sought to sabotage the "great leap forward" and that he had tried to use the government apparatus, of which he was head, to sidestep the Party leadership.[24] There was no direct evidence to suspect Yugov of this at the time. But even then it was noticeable that, for an incorrigible seeker of the limelight, he played a restrained role in public life for much of 1959, i.e., after the fall of Taskov. There was also the broader consideration that he was the head of an important faction in the Party, that he probably resented Zhivkov's elevation and, with Chankov out of the way and Chervenkov no longer the power he was, was able to assert himself in a troublesome way. He may well have hoped that, by keeping in the wings during the "great leap forward," he could await its inevitable failure, let Zhivkov thoroughly discredit himself, and then take the center of the stage for himself. Events were to show his great miscalculation, but the point is that, if Yugov was a malcontent during this period, then the unity of the Party must have been seriously undermined right at the outset of the "great leap forward."[25]

Economic Results of the "Great Leap Forward"

In his report to the National Assembly on December 16, 1960, Stanko Todorov, Chairman of the State Planning Commission,

[24] See Chapter 6.
[25] For a fuller discussion of the Party during this period, see Chapter 6.

claimed that the Third Five-Year Plan had been fulfilled in its main indices by the end of 1960, two years ahead of schedule.[26] Thus the "great leap forward" had been a success. On closer examination of some of the figures, however, it was evident that the regime could claim success only because of a very important modification of the whole intent of the "great leap forward" as it had been specifically defined at the beginning of the campaign. This was the shift from the concept of doubling (or trebling) the *actual volume* of production to that of doubling the rate of growth of production. That the government soon began to shift its ground was apparent in a speech by Zhivkov at the end of 1959 when he claimed progress on the basis of growth rates rather than total production.[27]

To anyone not remembering the Bulgarian leader's statement in 1958, the claims made at the end of 1960 for the success of the "great leap forward" might have seemed convincing. Thus in 1960 it has been estimated that 47.976 million leva of industrial production was produced.[28] In terms of the original schedule of the Five-Year Plan the total production would have been worth 49.312 million leva. The two figures are fairly close and, therefore, the government could quite justifiably argue that what was scheduled in 1962 had actually been achieved in 1960. But if one calculated by volume of production, then the real failure of the "great leap forward" in industry is clearly seen. The total volume of industrial production achieved for the three years 1958–60 was 125.68 billion leva. But the Five-Year Plan envisaged the total volume of production achieved for the whole five years to be valued at 209.576 billion leva. Thus, in terms of the regime's original intention—to produce in three years what originally should have been produced in five—"the great leap forward" failed in industry by about 84 billion leva.

The situation was similar in agriculture, where production was calculated on the basis of 1955 prices. In terms of the directives of the Five-Year Plan, a total of 90.07 billion leva of agricultural produce should have been achieved by 1962. By 1960 a total of

[26] *Rabotnichesko Delo*, December 17, 1960.

[27] Speech to the National Assembly, *Rabotnichesko Delo*, December 26, 1959.

[28] At 1956 prices; see the calculations in the excellent analysis of the results of the "great leap forward," by John Kalo, "The Bulgarian Economy," *Survey* (London), December, 1961, pp. 86–95. The following calculations are taken from this article.

52.876 billion leva worth had been achieved. Thus, the shortfall was over 37 billion leva worth of produce. But, in terms of the Five-Year Plan, 20.098 billion leva worth of produce should have been produced in 1962, while in 1960 the official figure for actual production was 20 billion leva.[29] Thus, calculating according to growth rates, the government could claim pre-fulfillment and success.

As far as national income was concerned, there was no official pretense that the 1962 target had been reached by 1960 even in terms of growth rates. Todorov told the National Assembly at the end of 1960 that the national income in that year was "shaping up to be about 37.2 per cent bigger than in 1957, while the directives [of the Third Five-Year Plan] envisaged that it should increase by 50 per cent."[30] Actually, the difference between what had been integrally planned for the five years (1958–62) and what was integrally produced in three (1958–60) was almost 100 billion leva.[31]

Perhaps the best comment of all on the results and effects of the "great leap forward" was in the targets set for industry and agriculture in the economic plan for 1961. These indicated not only a realization of failure but also an abandonment of the *Stürm und Drang* approach in the economy. The annual increase stipulated for industry was 7.8 per cent and for agriculture 10.9 per cent. Generally, in assessing this brief but turbulent period, the government must be credited—despite the over-all failure of "great leap forward"—with great quantitative increases in production which clearly would not have been achieved had there been no "leap into the dark." But quality, costs, and general economic efficiency had been sacrificed in the scramble for quantity. The economy as a whole, which had never received delicate treatment under Communist rule, was strained very seriously during this period and needed a good deal of respite for the damage to be repaired.

Perhaps even more important was the effect on the people and on the Party. The population was called on to make huge efforts and sacrifices during these two years. Though the Zhivkov Theses in 1959 had promised an increase of the minimum wage from 400 to 600 leva a month, because of higher prices and harder work the real standard of living cannot have increased much in two

[29] *Rabotnichesko Delo*, January 1, 1961.

[30] *Rabotnichesko Delo*, December 17, 1960.

[31] Kalo, *loc. cit.* Official calculations for National Income were based on 1952 prices.

years. As for the Party, its unity had been seriously impaired and its morale undermined both by failure and by the serious criticisms to which its rank and file had often been subjected during the course of the past two years. If one of the aims of the "great leap forward" had been to mobilize Party and people in support of a dynamic cause, then this aim failed in the end by as big a margin as did the economic targets.

6

Party and State, 1958–62

THE RUMBLINGS of discontent in the Bulgarian Communist Party, symptomized by the purge of Boris Taskov, have been discussed in the previous chapter. This chapter will deal with the broader aspects of the situation in the Party and government from the purge of Chankov, Terpeshev, and Panov to the Eighth Party Congress in December, 1962. It was an important period in the postwar history of the BCP because it marked the evolution from the factional struggles which followed the demotion of Chervenkov in 1956 to the final achievement of supremacy by Zhivkov at the Eighth Congress.

As was mentioned in discussing the July, 1957, purge, the fall of Georgi Chankov removed an important rival to Zhivkov—a man of about the same age, of greater ability and energy, with whom he could never feel quite safe. Chankov's removal was particularly important for Zhivkov because it further strengthened his control over the younger home Communist group with which the future evidently lay. His immediate job, therefore, was to strengthen the representation of this group in the top echelons of the Party. He was able to begin this process at the Sixth Party Congress held in June, 1958.

In many respects, however, the Party at the Sixth Congress gave the impression of great stability rather than great change. Its total membership, as compared with the Fifth Party Congress in 1954, increased by only about 30,000—from 455,251 to 484,255. The number of full members had, however, increased by almost 100,000 —from 368,142 to 467,546. But there had been a large drop in the number of candidate-members—from 87,109 in 1954 to only 16,709 in 1958.[1] One can assume, therefore, that most of the former candidate-members had now moved up to full membership. Thus, the number of completely new members cannot have been very large; similarly the number of members dropped must also have been quite small, a rather surprising constancy for a four-year period which saw the Twentieth CPSU Congress, the April plenum, and the Hungarian Revolution.

The greatest stability, however, was shown in the top body of the Party, the Politburo itself. Here there were no changes: all eleven full members were re-elected, but the number of candidates was reduced from four to three. The man dropped was General Petur Panchevski, the Minister of Defense, a Soviet-trained officer reportedly on close terms with Marshal Zhukov, who had been purged by Khrushchev in 1957. Panchevski was immediately released from his post as Minister of Defense but remained a Central Committee member and was subsequently made Ambassador to China.

The Politburo, therefore, again consisted of: Boyan Bulgaranov, Vulko Chervenkov, Georgi Damyanov, Raiko Damyanov, Dimitur Ganev, Ivan Mihailov, Encho Staykov, Boris Taskov, Georgi Tsankov, and Anton Yugov. The three remaining candidate-members were Dimitur Dimov, Todor Prahov, and Mladen Stoyanov.

In the Politburo, therefore, Zhivkov was still very much in a minority. In fact, he and Tsankov were the only two younger home Communists in the whole body. Of the full members, i.e., those entitled to vote, there were five older home Communists—Yugov, Bulgaranov, Taskov, Ganev, and Staikov—and four Muscovites—Chervenkov, Mihailov, and the two Damyanovs.[2] None of the candidate-members were younger home Communists.

But Zhivkov did succeed in increasing his strength in the Central Committee Secretariat. The number of secretaries was increased to five: one of the former secretaries, Dancho Dimitrov, was dropped, and two new ones, Mitko Grigorov and Pencho Kubadinski, were

[1] Zhivkov's report to Party Congress, *Rabotnichesko Delo* (Sofia), June 3, 1958.
[2] Raiko Damyanov was perhaps a borderline case between a home Communist and a Muscovite. Altogether he had spent about eight years outside Bulgaria before the war, some of them in Moscow, others abroad as a Comintern agent. For most of the war he was in prison in Bulgaria but in 1943 escaped and joined the partisans.

added. Both the additions were younger Party apparatchiks who were part of Zhivkov's growing patrimony. Grigorov, aged forty-six, had become head of the Central Committee's agitation and propaganda department the previous year, and Kubadinski, promoted to the Central Committee after the purge of Chankov, Terpeshev, and Panov, had been first secretary of the Party Committee in Russe since 1952. He was forty. The Secretariat, therefore, now consisted of Zhivkov himself as First Secretary, Bulgaranov, Ganev, Stanko Todorov, Kubadinski, and Grigorov. Todorov was also a Zhivkov follower, so there was a clear Zhivkov majority in the Secretariat.

The Secretariat could not match the Politburo either in numbers or the stature of its members. But it was the body responsible for the everyday running of the central Party apparatus. Zhivkov here was, consciously or unconsciously, following a practice of both Stalin and Khrushchev in the Soviet Union—building up strength in the Secretariat so as to mitigate the disadvantages of a difficult or divided Politburo. Later, several of the men he brought into the Secretariat were to pass into the Politburo, well-trained in their particular executive sphere and personally loyal to him.

In the new Central Committee elected at the Seventh Congress, Zhivkov also strengthened his position somewhat. The full membership now numbered 89 as against the previous 65. Of these, 62 full members were re-elected and 21 were promoted from candidate-membership; 2 were promoted from the Central Revision Commission and only 4 were completely new. The number of candidate-members was increased from 32 to 48. Of the new full and candidate-members, many, judging from their age and Party careers, seemed likely to owe their advancement to the First Party Secretary. Only three full members of the old Central Committee were dropped, again a remarkably small number in view of what had happened between the two congresses. Of these, the only notable case was that of Ivan Ilchev, a veteran Communist and friend of Yonko Panov. Ilchev had been appointed chairman of the Party Control Commission at the Sixth Congress but had been removed from this post in February, 1957, with no explanation. His dismissal may have been a prelude to that of Panov, Chankov, and Terpeshev.

The strain on Party unity imposed by the "great leap forward" has already been discussed. It should be stressed, however, that Boris Taskov, dismissed from the Politburo and his post as Minister of Trade in April 1959, was an older home Communist who probably looked to Yugov as his leader. His eclipse, therefore, and the shadow under which Yugov himself passed in that year, tended to undermine the strength of the group they represented at the highest level. In December of the same year Zhivkov again weakened this group and strengthened his own position in a series of important Party and governmental changes.

One of his most prominent supporters, Stanko Todorov, was taken out of the Secretariat and made a candidate-member of the Politburo; he entered the government as Chairman of the State Planning Commission and a deputy premier. At the same time, Boris Velchev and Tano Tsolov were brought into the Secretariat. Velchev had been First Secretary of the Sofia district Party committee since January, 1959, and prior to that had been head of the Party and Youth section of the Central Committee. Tsolov had previously been a Minister of Heavy Industry and immediately prior to his election to the Secretariat had been Chairman of the Committee for Industry and Technical Progress. Velchev's speciality was Party cadres and organization, Tsolov's industrial affairs. Both were considered appointees of Zhivkov, who had now, therefore, succeeded in further strengthening his grip on the Secretariat.

But more interesting was the weakening of Yugov's hold on the government apparatus over which he presided as Prime Minister. Todorov was foisted on him as a deputy premier. More significant, however, was Todorov's assumption of the leadership of the State Planning Commission at the expense of Rusi Hristozov, who was demoted to the Ministry of Internal Trade. Hristozov had served with Yugov at the Ministry of Interior in the infamous days immediately after World War II and in 1948 had succeeded him as Minister. He had become Chairman of the State Planning Commission after the fall of Chankov in 1957 but, like his leader, Yugov, was believed to be lukewarm toward the "great leap forward." Nor was this the only change affecting senior officials, past or present, at the Ministry of the Interior. Two deputy ministers, Georgi Kumbiliev and Stefan Gurov, were appointed to the Foreign Trade Ministry and the Committee for Construction, respectively. This was considered by observers at the time to be a move to weaken the hold of the older home Communist element at the Interior Ministry, a speculation apparently confirmed in 1962 when many of those associated with the Ministry of the Interior throughout the whole history of Communist rule were purged. They included Yugov (Minister from 1944 to 1948), Hristozov (Minister, 1948 to 1951), Tsankov (Minister, 1951 to

1962), and several former deputy ministers, including Kumbiliev.

It is quite possible that Yugov himself was in considerable danger during the second half of 1959. His hostile attitude toward the "great leap forward" and his machinations against Zhivkov, publicly revealed only in 1962, must have severely tested the artificial cohesion of the leadership. Indeed, but for the imperative need for unity during this period—especially after the purge of Tsankov—Zhivkov, in alliance with Chervenkov and his powerful faction, might have forced Yugov out. As it was, the lesson given him by the changes in December, 1959, seems to have been a salutary warning for Yugov against any future intrigues, for in 1960 he bounced back to prominence and, judging from his speeches, became a strong convert to official policy.[3]

The rebuffs given to Yugov, and his silence in the second half of 1959 followed by his rather ostentatious conformity in 1960, indicated that he had overreached himself. His following in the top echelons of the Party was insufficient to support a successful bid for power. Even had he been the unchallenged leader of the older home Communists, he would have found Zhivkov and the Muscovites, who looked on him as their old enemy, too much of a combination for him. But his claims to leadership of the older home Communists were now evidently being challenged by a man who had only recently come into the limelight: Dimitur Ganev.

Ganev—who, like Yugov, had suffered eclipse in the aftermath of the Traicho Kostov trial—had taken Chankov's Politburo seat in July, 1957. In November, 1958, he had become Chairman of the Presidium of the National Assembly (titular head of state) on the death of Georgi Damyanov. It was reasoned at the time, with strong validity, that this meant the end of Ganev as a serious contender for power and influence.[4] He was sixty at the time—a relatively advanced age in Communist politics—and the position of titular head of state was generally considered as a suitable reward to a political middleweight for yeoman service to the cause. But this was apparently not so. The impression in Sofia in 1959 and 1960 was that he carried considerable weight in the Politburo and that he was looked up to by many older home Communists in the Party who found Yugov personally distasteful (many did) or were

[3] See, for example, his speech attacking deficiencies in agriculture and local Party administration in *Rabotnichesko Delo*, April 26, 1960.

[4] Although no announcement was made of Ganev's relinquishing his appointment as Central Committee Secretary when he became head of state, it is probable that he did so.

put off by his opportunism. Ganev's personal relations with Yugov were probably not the most cordial, since at a national Party conference held in June, 1950, when both were in eclipse, Yugov—presumably in order to save himself—had violently attacked Ganev's performance as Minister of Foreign Trade.[5]

The Party Factions

During this period, one can speak of four factions in the higher ranks of the BCP: 1) the Chervenkov-Muscovite group, now out of favor in Moscow; 2) Zhivkov's group of younger home Communists; 3) the section of the older home Communists adhering to Yugov; 4) the section, also of older home Communists, looking to Ganev. Of these, it was the second that was rising steadily to the ascendency, thanks to Khrushchev's help and the inexorable aging of its rivals.

Factionalism has, of course, been endemic in all Communist Parties when not controlled by one man with all the forces of coercion at his disposal. Nor is it a phenomenon unknown in more democratic societies. But the extent to which it prevailed in the Bulgarian Party between 1958 and 1962 was unique in the Communist world at the time. In the Soviet Union, Khrushchev had gained mastery by the 1957 purge; Gheorghiu-Dej had also used the purge of Chisinevschi and Constantinescu in July, 1957, to consolidate his own position. In Poland, a widely-backed Gomulka was supreme, and in apathetic Czechoslovakia, Novotny was emerging as clearly the most powerful leader. In East Germany, the Hungarian and Polish upheavals in 1956 had eventually served to strengthen Ulbricht's position and in Albania, Hoxha's survival of the attempt against him in April, 1956, made him more powerful than before. In Yugoslavia, factions of reformers and conservatives had already formed and differences between the nationalities were always dangerous; but no one doubted Tito's ultimate supremacy. The situation most similar to Bulgaria's was probably that in Hungary where, in the first years after 1956, Kadar's centrist group was occasionally threatened and constantly thwarted by the large Stalinist faction in the leadership and the lower levels of the Party. But Kadar, strongly backed by Khrushchev—who had the most direct vested interest in his prospering—sought to extricate himself

[5] *Rabotnichesko Delo*, June 16, 1950.

from his difficulties by appealing to the population over the heads of the intransigents in his Party. Such a course also lay open to Zhivkov and probably a genuine reform program, such as that promised by Kadar, would have gained at least as much response as it did in Hungary. But Zhivkov lacked either the will or the inclination. Thus, when he did triumph in the Party, there was very little popular response to his victory.

In its disorderly situation, the Party could hardly help making a virtue out of necessity by stressing the collective character of the leadership and the iron obligation of democratic centralism. This was deemed especially necessary during the "great leap forward" when there was so much dissension and doubt. An authoritative article in *Novo Vreme* for June, 1959, is worth quoting at some length because it expounds the ostensible principles of Party leadership that have prevailed from the April plenum to present day. Entitled "For Adherence to Lenin's Principles and Collectivism in Work and Leadership," it summed up the concept of collectivism in the following way:

> Lenin's conception of collectivism requires that questions regarding Party and state policy and work be decided by the conviction of the majority of the leadership, after a collective consideration of the problems. Collective experience alone, the collective mind alone, allow the working out of correct decisions on one or another of the questions having the character of principle in socialist construction, and allow the avoiding of errors and the partial approach. It is not the majority that must adapt itself to the opinion of the minority; to postpone its decision until the last man in the leadership should surmount his doubts and hesitations would mean in practice that the leadership would postpone its decisions indefinitely. It is just the contrary: the minority has to conform with the opinion and the decision of the majority; from the moment a decision is taken, to dismiss its doubts and hesitations and to fight without any reserve for the realization of the decisions. This is what is called an ABC for every Communist.

Was the Bulgarian Party observing this principle?

Yes, it is being observed. The Central Committee of the Party, the Politburo, gives us an example of this. Since the April plenary session of the Central Committee of the Bulgarian Communist Party, there has not been a single important problem of our domestic or foreign policy which has been decided individually, without the collective. The important problems have been solved collectively—by the Politburo, the Central Committee, the Council of Ministers, and the National Assembly, while the fundamental problems of our development are discussed by a large Party, state, economic, and cultural active—by the large people's masses.

Then followed a strong affirmation of the authority of the leadership and an implicit warning to those who might challenge it:

> Not from others but from the great Lenin, from Georgi Dimitrov, and Vasil Kolarov, have we learned that in our socialist country there can be only one center—the Central Committee, the Politburo. The Central Committee is the brain of the Party, the militant staff of the Party, wherein is concentrated the wisdom of the Party, its experience of leadership and of socialist building. Lenin used to teach that there cannot be a real unity and discipline in the Party without a might-possessing and authoritative center. The existence of a leading center gives the Party the opportunity to subordinate all its activity to one will, to pursue one purpose; to correctly distribute and direct its forces. All important problems of Party and state policy are subject to discussions and solution at the Central Committee, at the Politburo. The decisions and directives of the Central Committee are the law and the basis for the activity of all Party organs and organizations, for every Party worker, for every Communist.

All this, of course, was copy-book Communism. Its authenticity, however, was rather undermined by the disunity which prevailed at the very center that was supposed to wield the authority.

The State at the Local Level

Most observers—if interested in Bulgaria at all—are interested in the character and machinations of the Party at the highest level. To most Bulgarians, however, other than those living in Sofia itself, the doings of the Politburo and Central Committee are only of distant or academic interest.[6] It is the Party at the local level which is their concern. So it should also be to serious observers wishing to make a real study of the impact of the Communist system on Eastern Europe. A thorough examination of a single county would in many ways give a much truer picture of Bulgaria under Communist rule than the whole of this book or better books that may follow it. In mitigation one can only plead the

[6] David Binder, *The New York Times'* correspondent formerly in Belgrade, once told the writer that on a visit to Rumania he had asked a peasant in Ploesti what he thought of Ceausescu. "Who is Ceausescu?" came the reply. Equivalent answers could have been evoked in Bulgaria and in any other Eastern European country.

insuperable obstacles in the way of doing this, notably the impossibility of spending enough time in the country or having sufficient liberty to make such a detailed and worthwhile study. Nor do the Bulgarians make the job easier by doing such studies themselves. In Hungary since 1964, superb and objective sociological works have been published about local conditions and situations. None such exist in Bulgaria. A systematic study of the local press would help in building up a picture of provincial Party administration, but this would demand a discipline and an effort that few are prepared to give.

Having confessed inadequacy to the task, one can only give a very sketchy outline of the Party at the local level. Certainly, however, the administrative-territorial reform announced in January, 1959,[7] probably had greater impact on the Bulgarian population as a whole than any other single government decision since the collectivization of agriculture. It affected both the central and the local apparatus, administrative and economic, and involved root and branch changes. Briefly, the previous administrative structure had been as follows:

The *central governmental apparatus* was composed of sixteen ministries, one commission, and four committees. These bodies centralized the whole management of the state.

The *local governmental apparatus* consisted of 13 districts (*okrugs*), 117 counties (*okolyi*) and over 1,930 village municipal communities (*obshtini*). Each district center had its district, county, and town people's councils; each county center had county and town people's councils; every village had its village people's council. The councils at all levels had their corresponding Party committees. The councils were elected by popular vote and acted as local government organs. Their functions, however, were limited to the execution of orders from the central government.

This system required a huge bureaucracy to run it. In 1957, Bulgaria had about 260,000 white-collar workers in a population of some 7.5 million, and nearly 7 per cent of the annual national income went for salaries of administrative employees.[8] The different chains of command were far too long. For example, in industry the following management chain operated: local enterprise —ministerial department—respective ministry—ministerial council.

---

[7] *Izvestia na Presidiuma na Narodnoto Subranie* (Sofia), January 24, 1959. The changes were originally announced by Zhivkov as part of the measures attendant on the "great leap forward."

[8] Kiril Lazarov (Minister of Finance), *Finansii i Kredit* (Sofia), March, 1957.

In agriculture, local industry or trade it was even longer: collective farm (or local enterprise)—district people's council—county people's council—respective ministerial department—respective ministry—ministerial council. Industry, depending on the type, was the responsibility of many ministries and departments. Many industrial enterprises, though closely linked in the production process and located in the same district, county, or town, often operated completely independently of one another, the only connecting link being the Council of Ministers in Sofia.

Such a system would have been cumbersome with even the most highly qualified personnel running it; but Bulgaria seriously lacked such personnel. Political loyalty was the prime requirement for occupying a key post and this hardly assured the best choice, especially when the apparatus was so huge. The underdeveloped economy needed specialists, but sufficient numbers of these were not available to satisfy the needs and to cope with the tremendous plans for development.

First Secretary Zhivkov himself acknowledged the inefficiencies of this organization when addressing the Central Committee plenum in January, 1959. Now, said Zhivkov, in the more advanced stage of socialist development in Bulgaria, the system was not only inadequate; it was beginning to be definitely harmful.[9]

The resultant reform was sweeping, especially as it affected local administration. The existing 13 districts (*okrugs*) and 117 counties (*okolyi*) were dissolved and replaced by 30 administrative units, also called districts or *okrugs*.

Essentially, this reorganization meant the passing from a branch to a territorial principle of administration. The district now united the whole political, state, economic, and cultural life of the respective territory. This decentralization brought the state management closer to the production process. The affinities with the Soviet system introduced in July, 1957, were obvious. The previously existing counties (*okolyi*) were very small administrative units. They had little industry and few construction sites on their territories. The old districts (*okrugs*), on the other hand, were too large to be convenient for a territorial principle of administration. Thus the necessity of creating new administrative units encompassing a greater number of prerequisites for a more efficient governing system.

Chervenkov, in his speech to the January, 1959, plenum, stressed

[9] *Rabotnichesko Delo*, January 20, 1959.

that the new, purely Bulgarian, element in this reform was precisely this passing from administrative centralization according to branches of the national economy to a system where most economic and administrative activity in a given district, was controlled by the district authority. The authority was the district people's council. The basic administrative units were the town and village people's councils. These bodies, responsible to the district people's council, took care of administrative, educational, cultural, and health services, local retail distribution, etc.[10] The basic economic units in the district were the collective farm in agriculture[11] and the industrial enterprise in industry. These units fell under the direct management of the district people's council.

The reforms of the central state apparatus, formally approved by the National Assembly in March, 1959,[12] were less important. Briefly, six ministries and one committee were disbanded. A new commission and three committees were created. The National Bank was taken from the jurisdiction of the Ministry of Finance and made directly subordinate to the Ministerial Council. Those ministries dissolved were the branch economic ones: Heavy Industry, Light Industry, Food Industry, Electrification and Water Economy, Construction, Construction Materials and Communal Economy, and Public Construction and Roads. Their duties were taken over by the district people's councils.

The reform did not diminish the role of the Ministerial Council itself. As the supreme executive and administrative organ it retained ultimate control over the whole economic and cultural life of the country at the state level. Centralized planned financing and auditing were maintained.

In December, 1959, further structural changes were made. To the existing four deputy premiers, three more were added, making an unofficial "inner cabinet" of seven. In addition, the Ministry of Trade was divided in two: one ministry for foreign trade and another for domestic trade. The Committee for Industry and Technical Progress, established in March, was divided into the Committee for Industry and the Committee for Technical Progress. Similarly, the Committee for Construction and Architecture

[10] *Novo Vreme* (Sofia), April, 1959.

[11] The area of authority of the village people's councils coincided with the territories of the amalgamated collective farms. Thus, there were about 1,000 amalgamated collectives and about 1,000 village councils.

[12] *Rabotnichesko Delo*, March 13, 1959.

was split into one committee for construction and another for architecture.

Clearly this administrative reform was a radical move toward decentralization, greater than the similar reform in Czechoslovakia the year before and even more sweeping than that in the Soviet in July, 1957. It is difficult, however, to gauge just how successful it was in increasing the efficiency of the administration and the economy. The official press registered general satisfaction about its effects, and there seems little reason to doubt the claims that it released a great amount of local initiative that had previously been paralyzed. The central bureaucracy was also cut considerably and some 2,000 trained experts were released for work in the provinces.

But the new system also produced serious difficulties. The most unfortunate was quick to appear and to be criticized. This was *mesnichestvo*—localism or parochialism. Local initiative, sorely needed, was definitely encouraged, but centrifugalism also appeared as its attendant. *Mesnichestvo* was constantly criticized and held responsible for many shortcomings: for lack of coordination between enterprises and for violations of agreements between them; for various districts failing to fulfill contractual obligations; for the stockpiling of valuable supplies by enterprises; for the inadequate distribution of fruit and vegetables (Sofia seems to have suffered particularly from this) and of manufactured goods; and for profiteering by agricultural and industrial enterprises at the expense of national requirements. In short, everyone was looking after Number One.

Many of the thirty new district people's councils seemed either bewildered or paralyzed by the power invested in them. Some were criticized for "passing incorrect and unlawful" decisions, others for shifting responsibilities to Sofia.[13] A large number of village people's councils were accused of failing to supervise the state purchases of food from the collective farm under their jurisdiction.

Nor were the overall cuts in the bureaucracy as great as expected. The 2,000 officials made redundant in Sofia have been mentioned above. Not surprisingly, most of these deeply resented the privilege of serving the nation at closer hand, and sought every way to return to the fleshpots of the capital as soon as possible. In the

[13] For the most authoritative criticisms of these and other deficiencies, see Zhivkov's speech on January 12, 1960; *Rabotnichesko Delo*, January 19, 1960; and Yugov's speech in April, 1960 in *Ibid.*, April 26, 1960.

countryside itself, after the amalgamation of the collectives in 1958, it became an "unwritten rule" that all the chairmen of the former farms became deputy chairmen of the new collectives, resulting in a diffusion rather than a concentration of responsibility.[14]

Finally, by way of extenuation, it must be said that the reform was introduced during a period hardly conducive to a smooth, efficient implementation. This was the period of the "great leap forward" when the economy was under the great strain of the astronomically high targets set for almost all branches. It was quite natural, therefore, for local leaders to subordinate everything to the fulfillment of their own plan. With the return to "normalcy" in 1960, the pressure relaxed and the new system began to work better. But many of the bad habits already acquired continued to persist.

Before leaving Communist rule at the local level it is worth mentioning two other features of it.

In the late 1950's throughout Eastern Europe, an important development in state administration was the devolution of certain governmental and juridical responsibilities to the mass organizations. In Bulgaria, this began only in 1960; it was heralded by Zhivkov's speech to the local Party and state officials on January 12, 1960. Such a devolution, said Zhivkov, was possible because of "the constantly growing consciousness and political activities of the country's workers and the further development of socialist democracy."[15] Zhivkov, however, like all Soviet and East European leaders when speaking on this subject, was quick to point out that this devolution meant no withering away of the state. On the contrary! In the present phase of the building of socialism, the importance of the state must increase. Any differing view was said to be the hallmark of Yugoslav revisionism.

The two most important new institutions to arise in Bulgaria from this policy of devolution were the voluntary detachments of workers and the comrades' court.[16] Both were imports from the Soviet Union.

The voluntary workers' detachments, which took over some of the order-keeping duties of the militia, were the result of a visit made by Interior Minister Georgi Tsankov to the Soviet Union in

[14] Zhivkov speech, January 12, 1960; *Rabotnichesko Delo*, January 19, 1960.

[15] *Ibid.*

[16] These are often mistakenly referred to as "comradely courts." They were often anything but comradely.

late 1959 to see how the "druzhin" system worked there.[17] They were officially introduced in Bulgaria by a decree the following March[18] and were charged with putting down not only such crimes as hooliganism, brawling and the like but also more important crimes against socialist property, theft, etc. Applicants for membership in these detachments had to be over eighteen and were to be enrolled through such mass organizations as the trade unions, Komsomol, and the Fatherland Front. Whether such enrollment was actually voluntary is doubtful and there was almost certainly a great deal of direct propaganda and indirect pressure to boost recruitment. A member of such a group was bound to incur a good deal of animosity and contempt from his fellow citizens. Their effectiveness was also doubtful. Their introduction in the Soviet Union in 1958 did not achieve outstanding success. Similarly, in Bulgaria they could not stem the disturbing increase in violence that occurred in public places—football matches and the like—in the early 1960's. During 1964 they fell into disuse.

The comrades' courts had become a bloc-wide institution by 1960. Zhivkov promised that they would be introduced in all enterprises, collective farms, higher educational establishments, public offices, and elsewhere. Their purpose would be "to contribute actively toward the education of our citizens in the spirit of a Communist attitude toward labor and socialist property, toward preserving the regulations of our socialist community, and respecting the rights, dignity, and honor of our citizens."[19] They were introduced in the Sofia district in March and later spread to all Bulgarian villages and towns. The unpopularity of such public tribunals can readily be appreciated. At the Rumanian Party Congress in June, 1960, the Minister of the Interior, Alexandru Draghici, quite candidly reported that defendants preferred to have their cases heard in the regular courts because of the humiliation which they had to undergo in these new institutions.[20] The same was doubtless true in Bulgaria and everywhere else.

The Party at the Local Level

As a result of the administrative reorganization of the country, the Communist Party structure at the local level also had to be

[17] Zhivkov; *Rabotnichesko Delo*, January 19, 1960.
[18] Announced by Radio Sofia, March 10, 1960.
[19] *Rabotnichesko Delo*, January 14, 1960.
[20] *Scînteia* (Bucharest), June 23, 1960.

adapted to conform with the new territorial units. Thus there emerged thirty district (*okrug*) Party organizations and 1,000 village (*obshtini*) organizations.

Completely new Party organizations therefore had to be set up and there is ample evidence to show that considerable dislocation and inefficiency resulted. Zhivkov himself, in his speech to a large conference of Party officials in January, 1960, was very frank on this subject. The conference had probably been called because of the confusion that had arisen and Zhivkov took the opportunity not only to criticize but to explain precisely what the functions of the village Party committees were. Since these were the new organizations that had been set up, it was natural that Zhivkov should address himself mainly to this subject.

The village Party organizations were placed in direct control of primary Party organizations in collective farms, schools and all other sectors of life in the village except for large enterprises, state farms, and Machine Tractor Stations, whose primary Party organizations came directly under the *okrug* Party committees. Judging from Zhivkov's remarks, there was a great deal of resentment on the part of collective farm chairmen over the interference of these Party committees. Some collective farm chairmen had ignored the village committees, former county (*okoliye*) Party leaders, who had been transferred to collectives and now found themselves having to take orders from officials of "lower" rank, expressed a good deal of personal hostility. The village Party organizations were regarded as inferior interlopers. There was also the problem of the 2,000 officials freed by administrative reorganization for work at the local level. For most of them, this was a freedom that they wished more than anything to avoid. The result was instability and a quick turnover in personnel because many officials were refusing to stay at the posts to which they had been assigned. Such "fluctuations," said Zhivkov, would have to be watched carefully by the Central Committee.[21]

Another factor causing considerable local irritation was the establishment of Party control commissions in every section of the economy. Again, following the Soviet example, these commissions had been set up at the beginning of 1959. This meant a proliferation of Party officials and the ever-present danger of clashes with the village Party organizations.

The main aim of these control commissions was to strengthen

[21] *Rabotnichesko Delo*, January 19, 1960.

the Party's grip over the activities of economic and administrative management. They ensured and strengthened the Party's presence in every walk of life. Literally thousands of them sprang to life, comprising hundreds of thousands of Party members and candidate-members. To get some idea of how omnipresent these commissions were, one need only state that in June, 1960, in Sofia alone, there were 148 commissions in industrial enterprises to control the quality of production, forty to control technical progress, twenty-six for economization in materials, twenty-five to control the scheduled fulfillment of the production plan, and thirty-one for the introduction of rationalizations and workers' suggestions. In commercial enterprises, nineteen commissions to control the supply of goods to stores had been set up. In the Lovech *okrug*, an agricultural area, thirty-four commissions to control corn cultivation, ten to increase the milk yield in dairy farms, nine to ensure the fodder base, and six to control land reclamation and irrigation construction had been organized.[22]

The "busybody" psychosis these commissions engendered is not hard to imagine. The situation was absurdly complicated by the fact that the members of commissions frequently were supposed to supervise and check the work which they themselves were doing in their professional capacities.

It was not surprising, therefore, that the morale of the Party at the local level was also a subject of complaint by Zhivkov in his speech to the conference of Party officials in January, 1960. On top of it all was the neurotic atmosphere created by the "great leap forward" itself. Bulgaria between 1958 and 1960 came closer to having a "Chinese" flavor than any other Eastern European country in any period since 1945 (except possibly, Albania in 1966 and 1967, when the regime there consciously copied Peking's cultural revolution).

If the morale of the Party at the local level was not high, neither were the morals of some of its members at any level. Zhivkov's speech was full of criticisms of the opportunism and corruption of many officials. No one, said Zhivkov, was against a better standard of living, but everyone must "cut his coat according to his cloth, within the salary paid to him by society for his work." There were, he continued, unscrupulous careerists whose only concern was to hunt better posts. There was a system of patronage and promotion by connections and "certain leaders who, because of

[22] *Partien Zhivot* (Sofia), June, 1960.

their wrong activities and behavior," were encouraging this. Some leaders were also forgetting that they were sons of the people and treated the public haughtily, even contemptuously. Finally, there were some cases of downright immorality and neglect of family obligations. There was a danger of Party men "changing from fighters and revolutionaries into mere philistines," thinking only of themselves and their personal comforts.

This Lenin-like outburst by Zhivkov was doubtless justified in many cases and, in the topmost ranks of the Party, men like Yugov and Chervenkov hardly set the right example. It would be unfair, however, to overlook those Party officials who, struggling under the most harassing conditions, did their honest best and to whom Communist devotion and idealism still meant something. But power was tending to corrupt many and devotion and idealism were becoming increasingly something for others.

Interrelation of Party and Government

That the Communist Party controls the government is, of course, a truism which only the developments in Yugoslavia in 1967 and in Czechoslovakia before August 1968 seemed likely to challenge.

In the Stalinist period, this control was most clearly illustrated by the fact that the Party leader also held the post of Premier. From 1950 to 1954, Chervenkov in Bulgaria held both these posts. After Stalin, when the principle of collectivism was ushered into Soviet practice, these two posts were no longer held by one man. As mentioned above, Zhivkov became First Party Secretary in 1954 with Chervenkov retaining the premiership. When Chervenkov was demoted after the April Plenum, Yugov became Premier. Later, after the consolidation of Khrushchev's power in the Soviet Union, the old Stalinist practice of uniting the two posts in one man was revived: Khrushchev assumed the premiership when Bulganin was forced out of office in 1958. The Eastern European response to this development was, however, far from uniform. In Poland, there was none at all. In fact, only in Hungary and Bulgaria was it followed exactly and then only with much delay. Kadar became Prime Minister in Hungary in 1961, and Zhivkov became Premier in Bulgaria after the purge of Yugov at the Eighth Party Congress in 1962. In the German Democratic Republic, Czechoslovakia, and Rumania, however, the practice was adopted of making the First Party Secretary head of state, thereby symbolizing the supremacy of the Party in the whole of public life. Thus Novotny in 1957, Ulbricht in 1960, and Gheorghiu-Dej in 1961 became, in effect, presidents of their respective states.[23] After the fall of Khrushchev in October, 1964, the division principle was once again revived under Brezhnev and Kosygin and, in 1965, the Hungarians followed suit with Kadar stepping down from the premiership in favor of Kallai. Surprisingly, however, a similar change did not happen in Bulgaria. Thus Zhivkov became the only First Party Secretary in the Communist world who was also Premier.

The fact that the Eastern European states responded in widely differing ways to the change in Soviet practice after Stalin's death, and to the further changes in 1958, demonstrates the greater autonomy these states gained in the middle 1950's. Within a period of only five years, the exigencies of the *domestic* situation—rather than developments in Moscow—were playing an increasingly important part in shaping the policies of these states. In the case of Bulgaria in 1958, these exigencies were such that only blatant Soviet interference in favor of Zhivkov could have forced Yugov out of the premiership. The situation within the regime was still very delicately balanced; Zhivkov—unlike Khrushchev in 1958, Kadar in 1961, and Zhivkov himself in 1962—did not hold the undisputed authority that warranted uniting the two posts in his person. On the contrary, Yugov's behavior during this period, as was later revealed at the time of his fall, clearly showed that he was not even prepared to recognize Zhivkov as *primus inter pares*.

In fact, for most of his premiership Yugov, despite the opposition his personality aroused, probably enjoyed greater standing than almost any other Premier in the Eastern European states. His authority was clearly greater than that of any Premier since Imre Nagy between 1953 and 1955. He was certainly a more powerful figure than Stoica in Rumania, Ferenc Munnich in Hungary, Siroky in Czechoslovakia, Cyrankiewicz in Poland, or Grotewohl in East Germany. Only Mehmet Shehu in Albania seems likely to have enjoyed greater status in his own country than Yugov in Bulgaria. (Shehu was the acknowledged second man in the regime after Hoxha and had been since the execution of Koce Xoxe in 1948.)

Therefore, until Zhivkov could install some of his own men in

[23] On the death of Gheorghiu-Dej in 1965, the practice was interrupted, but was revived again in December, 1967, when Ceausescu became head of state.

the governmental apparatus, he had little chance of exerting control over the regime as a whole. This is why the personnel changes announced in December, 1959 (and mentioned above), were so important. Not only was Todorov made a deputy premier and Chairman of the State Planning Commission, replacing Yugov's supporter, Hristozov, but other changes pointed to a successful encroachment by Zhivkov supporters. The most important of these was the promotion of Zhivko Zhivkov (no relation to Todor) to a deputy premiership.

Zhivko Zhivkov, some three-and-a-half years younger than Todor Zhivkov, later came to be recognized as one of the most able men in the Bulgarian leadership. He had already had a many-sided career. The holder of a prewar law degree from the University of Sofia, he became head of the Bulgarian Komsomol in the first few years after World War II. (This was first called the Union of National Youth and then the Dimitrov Union of National Youth.) At the Fifth Party Congress in 1948 he became a candidate-member of the BCP Central Committee. After a year as deputy chief of the Central Committee's *agitprop* section, he became a deputy foreign minister in 1950 but, a year later, returned to Party work as secretary of the district committee in Haskovo. In September, 1952, he began a long connection with economic questions when he became Minister of Foreign Trade at the young age of 37. In 1957, his career suffered a temporary check when he became first deputy minister of trade[24] and then again deputy foreign minister. At the Seventh Party Congress in 1958, he was reelected to the membership in the Central Committee, that he had first acquired in 1954, and immediately afterwards he became Minister of Education and Culture in place of Chervenkov. It was this post he gave up when made a deputy premier in 1959. In 1962, with the full triumph of Todor Zhivkov, he became a full member of the Politburo and first deputy premier in place of Rayko Damyanov. After Todor Zhivkov, he thus became perhaps the most powerful man in the government apparatus.

Other young Party apparatchiks introduced into the lower echelons of government in December, 1959, could be classified as members of Zhivkov's patrimony. In all, five Party secretaries of district committees were transferred to posts at the deputy-ministerial level. Some of these soon fell by the wayside; among those who did not was Marin Vachkov, who became first deputy chair-

---

[24] In February, 1957, the Ministries of Foreign and Internal Trade were amalgamated.

man of the State Planning Commission. He was later to become
an enlightened and quite successful Minister of Agriculture.

The new junior minister who was to go the farthest, however,
was an apparatchik, not from the provinces, but from the Party
apparatus in Sofia. Luchezar Avramov, aged 37, chief of the
agitprop department of the Central Committee, became first deputy minister of foreign trade. Avramov was from a family that had
rendered notable service to the Communist cause. His father was
killed by the royalist police in the late 1930's, and his family then
emigrated to the Soviet Union, where "Lutchko" finished his
schooling. He parachuted into Bulgaria in 1941 to help the Partisan movement but was captured and imprisoned. His first post of
note under the Communist regime was that of first secretary of the
Komsomol, a post he held from 1950 to 1955. He lost this post
in circumstances that suggested some disgrace (he was said to have
been involved in a personal scandal) and then became first secretary of the Dimitrov rayon Party Committee in the city of Sofia.

After holding this post for two years, he became chairman of
the innocuous Bulgarian Committee for Physical Culture and
Sport. The impression that his career had been temporarily checked
was confirmed at the Seventh Party Congress in 1958, when he was
only re-elected to the candidate-membership of the Central Committee that he had held since the Sixth Congress in June, 1954.
(Only three candidate-members of twenty-nine were not promoted
to full membership.) In June, 1959, however, he became head of
the Central Committee's *agitprop* department and in December
was transferred to the government as first deputy minister of foreign trade. After that he rose steadily. He assumed responsibility
for Bulgaria's foreign trade balances, a post which subsequently
gave him supreme control over all foreign trade questions. In 1961,
he at last became a full member of the Central Committee. At the
Eighth Congress in 1962 he was elected to the secretariat. A year
later he added to his responsibilities by becoming head of the
government commission for the development of tourism, a post
in which he has achieved outstanding success. In March, 1966,
he was appointed to the newly created Bureau of the Council of
Ministers, another version of the "inner cabinet" composed of
deputy premiers. Avramov had vigor, brains, and youth and seemed
destined for even higher things.

These, then, were some of the promising young men Zhivkov
used to strengthen his stake in the government and to weaken
Yugov. In fact, the reshuffle in 1959 may be considered as the first

important sign that Yugov was losing in the power struggle. The momentum that had brought him back from the brink of physical liquidation in 1950 to the premiership in 1956 had been definitely stopped. From then on, despite his renewed activity in 1960, his long and checkered career began to draw to a definite close.

Moscow's Concern About the Bulgarian Party

Political issues and power struggles are often so intertwined as to become inextricable. This is all the more obvious in the politics of Communist states, where the absence of any formal and accepted opposition often prevents, or obscures, that crystallization of issues which is still sometimes possible in the liberal democratic systems. In Bulgaria after 1956, the problem of disentanglement was often very difficult. Issues there certainly were, but it was impossible to tell whether the stand taken on them by a certain leader or faction was sincerely held or used simply as a means to discredit the opposing leader or faction. Thus, if Yugov opposed the "great leap forward," was his opposition based on some kind of principle or was it simply an attempt to embarrass Zhivkov? Later, in 1962, did Zhivkov espouse the cause of reform because he believed in it, or because he could use it, with Moscow's help, to bludgeon his opponents whom he denounced as Stalinists?

In 1960, this problem also presented itself. Then the issue was the Sino-Soviet dispute and Bulgaria's attitude toward it. The evident fascination in Bulgarian ruling circles for things Chinese has already been discussed. It ceased, at least officially, immediately after Moscow expressed its displeasure over the ideological pretensions of the Chinese communes. But as the Sino-Soviet dispute gathered momentum, many eyewitness reports from Sofia maintained that the Bulgarian Party was by no means united behind its leadership in its attitude toward it. The official Party line was completely pro-Soviet. At the Communist "little summit" in Bucharest in June, 1960, where the first public collision between the Soviets and the Chinese occurred, Zhivkov, as he himself put it, "supported every word" of Khrushchev's speech.[25] Immediately on his return from Bucharest, he called a Central Committee plenum, which published a resolution wholeheartedly endorsing the Khruschev line.[26] In articles, speeches, and broadcasts, the same

[25] Radio Sofia, June 24, 1960.
[26] *Ibid.*, July 13, 1960.

theme was driven home. A Party leadership once considered one of the most dogmatic of all now hewed with touching faithfulness to the anti-dogmatic line.

But these official pledges evidently did not accurately reflect prevailing sentiment in the Party as a whole. A large group was said to be profoundly suspicious of Khrushchev's policy; its leader was reported to be none other than Chervenkov himself. Any evidence that existed to support these rumors was of a circumstantial rather than a direct sort. None of it pointed to the existence of a "Chinese wing" of the Party that would have wished Bulgaria to take the same course as Albania was soon to do. What probably existed was a large number of members who were bewildered by what they considered the dangerous course of Soviet foreign policy and by the prospect of a profound split in the world Communist movement. All the Eastern European Parties at the time must have harbored groups that regarded peaceful coexistence not only as ideologically wrong but also as practically dangerous. What might be feasible for the solidly entrenched CPSU in the Soviet Union could prove suicidal for the Eastern European regimes, only recently installed and still lacking real roots.

As for Chervenkov himself, it was not difficult to visualize him as an opponent of Khrushchev's policy. The antipathy each man held for the other was so often reported as to be taken for a fact. Chervenkov also had Khrushchev to thank for his demotion in April, 1956. Moreover, as an orthodox Marxist-Leninist of long experience and some note, he might well have despised the crude pragmatism of Khrushchev. He probably had much more sympathy with the militancy and personal dignity of Mao. At any rate, it was a most noticeable omission that after the June conference in Bucharest, Chervenkov did not contribute one word to the flood of official support for Khrushchev's stand.

But the strongest circumstantial evidence of all that there was disunity, or at least confusion, over official policy toward the Sino-Soviet dispute occurred toward the end of August, 1960, when Frol Kozlov, then number two to Khrushchev in the Soviet Union, and Nikolai Ignatov, a Central Committee secretary, visited Bulgaria. The reason for their visit was not given, but almost immediately after their arrival they had a conference with several full members of the Politburo, one candidate-member, and one member of the Secretariat.[27] The fact that the one candidate-member present was

[27] *Ibid.*, August 27, 1960.

Dimitur Dimov who, as Chairman of the Party Control Commission, was specifically charged with Party discipline, and that the Secretariat member was Mitko Grigorov, the Party secretary responsible for matters of ideology, certainly suggested that questions of an ideological-disciplinary nature were discussed. In their ten-day tour of Bulgaria, the two important Soviet visitors also made several speeches "explaining" the foreign policy of their country to Bulgarian Party activists. This also suggests that there was some concern about the reaction of the rank and file to the Sino-Soviet dispute. There was also the fact that Kozlov and Ignatov apparently did not meet Chervenkov, at least officially, until shortly before their departure from Sofia airport. He certainly did not attend the key meeting at the beginning of their stay.

During and immediately after the visit of the two Soviet leaders, the official Bulgarian attacks against dogmatists continued with ever greater intensity, although these were always accompanied by the usual attacks against revisionism. On August 26, Todor Pavlov, the president of the Academy of Sciences and a "Stalinist" if ever there was one, attacked dogmatism.[28] On September 9, Politburo member Encho Staikov in *Pravda* lashed out at "dogmatists, doctrinarians, and sectarians." In his September 9 anniversary speech, General Ivan Mihailov attacked dogmatism and referred to China only as "becoming a mighty industrial state,"[29] and on September 22, an article in the Sofia *Vecherni Novini* stated that dogmatism was "characteristic of religion" and was "incompatible with Marxism-Leninism." These attacks were certainly leveled at dogmatists in general but were probably intended for Bulgarian dogmatists in particular.

To the world conference of Communist Parties in Moscow in November, 1960, Bulgaria sent the strongest delegation ever to leave her borders. It included Zhivkov, Yugov, Ganev, Grigorov (the man obviously being groomed to replace Chervenkov as chief ideologist), and Ruben Avramov, the head of the Central Committee department for science and culture who, as Ruben Levy, had had a romantic career in the Comintern. But it also included Chervenkov and, if the foregoing analysis is correct, then his inclusion could be explained only by the desire to present a front of real Party unity on this matter, or to identify and bind Chervenkov with the decisions that were to be taken in Moscow. Whatever the wish, it was successful. All reports of the Moscow conference indicate complete Bulgarian loyalty to Khrushchev. Chervenkov, for his part, publicly went along with the decision of his delegation. Shortly after his return from Moscow he broke his long ideological silence and came out strongly for the Declaration and Appeal issued at the end of the conference.[30] So, for a time, the matter rested.

This description of the evident wavering in certain sections of the Bulgarian Party has been necessary because it concerned the most important issue ever to arise in the international Communist movement. The question of how much this issue was used in the power struggle within the Bulgarian Party is difficult to answer. There was probably much opportunism in the pro-Khrushchev stand of the Zhivkov leadership, which built its policy on a foundation of unwavering support for Moscow. As for Chervenkov's opposition, a knowledge of the man would suggest that it was prompted by some sincerity. But part of it—and much of his supporters' opposition—may have been simply a reaction of the "outs" against the "ins." Many members of the old Bulgarian apparatus were being replaced by younger men, and these newcomers had the support of a Soviet leader whose influence in the process of replacement had been decisive. The only recourse, therefore, albeit a desperate one, was to oppose what their opponents supported, thereby instinctively gravitating toward the other center of the world movement, which was challenging Moscow. The recourse, as it turned out, was a hopeless one, but in 1960 it may have seemed rather less unrealistic than it does, in retrospect, today.

Dissension on the Right

The Moscow conference for a time brought the centralist Zhivkov leadership some relief from the obstinacy of the dogmatist forces on its left. The early part of 1961, however, brought trouble on its right flank.

At the end of 1960, the "great leap forward" was officially wound up, with the regime protesting loudly that the goals originally set for 1962 had already been achieved.[31] Few knowledgeable Bul-

[30] Radio Sofia, on December 20, 1960, broadcast a speech he made at Plovdiv. Next day it repeated the broadcast twice. A Central Committee plenum in support of the Declaration and Appeal was held on December 10; Bulgarian Telegraph Agency, December 12, 1960.

[31] See Chapter 5.

garians could have been deceived by these claims, and the disappointment and bitterness which must have followed in the wake of this venture were soon reflected in mounting dissension against the Party leadership.

The first intimation of this dissension was contained in the April issue of the Party monthly, *Partien Zhivot*. In an editorial entitled "Five Years," ostensibly dealing with the half-decade since the April 1956 plenum, *Partien Zhivot* savagely attacked the "anti-Party group" of Chankov, Terpeshev, and Panov, purged in 1957. But it also revealed that a group of "coffee-house conspirators" was still up to mischief and once again named Panov and Terpeshev. Linked with them, however, and now their leader, was Nikola Kufardzhiev, a fairly obscure secretary of the Central Council of Trade Unions since 1957, who was reportedly the son of a prominent "left-sectarian" member of the BCP between the wars. These were the only three conspirators named and *Partien Zhivot*, after mentioning in passing that they had been expelled from the Party, tried to dismiss the whole band of conspirators as being pitifully small. But the fact that it gave them so much space and vehemence would seem to belie this contention. Soon afterwards *Novo Vreme* took up the subject. In an editorial harmlessly entitled "Actual Problems of Party Work," it used a milder tone than *Partien Zhivot* but was more precise about the sins of the evildoers. After reviewing the achievements of the Third Five-Year Plan, it continued:

> In the light of these great successes of the Party policy, the miserable attempts of a small group of former members of the BCP, headed by Nikola Kufardzhiev, Dobri Terpeshev, and Yonko Panov, become still more culpable; those who have broken away from the people, those politically demoralized functionaries who deny the Party line for accelerated economic development and offer foreign revisionist solutions, who, because of their pessimism, see nothing positive in our socialism, who speculate with the difficulties of our development, hiding their unhealthy, careerist, and power ambitions behind the basest demagogy.[32]

The most explosive charge here was that the conspirators were offering "foreign revisionist solutions." Charges and countercharges in Communist polemics must always, of course, be taken with a grain of salt. But the behavior of Terpeshev and Panov since the April, 1956, plenum, and their evident wish to proceed further

[32] *Novo Vreme*, May, 1961.

and faster with reform, make such a charge not entirely incredible.

This was also a period of great strain in Bulgarian-Yugoslav relations. Belgrade was incensed at the anti-Yugoslav revisionist passages contained in the Declaration and Appeal of the Moscow conference in November–December, 1960. Usually when Yugoslavia's relations with Moscow were bad, her relations with Bulgaria, the traditional enemy, were very bad; this time was no exception. Relations probably reached their lowest point since the Stalin period when the Yugoslav press attaché in Sofia, Vladimir Sindjelic, was expelled from the country in March, 1960. This occasioned a real onslaught against the Bulgarian government, which was accused of extreme provocation against Yugoslavia under the guise of the struggle against revisionism.[33]

There is no direct evidence linking the expulsion of Sindjelic with the activities of the Bulgarian conspiratorial group but, from the sequence of events, the charges made, and the political profiles of men like Terpeshev and Panov, it was likely that the group did lean toward Yugoslav revisionism and that it had contacts with the Yugoslav Embassy.

The revelations about Kufardzhiev, Terpeshev, and Panov were immediately followed by the dismissal of the first secretary of the district Party committee, Petar Chushkarov, and the chairman of the district People's council, Georgi Milchev, in Pleven, in northern Bulgaria.[34] No reasons were given and the two men concerned were of little prominence, but it was probable that they too were part of the dissident group.

A far more important purge occurred at the end of May. Todor Prahov, Chairman of the Central Council of Trade Unions, was transferred to the chairmanship of the innocuous Union of Bulgarian Fighters against Fascism and Capitalism. Three secretaries of the Central Council were also dismissed: Maria Kiritova, Nikola Aleksiev, and Boris Blagoev.

These changes were certainly the most dramatic since the purge of Boris Taskov in 1957. If Prahov was not in the BCP's top ten, he was certainly in its top twenty. A veteran Communist, he had been a candidate-member of the Politburo since 1954 and head of the trade unions since 1951. Though much of his early life had been spent behind bars in royalist Bulgaria, there was no reason to

[33] See, for example, *Borba* (Belgrade), March 11, 1961; *Politika* (Belgrade), March 18, 1961.
[34] Radio Sofia, April 6, 1961.

believe that his health was the cause of his demotion, since he had been very active immediately prior to his transfer.

Nor should the importance of his three purged colleagues be underestimated. A secretaryship of one of the regime's most important transmission belts was of some consequence and, in addition, Kiritova was a full member of the Party Central Committee and Aleksiev a candidate-member. Blagoev was less well known, but had been an important trade union figure since 1950 and a Central Council secretary since 1957. These three officials comprised half the Central Council secretariat.

As in the cases of Chushkarov and Milchev, no reasons were given for the purges at the time and it is still not easy to account for them. It is doubtful that the reasons were other than political, but it is by no means certain what kind of politics was involved. Prahov, for example, hardly fits into the image of a revisionist or even of a "doubter" on the style of Taskov. In fact, certain connections with Chervenkov might point to his being a representative of the dogmatic left. Both were from the same town of Zlatitsa, east of Sofia, and Prahov had been appointed trade union chief when Chervenkov was at the height of his power. Then again, *Trud*, the daily organ of the Bulgarian trade unions, was the only Eastern European paper to print a report of the show trial in Albania of Teme Sejko and his codefendants.[35] This was construed by the Yugoslavs as an example of Bulgaria's pro-dogmatist, anti-Belgrade attitude. It certainly caused a minor sensation at the time and occurred only two days before the dismissals of Prahov and company were announced, thus suggesting a disciplinary move. But, if true, this was a very severe reprisal indeed; the dismissal of *Trud's* editor would have seemed sufficient but this, in fact, did not occur. It seems more likely that the report was carried inadvertently.[36]

The most likely explanation springs from the fact that Nikola Kufardzhiev, the new leader of the "anti-Party group," was also a secretary of the Central Council of Trade Unions. It is possible that Kufardzhiev, evidently a forceful man, used his trade union post as a base for his nefarious activities, and either the three dismissed secretaries supported him, actively or passively, or they simply had not been watchful enough. As for Prahov, it is possible

---

[35] See William E. Griffith: *Albania and the Sino-Soviet Rift* (Cambridge, Mass., 1963), pp. 80–82. The *Trud* report appeared on May 28.

[36] *Ibid.*, p. 81.

that he was not in command of the situation and allowed dissension and demoralization to grow dangerously in his "empire."

The Party and the Twenty-Second CPSU Congress

The Twenty-Second CPSU Congress profoundly affected the entire world Communist movement. It was a turning point in the Sino-Soviet dispute and marked the virtual expulsion of Albania from the Soviet bloc. It also sought to exorcise the spirit of Stalin from the Communist body politic forever. Its effect on Eastern Europe, though less explosive than that of the Twentieth Congress five years before, was nevertheless considerable, though very uneven. In Poland, for example, it was not allowed to deter the steady retrogression from October that had been going on since 1959. In Hungary, it was of massive political and psychological help to Kadar in pressing ahead with his new course. In Czechoslovakia and Rumania, it stirred up many foul pools in the history of the two Parties, with the leaders of both, Novotny and Gheorghiu-Dej, seeking to exculpate themselves and avoid the necessity for real reform. Gheorghiu-Dej was conspicuously successful; for Novotny, however, it was the beginning of the long road that led to his overthrow in January, 1968. Ulbricht, bowing deferentially to the mood in Moscow, carried on very much as before; the changes in East Germany domestic policy that occurred in 1962 and 1963 were due more to the building of the Berlin Wall in August, 1961, than to the Soviet congress the following October.

Nowhere was the effect more profound than in Bulgaria; nowhere did it produce more change or more reaction to that change. It was obvious that, as a result of this second bout of destalinization, Chervenkov would have to go. For him to stay would have meant not only an open defiance of Khrushchev but also an implicit admission of the fact that he was still the real ruler of the country.

But finally to topple a man who had been his country's outstanding personality for eleven years, and who still had strong support in the Party, was a task that needed preparation. It was not surprising, therefore, that the Central Committee plenum—called ostensibly to hear the report by Zhivkov on the Twenty-Second Congress, but actually to purge Chervenkov—occurred a full month after the Soviet congress ended. What went on behind the scenes during this month is not known, but it is believed that the elaborate case against Chervenkov was prepared by Bulgaranov, an old enemy who had suffered much at his hands.

The plenum took place on November 28 and 29; Chervenkov was dismissed from the Politburo, the Central Committee, and his deputy premiership for his "mistakes and vicious methods,"[37] both before *and after* the April plenum in 1956. Zhivkov, in his report,[38] comprehensively attacked Chervenkov. He was at pains to destroy the myth that still clung to the man.

> The Politburo of the CC of the BCP thinks also that it is necessary to carry to its end the clarification and the dispelling of the personality cult of Comrade V. Chervenkov, which was created in the past in our country. This cult, as is known, was systematically imposed in the course of many years with the aid of all ideological, political and organizational methods . . . Comrade V. Chervenkov is just one of the officials of the Bulgarian Communist Party and it is entirely improper and artificial that he was extolled and placed above the collective, above the Politburo and the Central Committee of the Party. Therefore, we think that it is necessary to clear away all exaggerations of the role and merits of Comrade V. Chervenkov, all remnants of the false aura with which, here and there, people still surround his personality.

But Zhivkov insisted on preserving the myth of Georgi Dimitrov. The worst crimes under Communist rule had been committed *before* Chervenkov attained supreme power, i.e., under Dimitrov. But Zhivkov explicitly denied this and praised the Dimitrov period:

> Everybody knows that the setting after World War II, in which Georgi Dimitrov lived and worked, was much more complicated and more difficult. International relations were much more tense, the international situation of the People's Republic of Bulgaria was considerably more serious, in the country the opposition was working actively, the exploiting classes were not as yet defeated, the class struggle was waged both openly and secretly.
>
> In this complex setting, Georgi Dimitrov always observed Lenin's principles of leadership; he observed the method of collectiveness in work, did not misuse his power, and did not infringe legality in the country. The laws were observed also toward the most intemperate enemies of the people's rule.

Zhivkov then listed Chervenkov's mistakes in various branches of public life: in agriculture where, before 1956, his policy had

[37] Radio Sofia, November 30, 1961.
[38] *Rabotnichesko Delo*, December 2, 1961.

been responsible for the pitifully low incomes of many farm workers; in industry, where "erroneous doctrinaire concepts" had been responsible for what was now considered to be the slow development of industry before 1956; in Party and state leadership, where his mania for centralization had reduced to impotence, not only the Party and government agencies, but all the mass organizations as well. He was particularly criticized for his attitude toward the Bulgarian Agrarian Union, which he was charged with relegating to a position of complete insignificance. Since 1956, said Zhivkov, the BCP's relations with the Union had been placed on a fraternal footing. It was now recognized as having an important place in the building of socialism. Moreover, its international ties "with a large number of similar parties and organizations abroad are very useful and necessary."

Zhivkov's attack on Chervenkov was followed by other speakers at the plenum and was taken up by the radio and every section of the press in the following weeks. Now the assault was heavier than the relatively polite criticism of him at the April, 1956, plenum and after. Though many of the charges leveled at him were true, others were manifestly false.[39] There were two reasons for this massive onslaught. First, it showed that Chervenkov was now really at the end of his power; there would be no repetition of 1956 when he faded from the limelight and then re-emerged as a still-powerful force. Second, the very strength and persistence of the campaign against him showed that Chervenkov still had great support in the Party and that a massive attempt was needed to break it. Chervenkov, like Molotov earlier in the Soviet Union, never made a self-criticism. Thus, though finally beaten, he would not concede defeat. Many of his supporters therefore felt less inclined to abandon their own opposition and quietly accept the new leaders and policies. They could not go along with the new and total denunciation of Stalin (and hence of Chervenkov) and expressed their opposition to it openly. Zhivkov himself admitted this in his plenum speech:

> There are some Party members who do not understand the need for the full unmasking of the Stalin cult and the fractional group, do not see the enormous principled meaning of this decision of the Twenty-Second Congress for all fraternal Parties; they think that now in the Soviet Communist Party a fight is being taken up against some old-time Bolsheviks. There are also those who do

[39] For the most comprehensive single attack on Chervenkov, see *Novo Vreme*, January, 1962.

not want to understand the truth, the essence of the decisions of the Twenty-Second Congress, and who try to open a discussion. Their deportment hides dangers, they do not take into consideration Party discipline and the Party policy; they have just got an idea in mind and without caring about the actual facts, poison with their unhealthy moods and talks the atmosphere around themselves.[40]

This opposition did not quietly fade away, but persisted and caused nervousness in both Sofia and Moscow. At the end of 1961 and the beginning of 1962, "not a few members and candidate-members were expelled from the Party" at the local level.[41]

Obviously the purge of Chervenkov had given Zhivkov a big boost in his patient quest for supreme power. At the November plenum, Stanko Todorov and Mitko Grigorov, two of his own group, had been elected full members of the Politburo. But tightening his grip on the leadership was one thing, and asserting his authority in the Party as a whole was another. His difficulties in the political and ideological field were dramatically reflected in April by the arrival of a Soviet delegation headed by Party secretary and ideologist Leonid Ilichev, who had to leave the session of the newly elected Supreme Soviet to attend a hurriedly-called conference on ideological questions in Sofia. The deliberations of this conference were not reported, but the split in the Party ranks was clearly reflected in the resolution of a Central Committee plenum called immediately before it. This admitted the existence of Communists "who are inclined to minimize the harmful effects of the personality cult, thinking that everything has passed away and been corrected, without seeing that in many places things still are as they used to be. Others are inclined . . . almost to deny the Party line and the successes that were achieved during the period of the cult."[42] Thus the old "double" enemy was referred to again: the dogmatists on the left and the reformers and revisionists on the right. But from all the evidence, it would seem that by far the greater danger came from the left.

The Khrushchev Visit

Khrushchev arrived in Sofia on May 14, leading a big Soviet Party and government delegation which included Foreign Minister Gromyko and Central Committee secretary Ponomarev. He had

[40] *Rabotnichesko Delo*, December 2, 1961.
[41] See *Partien Zhivot*, April, 1962.
[42] *Rabotnichesko Delo*, May 5, 1962.

not been to Bulgaria since his appearance at the Seventh Party Congress in June, 1958. The Eighth BCP Congress was originally scheduled for August, 1962, and it might have been expected that he would have attended that. Instead, he came in May, at relatively short notice. The purpose of his visit was clearly to back Zhivkov in his struggle against his opponents and in his acceptance, however reluctant, of Moscow's new attempt at *rapprochement* with Yugoslavia. For many in the Bulgarian Party, Moscow's new shift in Yugoslav relations was yet another cause of deep dissension.

Even for the Zhivkov leadership, Khrushchev's efforts to improve relations with Tito, which accelerated noticeably at the beginning of 1962, must have been a bitter pill to swallow, not only because of its own reluctance on the matter but also because it produced yet another divisive element in the Party. Zhivkov would probably have been happy to have relations with Yugoslavia continue on the old basis: state relations "normal," Party relations nonexistent. In his report to the Central Committee after the Twenty-Second CPSU Congress, he repeated this formulation and described with satisfaction how the "representatives of the revisionist, anti-Leninist views" of the Yugoslav Communist League were meeting with constant rebuff. If the Yugoslav leaders did not renounce these views there could be no hope of better Party relations. State relations, however, were different: economic, governmental and cultural contacts were developing and Bulgaria would do everything in her power to extend them.[43]

Khrushchev evidently pressed the Bulgarians on this subject during his visit and even though Zhivkov complied, it was still possible to detect a note of caution and skepticism in his allusions to it. For example, in his speech in Sofia on the eve of Khrushchev's departure, he said the following:

> It must be noted that our relations with neighboring Yugoslavia are steadily improving; the economic and cultural relations are developing and mutual contacts increase. In the future we shall do our best—everything that is called for on our side—for the further development of Bulgarian-Yugoslav relations.[44]

This was evidently his way of saying that it takes two to make a friendship and that, willing though the Bulgarian regime was, there were problems attendant on a Yugoslav-Bulgarian *rapproche-*

[43] *Rabotnichesko Delo*, December 2, 1961.
[44] Radio Sofia, May 19, 1962.

ment that could not be solved simply because Khrushchev wanted one. However, Zhivkov's remark was deemed a "positive and constructive approach" by the Yugoslav Foreign Ministry.[45]

As for the domestic Bulgarian aspects of the visit, Khrushchev left no doubt about his support for Zhivkov. On his "whistle-stop" tour throughout several parts of the country, he used every opportunity to praise "the Central Committee of the BCP headed by Comrade Zhivkov." The best example of this was in a speech at Obnova in the Pleven district, where he emphasized that it was since Zhivkov's election as Party First Secretary that much had been done to normalize the situation in Bulgaria. "Therefore," continued Khrushchev, "I repeat that we have best relations with the BCP, the best relations with its Central Committee, and personally with Comrade Todor Zhivkov. We admit, and are proud of, the achievements of the BCP in respect to the solidarity of the ranks of the Communist Party, the Central Committee, and the correct Marxist leadership."[46]

On two occasions during this visit, in which he was at his colorful, arrogant best, Khrushchev seemed to make a point of expressing a preference for Zhivkov over Yugov. Speaking in Varna, he said: "Previous to me, Comrade Yugov spoke well; also today, at the shipyards, Comrade Zhivkov spoke wonderfully."[47] Later, at Obnova, he said: "We have good relations between the governments, between me and Comrade Yugov . . . Our relations with the Bulgarian Communist Party are such that we cannot conceive of or wish for better. We have the best personal relations with Comrade Zhivkov."[48] This difference was noted at the time and considered important because now, with Chervenkov finally disposed of, the ring had been cleared for a direct confrontation between Zhivkov and Yugov. It was also significant in view of the rumors that Yugov was now considered by the conservatives as their best hope of stemming the tide that was threatening to engulf them. Finally, it was the first indication that Yugov's position might be weakening.

In general, Khrushchev's visit was a great triumph for Zhivkov. Not only in Bulgaria but in the Communist world as a whole, it left no doubt as to who had Moscow's backing. But, at the time when the centrifugal tendencies throughout Eastern Europe were

[45] *Tanjug* (Belgrade), May 25, 1962.
[46] *Rabotnichesko Delo*, May 19, 1962.
[47] *Ibid.*, May 17, 1962.
[48] Radio Sofia, May 19, 1962.

gathering force, it made Bulgaria more of a satellite than ever. His hosts had to sit and smile while Khrushchev lectured them in the most blatant manner, whether the subject was foreign policy or corn-growing. And Zhivkov seemed to revel in his subordination. A few days after Khrushchev's visit, in a speech at Razgrad, he admitted that the visit had been "a check of our road toward socialism and Communism, and we must say," he continued, "that our political watch-dial is exact to the second with the watch of the Soviet Union, that our watch is working toward Moscow time. This is a matter of great pride for all Bulgarian people."[49]

The Enhancing of the Agrarian Union

During his visit Khrushchev made a special point of praising the Bulgarian Agrarian Union, under the leadership of Georgi Traikov, as a faithful ally of the BCP, and as an example of Communist collaboration with non-Communists that was a lesson for the whole socialist movement. At Obnova he singled out Traikov in the following, inimitable way: "I should like specially to point out Comrade Traikov, but somehow you don't know him, you don't understand who he is . . . He leads the peasant movement and he is not a Communist. I am a Communist, but between us there are no differences on the questions concerning the construction of socialism. God give us more such non-Communists."[50]

A short time before Khrushchev's visit, at the end of April, the Thirtieth Congress of the Agrarian Union had been held. Zhivkov and a whole array of Party notables were present, and the importance of the Union as an ally of the Party and a factor in the construction of socialism was stressed as never before. Clearly a deliberate effort was being made to infuse the Union with new life and importance in order to rally the now completely collectivized peasantry to the cause of socialism. As mentioned earlier, the regime, always conscious of peasant indifference or hostility, had sought to use the great tradition of the Agrarians to win support in the countryside. But Chervenkov had always relegated the Agrarian Union, as an institution, to the status of a despised anachronism. For this, as mentioned earlier, he was to be roundly

[49] *Rabotnichesko Delo*, May 28, 1962.
[50] Radio Sofia, May 19, 1962.

criticized when finally disgraced after the Twenty-Second CPSU Congress.

The reasons for the rehabilitation of the Agrarian Union had both internal and foreign relations aspects. Numerically, the Union was by no means negligible: at its Thirtieth Congress, it had some 120,000 members, of whom 100,000 worked in the collective farms. It was, therefore, a mass organization, the Party's main transmission belt to the countryside. After the completion of collectivization and the merger of collectives, when more attention was being paid to agriculture through greater resource allocations, it was evidently considered that the Union, if given a greater role in public life, could become a useful instrument to improve the morale and psychological climate of the peasantry. Externally, the Union was considered a good public relations vehicle through its contacts with foreign Agrarian parties and peasant associations, especially in non-Communist countries. The impression was given abroad that the great party of Stamboliski was still alive and kicking, an independent but faithful ally of the Communist Party. It was noticeable that, since 1962, Zhivkov has usually taken one of the Agrarian ministers in the government along with him on top Party-government delegations.

The climax of this new policy toward the Union was to come in April, 1964, when its leader, Traikov, was elected titular head of state (chairman of the Presidium of the National Assembly) on the death of Dimitur Ganev. Born in 1898, Traikov was, for most of his life, associated with the city of Varna. He joined the Agrarian Union in 1919 and worked in Varna as one of its full time organizers. In 1934, after the seizure of power by the "Zveno" group, Traikov became deputy mayor of Varna. Always on the left wing of the Agrarians, he maintained contacts with the underground Communists up to and during the war. In 1943, he joined the Fatherland Front. In 1946, he became Minister of Agriculture and was a permanent feature in the Council of Ministers thereafter. A deputy premier in 1949, he became first deputy premier after the April plenum and the demotion of Chervenkov in 1956.

Many Agrarians regarded Traikov as a traitor for his collaboration with the Communists. Between 1944 and 1948, when different groups of Agrarians, led by Dimitur Gichev and by Nikola Petkov, wished to preserve the independence of their Party, the BCP had a faithful ally in Traikov in their attempts to break the Agrarian opposition. After this was achieved through the execution of Petkov, Traikov became chairman (the title was later changed to secretary) of the now completely subordinate Union. By April, 1964, he could hardly complain that his efforts had gone unrewarded.

The Eighth Party Congress

The Eighth Party Congress originally had been scheduled for August but was postponed until November.[51] The main reason was obviously the instability in the Party. During the spring and summer of 1962, this was accentuated by a deteriorating economic situation which aroused considerable discontent in the country as a whole.

In late July, a series of price increases were announced that affected several important items of household supply. This was followed by serious warnings to the population against expressions of discontent. One warning accused "bourgeois remnants," now united with the "anti-popular scum of society," of trying to create "doubts and unhealthy" moods.[52] Another accused some Party members who "constantly protest and grumble against Party measures and undertakings." Anyone caught spreading slanders or rumors would be handed over to the State Prosecutor. The same warning ended with a significant admission and an ominous threat:

> People whose sole occupation it is to fabricate and spread rumors are to be found in plenty in Sofia. They must know, however, that their hostile activities cannot and will not remain unpunished, and that they themselves do not deserve to be citizens of our capital.[53]

The regime was clearly concerned about the mood in Sofia itself and raised the threat of deportations to the countryside—a common device for dealing with malcontents. It was a powerful threat since to live in Sofia, despite the crowded housing conditions, had come to be regarded as one of the great privileges of life by many Bulgarians.

It was in this atmosphere that preparations for the Party congress took place. Already there were hints of the drama that was to come. In a series of government changes announced in March, 1962, Georgi Tsankov lost his post of Ministry of the Interior and

[51] *Rabotnichesko Delo*, June 17, 1962.
[52] *Ibid.*, July 31, 1962.
[53] *Ibid.*, August 4, 1962.

was formally "promoted" to the rank of deputy premier. Thus Tsankov was eased out of the power base he had controlled since January, 1951. From being one of the most powerful men in Bulgaria, in command of the whole police and security apparatus, he became just another deputy premier with no portfolio and no power base. His place was taken by General Diko Dikov, a partisan general, a former deputy minister of defense and, more recently, head of the Administrative Organs (military) department of the Central Committee. A more popular, flexible man than Tsankov, Dikov set about mitigating the sinister reputation the Interior Ministry had acquired.

The changes at the Ministry of Interior in March, 1962, followed the pattern established by the changes of December, 1959. Present and past officials of the ministry were demoted. Apostol Kolchev, first deputy minister under Tsankov, lost his post and became secretary of the Presidium of the National Assembly, a rather ludicrous appointment for a secret policeman. Georgi Kumbiliev who, in December, 1959, lost his post as deputy minister of the interior to become Minister of Foreign Trade—another bizarre transfer—now became Ambassador to Peking and was replaced by Luchezar Avramov. Finally, Rusi Hristozov, Minister of the Interior from 1948 to 1951, later Chairman of the State Planning Commission and, after December, 1959, Minister of Internal Trade, left the government completely. And, a rather pathetic footnote to these changes, Kimon Georgiev, aged seventy-nine, one of the leaders of the "Zveno" *coup* in 1934, first Prime Minister after the September 9, 1944, "liberation," and a hanger-on in high places ever after, finally lost his deputy premiership. Never formally a member of the Communist Party, Georgiev had nevertheless served it well and, even now, was nicely compensated by being elected a member of the National Assembly Presidium. He never lacked ability nor, without knowing the inner workings of the man's mind, can it be automatically assumed that he lacked all principle. Nevertheless, a man who began his career with a good deal of respect ended it in an aura of amused or sad contempt.

During the spring and summer there were some signs, small but clear, of a deterioration of Yugov's position. The differentiation between him and Zhivkov made by Khrushchev during his visit in May has already been noted. At the beginning of September, when the agenda for the forthcoming Party congress was published, Yugov was not listed as one of the main speakers, although it is customary for Premiers to give the report on the new economic plan. This time a Twenty-Year Plan was to be outlined and its *rapporteur* was to be Zhivkov himself. Later, a state visit by Yugov to Ghana, scheduled for the middle of October, was called off without explanation. These signs, of course, were by no means conclusive and Yugov, in many respects, continued to be very active. When Kirilenko, for example, visited Bulgaria in August—the third top Soviet official, after Ilichev and Khrushchev, to visit Bulgaria in 1962—Yugov figured prominently among those with whom he conferred. But, taken together with the recurring speculation about the Premier's position since 1959, they were viewed as storm signals not to be ignored. In Tsankov's case, also, there were, in the spring and summer, various criticisms made of the activity of the Ministry of the Interior which spelled danger for him.

Yet, his fate, and that of Tsankov, was evidently not settled until the very eve of the Party congress. The congress began on November 5; two days before, Yugov, in his capacity as Premier, had received the new Ambassador from Afghanistan. In fact, on the night before the Congress, his portrait and Tsankov's were still hanging in the congress hall with those of the other Bulgarian leaders.[54] The mystery is hard to explain. On October 31, a plenum of the Central Committee was held at which it was presumably announced that Zhivkov would be assuming the premiership immediately after the congress, following the trend that Khrushchev and Kadar had set. It may also have been announced that Yugov would suffer some further demotion. In addition, Zhivkov may have revealed that he planned to denounce several members of the old security apparatus, including Tsankov, Hristozov, Kumbiliev, and Kolchev. This may have led to an open clash in which Yugov and Tsankov made their last bid to rally support in the Central Committee against Zhivkov, not to overturn him—this was impossible by now—but to prevent their own humiliation.

The plenum was then interrupted while Zhivkov made a hurried visit to Moscow, where he conferred with Khrushchev. He returned on the evening of November 3, when the plenum was resumed. This was during a period when all the Eastern European Party leaders were making individual trips to Moscow, presumably to discuss the aftermath of the Cuban crisis the previous October. But it is hard to believe that Khrushchev and Zhivkov talked about

[54] *Tanjug*, November 5, 1962.

much else than the crisis within the BCP. There was considerable speculation at the time that the purge of Yugov was ordered by Khrushchev personally because he had criticized the Soviet leader's "cowardice" in bowing to Kennedy's ultimatum over Cuba. But to think that Yugov would risk everything on an issue of principle would be to overrate his integrity, and to imply that he considered it possible to unseat Zhivkov over an issue like Cuba would be to underrate his intelligence. He may have genuinely differed with Zhivkov over such issues as the "great leap forward" and the new Twenty-Year Program of economic development but, in the end, the issue boiled down to a struggle for power, a struggle that became more uneven as time went on until it was a question of Yugov making a last effort, not to improve his position, but to save it.

Zhivkov's opening address to the Party congress on November 5 was one of the most sensational delivered at any Communist congress for many years.[55] He announced the expulsion of the current Premier (Yugov) and a current deputy premier and Politburo member (Tsankov) from the Central Committee, and of a former Premier and party leader (Chervenkov) from the Party itself. Purges of this magnitude, if made at all, are usually made at Central Committee plenums and not at congresses, which are usually designed as demonstrations of unity. The fact that Zhivkov had to take such an untoward step showed the gravity of the dissension existing in the Party right up to the congress.

Others were also denounced in Zhivkov's speech: Hristozov, Kolchev, and Kumbiliev, all of whom, as already mentioned, had been on the slippery slope some time. Ivan Raikov, a veteran deeply implicated in the trial of Traycho Kostov, was also expelled from the Central Committee and Hristo Boyev, a deputy minister of the interior in the early 1950's and now Ambassador in Japan, was bitterly attacked by Zhivkov.

All the victims were sacrificed on the altar of destalinization. Yugov was guilty of "crude violations of socialist legality" and of actions against Party unity. Chervenkov's sins were similar, but Zhivkov also charged him with creating an atmosphere in the Party and in the country "alien to Marxism-Leninism," an indirect tribute to the influence this man still possessed despite his demotions. Tsankov and the lesser security men were all charged with violations, in varying degrees, of socialist legality.

---

[55] *Rabotnichesko Delo*, November 6, 1962.

The Case Against Yugov

The charges against Yugov, given only in outline by Zhivkov himself, were spelled out by other speakers at the congress and later *ad nauseam* by the press. Mitko Grigorov—who, as a result of this congress, became the second most powerful man in the Party after Zhivkov—devoted an important part of his congress speech to a listing of Yugov's sins. These are worth noting in some detail, since they shed considerable light on Yugov's career, although they should perhaps not all be taken as gospel truth.[56] The charges were:

Violations of Socialist Legality: Yugov, as Minister of the Interior from 1944 to 1948, committed crude violations of socialist legality, being guilty and responsible for the arrest and ill-treatment of Party and state officials who had not committed any offense whatsoever. Grigorov stressed that during Yugov's time "the Secretary of our Party, Traicho Kostov, was arrested." This was the first time that Kostov had been referred to as "the Secretary of our Party" since his execution in December, 1949. In this connection, Grigorov revealed that the November, 1961, plenum (i.e., the one held after the Twenty-Second CPSU Congress) had elected a commission, headed by Todor Zhivkov, to examine the cases of condemned Communists. This commission had recommended the full rehabilitation of those who had been condemned, and the Central Committee endorsed the recommendation.

Grigorov added that, during Yugov's tenure at the Ministry of the Interior, the perfidious network of alleged spying and sabotage centers was prepared, into which many Communists later fell and by which some were killed.

Denial of Guilt: Yugov had not admitted his guilt to the Party and the people, and did not draw the moral from this difficult period. At the April, 1956, plenum, Yugov not only failed to reveal the truth about his activity but, according to Grigorov, even attempted to deceive the Central Committee and the Party and to represent himself as a "fighter against the cult of personality." (This was the plenum which sanctioned the appointment of Yugov as Premier in place of Chervenkov.)

Anti-Party Plotting: Yugov, fearing that the whole truth might be revealed about his activity during the period of the personality

56 *Rabotnichesko Delo*, November 7, 1962.

cult, and that he might lose his positions, entered into an anti-Party plot with Chervenkov and Georgi Chankov and "began to lead a factional struggle for the seizure of the Party leadership." This seems hardly credible, since it was Chankov who had good reason to resent Yugov's elevation to the premiership in 1956. But Grigorov continued, saying that after the July, 1957, purge of Chankov, Terpeshev, and Panov, Yugov and Chervenkov were categorically warned that, if they continued their anti-Party activity, the statutes of the Party would be most strictly applied against them.

Ambition to Become "The First Man in the Country": Despite this warning, said Grigorov, Yugov did not discontinue his subversive activity and did not renounce his "morbid" ambition to become the first man in the country. He only changed his tactics. Outwardly, he represented himself as a warm supporter of the line of the April plenum and he constantly quoted the opinions of Todor Zhivkov. In reality, according to Grigorov, he secretly continued his unprincipled anti-Party attempts to win over the members of the Central Committee and other Party cadres to his subversive activity against the Party leadership and the Party line.

Creation of a Second Party Line: After the April plenum, when he became Premier, Yugov used "his high Party and state position" for a struggle against Party unity, and began the creation of a second center in the Party and in the country, and of a second Party line. (This charge would certainly fit into the warnings made in 1959 and 1961 against factionalism.)

Opposition to the "Great Leap Forward": Yugov accepted "only with words" the policy of accelerated economic development. In reality he began to work against it, exploiting the inevitable difficulties and expressing doubts about the correctness of the line. He also opposed the administrative reorganization of the country in early 1959. During that period of intensive work, Yugov, according to Grigorov, not only did not do his duty of organizing the work of the Council of Ministers, but by his conduct he incapacitated the Council of Ministers, the central departments and the District Councils. (This charge would fit in with Yugov's relative reticence during that period.)

Incompetence as Premier: Grigorov said that at the last plenum of the Central Committee (i.e., the one held immediately before the congress) the ministers under Yugov had attested to his personal incompetence. Because of his incompetence, the basic problems in Bulgarian policy had to be worked out by the Central Committee of the Party under Zhivkov.

Dishonesty, Rudeness, Vanity: Grigorov drew a very unflattering picture of Yugov's character. Apart from his dishonesty and his two-faced relations with his colleagues and with the Party leadership, and in addition to his rudeness towards his co-workers, a characteristic feature of Yugov's conduct was his unrestrained vanity and his desire to win fame and popularity. Grigorov ridiculed Yugov's evident desire always to stand next to Zhivkov when being photographed, his great interest in the pictures of himself published in the press, the place where his speeches were printed, and so on. In connection with his vanity of Yugov, said a coy Grigorov, "such scandals have taken place that I feel ashamed to mention them."

This was a truly impressive list. One can discount Grigorov's lumping together of Yugov, Chervenkov, Chankov, Terpeshev, and Panov as part of the same recalcitrant group. But his other charges, except that of incompetence, carry the ring of truth, even if exaggerated. However, the fact that Yugov was guilty of so many sins and yet held onto the premiership for over six years, attests once again to the severity of the power struggle in the top ranks of the Party leadership.

Victory over the Security Organs

The fall of Yugov marked the final triumph of Zhivkov in the top echelons of the BCP and the end of a man who had been one of the most important personal and political elements of Communist rule in Bulgaria. But the fall of Georgi Tsankov, and of lesser past or present security chieftains like Hristozov, Kolchev, and Kumbiliev, was probably of even more basic importance. None of these men were of outstanding importance in themselves, but they represented an institution of huge significance: the security apparatus vested in the Ministry of the Interior, which had contested the supreme and ultimate power with the Party itself. In this sense, the fall of Tsankov was more momentous than that of Yugov; indeed, it may well have been the most important single instance of progress in the whole course of Communist rule in Bulgaria.

While Chervenkov held supreme power in Bulgaria, the various institutions of the Communist regime—Party, state, security apparatus, army, to name the most important—were, with the possible exception of the army, firmly under his subordination. When his personal rule ended, these institutions had the opportunity to reassert their own identities, and each took on a more separate and individual importance. It then became the task of his successor, Zhivkov, to try to establish his own complete control over them. This task was all the more difficult because, in the early stages, his control over the Party itself was very shaky. But gradually he succeeded. He steadily tightened his hold on the Party. His purge of Yugov and his assumption of the premiership brought the state apparatus more firmly under his control. His purge of Tsankov and the lesser security lights broke the independence of the security apparatus. Later it will be shown that the Bulgarian Army remained an element not completely under control, as the April conspiracy in 1965 was to demonstrate.[57] With the crushing of that conspiracy the army, however, also appeared to have been placed in safe subordination. But of all the institutions a Communist leader must control before his authority is unchallenged, the security apparatus is the most potentially dangerous because of its power and its intrusion into so many aspects of government and of public life. That is why Zhivkov sought to humiliate Tsankov and almost every other important security official over the previous fifteen years.

The Bulgarian situation has close parallels in several other Eastern European countries. In the Soviet Union, the problem of Beria after the death of Stalin springs immediately to mind. In Rumania, the parallel has been astonishingly similar. What Tsankov was to Zhivkov, so Alexandru Draghici was to Ceausescu, and Draghici in 1968 had to be humiliated in the same way as Tsankov. In Yugoslavia, the Rankovic case shows also similarities, although here Tito wisely anticipated the situation that would arise after his death. But even under his acknowledged supreme rule, the security forces under Rankovic were almost an untouchable power. In Czechoslovakia, there developed a struggle for power between Novotny, the Party leader, and Rudolf Barak, Minister of Interior, which led to the purge and imprisonment of Barak in 1961. Here, the circumstances may have been different in that Barak may have stood for a more reformist political course than Novotny, but the basis of their struggle was the same: Barak with the institution at his command was against Novotny and the Party apparatus. In Poland, General Moczar, while at the Ministry of the Interior, was a powerful force in the struggle for the succession to Gomulka. In Hungary, a similar situation could develop; Bela Biszku—for several years Minister of the Interior under Kadar and still in

[57] See Chapter 8.

charge of the security apparatus—will certainly be a contender for the succession to Kadar. If he succeeds, it will be due mainly to this power base which he controls within the regime. If he is passed over and another man succeeds Kadar, then a struggle is likely to develop between the new leader and Biszku.

Thus, in Eastern Europe, it has been a safe rule of thumb that a well-entrenched Minister of the Interior is a threat to a new Party leader more by virtue of the institution he controls than in his own person. It was certainly the case in Bulgaria, and it took Zhivkov eight years—from 1954 to 1962—before he was strong enough to remove the threat completely.

The Zhivkov Team

As was to be expected after the sensations of the congress, the new Politburo and Secretariat showed a considerable shift in favor of Zhivkov. Two of his close associates, Boris Velchev and Zhivko Zhivkov, entered the Politburo, and Pencho Kubadinski and Tano Tsolov were elected candidate-members. Nacho Papazov, previously chairman of the State Committee for Science and Technical Progress, was elected to the Secretariat, as was Luchezar Avramov, the Minister of Trade. Immediately after the congress, Ivan Prumov, former Minister of Agriculture, also entered the Secretariat.

After the Eighth Congress, the Politburo consisted of the following full members: Boyan Bulgaronov (re-elected), Dimitur Ganev (re-elected), Mitko Grigorov (re-elected), Ivan Mihailov (re-elected), Encho Staykov (re-elected), Stanko Todorov (re-elected), Boris Velchev (newly elected), Todor Zhivkov (re-elected), Zhivko Zhivkov (newly elected). Candidate-members were: Dimitur Dimov (re-elected), Pencho Kubadinski (newly elected), and Tano Tsolov (newly elected). The Secretariat of the Central Committee included First Secretary Todor Zhivkov (re-elected) and Luchezar Avramov (newly elected), Boyan Bulgaranov (re-elected), Mitko Grigorov (re-elected), Nacho Papazov (newly elected), Ivan Prumov (newly elected), Boris Velchev (re-elected).

The former full Politburo members not re-elected were Tsankov, Yugov, and the veteran Raiko Damyanov. During the congress, Damyanov—a first deputy premier under Yugov—had admitted personal responsibility for some of the defects in the work of the

Council of Ministers,[58] and his departure, therefore, was no surprise. Of the former candidate-members, Mladen Stoyanov and Todor Prahov were dropped. Stoyanov had been elected to this position in July, 1957; his demotion had little political significance and he remained a member of the Central Committee. Prahov, however, was not even re-elected to the Central Committee; he was obviously paying the price for his earlier misdemeanors as head of the Central Council of Trade Unions.[59]

In a full Politburo of nine, therefore, Zhivkov had a majority of his own supporters for the first time. These were Zhivko Zhivkov, Velchev, Grigorov, and Todorov; together with Zhivkov, these made five out of nine. Three of the others—Staikov, Ganev, and Bulgaranov—were older-generation home Communists. The only Muscovite left was General Mihailov. Two of the three Politburo candidates—Tsolov and Kubadinski—were Zhivkov men, and the whole Secretariat, except for Bulgaranov, owed their rise to him.

The new Central Committee also bore the imprint of his victory in the power struggle. The number of full members was enlarged from 89 to 101 and that of the candidates from 44 to 67. Twenty-eight former full members and fifteen candidates were dropped. Among these were some figures of considerable note in the past. Apart from Yugov, Tsankov, and those personally denounced at the congress, they included Prahov; Karlo Lukanov, Minister of Foreign Affairs and an associate of Chervenkov from the very early days of the regime; former Minister of Defense Petur Panchevski; General Velichko Georgiev, commander of the Plovdiv garrison whose name had been associated with a rumored army conspiracy two years before;[60] Elena Dimitrova, wife of Chervenkov and sister of Georgi Dimitrov; Hristo Radevski, Secretary-General of the Writers' Union at the time of "the cult of personality"; and Todor Zvezdov, First Secretary of the Plovdiv Party committee and a close ally of Yugov.[61]

Easily the most conspicuous of the new Central Committee members were the veterans Petko Kunin and Titko Chernokolev.

[58] *Rabotnichesko Delo*, November 10, 1962.

[59] Prahov, however, was elected Chairman of the Central Revision Commission.

[60] See Chapter 8.

[61] Zvezdov was immediately removed from his Plovdiv post. Plovdiv was considered one of the bastions of the Yugov faction. Zvezdov was replaced by Kostadin Gyaurov, who at the Ninth Party Congress in 1966 was elected a candidate-member of the Politburo. Gyaurov is a brother of the famous singer Nikolai Gyaurov.

Kunin, a former Politburo member and Minister of Industry, had been one of Traycho Kostov's closest associates. It was Kunin who, in December, 1947, carried out the nationalization of Bulgarian industry. In 1951, in the delayed aftermath of the Kostov execution, he was sentenced to fifteen years' imprisonment, but was released in 1956. His election to the Central Committee showed that the Party leadership was carrying out its pledge to rehabilitate the Kostovites. Chernokolev had also been a member of the Politiburo and Minister of Agriculture but was comprehensively purged in 1951 after being attacked by Chervenkov and Chankov for having "wrong conceptions" about the development of agriculture. (He is believed to have opposed the hasty collectivization of agriculture.) More recently, Chernokolev had been partly rehabilitated through his appointment as President of the Academy of Agricultural Sciences. Now, his election to the Central Committee constituted a full rehabilitation.

Generally, the new Central Committee had a younger and, at the same time, more professional look than any of its predecessors. A considerable number of younger apparatchiks, supporters of Zhivkov, figured in it, and there was a fair sprinkling of technical expertise, which reflected a genuine concern for economic improvement.

The new government, now under Premier Zhivkov, was the complement to the new Central Committee. As elected by the National Assembly at the end of November, 1962,[62] it contained a number of structural modifications and the names of some ministries were changed. The most important innovation was the Committee for Party and State Control, which replaced the old Commission for State Control and was obviously modeled on the similar body recently set up in Moscow. This committee, headed by Boris Velchev, was answerable jointly to the Central Committee and the Council of Ministers. Another interesting experiment was the introduction of six new ministers without portfolio. In introducing the new government, Zhivkov explained that this was to provide for a more expert administration of the national economy, science, and culture. The new ministers appointed to these posts were to be prominent Party, public, or economic officials, or outstanding scholars or experts. The six were: Grigorov; Luchezar Avramov; Stoyan Tonchev, a secretary of the Agrarian Union; Lyubomir Krastanov, acting chairman of the Academy of Sci-

[62] *Rabotnichesko Delo*, November 28, 1962.

ences; Titko Chernokolev; and Evgeni Mateev, an economic expert.

The new cabinet now consisted of twenty-eight members. Under Premier Zhivkov were two first deputy premiers, Zhivko Zhivkov and Traikov, and four deputy premiers—Todorov, Mihailov, Tano Tsolov, and Kubadinski. Traikov was also Chairman of the Council for Rural Economy, Tsolov was Chairman of the Council for Industry and Construction, and Kubadinski Minister of Transport and Communications. Altogether there were fifteen newcomers. Apart from the new ministers without portfolio, the most notable among these were Ivan Bashev, Lukanov's replacement as Foreign Minister, and a very capable, attractive man; Apostol Pashev, Chairman of the State Committee for Planning; and Ivan Popov, Chairman of the State Committee for Science and Technical Progress. Like the new Central Committee, it, too, was a more businesslike body than any of its predecessors. Indeed, there were men of real ability among both the politicians and the technocrats. Zhivkov's team, both in Party and state, looked like a promising one for the new deal which had been promised to the nation at the Eighth Congress.

7

Trends in the Economy After 1960

I. PLANNING AND PERFORMANCE

AFTER THE "great leap forward" was wound up at the end of 1960 with the regime spuriously claiming its targets already achieved,[1] it was evidently decided that 1961 should be a year of retrenchment. The economic plan for 1961 was startling in its modesty. In industry, a 7.8 per cent increase in the value of the volume of production over 1960 was envisaged—a very low planned increase compared with the 15.2 per cent and the 27.8 per cent increase planned for 1959 and 1960 respectively; in fact, the lowest planned increase since 1948.[2] It was lower than the planned increase of 8.18 per cent in the Soviet Union and considerably lower than the 13.5 per cent increase planned in neighboring Rumania. For agriculture, a 10.9 per cent increase was planned[3]—again, a remarkably unambitious estimate compared with previous years. The capital investment plan was just marginally bigger than what had been achieved in 1960. As for national income, no specific planned percentage increase was given; it was simply stated that it was to reach the value of 48.035 million leva by the end of 1961. This information was of

---

[1] See Chapter 5.

[2] From 1948 to 1958 inclusive, the average annual increase of production was about 16 per cent; *Novo Vreme* (Sofia), March 1959.

[3] Radio Sofia, December 30, 1960. In the parliamentary bill which included the state plan, no percentage increase was stipulated; *Rabotnichesko Delo* (Sofia), December 21, 1960.

little help, however, due to the difficulty in comparing the volume of national income in the period 1958–60, because of the differing price bases and indices the regime evidently used.[4] But judging from other sectors of the economy, the planned increase for the national income must have been small indeed.

Clearly, the havoc created by the "great leap forward" demanded a year of consolidation and respite before the next great effort on the economic road to Communism was made.

Bulgaria Revalues and Devalues

Before turning to Bulgaria's Twenty-Year Plan of economic development, it is worth discussing briefly the rather curious revaluation of the lev which came into effect during the first three months of 1962.[5] Ten old Bulgarian leva were exchanged for one new one. A decimal point was simply moved up, and wages and prices were readjusted accordingly. Thus the revaluation of the currency, the creation of the "heavy lev," was a carbon copy of the creation of the heavy rouble at the beginning of 1961 and of the heavy franc a little earlier. All prices and wages were recalculated at the ratio of ten to one.

The whole move was curious because Bulgaria was the only Eastern European state to follow the Soviet example. When, at the beginning of 1961, the Soviets carried out their currency revaluation—which was actually a devaluation—none of their allies followed suit. The new Eastern European "non-commercial" exchange rates to the rouble were divided by 10, this representing the rate of decrease in prices in the Soviet Union carried out since the beginning of 1961. The new Eastern European commercial rates to the rouble, when published in March, 1961, simply corresponded to the increase of the gold content of the rouble which became effective also at the beginning of 1961, and this caused a marked upgrading of their currencies in terms of the rouble.

This seemed at first glance to be a major concession to the

---

[4] An example of how difficult comparisons are is provided by the Statistical Yearbook of the Peoples Republic of Bulgaria (hereafter referred to as *Statistical Yearbook*) for 1959, page 68. It gives the 1958 national income at 1938 prices (119.026 billion leva) at 1952 prices (40.874 billion leva) and at 1958 prices (33.900 billion leva) but gives no indication of the different methods of calculation.

[5] The revaluation was first announced by the Bulgarian Telegraphic Agency on July 18, 1961.

Eastern Europeans, or at least a major confession that the rouble
had been overvalued against their own currencies. But most of the
benefit was on paper only. For example, Soviet loans consist generally of commodity or foreign currency credits and are paid back
in goods or in foreign currency. In trade between the Soviet Union
and the Eastern European states, the position is similar. The value
of goods contained in the price lists of foreign trade is established
on the basis of world market prices—and these are dollar prices;
consequently the international dollar rate of exchange is converted
into roubles. Therefore, the rouble remained the basis of calculation and the value of Soviet-Eastern European trade transactions
was not affected by the relationship between the rouble and the
local currency (lev-rouble, etc.).

The mystery over the purpose of the move deepened when the
new gold content of the lev and the new foreign exchange rates
were announced. At the end of 1961, it was reported that the new
purchasing price of gold at the Bulgarian National Bank had been
fixed at 1.32 new leva for one grain of gold.[6] The previous price
had been 28.80 old leva for one grain of gold. At the same time
the new exchange rates with Western currencies—especially the
dollar—showed a considerable devaluation of Bulgaria's currency.
The previous official rate had been one dollar to 6.80 old leva;
the new was one dollar to 1.17 new leva.

It soon became clear that all these new figures were fictitious.
The state purchasing price of gold was soon quietly increased by
over 100 per cent—from 1.32 leva to 2.88 leva.[7] Since the former
purchasing price was 28.80 old leva, there had obviously been no
change, since 28.80 old leva equaled 2.88 new leva. Similarly, the
new exchange rate with the dollar was still unrealistic. On the basis
of prices of gold in dollars and in new leva (at the quietly announced new price), the real exchange rate could be calculated as
follows:

Price of gold	
One ounce	$35.00
One grain	$ 1.235
One grain	2.88 LV

Therefore, $1.235 equals 2.88 leva. Thus, one dollar equals 2.32
leva. This contrasted with the new official rate of one dollar to 1.17

[6] *Rabotnichesko Delo*, December 30, 1961.
[7] Advertisement in *Zemedesko Zname* (Sofia), January 19, 1962.

leva and was very close to the reported new black market price of the dollar.

Still, in spite of this continued unrealism, the devaluation of the lev against Western currencies was a sensible move designed to stimulate Bulgarian exports to the West, and in this sense it was successful. Just how it affected Bulgaria's trading position with the Soviet Union, easily her dominant trading partner, is not known. It constitutes one more of the puzzles in which Soviet-Eastern European trade continues to be wrapped.

The Vehicle to Communism: the Twenty-Year Plan of Economic Development

On September 16, 1962, the Party daily, *Rabotnichesko Delo*, published the draft directives of a Twenty-Year Plan of Economic Development. These directives were then submitted for "nationwide" discussion and approved at the Eighth Party Congress the following November.

The basis, and the inspiration, of the Bulgarian Twenty-Year Plan was the Twenty-Year Plan of the CPSU, approved the previous year at its Twenty-Second Party Congress, which aimed at "a more or less simultaneous transition, in the frame of one historical epoch, of all socialist countries toward Communism."[8] Or, as Khrushchev expressed it in his report at the Twenty-Second Congress:

> The coordination of the efforts for the development of the national economy of each socialist country with the mutual efforts for strengthening and expanding the economic cooperation and mutual help— this is the broad road for further upsurge of the world socialist economy.[9]

The Bulgarian Twenty-Year Plan envisaged by 1980 "the completion of the material-technical basis of socialism in Bulgaria and the gradual extended building of the material-technical basis of Communism."[10]

To put these directives in the perspective of general economic development, the following table shows the planned percentage increase figures for the main industrial and agricultural products

[8] *Novo Vreme*, October, 1962.
[9] *Rabotnichesko Delo*, October 18, 1962.
[10] *Ibid.*, September 16, 1962.

for 1961 to 1980 compared with the percentage increase in production achieved for 1939 to 1961 and, within that period, for the years 1951 to 1960. The total value of production for 1960 is included for purposes of comparison:

	1939–60[a]	1951–60[a]	1960[a]	1961–80[b]
National income	180	100[c]	4,457,000,000[d]	400
Total industry	1,100	300	4,838,100,000[e]	600
Heavy industry (Group A)	2,600	420	2,416,500,000[e]	800–850
Light industry (Group B)	690	220	2,421,600,000[e]	400
Electric power (kwh)	1,600	480	4,657,000,000	970–1,080
Steel (tons)	4,400	4,840	253,460	1,640–1,870
Coal (tons)	670	190	17,147,000	360–390
Cement (tons)	600	160	1,586,000	530–590
Rural production	50	80	1,834,000,000[f]	150
Grain crops	20	56	385,000,000[f]	—
Fruit	21	57	207,000,000[f]	300
Meat (tons)	30	34	417,285	230
Eggs	64	110	1,221,000,000	200

[a] Values of production for 1960 and all percentage increase calculations are based on figures from *Statistical Yearbook*, 1961, pp. 96, 100, 102, 105–106, 170, and 221.

[b] All are percentage increases from *Rabotnichesko Delo*, September 16, 1962.

[c] Increase 1953–60, from *Statistical Yearbook*, 1961, p. 96.

[d] New leva at 1957 comparative prices, *Statistical Yearbook*, 1961, p. 96.

[e] New leva at April 1, 1956, comparative prices, *ibid.*, pp. 100 and 102.

[f] New leva at 1955 comparative prices, *ibid.*, p. 170.

Before turning to the 1961–80 plan, it is worth examining the increases during the periods 1939–60 and 1951–60. These show that, except in the cases of steel and rural production, the *percentages* of increase during the decade 1951–60 represent only a small part of the increase for the two decades 1939–60 as a whole. The main reason for this is, of course, the very low 1939 bases—in some cases practically nonexistent—for most of the industrial products mentioned. But still, these figures do underline the great industrial progress made in the 1940's.

This comparison makes the new Twenty-Year Economic Plan look relatively moderate, until it is remembered that the level of production in 1960—the basic year of comparison for the Twenty-Year Plan—represents a relatively advanced stage of economic progress and a far less favorable springboard for spectacular increases than 1939. In fact, the targets of the 1961–80 plan are very high, indeed, for industry. This can be seen from the following table, which gives the average annual increases in absolute figures and, for the sake of comparison, the increase achieved in 1961, the first year of the new Twenty-Year Plan, over 1960.

In total industrial production, therefore, the planned average annual increase was even higher than that envisaged by the Zhivkov Theses and, in every case, it was higher than the average annual increase attained between 1951 and 1960.

Some Components of the Plan

The plan as approved at the Eighth Party Congress[11] showed some modifications compared with the draft directives, the most important being a reduction in the planned total of limited capital investments by about 23 per cent. But, apart from this, there were no differences that would really change the character of the draft directives as a whole.

The national income was envisaged as increasing 2.3 times by 1970, or 130 per cent, and about five times, 400 per cent, by 1980. A measure of the ambitiousness of this target is seen from the fact that between 1939 and 1960, the national income increased only 2.8 times and the 1939 base was much lower than that of 1960. Another important aspect of the national income plan—and one not too cheerful for the standard of living—was that the annual part allocated for accumulation would be "about" 27 per cent over the twenty-year period as against 27.5 per cent in 1960. This is a high rate for the accumulation fund. In fact, excluding the "great leap forward" years of 1959 and 1960, it is a higher rate than for any year since 1954. In the five years between 1954 and 1958, when a real effort was made to improve the standard of living, the accumulation fund never exceeded 20.7 per cent.[12]

Obviously, the high percentage set aside for accumulation was mainly designed to enable larger sums to be allocated for limited capital investments. Despite the scaling down of planned capital investments as first envisaged by the draft, it was this aspect of the plan that was probably the most ambitious of all—a surprising

[11] *Rabotnichesko Delo*, November 17, 1962.
[12] See Appendix IV, Table 7.

	1951–60[a]	1958–65 Zhivkov Theses[b]	1961 increase over 1960[c]	1961–80[d]
National income (new leva, 1957)	281,000,000	911,000,000	129,000,000[e]	891,000,000
Total industry (new leva, 1956)	362,000,000	963,000,000	420,000,000[f]	1,451,000,000
Heavy industry (Group A)	195,120,000	—	—	991,000,000
Light industry (Group B)	166,780,000	—	—	484,000,000
Electric power (kwh)	386,000,000	918,000,000	749,000,000	2,392,000,000
Steel (tons)	24,833	92,603	87,000	224,830
Coal (tons)	1,122,000	3,750,000	1,453,000	3,267,000
Cement (tons)	98,400	265,000	181,000	445,700
Rural production (new leva, 1955)	81,830,000	560,838,000	*less than 1960*	137,535,000
Grain crops (new leva, 1955)	13,920,000	—	—	—
Fruit (new leva, 1955)	7,600,000	—	—	31,000,000
Meat (tons)	10,700	111,600	70,000	47,987
Eggs	63,600,000	741,000,000	192,000,000	122,120,000
Fowl	1,366,000	7,590,000	560,000 *less than 1960*	582,000

[a] Calculations are based on figures in *Statistical Yearbook, 1961*.

[b] Calculations are based on Zhivkov's report, published in *Rabotnichesko Delo*, January 20, 1959, and *Statistical Yearbook, 1961*.

[c] Figures for electric power, steel, coal, cement, and rural production are based on information in *Rabotnichesko Delo*, January 28, 1962; calculations for meat are based on information in *Kooperativno Selo* (Sofia), September 8, 1962; for eggs, in *Zemedelsko Zname*, February 22, 1962; for fowl, in *Rabotnichesko Delo*, April 5, 1962.

[d] Calculations are based on Draft Directives published in *Rabotnichesko Delo*, September 16, 1962, and *Statistical Yearbook, 1961*.

[e] Calculations are based on information in *Rabotnichesko Delo*, January 28, 1962.

[f] Calculations are based on information in *Rabotnichesko Delo*, December 17, 1962, and January 28, 1963. Values are given in 1960 comparative prices.

feature in view of the consistent failure in the past to fulfill capital investment targets. The greater part of the capital investments would be used for what it had become the fashion to call "material production," i.e. heavy industry. (The expression "heavy industry," though still used, was now less conspicuous, probably because of its unpopular connotations.) It was also planned—and this was eminently reasonable—to increase considerably the relative weight of investments in machines and installations as compared with industrial buildings. The aim here was to increase productivity by replacing outdated equipment even in many recently-built plants.

Standard of Living

Despite this stress on heavy industry, the government made clear its intention to use the Twenty-Year Plan as a vehicle for appreciably raising the standard of living. It was envisaged that the relative weight of limited capital investments allocated for cultural life and living conditions generally would steadily increase from 9.6 per cent for the period 1961–65 to reach 34.1 per cent for the last five years of the plan, from 1976 to 1980.[13] Clearly, once industrialization had reached a certain stage, the intention was to go over to a campaign to raise the standard of living—the classic Communist formula and order of priorities. How this thesis would cope with the constant need to readapt industry to continuous changes in science and technology remained to be seen.

One grave deficiency (by no means confined to Bulgaria) to which the directives particularly addressed themselves was the housing shortage. The government promised to overcome this shortage by 1970 and to guarantee each member of a family, in both villages and towns, not less than nine square meters of living space. By 1980, this minimum should increase to sixteen square meters. The housing shortage was not felt in the villages; with the migration of younger peasants to the cities, housing space and general conditions in the villages were now relatively good. The real need, therefore, lay in the towns and cities and, since the Twenty-Year Plan provided that by 1980 the number of people engaged in rural production would drop by 30 per cent,[14] the urban housing shortage would become very great unless tackled resolutely.

[13] *Novo Vreme*, October, 1962.
[14] *Ibid.*

The fact that the population of Bulgaria was expected to increase to 9,200,000 in 1980 (it was 7,900,000 in 1960) only added to the urgency.

Industry

The draft provided that by 1970, the total industrial production would increase by about three times (200 per cent) and by 1980, by about seven times (600 per cent) as compared with the total industrial production in 1960, which amounted to 4.838 billion new leva at 1956 comparative prices.[15] In this case, the directives did not indicate whether the increase was to be in volume, or in value at current or comparative prices. The following analysis is based on the assumption that the increase is planned in volume and expressed in comparative prices with 1956 as a base; this method was used in the Statistical Yearbook for 1961 for the figures on industrial production.

The directives envisaged the development of the heavy industrial branches (Group A) as taking place at a faster rate than that of the light industrial branches (Group B). By 1980, the heavy industrial production (Group A) is to increase 9 to 9.5 times (800–860 per cent), while the production of light industry (Group B) is to increase more than five times (400 per cent). This was compared with 1960, when the production of heavy industry amounted to 2.416 billion new leva and that of light industry to 2.422 billion new leva.[16] These figures show that 1960 was the year when the production of heavy industry had practically reached the level of light industry, while by 1980 the production of heavy industry was scheduled to surpass by far the production of light industry.

The directives made it clear that Bulgarian industry had the task of achieving rapid technical progress and technical reconstruction through the increasing division of labor within the socialist system and by the extension of trade. Both in industry and in the other branches of the country's economy, this technical progress was to be achieved through a broad implementation of electrification, mechanization, and automation of production, by improving existing techniques and developing new ones. At the same time,

[15] *Statistical Yearbook*, 1961, p. 100.
[16] *Ibid.*, p. 102.

both the variety and quality of consumer goods had to be improved.

The directives provided that by 1980, the productivity of labor in industry was to increase by not less than four times (300 per cent). In order to ensure the gradual shortening of the work days, the productivity per hour was scheduled to increase six times (500 per cent) as compared with 1960.

The industrial branches receiving the strongest preference in the plan were electric power, coal, oil, ferrous and non-ferrous metals, machine and chemical production. Bulgaria's fuel and energy base had always been precarious; electricity in particular was often in short supply in the 1960's, with householders having to suffer lengthy cuts. Now, of the 64–65 billion kwh planned for 1980, home production was to account for 50–55 billion with the remainder being imported from the Comecon grid. Of special interest were the ambitious plans for a Bulgarian oil industry which had been practically non-existent until the middle 1950's. By 1980, production at the huge new Burgas oil refinery was scheduled to reach four million tons. Coal production was scheduled to reach 80–85 million tons, of which 70 million should be lignite brown coal. The large Maritsa-East fuel complex was scheduled to ensure 70 per cent of the total coal production, as well as 45 per cent of the total electric power of the country.

All these figures for fuel and power will probably be revised downwards in the fairly near future, because Bulgaria has taken the plunge into nuclear power. She had been conservative in this respect compared with Czechoslovakia, Rumania, and Hungary. Czechoslovakia's first nuclear power plant was due to go into (long-delayed) operation in 1969; Rumania, bent on having the most modern equipment, negotiated with several Western firms but, by the middle of 1968 had still not made a purchase, while Hungary announced in 1967 that she would purchase a Soviet reactor. When Bulgaria finally made the decision it was, of course, the Soviet Union to whom she turned. By 1973, Soviet specialists will have completed the first part of an 800-megawatt reactor; the second part should be completed a year later.[17]

Throughout the course of Communist rule, the ambitiousness of Bulgaria's industrialization drive has nowhere been expressed more dramatically than in the attention given to ferrous metallurgy. The Twenty-Year Plan intensified this concentration. By 1980, Bul-

[17] Tass (Moscow), July 15, 1968.

garia was scheduled to be producing four to four-and-a-half million tons of pig iron, four-and-a-half to five million tons of steel, and about four million tons of rolled iron. This production was to be concentrated in two huge complexes: the Lenin Metallurgical Plant in Dimitrovo, a plant originating in the pre-Communist era, which had already been greatly enlarged and was now scheduled for still further extension and renovation; and the huge Kremikovtsi combine near Sofia, begun in 1960 and designed to be the greatest single economic showpiece for Communism in Bulgaria.[18] Nonferrous metallurgy—lead, zinc, and copper, in which Bulgaria was relatively rich—was to increase by 350 per cent at the end of the twenty-year period.

The greatly expanded ferrous metallurgical industry was to serve as a foundation for the Bulgarian machine-building industry, whose total production was supposed to increase by 1,600 per cent by 1980. This industry was to specialize in those fields that consumed the least amount of metal: metal-cutting machines, electrically- and mechanically-driven trucks, electro-tippers, and internal-combustion engines, including ship engines. The electrical industry was to specialize in electric motors, transformers, electrical tools and other devices, batteries, cables, and wires. Obviously, Bulgaria was to specialize in these machine products under the terms of an agreement with her Comecon partners. The electronics industry was to concentrate on the development of technology for the automated production of semiconductors, transistors, vacuum tubes, etc. As for automobiles, the plan provided for the domestic production of 120,000 by 1980. The importance placed on machine construction was once again shown in November, 1962, after the Eighth Party Congress, when a new Committee for Machine Construction was created and its chairman given a place in the cabinet.

Finally, the chemical industry—which, because of the economy's underdeveloped state, had never received the attention accorded it in the more advanced Eastern European states—now came more to the center of the industrial stage. Like ferrous metallurgy, it was to be one of the future raw-material bases for industry, construction, and agriculture. Its total production was planned to increase twenty-seven times by 1980, as compared with 1960, and special attention was to be paid to synthetic materials which could replace metals in the machine and furniture industries and in building

[18] See pp. 22–28.

construction. An example of how the chemical industry was to service agriculture was seen in the target for chemical fertilizers: 1.3 million tons by 1980, or ten times more than the production in 1960.

A New Look in Agriculture

The Twenty-Year Plan, even if its provisions are only partly fulfilled, will transform Bulgaria into an industrial country. Its agriculture, while not neglected, will change quite radically in character. In all types of agricultural production, the main trend will be on intensification. The Twenty-Year Plan provided for an increase of total rural production by 2.5 times (150 per cent) compared with 1960, with a special acceleration for livestock breeding.

If the plan is carried through, two of Bulgaria's traditional basic crops—wheat and tobacco—will cease to have the importance they once held. No figure was given for the production of bread grain crops; it was simply stated that it would be enough "to ensure the full satisfaction of the needs of the population and the necessary reserves."[19] This means that the area given over to wheat will considerably decrease because of the greater yield per hectare that may be expected through the use of better seed and fertilizer.

The total production of tobacco in 1980 was planned to be increased by only 10 per cent as compared with 1960, when 61,898 tons of Oriental and Virginia tobacco were produced.[20] Thus, the production of tobacco in 1980 was planned to reach only about 68,000 tons, while in 1961 and in 1962 the plan for Oriental tobacco alone provided for a production of about 90,000 tons.[21] The target for 1962 was later raised to more than 100,000 tons.[22] This decrease in tobacco production targets can best be explained by a Soviet intention to increase the purchase of low-quality

[19] *Rabotnichesko Delo*, November 17, 1962. In the original draft directives it was stated that bread grain crops would be kept almost at the level of 1960, since this would ensure full satisfaction of popular needs and the necessary reserves. In the final directive, however, the reference to 1960 was left out, possibly because someone remembered that the population would increase in the next twenty years.

[20] *Statistical Yearbook*, 1961, p. 193.

[21] Todorov's speech to the National Assembly, November, 1961; *Rabotnichesko Delo*, November 2, 1961.

[22] *Kooperativno Selo*, June 7, 1962.

tobacco from underdeveloped countries such as India.[23] The Twenty-Year Plan directives provided that, in field production, the highest rates of increase must be achieved in fodder for livestock breeding, and in the production of grapes, fruits, and vegetables for home consumption and for export. Tobacco was omitted from this list. Evidently, Bulgaria will, in the future, produce only high-quality tobacco for export and for internal consumption.

This rather narrow concentration on a few high-earning export crops will necessitate increased imports of sugar, cotton, and fodder. All in all, one can say that the plans for the future of Bulgarian agriculture are bolder and more businesslike than those for industry. Of course, it can be argued that nothing is bolder than some of the industrial targets mentioned above. But these targets simply represent an intensification of the orthodox Communist preoccupation with heavy industry and are based on the dictum of "produce everything—only more." In agriculture, the production of some staple products was being curtailed or virtually eliminated in favor of others that are better money-spinners in today's market, and this policy has already begun to achieve considerable success for Bulgaria in Western markets.

As already mentioned, *intensification* is the basic trend in Bulgarian agricultural planning, along with specialization. By 1980, the chemical industry was to supply 1.1 million tons of artificial fertilizer, which would amount to 22 or 23 kilograms per decare of arable land as compared with 3.2 kilograms per decare in 1960.[24] Mechanization, essential not only for agricultural efficiency but also to free rural manpower for industry, was scheduled to be extended greatly. The number of tractors by 1980 was planned to be from four to five times greater than in 1960, for a total of 180,000 15-horsepower units.

All these plans for the radical transformation of agriculture were due to be financed by a total capital investment outlay of 13 billion new leva. Much of this would come from the funds of the collective farms themselves and from bank credits (which, of

[23] In October, 1962, the Soviet Union contracted to buy 17,000 tons of tobacco from India; Tass, October 29, 1962. This type of agreement with the third world could become a regular feature.

[24] Deputy premier Stanko Todorov stated as early as 1956 that Bulgaria needed an annual supply of 1.3 million tons of fertilizer: *Za Kooperativno Zemedelie* (Sofia), December 23, 1956. In 1956, Belgium used 300 kilograms of fertilizer for the equivalent of a decare, Switzerland 137, and Great Britain 120; E. Valev, *Bolgaria* (Moscow, 1957) p. 210.

course, have to be paid back). Nevertheless, the planned annual agricultural investments for the twenty-year period were an average of 50 per cent higher than the amount invested in the rural economy in 1960 and 1961.

Generally, the plans for agriculture seemed more realistic, shrewd, and rational than those for most sections of industry. They reflected a courageous effort to diversify and an awareness of the opportunities on the capitalist markets—more than can be said for the "Sturm und Drang" approach which characterized industrial planning. The total target of a 150 per cent increase seemed attainable, given good weather, the required application of technology, and the right incentives to the farmers themselves. This last requirement might well be the most difficult to meet but the authorities were aware of the problem and would do their utmost to solve it—within the framework of collectivization, of course.

Kremikovtsi—A Communist Showpiece

The Kremikovtsi Metallurgical Combine was formally opened on November 5, 1963. This "giant of Bulgarian ferrous metallurgy," the "child of Bulgarian-Soviet friendship," was intended to become the most important single factor in Bulgaria's drive for total industrialization. It was the Bulgarian equivalent of Galati in Rumania, the East Slovak Iron Works in Czechoslovakia, Dunaujvaros (formerly Sztalinvaros) in Hungary, Nowa Huta in Poland, and the Schwarze Pumpe complex near Dresden, East Germany—all Stalinist economic monuments reflecting the essentially autarchic approach to economic development that, despite Comecon, is still so deeply ingrained in the minds and habits of the Eastern European leaders. Regardless of what changes the future brings to Bulgaria, it will always remain a monument to Communist rule and, as such, is worthy of some attention.

The combine, about twelve miles from Sofia, was begun in the spring of 1960 and only the first part of it was commissioned in November, 1963. These parts were: a mechanical repair shop; a shop for metal construction materials; a thermo-electrical power station with a power of 56,000 kilowatts; a coking-chemical plant with a capacity for 350,000 tons of metallurgical coke; the first high oven with a capacity of 560,000 tons of pig iron per year.[25]

[25] *Rabotnichesko Delo*, November 6, 1963.

In November, 1967, a second part was commissioned consisting of ten new units. These were: a pit with an output capacity of five million tons of iron ore annually; an ore-dressing factory with an annual capacity of three million tons of processed ore; a pelletization factory with a capacity of two million tons of pellets; a second coke battery for 392,000 tons of coke; a second high furnace for 517,000 tons of pig iron; a steel production complex with a 100-ton electric oven for 130,000 tons of steel and with three 100-ton convertors for 1,140,000 tons of steel; a ferro-alloy shop with a capacity of 26,000 tons of ferro-manganese; a lime-dolomite shop with a capacity of 160,000 tons of lime; a shop for the separation of air with a capacity of 119 million cubic meters of oxygen; a blooming mill for the production of 3 million tons of metal ingots; and a "1700-mill" for the production of 1.5 million tons of sheet iron.[26] The whole plant is designed to be at full capacity only by 1980, when it should be producing 3,000,000 tons of pig iron, the same amount of rolled iron and 3.6 million tons of steel.[27]

The combine is built near large iron ore deposits which were known and exploited on a very small scale before World War II. During the war, however, and for several years afterward, exploitation of the Kremikovtsi ore was discontinued. Geological research into the ore deposits began again in the 1950's and, by 1958, it was estimated that deposits totaled nearly 250 million tons of iron ore. The first plans for the construction of the combine probably originated at the Soviet-Bulgarian talks in Moscow in February, 1957, when the Soviet Union agreed to help Bulgaria to carry out "investigations for determining the methods of enriching the iron ores recently discovered.[28] At least, when the draft directives of the Third Five-Year Plan (1958–62) were issued, the construction of the combine had been decided on. These directives stipulated that the first stage of the combine should be completed by 1964. Construction, therefore, was completed ahead of schedule. It is interesting to note that, but for the attitude of Chervenkov, the combine would probably have been begun earlier. In 1955, when the first big deposits were discovered, Chervenkov (in the words of a later accusation) "assumed a scornful attitude to the discovery" and through his attitude "caused the delay in settling

26 *Zemedelsko Zname*, November 2, 1967.
27 *Rabotnichesko Delo*, November 6, 1963.
28 *Ibid.*, February 21, 1957.

the question of building the metallurgical combine in Kremi-kovtsi."[29]

There must have been considerable debate among the experts over whether the large Kremikovtsi deposits were, in fact, worth fully exploiting. The iron content of the ore was rather low. It contains only 31 per cent iron, nearly 19 per cent barite, 6.2 per cent manganese, and 0.4 per cent lead.[30] (By contrast, the iron content of the ore in the mines around Lake Superior in the United States runs as high as 55 per cent.) This means that the ore has to be enriched in order to reach an iron content of 48 per cent.[31] Zhivkov himself, in an interview given to a French journalist in 1961, admitted that it would not be profitable to exploit the ore solely for its iron content and, for this reason, Kremikovtsi would have to be designed so as to exploit all the components of the ore.[32]

Besides the quality of the Kremikovtsi ores, their actual quantity, though seemingly large, hardly seemed vast enough to justify the construction of such a huge combine. If five million tons of ore were mined each year, the deposits located so far would last fifty years; if seven million tons were mined annually, they would last for thirty-five years—and seven million tons corresponds to a production of two million tons of metal, i.e., to only 65 per cent of the planned final capacity of the combine. Thus, unless substantial new iron ore deposits are discovered in Bulgaria, large amounts of ore will have to be imported. The government showed itself well aware of this problem and from 1964 onwards contracted to import substantial supplies from Algeria, Brazil, and India.

Nor were the quality and quantity of much of the coke available for Kremikovtsi such as to inspire any great confidence. Part of it was to be produced in the coke-chemical plant of the combine itself from coal of the local "Balkanbas" mine. But this coal is of such poor quality that it has to be enriched before going to Kremikovtsi. Moreover, the total coal deposits of the "Balkanbas" mine have been put at forty-one million tons.[33] The capacity of the mine was planned to reach one million tons by 1965. Thus the deposits will be exhausted in about forty years. Other coal supplies

[29] Tano Tsolov at the Eighth Party Congress; *Rabotnichesko Delo*, November 13, 1962.

[30] Interview with Academician Yovcho Yovchev, *Rabotnichesko Delo*, November 3, 1963.

[31] *Ikonomicheska Misal* (Sofia), No. 4, 1962.

[32] *Rabotnichesko Delo*, October 21, 1961.

[33] *Minno Delo i Metallurgia* (Sofia), No. 11, 1961.

for Kremikovtsi come from Poland and the Donets Basin in the Soviet Union and considerable quantities of Soviet coke are also imported. Evidently, when the combine is working at full capacity at some undisclosed date in the 1970's, considerably increased imports from Poland and the Soviet Union will be necessary. (It is this obvious necessity to import which throws doubt on the wisdom of the very location of Kremikovtsi, in the hills near Sofia, far from the sea and the waterways.)

The Soviet Union played a large role in both the planning and building of Kremikovtsi. The Moscow planning organization, "Gipromez," presented the technical and economic report on the planned construction, while the plans for the pit of the Kremikovtsi mine were worked out by a Leningrad firm.[34] A group of Soviet engineers was on permanent duty there in the first five years of the combine's operation. When the plant was opened in November, 1963, 64,000 tons of machinery out of the total of 77,000 was of Soviet provenance.[35] For this equipment, as well as for that of the "Maritsa-East" thermoelectric power station, the Soviets granted a credit in December, 1960, of 650 million old roubles.[36]

Without Soviet aid, therefore, Kremikovtsi would have been inconceivable. Having granted this, however, the question arises whether this Soviet help has built a combine capable of approaching, let alone meeting, the standards of modern metallurgy. By these standards, Soviet equipment is generally insufficient even when it is new—and much of the equipment supplied to Kremikovtsi was probably not new. A good example of the antiquity of much of the Soviet equipment supplied to Bulgaria is seen in the other large Bulgarian metallurgical plant, the "Lenin" combine at Dimitrovo. This combine, also commissioned in 1963, was fitted out by the Soviets, but the Fourth Five-Year Plan (1961–65) called for its complete reconstruction and mechanization. Later, after 1965, the Bulgarian government followed the example of other Eastern European states (notably Rumania) and began looking to the West for heavy industrial equipment. Some German machinery was bought for Kremikovtsi; but the Galati combine in Rumania is mostly equipped with Western plant and machinery and has, therefore, been more competitive from the beginning than Kremikovtsi.

[34] *Ibid.*, Nos. 7–8, 1960.
[35] *Rabotnichesko Delo*, November 6, 1963.
[36] *Ibid.*, January 1, 1961.

Thus, Kremikovtsi has many disadvantages, some of them seemingly insuperable. In fact, this costly enterprise—in 1962 and 1963 one-fifth of the total capital investments in industry were spent on it—has been privately called the "graveyard of Bulgaria's economy" by some Bulgarians. On the other hand, many other Bulgarians, whether aware of its disadvantages or not, take some degree of pride in the erection of this giant—not as a showpiece of Communism but as a monument to the national effort. They may criticize it among themselves but to foreigners they will defend it. It may be a white elephant but at least it is theirs!

II. ECONOMIC REFORM IN BULGARIA

The preceding discussion of Bulgaria's plans for economic development shows that, in spite of the clear intention to avoid the excesses of the "great leap forward," the country's economic planners were still motivated by the "boom" mentality, and their plans envisaged large-scale expansion in every sector of industry. At the same time, however, the Eighth Party Congress in November, 1962, approved a resolution indicating an awareness of the need for a new system of planning and management. This resolution accepted in principle the need for a new economic mechanism, for increased worker participation in the drawing up and implementation of plans, and for the enhancing of material incentives throughout the economy.[37] The following May, a Central Committee plenum confirmed these decisions and announced some "groundwork" moves, including the merger of some industrial enterprises and the reorganization of economic administration in all twenty-seven districts throughout the country.[38]

In a way it was surprising that the Bulgarians should have been considering serious economic reform so early. The Bulgarian economy was still largely undeveloped; partly as a consequence of this, it had maintained an impressive rate of growth, and it was still on the wave of an investment boom. Between 1948 and 1964, the average annual growth rate of industry was 14.7 per cent.[39] Bulgaria (and, to a lesser degree, Rumania) seemed for the moment reasonably well suited to the classical Communist system of plan-

[37] *Rabotnichesko Delo*, November 16, 1962.
[38] *Ibid.*, May 19, 1963.
[39] These are calculations based on statistics given in the *Statistical Yearbook, 1964.*

ning and management. But it was apparently decided that weaknesses in the national economy were already serious enough to warrant action, or the preparation for action. For while great quantitative progress had been achieved in heavy industrial production, the country's very success in this respect had led to failure in others. The performance in agriculture had been depressingly poor, causing an unhealthy imbalance in the economy as a whole. And in all sectors of the economy, qualitative factors—the quality of goods, rentability, costing, accurate pricing, etc.—had been neglected. Inefficiency and cumbersome planning at every level were creating problems which largely offset the achievement of a high rate of growth, and the strain of maintaining this high rate was in turn aggravating the weaknesses and contradictions inherent in the economic system.

It should be remembered, of course, that this was not Bulgaria's *first* attempt at economic reform. The administrative-territorial reform of 1959, discussed in Chapter 6, did provide for a large measure of decentralization on the territorial principle. But this had only scratched the surface, since the *mechanism* remained largely the same as before. Bulgaria had never seen anything like the abortive economic model in Poland or the Yugoslav reforms, but in 1962, basic economic reform was very much in the air in Eastern Europe. Inspired by Professor Yevsei Liberman's now famous article in September, 1962,[40] an intense round of discussions began on the ways and means of achieving greater economic efficiency. It was not surprising that the two most advanced states in Eastern Europe, the G.D.R. and Czechoslovakia, were the first to publish thoroughgoing reform measures, since the complexities of their economies made the need for change more urgent. But it should be noted how soon the Bulgarians took the first steps to change their own system.

Coincidental with the May, 1963, Central Committee plenum, discussion on economic reform began in *Novo Vreme*, the most authoritative Party journal. The discussion warmed up later in the year, with an article by Professor Angel Miloshevski on material incentives and worker participation. What Miloshevski proposed was nothing less than the adoption of the Yugoslav workers' council system:

> We find that, in order to reach a more complete solution to the question of increasing the interest and the activity of the workers in the state enterprises, a form of management must be estab-

[40] *Pravda* (Moscow), September 9, 1962.

lished which ensures the workers' more immediate participation in the management of enterprises, and in the disposal of the means of production. Parallel with the rights of the directors, the rights of working people—of the individual plant—must be increased. It can be considered that the conditions are already ripe for the creation of such an organ in our state enterprises through which the workers shall participate in the solution of many questions of production, connected with the organization of labor, with labor remuneration, with the distribution of profit; that they shall have a word to say even in the appointment of the director of the enterprise . . .[41]

Miloshevski's proposals were not subsequently adopted by the regime, but it was significant that they could have been voiced at all.

Even more important was an article published in the December issue of *Novo Vreme* by Professor Petko Kunin. A rehabilitated follower of the executed Traicho Kostov, Kunin, before his disgrace, had been considered one of Bulgaria's most able economists. His article was more comprehensive than Miloshevski's. He argued that all factories should be self-supporting, that they should operate "without being 'financed by the state.'" He called for a new system of planning and accounting that would give full scope to real economic competition among the factories, the "most rational and economic use of basic and working capital funds and of the labor force, for profits and profit-sharing to be used as a 'stimulating device.'" Profits, he argued, should determine the remuneration of managers and be the main source of increases of wage payments. (It should be noted that, in Bulgaria as in all of Eastern Europe, profits are defined differently than in the West. In the East, profits are gross revenue minus all costs except labor costs. In the West, they are gross revenues minus *all* costs, including labor costs.) Those who expected the regime to put up orthodox economists to counter Miloshevski and Kunin were agreeably disappointed. In fact, early in 1964, the regime itself introduced some clearly reformist measures.

At the beginning of the year, an experiment along the lines suggested by Kunin was begun at the "Liliana Dimitrova" textile plant in Sofia. It involved "non-state financing" and a system of remuneration and premiums based on profit. The first results on the operation of the system were very encouraging.

In February, 1964, a national conference of industrial accountants was held in Sofia at which it was disclosed that a com-

[41] *Novo Vreme*, November, 1963.

pletely new system of planning and management was being prepared. According to a speech made by the Minister of Finance, Dimitur Popov, experiments in the new system were to begin the following June and would be continued into 1965; by the end of 1966, it was hoped, the new system would be applied throughout the country. The regime did not come out with an official blueprint for reform, but from various articles, it was possible to see the course the reforms would take.

The first really specific article on economic reform, written by Ivan Mironov, was published in May, 1964.[42] Mironov began by advocating that wages and capital accumulation be tied to the profit level of individual plants. He also proposed that each enterprise be subjected to a property tax reflecting true wear-and-tear and obsolescence. This idea carried Kunin's idea of enterprise self-sufficiency one stage further, since it would enable the factory to replace its own capital without having to avail itself of "free capital" from public funds. As a consequence of these measures, capital would become more expensive and would be more intensively used. Tax and interest rates would not be the same for all branches but would be varied by the regime according to whether it wanted to encourage or discourage certain industries. Furthermore, since factories would now be charged for the capital in their possession, it would be necessary to have free sales of capital among enterprises and to permit one enterprise to lease capital—e.g., a building or a large machine—to another.

Mironov believed that, when the accumulations of each plant (and a considerable part of the wages) depended on the rise of the profit, the workers could not be indifferent to the problems of management and the result of the work of their enterprise. He was also specific in saying that, in effect, every socialist enterprise should follow the path of its capitalist counterpart by trying to maximize its own profits.

Articles like Mironov's, helpful though they were as pointers, did not indicate which proposals were actually being implemented in the fifty-odd pilot experiments being conducted at the time. Later, however, two articles written by a Yugoslav reporter accredited in Bulgaria, Frane Barbieri, gave some idea of the nature of these experiments.[43] The first was particularly valuable because it described the reforms at the "Druzhba" (Friendship) bottle- and jar-making plant near Sofia. If this description is compared to

[42] *Ikonomicheska Misal*, May, 1964.
[43] *Politika* (Belgrade), October 15 and 18, 1964.

some of the more radical proposals of the Bulgarian economists, it is possible to arrive at a reasonably accurate picture of the nature and scope of the experiments.

Since the way prices were determined would greatly affect the degree of overall freedom granted to each plant or factory, it was not surprising that this question loomed large in the discussions of the reforms. In 1964, the Bulgarians seemed rather conservative in this respect. D. Nachev, in an article in the September issue of *Partien Zhivot*, another monthly journal of the Party Central Committee, revealed the dilemma of the planning authorities when he urged that prices be "realistically fixed" to "reflect the relationship between producer and consumer." But he added the ominous proviso that they should "not diverge from the interests of the state," at the same time taking comfort from the fact that instructions had been given to the price-fixing bodies to fix prices which would more accurately reflect market forces.

It was clear, therefore, that prices would continue to be centrally fixed, and it was simply hoped that the planning organs would be flexible and realistic in their decisions. This was strongly confirmed by Barbieri, who quoted Grisha Filipov, a vice-chairman of the Bulgarian State Planning Commission, as stating that the "market can establish neither prices nor production, for this leads to disorganization. They would remain established strictly according to plan." Nor could there be any question of the factories' freedom to contract. At one plant, Barbieri found, the management had to try to maximize its profits within the framework of price, production, and distribution plans all still fixed by the state. Only within these preconditions was the profit motive allowed free reign. Obviously, as far as the determination of commodity prices was concerned, the Bulgarians had scarcely dared to dip more than their big toe in the water.

On the pricing of capital, however, the steps taken were already far greater. Here, Mironov's and Kunin's ideas about abandoning the system of providing state funds or free capital to enterprises were being put into practice. The enterprises themselves were now required to supply most of their own new capital—which would originate either out of the capital funds already in their control or from funds obtained from banks as repayable credit. The internal capital funds, the two components of which were depreciation and the firm's share of profit, were lumped together in "Development and Technical Improvements Funds." These funds were deposited in banks which were required to pay interest to the enterprises on their deposits. Although the depreciation rates had not been announced, a small percentage of the depreciation allowance reverted to the state. The rest, amounting to well over half, went to the banks in the name of the factory concerned.

Factories were also allowed to sell unneeded capital, once permission had been obtained from higher authority. To encourage such sales, the regime began to levy a 6 per cent charge on both fixed and circulating capital. It was not clear, however, whether this rate was on the gross value of capital, as in Hungary, or on the net value, as in Poland. The purpose behind the introduction of a capital interest rate will be dealt with more fully in the section devoted to economic reform in Hungary. It was an important instrument in promoting the more efficient and intensive use of capital and in facilitating a better evaluation of it; it was also useful in unearthing new sources of investment funds. The levying of the charge meant that if an enterprise manager held on to capital equipment he did not need (a common practice in all Communist states), the enterprise's wage fund would be affected. Thus, it paid the manager and the workers to get rid of surplus capital.

The factories' freedom to use their investment funds as they wished was still restricted in Bulgaria. Filipov, in his conversation with Barbieri, said quite openly that it was still essential to accumulate and distribute investments centrally, since the state still had "too many obligations" and needed "too great an amount of funds." To illustrate what he meant, he pointed to huge investments that the state had to find for the Kremikovtsi metallurgical complex. In a way, this official position was understandable. As long as there was an "investment boom"—and in 1965 Bulgaria still seemed in the middle of one—controls on investment expenditures could be reduced only very slowly. The need to meet investment plans and eventually to pay off the massive debt to the Soviet Union made genuine decentralization of investments a future rather than a current proposition. Such decentralization would only become easier after a reduction in the proportion of income devoted to investment.

Under the Bulgarian reform, as in all the others, the turnover tax, an old Communist favorite, continued to be used to adjust sales prices so that they would more closely approach the market value. Another tax designed to play an important part was the so-called progressive profits tax, which replaced the previous "deduction from profit." This apparently was not a real profits tax but rather a tax on what were sometimes called "the earnings of the enterprise." The "adjusted" earnings were considered to be equal to the gross receipts of the enterprise minus the turnover tax and the non-labor operating costs. Expenditures that were not considered economically justified were not counted as costs until after the progressive profits tax had been levied. This was a state device for having these economically-unjustified expenditures taken out of the wages fund rather than out of the sum that would go to the state in the form of the progressive profits tax. It was another attempt to cut down the wastefulness that characterized the Bulgarian and other East European economies.

The wages themselves were to be very closely tied to the earnings of the enterprise. The wage fund was to consist of whatever was left after deducting from the achieved output all the taxes, contributions, interest rates, economically unjustified costs, assessments for various material funds, and ordinary non-labor operating costs. The fund was then assessed for social-security contributions, which went directly to the state. The money remaining for individual distribution was divided into two categories: "guaranteed" wage payments and "variable" wage payments.

"Guaranteed" wages were to be paid to the employees regardless of the total performance of the enterprise. For the ordinary worker, this part of his wages amounted to about 90 per cent of his basic wage; for the management staff, it was considerably less, some 70 to 75 per cent. The "variable" wage was to consist of bonuses or awards; as far as the worker was concerned, its amount would depend on individual or group performance. Obviously, the regime hoped that the "variable" wage would be the main source of material incentive.

In the sphere of worker participation, the 1964 Bulgarian experiments did not go nearly so far as, for example, Professor Miloshevski had hoped his *Novo Vreme* article of November, 1963. The Yugoslav example still remained safely over the Serbian border. But while the system of "one-man management" was essentially preserved, the director, "the representative of the state," had to consult with the enterprise's "production committee." This committee generally included five or six members for every 100 employees, with a number of officials serving *ex officio*. It was to help the management in promoting the increase of labor productivity and the profitability of production. It was also supposed "actively to influence" all questions relating to the organization of labor and production. It would have the main say in the distribution of the variable wages and—significantly—"an active say in all questions of management." Of course, it remained to be seen what this last privilege would really amount to. In the meantime, it seemed that any decision of the production committee was not effective until signed by the director. In case of a dispute between the two sides, there was no arbitration court that could decide the issue; the manager, in effect, was always right.

The Official Theses

The official Politburo "Theses" outlining the plan of reform were published in December, 1965,[44] over three years after the intimation at the Eighth Party Congress that reform was being contemplated. Hesitation over how "liberal" or "conservative" to be on such important issues as prices and the degree of centralized control, as well as the desire to give the experiments a thorough trial, probably caused the Bulgarians to delay the publication of their officially approved plan. An official announcement had been expected early in 1965. In July, 1965, Premier Zhivkov told a group of Austrian journalists that the official Theses would be published in about a month. There was, therefore, a definite delay; differences of opinion on "how far to go" could well have been mainly responsible for it. Economists themselves seem to have been seriously divided on the question, and it is noteworthy that Professor Eugeni Mateev—a minister without portfolio in the cabinet, a first-rate economist, and the man who initiated the series of discussions in *Novo Vreme* in May, 1963—was described by Zhivkov as being "against the [new] system."[45] Mateev was no dogmatist, but he may have regarded the application of an advanced system of reform to a relatively primitive economy as being dangerously premature. He might have agreed with the point Filipov (also a trained economist) was trying to make: that a great degree of centralized control was still necessary.

If some trained economists considered the reform too liberal, it can well be imagined what many party apparatchiks thought of it. "Stalinist" opposition to reform of all kinds in Bulgaria had been very strong since 1956 and had been responsible for frustrating more than one promising development. Understandably, the fundamental changes involved in any radical economic reform would arouse the strongest apprehensions in the party.

[44] *Rabotnichesko Delo*, December 4, 1965.
[45] *Die Presse* (Vienna), July 17, 1965.

Yet the leadership was able to play an important card: by conducting preliminary experiments, it could produce statistics—perhaps accurate, certainly politic—to show that in the first half of 1965 the growth of industrial production in those enterprises operating under the new system averaged 15.6 per cent, as compared to only 11.5 per cent for those still operating under the old system.

With the publication of the Theses, everybody finally got a chance to see what the new system was all about. Its reformist character was based on the following general principles: considerable decentralization of economic decision-making, with major responsibility assigned to the so-called industrial association, or trust (see below); increased use of the profit motive; a system of wages tied to production results; "full use" of economic levers, including profit, prices, credit interest, and taxes.

On decentralization, the Bulgarian Theses followed the pattern set by the East German, Czechoslovak, Polish, and Soviet reforms. The economic associations, or trusts, were to be the new centers of power and would largely determine the degree of autonomy which individual enterprises would enjoy. Only in Yugoslavia (and, later, in Hungary) were individual enterprises to escape this control at the association level. In Bulgaria, the business of the associations and of the individual enterprises would be conducted on the basis of contracts. Priority in contracts was to be given to commodities listed in the centrally-fixed plan, and not all contracts would be officially approved. "Free contracting" would be allowed in the light of production possibilities and according to market needs. The degree of freedom which this new contracting system would allow would depend on the size of the priority list fixed by the central authorities.

The decentralization reform reflected the government's obvious intention to shift part of the task of handling investments off its own shoulders and onto the enterprises. The responsibilities thus transferred were to be financed by the enterprises out of their own funds and through repayable bank credits. Within the enterprises —and here again Bulgaria conformed to the general pattern—a number of special investment funds were to be created; these included a development and technical improvement fund (the amount to be determined as a percentage of capital funds); a new products fund; a social-cultural fund; and a wage reserve fund. The development and technical improvement fund would be used to finance capital investments and capital repairs. Resources from this fund could be used to finance the development of new products. Its amount would be a fixed percentage of total production costs. The percentage of the enterprises' contribution to the social-cultural fund was to be a fixed percentage of the total wage fund. Under the new system, wages would be made up of two components: the guaranteed portion (easily the biggest), and the incentive portion, which would, of course, vary. Here the Bulgarian system was very much like the Czechoslovak—but unlike the Soviet, Polish, and East German, where the state itself still fixed the overall level of each enterprise's wage fund.

On the key question of price formation policy, the Bulgarian reform was (on paper) a relatively advanced one. Like the programs adopted in Czechoslovakia and later in Hungary, it was to have a three-price system of categories—fixed, variable, and free. The prices of basic production goods and the most important consumer goods would be fixed by the state. On other goods there were to be fixed maximum and minimum prices, or, in some cases, a fixed maximum only. A last (small) category of goods, composed mainly of seasonal and locally-produced items, would be priced freely.

To sum up, it is fair to describe several features of the new Bulgarian system—on paper at least—as "liberal" or "advanced." Other features—in particular the scheme for more participation by workers in decision-making—could be termed "liberal" by Bulgarian standards, though timid and orthodox compared to Yugoslavia's reforms.

Finally, the program had its conservative aspects. While the Bulgarian leaders showed their determination to ensure a more flexible and responsible economic system, they also took precautions to see that the trend toward greater freedom would not get out of hand. Thus a large number of controls were retained by the regime. As the Theses themselves said, the state would carry out "a uniform policy in the spheres of technical programming, capital investment, foreign trade, prices, remuneration of labor, and finance." Central planning continued to be the backbone of the whole system, and unlike the proposed Hungarian model, which anticipated the complete abandonment of compulsory, centrally-directed indices, the Bulgarian program simply stipulated a reduction. The obligatory indices that would remain included the volume of basic production in real terms; the limit on capital investment; the limit for basic raw materials; and foreign currency limits for imports and exports.

There was a good deal of economic logic in the retention of such controls as these, and in most of the conservative aspects of the reform, in view of the still-undeveloped state of the Bulgarian economy. But this seemed less a calculating conservatism than another example of the timidity that has become the hallmark of the Zhivkov leadership.

The Politburo Theses were approved by the Central Committee at a plenum in April, 1966, at which Zhivkov gave a major address on the reform.[46] The Theses had been thrown open for public discussion in which, according to Zhivkov, 1.8 million people had taken part in more than 28,000 meetings. The discussions had apparently been brisk and at times quite critical. For example, Zhivkov had to answer the general charge, made throughout East Europe, that the new trusts represented the danger of monopoly. This he countered with the thoroughly unconvincing argument that, though there was this danger, a socialist monopoly had not the same sinister implications as a capitalist one. On price formation, he also had to answer criticism that the system envisaged was still much too rigid. A young economist, Professor Georgi Petrov, had even been allowed to publish an article in the Party daily urging more elasticity in this respect.[47] Zhivkov readily acknowledged the key importance of price formation and promised, as had the Theses, that a complete reform of prices and of the system of price determination would be carried out. He agreed that the new prices must be flexible, that they must reflect the cost of production and "represent a scientific measure of the labor involved." The new system must also do away with the discrepancy between domestic prices and those on the international market, he continued. But Zhivkov admitted that no one quite knew at the moment how all this was to be done. It was necessary to work cautiously and experiment thoroughly.

On the whole, it was an impressive performance from Zhivkov; he followed it up at the Ninth Party Congress in November, 1966, by giving encouraging figures on the performance of factories operating under the new system in the first half of 1966. The following percentages compare the growth of enterprises operating under the new system as against those still working under the old system.[48]

[46] *Rabotnichesko Delo*, April 29, 1966.
[47] *Ibid.*, January 13, 1966.
[48] *Ibid.*, November 15, 1966.

	New system	Old system
Total industrial production	16.6	14.1
Productivity	15.3	6.3
Net production	26.4	14.2
Accumulation	40.4	20.4
Wage fund	13.6	9.6

Despite this genuine progress, however, it gradually became apparent that it was taking an unconscionable time for some of the important new features of the system to be applied at all. Thus, though it was claimed that in 1967 the new system was to be applied in 70 per cent of all industrial operations, the whole rural economy, automotive transport, and some trade enterprises,[49] the new pricing system was not applied at all in 1967. Zhivkov had promised in his speech to the April, 1966, plenum that work on this system would be finished by the middle of 1967, but it was later announced that a reform of factory prices only (inter-enterprise prices) would go into effect in the middle of 1968.[50] In general, throughout the whole of 1967 there was a noticeable falling off in enthusiasm for the whole notion of economic reform and far less publicity than before was given to its progress.

This impression that things were going wrong or, in some important respects, hardly going at all, was borne out by an important decree published in the official gazette, *Darzhaven Vestnik*, in November, 1967. This decree "On Increasing the Profitability of the Economy" amounted to a correction and revision of some important aspects of the Theses published two years before and was obviously designed to infuse some life into the system. It made provisions for improving the organization of production, labor, and management in the individual enterprises; bringing the quality of production closer to foreign standards; "correcting" (raising) labor norms, some of which had become far too low since the adoption of more modern machinery; introducing a multifactoral system of wages based on separate indices for the results of each worker's contribution; increasing interest rates on bank loans; and financing investments by the enterprises themselves through their own funds or from bank loans instead of from the state budget.[51]

That these new provisions were a reflection on how the reform was working was admitted in the preamble to the decree. This

[49] *Ibid.*, December 13, 1966.
[50] *Ibid.*, November 15, 1967.
[51] *Darzhaven Vestnik* (Sofia), November 10, 1967.

stated that, though the economic tasks set by the Ninth Party Congress in November, 1966, were being performed successfully, they "nowhere near exhausted the immense possibilities and advantages of the socialist order and do not correspond to the conditions created by the new economic system for the further development of the country's economy." It went on to complain that the correct groundwork had not been laid for the correct implementation of the new system and urged the elimination of "apathy and conservatism" in all branches of government and the economy.[52]

This decree expressed a considerable dissatisfaction with the workings of the new system—a dissatisfaction that evidently led, in the following months, to a complete reappraisal of the whole economy. The result was a very important modification in the whole concept of economic reform, which was announced by Todor Zhivkov at a Central Committee plenum in July, 1968. The modification was essentially a return to greater centralization in planning, a move which struck at the basic precept of the whole economic reform movement in Eastern Europe. Zhivkov argued that the scientific-technical revolution, through which he considered Bulgaria was passing, "calls for the central determination of the national economic ratios and the structure of the national economy through the state plan." This, he admitted, would "introduce a major change in the current concept that the state plan must be built essentially from the bottom upward."[53] However, other features of the reform program, notably rationalization through the use of financial levers, would be maintained and even strengthened. Zhivkov also urged the complete rejuvenation of the nation's economic cadres so that the economy would have the necessary expertise to face the new technological era.

It is still too early to say just what the new concept of recentralization will involve, or to estimate whether it will achieve the results for which the regime has been groping. Much will depend, of course, on the quality of cadres available and, more particularly, whether they will at last be given their chance. There is talent available, but, in spite of the many promises made, it has never been given sufficient authority or reward. Hopes for a large-scale removal of older Party cadres at the November, 1966, Party Congress were bitterly disappointed. Now the same thing was being promised two years later. Whether Zhivkov would now have the courage to face the many implications of his intentions—something he has never shown in the past—remains a very big question.

[52] *Darzhaven Vestnik*, November 10, 1967.
[53] *Rabotnichesko Delo*, July 26, 1968.

8

Politics Since the Eighth Congress, 1962–68

AFTER HIS TRIUMPH at the Eighth Party Congress in 1962, Zhivkov had no serious rival in the top echelons of the Bulgarian Communist Party. It had been eight years since his appointment as First Party Secretary. In that time, aided by circumstance, Moscow, and his own maturing skill, he had successfully removed Chervenkov, Georgi Chankov, and Yugov from the political scene —even though all three men were of greater stature and were initially more powerful. Bulgarian politics now seemed set on a more even course, with both Party and nation quiescent, or at least resigned to the situation.

But then, after the storms seemed to have calmed, the most dramatic and extraordinary incident in the history of Communist rule in Bulgaria occurred.

The April Conspiracy

On the night of April 7, 1965, Ivan Todorov-Gorunya, a senior member of the Bulgarian Communist Party, shot himself in his Sofia apartment to avoid arrest by the security police. His death marked the end—before it had had a chance to begin—of a political-military conspiracy designed to overthrow the Zhivkov regime.

Political conspiracies and military *coups d'état* have, of course, been staple breakfast reading over the last twenty years, since the breakup of colonial rule in most parts of the world. Before World War II they were commonplace in the Balkans, nowhere more so than in Bulgaria itself. But this conspiracy occurred in Communist Bulgaria in 1965. True, all the Communist states had had their full share of real or imagined conspirators, factions, plots and traitors. East Germany, Poland, and Hungary had known open rebellion. But only in Albania, in the fall of 1960, had there been a previous case of a conspiracy aimed at seizing power through force of arms.[1] The April conspiracy in Bulgaria, therefore, was a rare phenomenon for Communist Eastern Europe.

The full story of what happened probably will never be known in the West. The Bulgarian regime did its best to belittle the episode. Before its own people it attempted at first to preserve a strict silence. But to the rest of the world it had to acknowledge that certain people "had broken the laws of the country" and that an inquiry was being held;[2] it also admitted that Todorov-Gorunya had committed suicide, "having fallen into a state of depression on learning that his criminal activity had been discovered." Later, however, in a speech to senior army officers broadcast by Radio Sofia on May 8, Zhivkov admitted the existence of a "plotting group" which he claimed comprised no more than five adventurers completely alienated from the army, the Party, and the people. Later, in interviews given to Western journalists, he was a bit more forthcoming but still revealed little.[3] The official reports of the trial of the conspirators, held in June, described them as "despicable power seekers . . . who, spurred by adventurist and careerist motives, committed crimes against the law."[4]

Piecing together the scanty bits of evidence, one can attest to a few facts and hazard a few conclusions from them.

[1] At the Fourth Congress of the Albanian Party of Labor in February, 1961, First Party Secretary Enver Hoxha announced there had been a military plot against his regime the previous fall, led by Rear-Admiral Teme Sejko. Hoxha accused the American Sixth Fleet, the Greek "monarcho-fascists," and the "Yugoslav revisionists" of being implicated. In reality, as was later admitted by the Albanians, it was a Soviet-inspired plot with its center at the Valona naval base. The essential difference between this plot and the Bulgarian conspiracy was that, whereas outside forces were involved in the former, the latter was a completely domestic affair.

[2] Bulgarian Telegraphic Agency, April 22, 1965; for foreign release only. The first news of the plot was given by a UPI stringer (a Bulgarian citizen) in Sofia on April 14, 1965.

[3] See, for example, interview with *Le Figaro* (Paris), June 5, 1965 and *Neues Oesterreich* (Vienna), July 17, 1965.

[4] Bulgarian Telegraphic Agency, June 19, 1965.

One safe conclusion can be made about the timing of the conspiracy. It was uncovered less than five months after the fall of Khrushchev, an event which sent tremors of instability throughout Eastern Europe—nowhere more so than in Bulgaria, where Zhivkov had been so dependent on Khrushchev's good will and support. The conspirators, therefore, probably decided to try and take advantage of this completely unexpected situation. The palace revolution in Moscow in October, 1964, prepared the ground for the conspiracy in Sofia the following April.

From here, however, the grounds for assumption become far less sure. At the trial held in June, 1965, there were nine defendants, all of whom "condemned their own criminal activities as plotters." Thus, with the dead Todorov-Gorunya, there were at least ten involved. These were almost certainly only the ringleaders; it may be assumed that numerous others knew of the conspiracy and had been counted on to join if ever the command had been given. Some of these passive supporters were later removed from their posts.

The leader of the conspiracy was undoubtedly Todorov-Gorunya. During the war Todorov-Gorunya was the political commissar of the most famous Bulgarian partisan group, the "Gavril Genov" detachment. (Gorunya—meaning "swine"—was a partisan appellation which he retained.) After the Communist takeover, Todorov-Gorunya was for many years secretary of the Vratsa district Party committee and it was in this area that he made a name as a conscientious chieftain, respected by Communists and many non-Communists for his devotion and his concern for the people he governed. (Vratsa had been the main theater of operations of the "Gavril Genov" detachment.) In 1957, he was elected a deputy to the National Assembly for the Vratsa district and soon began to achieve some prominence on the national level. In 1958, at the BCP Seventh Congress, he was elected a candidate-member of the Central Committee. In 1961, he was appointed a deputy minister of agriculture and, in 1962, the first deputy minister of agriculture. The same year, at the Eighth Party Congress, he became a full member of the Central Committee and, immediately afterwards, Chairman of the Directorate of the Water Economy. Todorov-Gorunya's importance, however, lay in the local power he held in Vratsa—the extent of which, as will be seen, was very great indeed. In the Balkans, local power has continued to be a factor of national political importance even in the Communist era. In Bulgaria, this tradition of localism has already been noted in the case of Yugov in Plovdiv. In Albania, several of the top national leaders owe much of their influence to the fact that they are all-powerful in certain areas of the country. Yugoslavia, with its ethnic, territorial, and historical diversities, is the most obvious example of this.[5] Todorov-Gorunya in Vratsa, therefore, had a base of power which made him a much more powerful man in Bulgaria than his official position would suggest.

The first reports of the attempted *coup* to reach the West suggested that its second most important leader after Todorov-Gorunya was Major-General Tsviatko Anev, the commander of the Sofia garrison. (This was not as important a post, incidentally, as the title might suggest. Anev had perhaps 500 men under his command. The most important military position in Sofia was that of commander of the first Bulgarian Army, which was based in the capital.) During the war, Anev had been second-in-command of the same "Gavril Genov" partisan detachment of which Todorov-Gorunya had been political commissar. He had been appointed to the command of the Sofia garrison at the end of 1961. At the trial of the conspirators, Anev received a twelve-year sentence.

Anev was certainly a key figure in the conspiracy; if his garrison had been loyal to him, it could, small as it was, have seized vital parts of Sofia (the radio, railway station, etc.) in the very first hours. But it seems that the main plotter after Todorov-Gorunya was Tsolo Krustev. In reporting the trial, BTA (the Bulgarian Telegraphic Agency) described Tsolo Krustev as a "former official" at the Foreign Ministry. His last known post was head of the Asian department at that ministry; from 1957 to 1960, he had been Ambassador to North Korea. During the war, he had been commander of the "Gavril Genov" detachment and for several years after it had served under Todorov-Gorunya as one of the secretaries of the Vratsa district Party committee. From 1954 to 1957, he was chairman of the "Voluntary Organization for the Collaboration with Defense" (DOSO). Krustev was sentenced to fifteen years' imprisonment at the trial.

Of the seven others sentenced at the trial, two need not detain us. Avram Chernev—who got three years—was described as a "former teacher" and Stoyan Milanovic was a former Yugoslav citizen; he also got three years. The five others, however, are inter-

---

[5] The case of Edward Gierek in Katowice in Poland and various secretaries of the Ostrava region in Czechoslovakia might be quoted as similar examples in Northeast Europe. Here, however, power springs from the *industrial* importance of the regions, rather than a tradition of localism.

esting because of their connection with the military. Two were Major-Generals on the active list: Micho Michev (ten years' imprisonment) and Lyuben Dinov (eight years). Michev, at the time of the conspiracy, was deputy chief of the general political administration of the army.[6] Dinov had worked in the army's general political administration in the early 1950's and became the head of it in 1953 or 1954, but he had lost this post in 1955. Since then he evidently had continued working at the Ministry of Defense in a capacity that, unfortunately, is not known. Two other conspirators, Ivan Velchev and Blagoi Mavrodinov, were, like the other military defendants, simply described as "former army officers." No other information on them is available, but the fact that Velchev was sentenced to fifteen years' imprisonment—only Krustev received a sentence so severe—suggests that, apart from being one of the main conspirators, he was an officer of high rank. Mavrodinov only received five years, an indication of his smaller role in the affair and probably of his more junior rank also. The last defendant, Boris Temkov, got ten years. BTA described him as a journalist and he is known to have been Radio Sofia's correspondent in Iraq in 1960 and 1961. Previously he had been employed in the Foreign Ministry, but—more important—during World War II he had been a partisan in the "Vassil Kolarov" detachment which operated in and around Plovdiv.

In a case so fascinating, about which so little is known, there is a great temptation to let speculation run wild. But, while resisting this temptation, one can draw some tentative conclusions from the evidence available.

There was obviously a strong personal bond between the ringleaders, based mainly on common partisan experience in World War II. Todorov-Gorunya, Anev, and Krustev were members of the same partisan detachment, and most of the other defendants are known to have been partisans. Moreover, Todorov-Gorunya and Krustev had their base of power in the same district—Vratsa. Finally, two of the generals involved, Michev and Dinov, had been "political" generals after the Communist takeover.

The strong army involvement in the coup was thoroughly in keeping with Bulgarian pre-Communist history. The army had always been an active—sometimes a decisive—factor in Bulgarian politics. Though not a militaristic nation in the accepted sense,

[6] He should not be confused with Lieutenant-General Misho Mishev, who was chief of the army's general political administration from 1957 to 1962.

the Bulgarians have always accorded their army a special and honored status among national institutions. This, and the awareness that it was often the most stable element in an unstable situation, had led the army to intervene on several occasions after the liberation from the Turks in 1878. Notable cases of this were in 1886, 1923, and 1934, and, of course, on September 9, 1944 when the last "bourgeois" government was overthrown. This tradition is worth remembering in view of the steady recurrence of historical patterns in Communist East Europe, particularly after the Stalinist *Gleichschaltung* had begun to lose its impact.

The partisan movement in Bulgaria was never very strong; it certainly did not compare with its counterpart in Yugoslavia nor, so far as the effect it had, with that in Albania. It had little popular support and fought not so much against the Germans, as is now claimed, but against Bulgarian army and police units sent to hunt them down. In the areas close to Yugoslavia, some Bulgarian partisans fought with the Yugoslavs. Still, the Bulgarian movement had a creditable fighting record and, when liberation came, its leaders were entitled to expect positions and privileges as a reward for their services to the cause. But, throughout most of Eastern Europe, the consolidation of the Communist system meant the victory of the Muscovites over the home Communists. Thus the Bulgarian partisans, both in the political and the military sphere, were denied the fruits of victory and some were physically persecuted— the case of Slavcho Trunski being the most famous of them all.[7] Soviet-trained generals, like Mihailov, Damyanov, and Panchevski, took over the armed forces, just as the Muscovite Chervenkov and his group seized command in the political sphere. In this respect, the fate of the Bulgarian partisans was similar to that of the Polish partisans, who quickly lost power and influence after the downfall of Gomulka in 1948.

By 1956, however, the period of intense sovietization in Bulgaria had come to an end and a policy of "re-Bulgarization" was ushered in. This, of course, was part of the general process of replacing Muscovites with home Communists in most parts of Eastern Europe. Particularly after 1960, it was noticeable that Bulgarian ex-partisans, many of them still quite young, were quietly but steadily replacing the older Soviet-trained commanders in most of the important military posts. (The new commanders, of course, almost invariably had had a period of training in Soviet military academies,

[7] See Chapter 4.

as had the prewar generation of leaders. But postwar training in the U.S.S.R. often had far less effect on the ethos and the loyalties of the men concerned.) This turnover reached its culmination in March, 1962, when General Ivan Mihailov was replaced as Minister of Defense by General Dobri Dzhurov, a former partisan. At the same time another partisan, General Diko Dikov, became Minister of the Interior.

Zhivkov himself had been a partisan, fighting mainly in the hills around Sofia. (He had no doubt fought honorably, though he can hardly have been the Achilles that some propagandists later made him out to be.) It is possible that the Party leader, pressed by conflict in the political leadership, sought to ensure a firm body of support in the army by the promotion of these partisan officers. If this was his intention, he was only partially successful. The bulk of the army did remain loyal at the time of the April, 1965, conspiracy, but obviously more than a few partisans were ready to carry their disaffection to the point of mutiny. Nor was this the first time that a group of partisans had shown a taste for rebellion. The "coffee-house" conspirators of 1961, Panov, Terpeshev, and Kufardzhiev,[8] had all been partisans. That summer, rumors swept Sofia that this group, together with elements in the regular army, had been planning a putsch, although this was later strongly denied by regime sources.[9] What is clear, then, is that many of the former partisans still formed a tightly-knit group, loyal to each other rather than to the regime—here the similarity with the Polish partisans is striking—and that, despite the rehabilitation of many of them, some still remained discontented.

Discontent in the Military

Before speculating on their discontent, it is worth discussing the interesting fact that two of the conspirators, Michev and Dinov, were political officers. Their peculiar branch of soldiering may have had no connection with their entering the conspiracy, but the relation between the political and the military in the Bulgarian armed forces seems to have caused considerable ill feeling. The fall of Marshal Zhukov in the Soviet Union in 1957 had its repercussions in Bulgaria. It evidently contributed to the disgrace of former Defense Minister Panchevski, who was reported to have been a

[8] See Chapter 6.
[9] See Tano Tsolov: *Rabotnichesko Delo* (Sofia), June 17, 1961.

close friend of Zhukov. But the principal charge leveled at Zhukov was that "he attempted to place the army outside the Party's control by curbing the work of the political administration and of the Party organizations in the army."[10] Zhukov's philosophy had also had its devotees in the Bulgarian army and a Central Committee plenum in October, 1958, dealt with the problems it had caused. Little was reported about the deliberations at the time but it was later revealed how serious the "underestimation" of political work in the army had become. The following passage from an authoritative article illustrates this:

> Our commanders come from the people and the Party has entrusted them with the great responsibility of training and educating the army, which is placed under the leadership of the Party. Thus, regardless of whether they are Communists or not, the commanders are the practical implementors and executors of the Party line in the army. The army being guided by the Party, and being educated, trained, and organized by the Party, the one-man commanders are obliged always to take this theory and the Party line as points of departure in their activity. There is no Leninist one-man command beyond this line and against this line, and any deviation from it is inadmissible and dangerous. Such a deviation may lead to serious shortcomings and failures in the training of detachments and to various abnormal phenomena. This is precisely why the October plenum of the Bulgarian Communist Party Central Committee most strictly condemned and put an end to the dangerous and harmful trend of underestimating party-political work and of restricting the activity of political organs, Party organizations, and military councils, and condemned and ended the numerous serious violations of Party principles in educating and training the army, which were the results of this harmful trend.[11]

From this passage it is clear that the October, 1958, plenum, while confirming the principle of one-man command in the army —where the commander of the unit was ultimately responsible for both military and political activity and training—also sought to put an end to the neglect of political training which this principle had tended to encourage. The task of harmonizing military effi-

---

[10] See Raymond L. Garthoff; "The Military in Soviet Politics," *Problems of Communism* (Washington), November–December, 1967.

[11] General Velichko Georgiev, "The Party Line in Organizing, Training, and Educating the Army," *Narodna Armia* (Sofia), October 15, 1960. It is interesting that Georgiev, commander of the Second Bulgarian Army, was reported to have been involved in the discontent of 1961. He later lost his CC membership and his seat in the National Assembly.

ciency with Communist indoctrination was a difficult one and, despite the great successes in this respect which were claimed for the October plenum, it is likely that it continued to remain unsolved and caused bitterness and dissatisfaction.

This may have been one important reason for discontent in the military, but it would seem a contributory rather than a primary cause. More important in individual cases may have been pure personal frustration. True, the partisans as a group were coming into their own, but there were only so many important jobs to go around and some conspirators may have felt that they had been unfairly left out when the spoils were being shared. This was a charge that was later to be leveled at Krustev and Todorov-Gorunya. It is the usual charge against beaten factionalists in any totalitarian state, but it may have been *partially* true—and not only in the case of Krustev and Todorov-Gorunya.

The Political Motives

Finally, there is the question of political motives. The official version was that they were adventuristic supporters of the Chinese line. (These charges were usually accompanied by official protestations of loyalty to the Soviet Union which, for sheer bathos, equalled anything over the previous twenty years.) Though this was a convenient charge, the conspirators were more likely rebelling against the subservient policy of the Zhivkov regime toward the Soviet Union, and probably wanted Bulgaria to adopt a foreign policy closer to the Rumanian or even the Yugoslav model. The "Chinese" accusation was dismissed as spurious by almost all observers. Yet it would be rash to be definite about this, mainly because the conspirators themselves could well have had different motives, being united only by a dissatisfaction with the existing state of affairs. Moreover, if one accepts that a more independent foreign policy was what they generally wanted, then the policy of China *vis à vis* the Soviet Union may have roughly filled their concept. If the conspirators tended to be conservative or dogmatist in domestic policy, opposing Khrushchev's reform policy as reflected in Zhivkov's policy in Bulgaria, then again there might have been some justice in the charge that they were pro-Chinese. What evidence there is, unofficial and official, does suggest that they were, in fact, hard-liners in domestic affairs. We have seen how the Chinese example had exercised a fascination over many in the Bulgarian Party and how Zhivkov (as well as his Soviet supporters) had many difficulties with the Party rank and file when the Sino-Soviet dispute came into the open in 1960 and 1961. Quite possibly a strong residue of pro-Chinese sentiment remained, not based on any doctrinal or intellectual clarity but simply on an instinctive tendency to support whoever most strongly opposed the present line of Soviet and Bulgarian policy.[12] On the other hand, Rumania, with her conservative internal policy and her independent attitude abroad, may indeed have represented what the conspirators were trying to introduce in Bulgaria. As for Yugoslavia, it is hardly likely that her domestic policy had much appeal, although her foreign policy may well have. Then, again, it would seem that some partisans did have a certain general sympathy for Yugoslavia. Terpeshev, Panov, and Kufardzhiev, the conspirators of 1961 who in a sense were the forerunners of those in 1965, were considered to be in favor of *greater* reform at home and may well have had connections with Tito.

All this speculation is not designed so much to confuse as to show how confused the situation was, as well as to point up the varied motives which were probably behind the conspiracy and the lack of precision in such categorizations as "pro-Chinese," "pro-Rumanian" or "pro-Yugoslav." In their opposition to the existing situation, the conspirators were probably driven by many conflicting sympathies and emotions.

Support for the Conspiracy

Another question that arises is how much sympathy the conspirators may have had in the higher echelons of the Party, the army, and the regime generally. None of those named as conspirators seemed to have had the stature to take over the government if the conspiracy had succeeded; thus it was felt that more prestigious personalities must have been involved. At first the most prominent man in the Party on whom speculation centered was Pencho Kubadinski, whom we have seen earlier as a youngish apparatchik, candidate-member of the Politburo, and the holder of several governmental posts. In the army, General Slavcho Trunski,

[12] In an article the author wrote for *The World Today* (London) of June, 1965, (Vol. 21, No. 6) called "The Bulgarian Plot," I dismissed summarily the possibility that the conspirators could have been pro-Chinese in some way. Now I am not so sure.

now deputy minister of defense, was widely reported to have been the commanding spirit of the whole affair, as he was said to have been in the alleged *putsch* attempt in 1961. Both men, however, after a rather suspicious delay, reappeared in public and afterwards rose higher in the regime hierarchy: Trunski became commander of the Air Force as well as deputy minister of defense, and Kubadinski at the Ninth Party Congress in November, 1966, became a full member of the Politburo. One cannot be sure. Perhaps the reports were completely unfounded; perhaps they had some substance but the two men concerned made their peace with the regime and Zhivkov, in his eagerness to appease, subsequently bought them off with promotions.

Two important military figures who, if not directly implicated in the plot, were centers of disaffection, were Colonel-General Ivan Buchvarov and Lieutenant-General Nikolai Chernev. Though he was a political commissar in the partisan movement, Buchvarov's army career nevertheless does not seem to have suffered throughout the Chervenkov period.[13] From 1950 to 1959 he was chief of the general staff and for the latter part of that period was also a deputy minister of national defense. In 1959 he became first deputy minister of national defense and held this post till the spring of 1962, when he was appointed head of the Administrative Organs Department of the Party Central Committee (a department also known as the Military Department). In August, 1965, however, it was announced that Lieutenant-General Angel Tsanev now occupied this post.[14] No new post was announced for Buchvarov, but early in 1966 he was appointed Ambassador to East Berlin. At the Ninth Party Congress in November, 1966, he was not re-elected a Central Committee member.[15] Buchvarov's name was associated with the conspiracy in some Western press reports and he is reliably reported earlier to have had serious differences with Zhivkov.

Perhaps even more significant, in view of the controversies over political control in the army, was the case of Chernev. Appointed head of the general political administration of the army in 1962, Chernev, a former partisan, was dismissed from this post in February, 1966, and appointed Ambassador to Warsaw. Though

---

[13] His *political* career did, however, suffer. In January, 1950, he and five others were removed from the Central Committee for "not coping with their work and for blunted vigilance." He was re-elected in 1954.

[14] *Rabotnichesko Delo*, August 27, 1965.

[15] Buchvarov was killed in a plane crash near Bratislava a few days after the congress.

there was no suggestion that Chernev was implicated in the conspiracy, he may have been blamed for lack of vigilance: General Michev, one of the condemned plotters, was one of his deputies. In addition, the very fact of the conspiracy might have been interpreted as a sign that political training in the army was not up to scratch. At any rate Chernev, like Buchvarov, not only had to leave his post but the country as well. At the Ninth Party Congress he was not re-elected a candidate-member of the Central Committee.

The Buchvarov and Chernev cases apart, Zhivkov's response to the discontent was one of appeasement. The sentences meted out to the conspirators was surprisingly mild: the death penalty for the ringleaders would hardly have been draconian. In the few months following the abortive *coup*, Zhivkov and his Defense Minister Dzhurov spoke on several occasions to meetings of military officers "explaining Party policy," but doubtless also seeking to ascertain the extent of the disaffection and to remove it by a policy of assurance and appeasement.

Precautionary Steps

Other organizational changes were made to try to prevent a recurrence of this dangerous and embarrassing incident. The most important of these was a restructuring of the Ministry of the Interior, which implicitly reflected on the vigilance of that ministry in connection with the plot.[16] The ministry was stripped of all its security functions, and these were vested in a new Committee of State Security attached to the Council of Ministers; in other words, under Zhivkov personally as Prime Minister. The head of this committee was Angel Solakov, former first deputy minister of the interior. The Interior Ministry was renamed the Ministry of Internal Affairs; it remained under Dikov who was now, however, reduced to a lightweight status in the governmental hierarchy.

But if the Bulgarian regime was concerned over the conspiracy, so also was the Soviet. Less than three weeks after it had been uncovered, a CPSU delegation headed by Mikhail Suslov visited Bulgaria. The choice of Suslov shows how seriously the Soviets regarded the situation. It was also interesting because Suslov had been the chief Soviet delegate to the BCP Congress in 1962, where he had witnessed (or presided over) the political liquidation of

[16] It was rumored in Sofia that Soviet secret police, not Bulgarian, had uncovered the conspiracy.

Yugov, Tsankov, and, finally, of Chervenkov. He may have been regarded by the Kremlin as its current senior expert on Bulgaria and, in any case, the official accusation that the conspiracy had been Chinese-oriented was likely to arouse more than the passing interest of the Soviet Union's chief ideologist. Suslov had intensive discussions with Zhivkov and his closest advisers and made a short tour of the Russe, Varna, and Burgas districts. Having evidently reassured himself that Zhivkov had the situation in hand, Suslov ended his visit with a demonstrative show of support for Zhivkov. He described the Bulgarian leader as "the great friend of the Soviet state" and the BCP as "united round its Central Committee headed by Todor Zhivkov." The BCP was also a Party that enjoyed "a well-deserved authority in the international Communist movement."[17] The Soviet leaders must have been concerned indeed. With the break with Yugoslavia in 1948, the defection of Albania in 1961, and the later partial defection of Rumania, Moscow's position in the Balkans had deteriorated seriously. Bulgaria, always strategically important, now took on a correspondingly increased value. The importance of Suslov's mission, therefore, can readily be appreciated.

A Surprising Aftermath

After the trial of the conspirators in June, 1965, the Bulgarian regime was at pains to signify that all was now well. To all appearances the trial had ended an isolated, if embarrassing, incident; references to the plot virtually ceased altogether.

Yet three years later this silence was dramatically broken in none other than the Vratsa district, the stronghold of Todorov-Gorunya and Krustev. At a plenum of the district Party committee in April, 1968, attended by Zhivkov himself, some startling revelations were made by Ivan Abadzhiev, First Secretary of the Vratsa Party committee and a candidate-member of the Politburo. Abadzhiev, a former First Secretary of the Komsomol and a tough, energetic official, had been appointed to Vratsa the previous September. From his speech it was obvious why a man of his caliber had been sent there.

Abadzhiev made a violent attack on the personalities and politics of Todorov-Gorunya and Krustev. In "unmasking their true

17 Radio Sofia, June 2, 1965.

image," he described them as corrupt, immoral power-seekers; their politics had been characterized by a failure to "understand or to implement the decisions of the Twentieth CPSU Congress." They were—again the Chinese accusation—"heralds of Maoism in Bulgaria . . . [who] wholeheartedly adopted the line of Mao Tse-tung's group against the CPSU and the rest of the fraternal parties."[18]

Even more important was Abadzhiev's testimony to the lasting influence these two "miscreants" had in Vratsa, even after the death of one and the incarceration of the other. Abadzhiev admitted that as late as April, 1968, there were "traces (of this influence) that have still not been eliminated." He charged that "during the last two or three years, after the discovery of the plot, the District Committee (of Vratsa) did not make a thorough evaluation of the event and draw the obvious conclusions from it" and that "a number of close friends of the plotters remained in various responsible posts." Abadzhiev then made a most interesting admission:

> The heightened tension of the international situation, and more specifically the events in the Middle East in June, 1967, was used by close friends of the plotters and people personally connected with them as an excuse to increase their activity. . . . They openly demonstrated their support of the plotters and their disagreement with the Party line.[19]

During the Arab-Israeli war of 1967 it had been known that public opinion in Bulgaria was generally on the side of Israel and against Sofia's policy. But no tension had been reported similar to that in Poland and Hungary. Now, however, it seems there was considerable tension and, in Vratsa at least, it was used by "mischief-makers."

Later, however (no doubt after the arrival of Abadzhiev), "a realistic evaluation of the situation was made and a number of energetic steps to correct it were taken on the initiative and with the active participation of the CC of the BCP." The steps were, indeed, quite energetic: "thirty-three people were expelled from the Party and thirty-nine others penalized . . . fifteen were removed from their positions, and several people were deported from

[18] *Otechestven Zof* (organ of the Vratsa District Party committee), April 18, 1968. Further quotations of Abadzhiev's speech are taken from this source. It is significant that the parts of Abadzhiev's speech referring to the conspiracy and its aftermath were not reported in the Sofia press or by Radio Sofia.
[19] *Ibid.*

the district." Abadzhiev revealed later in his speech that 359 people in the Vratsa district had lost their Party membership. Even now, said Abadzhiev, it was "still too early to be sure that the desired results have been achieved in unmasking this situation and strengthening the Party organizations affected by it."

Abadzhiev's report, published exclusively in an obscure provincial paper, was one of the most significant political documents to come out of Bulgaria in several years. The report referred to only one of Bulgaria's twenty-eight district Party organizations and, because of the very strong connections of two of the April, 1965, conspirators with Vratsa, one can assume that the situation in this district was far more acute than in any other. But could the situation in other districts have been as quiet as would have appeared from the official press? This is difficult to believe, and the fact that, between April, 1965, and June, 1968, eleven out of twenty-eight district First Party Secretaries in Bulgaria were removed from their posts only adds to the suspicion.[20]

Continuing Opposition

What these figures and the whole tenor of Abadzhiev's speech point to is the continuing opposition to the Zhivkov leadership by a strong minority of the Party rank and file. Zhivkov may have won power at the top but he had been unable to clear out dissidents from the lower echelons. Taking the Vratsa case alone, it seems extraordinary that such a situation should have been tolerated for over two years—until Abadzhiev was appointed to set things straight. One may assume that Zhivkov had the power to have moved against the Vratsa dissidents earlier but considered it politic not to use it, because there were dissidents in other areas too, and to use direct action might only have exposed Party divisions which he was anxious to paper over. Thus, despite the fact that the opposition now had no representative in the top leadership as it had previously had in Chervenkov and Yugov, it was still powerful enough to delay strong measures against it. Moreover, it was powerful enough to blunt the force of a new drive toward reform that Zhivkov seemed prepared to launch after the fall of Khrushchev.

---

[20] In only two of these cases did the change involve a clear promotion for the secretary in question. It might be noted that during the preceding three-year period (April, 1962–April, 1965) only four of the twenty-eight district First Secretaries had been transferred to other posts.

Khrushchev's fall certainly put the Bulgarian leadership in a panic—a craven panic, if one recalls that in their statement marking the events in Moscow they did not give even a parting nod to the leader who had done so much for them.[21] Apart from this, however, Zhivkov's reaction was a healthy one. The spurt of reform that was noticeable after the Twenty-second CPSU Congress in 1961 had not long survived the BCP's own Eighth Congress in 1962, which saw the fall of Yugov. Perhaps the high point of this reformist zeal had come at the end of 1962, when an amnesty was granted to 6,000 prisoners, including 500 political detainees.[22] Soon thereafter, a brake was applied to the reform process in both the cultural and the political field; it was very similar to that which had slowed down the promising developments after the April plenum in 1956. Now the time was once more deemed appropriate for reform. Having depended too much on outside help, Zhivkov now seemed to be trying to broaden the base of his support at home and thus to give his power a firmer foundation. The population was assured that the decisions of the April, 1956, plenum would be even more energetically implemented;[23] Zhivkov himself urged (and, to some extent, tolerated) more freedom of criticism than before.[24] The April conspiracy in 1965 brought an unwelcome interruption to this promising beginning, but once it had been crushed the move toward reform was resumed. In both domestic and foreign policy, Bulgaria seemed to be moving toward a more enlightened and dignified position. Toward the end of 1965 and in the first half of 1966, Zhivkov seemed at last to be fulfilling the promise he had shown for a period in 1956–57 and again in 1961–62. The measures for economic reform were—for Bulgaria—quite impressive in their boldness: greater latitude was allowed in literature and the arts, with serious efforts being made to encourage younger writers; important practical measures, like the introduction of the secret ballot in local elections, were introduced; and emphasis was given to the fact that the law *did* allow more than one candidate to be included on the electoral list.[25] Above all there was

[21] See CC Declaration of October 19, 1964; Bulgarian Telegraphic Agency, October 20, 1964. Among the other Warsaw Pact states, only the Rumanians did not pay some tribute to Khrushchev; they ignored his fall completely.

[22] Radio Sofia, December 30, 1962.

[23] See, for example, the leading article in *Rabotnichesko Delo*, October 22, 1964.

[24] See his speech on the eve of Student Day, December 8, 1964; Radio Sofia December 7, 1964.

[25] See the article in *Otechestven Front* (Sofia), March 3, 1966, on the first session of the newly elected People's Councils.

a noticeably increased tolerance for freedom of speech and—a longed-for freedom—it became easier for Bulgarian citizens to travel abroad than at any time since the beginning of Communist rule. The number of Bulgarians coming to the West did not remotely compare with the outflow from Hungary, Czechoslovakia or Poland, but still it did increase, and this new freedom was sincerely welcomed.

The Ninth Party Congress

This promising situation in 1966 raised great hopes for the Ninth Party Congress that was scheduled for November. Many younger Bulgarians—and many Western observers[26]—believed that a real breakthrough would occur, that the old Party hands would be honorably pensioned off from the Politburo and Central Committee and that the younger, better-trained leaders replacing them would push through the reforms already started. There seemed a good chance that Zhivkov's Bulgaria would take the same course in internal affairs that Kadar's Hungary had taken in 1961.

But these optimists underestimated the strength and the will to resist of the older generation of Party apparatchiks; they overlooked Zhivkov's lack of decisiveness. These two factors produced a disappointing congress, a compromise solution that slowed down the process of reform. In his Central Committee report to the congress, Zhivkov referred to the "generation" problem:

The raising of specialists to leading work in no way means disregard for the old revolutionary workers. We must also in the future aim at not pensioning off prematurely those of them who are still able to work, while the pensioners should, according to their possibilities, be used for non-payroll work. Moreover, it is, known that the Party has been taking care of the health of the old revolutionary cadres and has been securing their material situation, and it will continue to do so in the future. Thus, at the present stage, the problem of the old and the young cadres and of the basis for their cohesion has been given a new, contemporary meaning and content. . . . The task is to make the most purposeful use of the forces, abilities, and merits of the different generations and contingents, old and young. We must say that, with isolated exceptions, the majority of old revolutionary workers understand the wisdom of this line. We hope that

[26] This writer was one of them: see J. F. Brown, "Fruehlingstendenzen in Bulgarien?" *Osteuropa* (Stuttgart), No. 9, September, 1966.

its correctness will also be understood by those comrades who, for one reason or another, have not yet accepted it by conviction.[27]

The last sentence was an admission of the resistance of the older generation. The whole passage reflected Zhivkov's dilemma. It was a problem that confronted every Eastern European leader, and each responded to it with a different degree of courage. On a smaller scale, the acuteness of Zhivkov's problem was like that of Tito in Yugoslavia; but where Tito showed decision and foresight, Zhivkov chose to temporize. His words quoted above contained a hint of the bargain that was to be struck in the elections to the Politburo, Secretariat, and Central Committee. When the results of these were announced, however, they were received by many with incredulous surprise. The new Politburo consisted of the following: Boyan Bulgaranov (aged 70), Tsola Dragoicheva (68), Pencho Kubadinski (48), Ivan Mihailov (69), Todor Pavlov (76), Ivan Popov (about 60), Stanko Todorov (46), Tano Tsolov (about 50), Boris Velchev (52), Todor Zhivkov (55), Zhivko Zhivkov (51).

This new Politburo contained two surprising retentions and two astonishing additions. It had been expected that Bulgaranov and Mihailov would be retired; their retention, however, was clearly due to a recognition of their influence with the older cadres and was a symbol of the policy, forced on Zhivkov, of "harmonizing" the different generations, thereby avoiding conflict between them. In Mihailov's case the desire not to offend Soviet susceptibilities may also have been a factor: he was the only remaining member of the Politburo who could genuinely be called a Muscovite.

The inclusion of Dragoicheva and Pavlov, both of whom had practically retired from active political life, was such a grotesque effort to placate the veterans that it was almost risible. Tsola Dragoicheva had been a member of the Politburo from 1940–48, the only woman to have held membership in that body. She now returned to it after nearly two decades of obscurity. A teacher by profession, she had joined the Communist Party when very young. She was briefly imprisoned in 1923 and in 1925 was sentenced to death, a victim of the White terror that followed the unsuccessful attempt to assassinate Czar Boris by blowing up the Sveta Nedelia cathedral. While awaiting her execution in Plovdiv jail, however, Dragoicheva became pregnant and thus avoided the death sentence. (Her son, Chavdar, is well known in certain Sofia circles and

---

[27] *Rabotnichesko Delo*, November 15, 1966.

is hardly of the stern stuff of which his mother is obviously made.)
Dragoicheva was released in 1932 and was in the Soviet Union for
training from 1932 to 1936. She then returned to Bulgaria and continued her underground activity, being elected to the clandestine
Central Committee in 1937 and the Politburo in 1940. For a time
she was editor-in-chief of *Rabotnichesko Delo* and was one of the
main organizers of the Fatherland Front, of which she was Secretary-General from 1943 to 1947. She lost her Politburo seat in
1948 and suffered in the general decline of the home Communists
after the fall of Kostov and the triumph of Chervenkov. From
1947 to 1957 she was Minister of Post, Telegraph, and Telephones
and after 1957 was Chairman of the Committee for Bulgarian-
Soviet Friendship.

Todor Pavlov, by his election in 1966, became the oldest man
ever to have been a member of the BCP's Politburo. For many
years he was famous as the "grand old man" of Marxist-Leninist
philosophy in Bulgaria and was known as an inveterate dogmatist.
He was chairman of the Bulgarian Academy of Sciences from 1947
to 1962 and was then made honorary chairman of that body.
After 1962, he spent much of his time in sanatoria, but was nonetheless considered fit enough to take a Politburo seat in 1968 at
the age of 76! Pavlov had been a member of the BCP Central
Committee in the early 1920's; he was in the Soviet Union from
1932 to 1937 and for most of the war was in a Bulgarian concentration camp. From 1944 to the abolition of the monarchy in 1946,
he was one of the three regents appointed during the young Czar
Simeon's infancy. He was not re-elected to the Party Central Committee until 1954.

There can be no denying the strong characters of Pavlov and
Dragoicheva, although the latter marred a heroic record through
her role in the brutal persecutions after September 9, 1944. But
they had become political anachronisms long before 1966 and
they were completely out of touch and sympathy with the needs
of a modern socialist society. Age alone, of course, is not always
a reliable yardstick with which to separate conservatives from pro-
gressives: a veteran can be progressive and a young man hard-line
and dogmatic—there are many examples of this in the Communist
states. But Pavlov and Dragoicheva certainly conformed, in the
political sense, to the generalization about the hardening of ar-
teries. It might be argued that their election to the Politburo was
simply a gesture of appeasement and meant nothing in political
terms, that they were two "Chinese vases" of merely decorative

value. This, however, is to underestimate these two old warhorses—
and after his appointment, Pavlov at least played an active and
far from "progressive" role in cultural policy. Furthermore, the very
fact of their appointment cannot only have stiffened the resolve of
the veterans in the Party to resist the winds of change. It must also
have discouraged the true reformers and generally created a psychological climate unconducive to real advancement.

If the concessions reflected in the retention of Mihailov and
Bulgaranov and the addition of Dragoicheva and Pavlov had been
confined to elections to the Politburo, there still might have been
some justification in interpreting them as gestures bereft of political meaning. But the new Central Committee, though con-
taining some excellent choices, was hardly one to encourage hope
for comprehensive reform. It contained 137 full members against
101 in the old Committee elected in 1962. The following figures
give a comparison between the two bodies by age-groups:

	Ninth Congress, 1966	Eighth Congress, 1962
Under 40	3	4
40–49	43	41
50–59	49	30
60–70	24	16
Over 70	6	4
Unknown	12	6

The following is a breakdown of the newly elected full members
in 1966 by profession.[28]

Ministers and government officials	34
Functionaries of the CC of the BCP	22
District or local Party functionaries	25
Generals (including army and state security generals)	13
Scientific and cultural workers (including writers and journalists, scientists, etc.)	12
Industrial managers	1
Komsomol functionaries	1

[28] Each person is entered in one category only, although several belong to
two or more categories, e.g., generals who are, at the same time, deputy ministers or heads of CC departments.

Functionaries of other public organiza-
tions (including the National Assembly
Bureau and Presidium, the Fatherland
Front, the trade unions, etc.)   12
Diplomats (including both career diplo-
mats and party functionaries at present
holding diplomatic posts)   10
Old Party members, pensioners   7

TOTAL   137[29]

None of these figures reveals a Central Committee brimming
with youthful dynamism or with the kind of expertise which Zhivkov would evidently have liked to see receive greater recognition.
The overall impression was of a rather conservative committee, of
a compromise in personnel that begets compromise in policy.

Where Zhivkov *was* able to introduce representatives of the
younger Party cadres and of the technical classes was in the Secretariat and, to some extent, into the group of candidate-members
of the Politburo. There was even one hearteningly bold choice to
full Politburo membership: that of Professor Ivan Popov who had
never previously been a member even of the Central Committee.
Popov, a lifelong Communist, had graduated in electrical engineering from the University of Toulouse in the 1930's. In 1953, he had
become a professor of engineering at the Machine and Electro-
Technical Institute in Sofia and in 1962, he became Chairman of
the Committee for Technical Science and Progress. He was already
sixty in 1966, but his appointment was believed to have been welcomed among the economic and managerial classes.

Among the Politburo candidates, two—Dimo Dimov and Peko
Takov, the Minister of Internal Trade—were relative veterans,
former partisans, and men of little color or ability. Angel Tsanev,
who took Buchvarov's place as head of the Central Committee's
Military Department, also received candidate status. The rest, however, were more interesting. They included Luchezar Avramov,
whose abilities have been discussed in Chapter 6 and who certainly
deserved full Politburo status; he was, however, appointed a deputy
premier immediately after the congress. Also included were the
three provincial chieftains: Kostadin Gyaurov, forty-two; Krustyu

[29] One other figure worth noting is that, of those members whose background can be traced, 74 members of the 1966 CC had been either active
partisans or inmates of prisons or concentration camps. In 1962, the number
was 66.

Trichkov, forty-three; and Ivan Abadzhiev, thirty-six. They were interesting not only because of their relative youth, but because they were First Secretaries of very sensitive districts. Gyaurov, as stated in Chapter 6, took over Plovdiv, the former stronghold of Yugov, in 1962; Trichkov was First Secretary in Blagoevgrad (Pirin Macedonia) on the frontier of Yugoslav Macedonia which, by 1966, was once again becoming a bitter bone of contention between Sofia and Belgrade; Abadzhiev, as we have seen, was sent to clear out the hornets' nest in Vratsa. All three were prototypes of the new Bulgarian apparatchik—well educated, hard, determined, and very much on the make.

The new Secretariat numbered six as against seven in the old. Apart from Zhivkov, Bulgaranov, Velchev, and Ivan Prumov were retained. Stanko Todorov, forty-six, appeared again in the Secretariat after an absence of nine years; the completely new member was Venelin Kotsev, aged about 40. Kotsev had previously been head of the Central Committee department for culture and arts. He and Pavlov were now the men in the top bodies of the Party with general responsibility for culture and education. Pavlov had long been known for his conservatism; Kotsev, though it may be to early to judge, seemed more conservative than liberal during his first two years in office. For the first time, *members* of the Secretariat as well as Central Committee secretaries were elected, following the practice in Czechoslovakia. Two of them—Dr. Vladimir Bonev, vice-chairman of the Fatherland Front, and Stoyan Gyurov, Chairman of the Central Council of Trade Unions—were obviously chosen as representatives of the mass organizations; the third, Professor Stefan Vassilev, an engineer, was First Secretary of the Sofia City Party Committee. This was the most powerful local organization in the country (Zhivkov's political *alma mater*) and an odd place to find a technocrat in charge.

The elections to the top Party bodies contained one sad retirement and one very notable purge. Encho Staikov, sixty-five, Chairman of the Fatherland Front, was not re-elected to the Politburo. It was ironic that he was the veteran who had to go, because he was more reformist than the two who were retained and had a far better record than Dragoicheva or Pavlov. The notable who was purged was none other than Mitko Grigorov, Politburo member and Central Committee secretary, whom we have seen earlier as one of the earliest members of Zhivkov's coterie. Grigorov went quietly; he was neither denounced nor subjected to subsequent criticism and, like Staikov, he retained his full membership of the

Central Committee. But his demotion was still a major event since he had been considered by many as second only to Zhivkov in Party rankings. To account for it is not easy, either, since there seem to have been no major differences in policy between the two men. It was probably a case of excessive ambition on Grigorov's part, of Zhivkov's growing dislike for him, and of Grigorov's general unpopularity. His case recalls that of Gyoergy Marosan in Hungary who was dismissed by Kadar in 1962, not for reasons of policy, but simply because he was a troublemaker and had ceased behaving with due Leninist modesty.

These, then, were the main features of the elections at the Ninth Party Congress. They have been treated at some length because, more clearly than anything else, they mirror both the nature of the political conflict still going on in Bulgaria and the response of the Zhivkov leadership to it. The response was typical of that lack of decisiveness on Zhivkov's part which always seemed to undermine the good intentions he had professed. Three times in the previous twelve years—in 1956, 1961, and in 1965–66—the Bulgarian regime seemed to be embarking on a genuine course of reform, only to shrink away from it when many hopes had been raised. In 1966, these hopes had been particularly keen, because the regime was showing a new vigor both at home and in foreign policy. But the Ninth Congress seriously dimmed these hopes and subsequently Bulgarian policy, both at home and abroad, confirmed the pessimism which the congress had produced. The clock was not put back, just as it was not put back after the first two false alarms in 1956 and 1961. On the whole—there are exceptions in some spheres—Communist Bulgaria continued to inch forward toward a better, more efficient society, even a freer one. But in terms of the population's rising expectations, especially those of the younger generation, and in terms of the progress in other Eastern European states, the pace has been far too slow and has only increased the general frustration. Zhivkov may plead for patience for a few more years, until the older cadres can finally be put out to pasture and the sacrifices of the past can become the rewards of the present. But, after so many disappointments, how long will Zhivkov continue to be given the benefit of the doubt?

9

Agrarian Policy Under the Communists

THE DEVELOPMENT of agricultural production and the course of collectivization have already been discussed in the chapters dealing with the economy as a whole. This discussion, however, gave only the outlines of development in a branch of Bulgaria's economy which, despite industrialization, has remained extremely important. Therefore, a detailed description of the major changes in the structure and organization of Bulgaria's agriculture is necessary, since these changes have played a key part in the country's evolution.

Bulgaria was traditionally a country of small, private landowners. In 1934, almost 80 per cent of the more than six million inhabitants were directly dependent on agriculture; only 8.2 per cent were engaged in industry and 3.4 per cent in commerce, trade, and communications. The land-owning structure was the most egalitarian in Eastern Europe: in 1934, farms of over 50 hectares (500 decares) represented only 1.6 per cent of the country's arable land; at the end of 1946, the total arable land, including South Dobruja, amounted to 48,942,890 decares, distributed among 1,094,109 farms.[1] Bulgaria's small farms, however, were not compact units. They were divided into numerous, scattered plots: in 1934, the total arable land (without South Dobruja) was distributed among 884,869 farms which consisted of 11,862,158 separate plots.[2]

[1] Kiril Lazarov (later Minister of Finance), *Bulletin of the Bulgarian Academy of Sciences*, Vols. 1–2, January, 1951. South Dobruja was regained from Rumania by the Treaty of Craiova in September, 1940.
[2] *Statistical Yearbook*, 1940, pp. 20, 811.

If extreme fragmentation was one characteristic of prewar Bulgarian agriculture, the strong trend toward cooperation was another. The cooperative granting of credit was very widespread indeed. The Bulgarian Agricultural and Cooperative Bank was the largest credit institution in the country; it accounted for about 60 per cent of the country's bank deposits and extended credit to all branches of agriculture. Farmers also received credits from the Co-operative Popular Banks and the Agricultural Credit Cooperatives. The main role of these credit cooperatives, however, was to buy and sell agricultural produce and to furnish the rural population with machinery and equipment. Their importance increased greatly during World War II and it has been estimated that, on the eve of the Communist takeover, there were 3,000 of them with a total membership of one million.[3]

Nor was the collective possession of land unknown in Bulgaria. The family institution of Zadruga, famous in what was later Yugoslavia, was also well established in western Bulgaria during the period of Turkish domination and lingered on into the twentieth century. At the head of each unit of land was the eldest family member, who had virtually supreme power in allocating the work to be done. But in financial matters he had to consult with the other adult family members and could be removed if these considered him incompetent. The family members possessed no private property but, regardless of the volume of work done by any one of them, each had the right to take what was reasonable to cover his own needs from the common wealth of the family. Every Zadruga member was free to leave and, if he did, an agreed part of the common property was paid to him.

It is tempting to see in these precedents of cooperation and collective ownership a foundation or preparation for the collectivization that was to come and to conclude that, because of them, the Bulgarian peasant was not adverse to what the Communists had in store for him. But there seems little ground for such argument. Compulsory collectivization was completely different in spirit from anything that had gone before. There was active and passive resistance to collectivization, and in his attitude toward it the Bulgarian peasant was no different from his counterparts in the rest of Eastern Europe. This is not to imply that he was satisfied with his lot under the old system, or that this system was not inefficient and wasteful. Nor does it deny the advantages of large-scale farming or indicate that, no matter how the collective system is re-

[3] L. A. D. Dellin (ed.), *Bulgaria* (New York, 1956), p. 288.

organized in the future, it will always be a failure. This resistance is mentioned here simply to correct an impression based on glib historical analogies and fostered by quite effective official propaganda.

The Phases of Collectivization

Collectivization in Bulgaria lasted from 1944 to 1957. Within this period, three phases emerge: first, 1944 to 1947; second, 1948 to 1949; third, 1950 to 1957.

In the first phase the Communists, though masters of the country, did not move quickly to transform its economic structure. The first necessity was to rout out all political opposition. Also, an Allied Control Commission was installed in Sofia, since Bulgaria was a defeated country. This commission could not prevent Bulgaria from falling completely under Communist sway, but it may well have inhibited any massive pressure on the farmers. More important was the opposition of the Agrarian Party, led by Nikola Petkov, and the Social Democrats whose press, until it was banned in 1947, spoke out bravely against administrative tyranny. In short, the Communist Party had tasks of an urgent political nature which had to be carried out before it could concentrate on reorganizing agriculture on the collectivized pattern.

Thus, by 1947, only 3.8 per cent of the arable land had been collectivized and this seems to have been accomplished entirely through voluntary means. The Party had explicitly warned against any compulsion and any hostile propaganda against private farmers.[4]

The collectives' terms of membership in this first phase were also relatively liberal and were obviously designed to make membership as attractive as possible. Up to 1947, the collectives were generally organized on the framework of the existing village cooperatives and did not necessarily include all the land, equipment, or livestock of their individual members. A decree on Labor Cooperative Agricultural Farms (trudovo-kooperativno zemedelsko stopanstvo—TKZS, or LCAF's in English), issued in 1945, contained the provision that members of collectives retained all rights of ownership of the land they contributed, and could mortgage or sell it.

---

[4] Declaration of September 28, 1945, in *The Bulgarian Communist Party in Resolutions and Decisions,* Part IV, 1944–55 (Sofia, 1955), pp. 32–33. Hereafter referred to as *Resolutions and Decisions.*

All the members together, as a token of their ownership, were entitled to a rent for the land they contributed or a "percentage of the net income of the cooperative farm up to 40 percent."[5] Labor remuneration was based on the Soviet system of the trudoden, a system of piece work expressed in terms of labor days. Land ownership (however nominal) and the land rent were the peculiarities of the Bulgarian collectivized system. These features were not part of the Soviet system and Bulgarian theoreticians have often pointed out that they constituted a special contribution to the treasury of Marxism-Leninism. The land rent was sharply reduced during the 1950's and had practically been abolished by 1959. In addition to the liberal terms of membership, the collectives were granted financial and material benefits such as tax remittances, credit preferences, priorities in the supply of building materials, seeds, and fertilizer, and free agronomical and technical help.

During this initial phase a land reform was passed in June, 1946. Though ostensibly designed to help poorer peasants, this was actually part of the preparatory process for further socialization. Private land ownership was limited to 200 decares (300 in Dobruja). Any privately-held land in excess of that was nationalized. It was a small measure, affecting only about 1.75 million decares, or 3.6 per cent of the total arable land. About 1.5 million decares was distributed among some 129,000 farmers—a little more than ten decares to each farmer. The balance of a quarter of a million decares went to create the State Land Fund, the basis of the future State Farms.

The aim of this reform was partly political—to preempt the appeal of Nikola Petkov and the Agrarians, who had left the Fatherland Front government and gone into opposition in 1945. It was also designed, however, to weaken the prosperous farmers, the kulaks, and thus undermine the private agrarian structure. The ten decares given to 129,000 farmers did not strengthen their recipients at all. They were intended to win the peasants' confidence in the government and make them less suspicious of collectivization, as were the generous terms in which it was initially presented.

The Second Phase: 1948–49

On December 26, 1947, industry and banking in Bulgaria were nationalized. The new regime faced a big job in reorganizing

[5] Dellin. *op. cit.*, p. 293.

what it had just acquired, and therefore was chary of beginning a vigorous collectivization campaign. But, mindful of Lenin's dictum that "the existence of private peasant farms . . . in great dimensions gives birth to capitalism," it set about preparing the ground still more thoroughly for the campaign to come. This preparation mainly consisted of blows aimed at private property.

In February, 1948, the National Assembly approved a law for the "compulsory purchase" of the larger types of agricultural machinery belonging to private farmers. This involved some 80 per cent of all the agricultural machinery in the country—allegedly "owned by Kulaks."[6] The equipment thus obtained—tractors, threshing machines, tractor plows—became the basis of the state Machine Tractor Stations (MTS). Also at the beginning of 1948, the Machine Tractor Stations which then existed became state enterprises; they had previously been operating on a cooperative basis. A little later it was decided that the collective farm members must place at the disposal of the collectives all their fit animals as well as all the land they had given over to "permanent cultures" —orchards, vineyards, etc.

An eloquent indication of the hostility to collectivization even among Party members was contained in a Central Committee directive of September, 1948:

> The greater number of leading Communists, Party and Fatherland Front activists in the villages are not members of the collective farms, and not a few of them are carrying out an open campaign against them. . . . The foundation of TKZS in the village is not a private initiative, but the Party line. Therefore you cannot be a Party member and fight against TKZS. . . . If we remain with the small private farms we will return to capitalism.[7]

Another discriminatory policy against private ownership was ordered in November, 1948; it reduced the private plots of collective farmers to between two and five decares, depending on the intensity of production in the region concerned. The number of livestock on these private plots was limited to one cow, three to five sheep, two pigs, and an unlimited amount of poultry.

But despite measures such as these and the glaring favoritism shown to the collectives, the collectivized area increased at a snail's pace. By the end of 1948, it accounted for only 6.2 per cent of the

---

[6] *Otechestven Front* (Sofia), January 29, 1950.
[7] *Resolutions and Decisions*, Part IV, p. 101.

arable land. Instead of the four million decares set as the target for 1948, 2,923,800 were under the collectivized plow.[8]

The directives for the First Five-Year Plan (1948–53) provided that the arable land held by collective and state farms should have increased tenfold by 1953.[9] This meant an increase from some 3 to 30 million decares, about 60 per cent of the total arable land. But by the end of 1949, the collectivized percentage stood at only 11.3. One of the main reasons for this slowness was peasant resistance to the "energetic" measures employed to persuade them to enter or establish collectives. A Central Committee statement in June, 1949, contained the following admission:

> The Politburo and the Party organizations take timely measures for the decisive correcting of the faults and distortions allowed to happen with the founding of the collective farms. . . . The Plenum of the CC finds it necessary that special governmental commissions study the counties where these distortions are the most prevalent . . .[10]

It is not difficult to surmise what these "distortions—or the peasant reactions to them—were.

Other reasons for the disappointing lack of progress were the serious international and domestic distractions of the period. In June, 1948, Tito's break with the Cominform caused serious international tension; internally, the power struggle between the Muscovites and the home Communists led to the execution of Kostov in December, 1949. Once again other considerations had distracted the attention of the regime from the task of agricultural reorganization.

The Third Phase

The internal struggle saw the triumph of Chervenkov and the beginning of his personal rule. It was both a reflection of Chervenkov's character and policy and a sign of greater political stability that the greatest annual leap in the whole collectivization campaign occurred in 1950. The collectivized area increased from 11.3 per cent at the beginning of the year to 44.2 per cent at the end of it.

[8] Dellin, *op. cit.*, p. 296. Dellin gives the figure in hectares.
[9] *Resolutions and Decisions*, Part IV, p. 152.
[10] *Ibid.*, Part IV, p. 152.

The most important sign that the campaign was now on in earnest was the publication in May, 1950, of the Model Statute of the Collective Farms[11]—the organizational and procedural manual for existing and future collectives. This statute, similar to its Soviet counterpart except for the fiction of continued private ownership and the fact of the land rent,[12] remained in force with various amendments until March, 1967, when a completely new statute was approved.

Armed with this organizational framework, the authorities now set to the task of forcing the peasants into it. By the end of the year, an impressive collectivization figure had been reached, but at least some peasants had been forced into the collectives by pressure which went far beyond the bounds of normal "persuasion." The excesses in Kula county near the Yugoslav border, and in Teteven, northeast of Sofia, provoked rioting by the peasants, in which it was officially admitted that Komsomol members joined. A plenum of the Central Committee of the Dimitrov Youth Organization (DSNM—Komsomol) held in June, 1951, decided "to review the positions of those members of the DSNM who took part in the plundering of the equipment and animals of the TKZS, and to expel the organizers and inciters of these actions."[13] It was officially admitted that about four to five per cent of farmers already in the collectives wished to leave them;[14] one may assume that the real number was considerably higher.

Earlier in 1951—in March—the Party Central Committee had held a special session to discuss "the distortion of the Party and government policy in Kula county and in the village of Yablanitsa, in Teteven county." The entire Party committees of Kula county and Yablanitsa village were dismissed, some of their members expelled from the Party and some of these were even handed over to the Public Prosecutor.[15]

These open manifestations of peasant discontent seriously marred the satisfaction which the collectivization figures might otherwise have given. Finding a scapegoat for this embarrassing situation, Chervenkov dismissed his Minister of Agriculture, Titko

[11] *Darzhaven Vestnik* (Sofia), May 13, 1950.

[12] These liberal stipulations were, however, whittled down in the statute. Members of collectives could now sell their land only to the collective farm or its members and the maximum to be paid in land rent was reduced from 40 per cent to 30; Dellin, *op. cit.*, p. 297.

[13] *Narodna Mladezh* (Sofia), June 17, 1951.

[14] *Otechestven Front*, September 21, 1951.

[15] *Resolutions and Decisions*, Part IV, pp. 291–93.

Chernokolev, from his government position and from his Polit-buro and Central Committee posts early in 1951. A plenum of the Party Central Committee in September, 1951, then decided on general measures of consolidation of the collectives, improvement in the method of payment to the peasants, and a stepped-up prop-aganda campaign urging the advantages of collectivization.

After the turbulence and bitterness of 1950, progress in collec-tivization was minimal in 1951, a year of consolidation and ap-peasement. At the end of that year 47.5 per cent[16] of the arable land had been collectivized, an increase of only 3.2 per cent. The following year, however, saw another sizeable increase—to 60.5 per cent.[17] Unlike the "leap forward" in 1950, there is no reliable evidence to suggest that this increase was due to brute force and compulsion. The propaganda campaign, decreed in 1951, may have had some effect, together with the better conditions in the collec-tives introduced in the same year. Probably the most important reason, however, was the mood of resignation among large numbers of the private peasantry. The back of peasant resistance had cer-tainly been broken in 1950 and, once collectivization was resumed in earnest in 1952, many private peasants must simply have bowed to the inevitable.

In the three years between 1953 and 1955, collectivization was virtually suspended. At the end of 1955, the figure stood at 62.5 per cent of the arable land,[18] an increase of 2.5 per cent for the three-year period. The reasons for this stagnation were mainly political: this was the period of the new course following the death of Stalin in March, 1953. In 1956, however, the year of the April plenum which, in some ways was the culmination of the gradual reforms carried out after 1953, collectivization was stepped up again. At the end of that year, the collectivized percentage stood at 77.4. The pace was slackened again in 1957, which saw only a 2.6 per cent gain[19] but, in the first six months of 1958, the final spurt was made, obviously with a view to the Seventh Party Congress in June of that year. At the congress, Premier Yugov was able to announce that 92 per cent of the arable land had been collectivized; the rest, mainly the mountainous areas, was considered unsuitable for col-lectivization.[20] Bulgaria had become the first Communist state

[16] *Zemedelsko Zname* (Sofia), December 3, 1952.
[17] *Rabotnichesko Delo* (Sofia), February 26, 1954.
[18] *Statistical Yearbook*, 1956, p. 54.
[19] *Rabotnichesko Delo*, March 16, 1958.
[20] *Trud* (Sofia), June 6, 1958.

after the Soviet Union to have collectivized its agriculture. What had previously been Bulgaria's most outstanding physical characteristic—the patchwork quilt of tiny peasant holdings—had been completely transformed in a little over ten years.

State Farms

State farms, owned directly by the state and staffed by salaried government employees, have never played an important part in the Communist agriculture of Bulgaria, as they have, for example, in that of neighboring Rumania. By the end of 1956, their number stood at 49 and they covered 1,744,000 decares of arable land. By 1960, they numbered 67, with an average size of 33,673 decares, and this number has remained constant.[21] They are managed centrally by a special department of the Ministry of Agriculture in Sofia.

Though a permanent feature of every Communist agricultural system, state farms were known throughout Eastern Europe under the "bourgeois-feudal" regimes. In Bulgaria, they first appeared toward the end of the last century and by 1939 there were as many as 56, although they covered a total area of only 168,000 decares. They were model farms, managed by specialists, and were largely experimental. The Communist state farms are similar in character. They are favored with the best equipment and scientific know-how but their output has never been commensurate with their superior resources. They achieved a profit for the first time only in 1957 and, like their counterparts elsewhere in Eastern Europe and the Soviet Union, have continued to be one of the biggest disappointments in a generally disappointing sector of the economy.

The Merging of the Collective Farms

The merging of collective farms—the amalgamation of a number of smaller farms into one large farm—was a preparatory measure for the "great leap forward" of 1959 and 1960. Isolated mergers of some very small farms had taken place as early as 1953, but the practice had been discontinued. As late as December, 1957, Todor

[21] *Bulgarian Pocket Statistical Yearbook,* 1960, p. 80. The area covered by the State farms is, for convenience, included under *collectivized* land. Strictly speaking, the land covered by both collectives and state farms should be called *socialized* land.

Zhivkov was cautioning against hurried mergers. He was not against mergers in principle but advised careful preparation, quoting the old Bulgarian proverb: "Three times measure and then cut."[22]

Nine months later, however, against all forecasts and expectations, the merger campaign was in full swing with the same Zhivkov defending it on the grounds that small farms up to 10,000 decares were "not profitable and . . . unable to make a big enough contribution to rapidly increased and cheaper rural production." Merging would greatly increase the financial resources of the collectives and thereby ensure bigger capital investment in agriculture as a whole. However, there must be no "force or administrative pressure" applied; "the cooperative farmer must be persuaded," said Zhivkov.[23]

The merger campaign was carried out in whirlwind style and there must have been considerable chaos in the countryside during the second half of 1958. It was during this campaign that the confusion about the whole of Botevgrad being transformed into one gigantic farm or commune arose.[24] Zhivkov's earlier warning that the matter needed careful preparation obviously went by the board. It was first announced at the end of 1958 that merging was virtually completed and that all but a few of the existing 3,450 collectives had been merged into 644 new farms averaging about 70,000 decares in size.[25] This was considerably bigger than the average size of a kolkhoz in the Soviet Union and far bigger than anything in the rest of Eastern Europe. Later, however, the number was increased to 932 and the average size decreased to 42,000 decares. This made the Bulgarian collectives somewhat smaller than their Soviet counterparts but still much the biggest in Eastern Europe.

The mergers had a good deal to recommend them. They enabled large-scale work methods to be applied and, as Zhivkov forecast, increased the financial independence of the collectives by strengthening their "indivisible funds"—the central fund of each collective from which major expenses were met. The indivisible funds were also strengthened by the steady abolition of the payment of land rent, a distinctive feature of the Bulgarian collective system. By the end of 1958 it had been abolished in half the collectives and by

[22] *Rabotnichesko Delo*, December 3, 1957.
[23] *Ibid.*, October 25, 1958.
[24] See Chapter 5.
[25] Radio Sofia, December 25, 1958.

the end of the following year had been practically abolished altogether.

The reorganization also had the effect of making the MTS (Machine Tractor Stations) less necessary than before. By 1960 there were 209 MTS's. Like the state farms, they were directly owned and operated by the government. The Party's watchdog in the countryside, they were controlled by a manager, a trusted Communist who was not only responsible for the work of the station but also for general supervision of agricultural policy in the area under his sphere of competence. The administrative-territorial reform of 1959, however, had led to many former local Party officials becoming managers of collective farms and this automatically meant a diminution of the authority of the MTS manager over the collective. Moreover, the greater financial strength of the merged collectives would enable them to purchase their own machines and thus be less dependent on the MTS. This seems to have been the aim immediately after the mergers were completed; the Zhivkov Theses of January, 1959, envisaged the gradual purchasing of MTS inventory by the new collectives. (In 1958, this practice had begun on a large scale in the Soviet Union.) This was delayed, probably because the original hopes for the financial strength of the collectives were too rosy. But in February, 1962, a government decree authorized 250 of the more prosperous collectives—about one quarter of the total—to begin purchasing MTS equipment that was "new and in good condition."[26] By 1965 the number of MTS's had dwindled to 82.[27] This gradual elimination of the MTS continued, and by 1967, these former "rural bastions of the Party" were operating only in areas where the collectives were still not in a position to buy them out.

Perhaps the greatest weakness of the merged collectives was that, by their very size, they further weakened the sense of participation on the part of the member. The regime was not unaware of this problem. For instance, the merging of the farms led to a considerable increase in the size of the work teams and the farmers were rewarded on a group rather than on an individual basis. On realizing that this was decreasing incentive, the regime switched back to smaller working teams and individual payment. Again, after the consolidation of collectives, it was impossible to continue the direct participation of all members in meetings. Representatives were sent from the various farms units to a central meeting

[26] *Rabotnichesko Delo*, February 22, 1962.
[27] *Statistical Yearbook*, 1966, p. 211.

point. This reduced any small sense of participation and belonging which may have existed and the feeling grew that all decisions were imposed from above. To counteract this feeling, the regime continually urged collective farms to cultivate "intra-cooperative democracy" so that all members would have a say in matters affecting finances, remuneration, norms, organization, etc. It was, however, difficult to see how "intra-cooperative democracy" could work properly on 42,000 decares.

The Private Plots

All collective farmers are entitled to private plots. Every household, according to the Collective Farm Statute, had between two decares and five decares of land at its disposal for private use. In the intensively cultivated areas the plots were nearer to two decares; in the grain-growing districts they were closer to five. The general assembly (the governing body of each collective) determined the exact size of the plots but the decision of which areas were "intensive" or "extensive" was left to the Ministry of Agriculture.

The private plot is not the same as privately-owned land. The private plot cannot be sold and no hired labor can work on it. The livestock on the private plot, which *is* the private property of its owner, is limited under the statutes as follows: one cow or buffalo cow with offspring, or one to two nanny goats with offspring; up to two sows with offspring; three to five sheep with offspring; one donkey or mule; an unlimited number of poultry, rabbits, and beehives.

In the Bulgarian, as in the other collectivized systems of Eastern Europe, the private plots have always occupied a special and controversial place. They are the closest thing to private peasant ownership still remaining under the collective system. Hence they are an affront to the dogmatic purism of many Communist officials. But there have always been more practical reasons for local officialdom to dislike them. Since they were *private* plots, it was inevitable that the collective farmers would tend to spend much more time working on them than on common land. Hence on many farms the authorities were tempted to violate the farm statutes by encroaching on the integrity of the plots, illegally reducing their holdings of livestock, cutting down their size or, in some cases, seeking to abolish them altogether. By 1959, the situation had become so serious that the central authorities felt compelled to intervene; they warned collective farm chairmen against interfering with the plots and defended the necessity of their continuance.[28]

The reason for their benevolence was the vital role the plots played in the agricultural production of the nation. In 1958, one third of all the sheep, 38 per cent of all the cattle (57 per cent of the cows) and 40 per cent of the pigs were in private ownership. They produced 52 per cent of the total output of meat and 40 per cent of the milk.[29] Three years later the percentages were considerably lower: 27 per cent of the meat and 26 per cent of the milk.[30]

Generally, the relative importance of the plots to total production has continued to fall off in recent years, mainly because of the gradual strengthening of the collective sector and the preferential treatment it has received in fertilizer and scientific techniques. But it is still significant enough to force the government to continue, and even strengthen, its encouragement of private plot production. The new model statutes of the collective farms, published in 1967 and completely replacing the statutes of 1950,[31] allowed the farmers to own equipment and building machinery for the cultivation of their private plots. They also allowed the plots to own seven pigs instead of the previous two. In the last few years the government has also been far more solicitous than before in providing fodder, artificial fertilizer, and insecticides for the use of private plot members. One should note, however, that the new model statutes did contain some rather restrictive provisions on the private plots which the old statutes did not. For example, it was stipulated that the plots should be used "mainly for the production of fodder" (of which Bulgarian agriculture has always been very short) and that the plots could be subjected to "cultivation in common" if the general assembly of the collective so decided. These were ominous provisions and can best be interpreted as an attempt to diminish the "privateness" of the plots and bring them firmly under the jurisdiction of the collective. Whether this will have any serious practical effect on their operation remains to be seen.

[28] See, for example, the speech by Minister of Agriculture Ivan Prumov to an agricultural conference in Sofia in November 1959; *Rabotnichesko Delo*, November 26, 1959.

[29] U.N. *Economic Survey of Europe*, 1960, chap. VI, p. 32.

[30] "The Performance of the Private and Public Sectors in Bloc Agriculture," Radio Free Europe Research (Munich), January 20, 1965.

[31] *Rabotnichesko Delo*, February 23, 1967.

The New Collective Farm Statutes

Though the model collective farm statutes of 1950 had been considerably amended in 1953, 1955, and 1957, it was becoming clear by 1965 that they were very much out of date and that, in any case, Bulgaria's new economic reform would necessitate extensive changes in collective farm organization. The fact that the government took this matter very seriously was shown by its cancellation of its original intention to publish a new statute in November, 1965, and its decision to refer the draft which had already been prepared to a special commission, headed by Todor Zhivkov himself, for further deliberation and more public discussion. This discussion, in specialized journals and the daily press, was extensive and "democratic" by all previous standards. The final draft was published in all major Bulgarian newspapers on January 23, 1967, and finally approved at a Congress of Collective Farms the following March. It was at this congress that a national Union of Collective Farms was established. In 1966 and 1967, similar unions were established in Hungary, Rumania, and Czechoslovakia. It was an encouraging move, since it created an institutional framework for what could develop into an agricultural pressure group in the countries concerned. More immediately, the union would serve as some counterweight to the large and powerful agricultural-economic "trusts" established by the new economic reform, such as "Bulgarplod," and to the agricultural procurement agencies.

The new statutes had several interesting features, apart from the changes affecting the private plots which have already been mentioned. Basic to the document was the entirely new concept of placing agriculture on the same level as industry, as an integral and important sector of the national economy. Equally basic was the ideological shift away from the original concept that the Bulgarian collective farm was an institution in which the peasants had "voluntarily" placed their private land, which was still essentially theirs. Thus the payment of land rent, virtually discontinued in practice by 1959, now disappeared completely from the new statutes and, with it, Bulgaria's "unique" contribution to the history of collectivization. Similarly, in those passages of the new statutes dealing with ownership and the terms of settlement on expulsion from the collective, no mention was made of the right of the farmer or of his heirs to restitution of his land, or of the amount of land equivalent to the holdings he had originally brought into the collective. In the case of the private plots, as mentioned above, though further material support for them was decreed, there were other stipulations obviously designed to undermine their "privateness."

In their practical aspects, however, there was much that was progressive and encouraging in the new statutes. Bulgaria's collective farmers now received benefits and rights which had never officially been theirs, but had belonged to the working class. They were granted periods of paid vacation and brought under the purview of the national Labor Code regarding work safety and health. The wives of the collective farmers were now also entitled to maternity benefits and to children's allowances and the farmers themselves to compensation for temporary or permanent disablement. In addition, the collective farm was now legally obliged to give assistance to its members for the construction of cottages and other household needs.

Most important were the stipulations which now officially guaranteed every collective farmer a minimum wage. Thus Bulgaria achieved a new "first" in Eastern European Communist agriculture by doing away with the *trudoden*, or labor day, system of payment. Payments under this system were determined first by deducting operating costs from the gross income of the farm, then by deducting the necessary allocations to be made to the farm's "indivisible" (central) fund, and then by dividing what was left of the gross income by the total number of labor days worked on the farm; this determined the average payment per labor day unit. This system provided no incentive for the farmer, since working harder or more efficiently had no visible effect on earnings. Actually, a rudimentary guaranteed wage system, combined with a modified *trudoden* system, began to be introduced in Bulgaria in 1962. The guaranteed minimum was fixed at 1.8 (new) leva per labor-day. The aim was to equalize the wages of collective farmers with those of state farm workers and the novelty of the scheme was that the state made a direct contribution to the wage fund of each farm, the size depending on the harvest outcome. Now the new statutes implicitly abolished the *trudoden* and went over completely to a direct wage system.

After setting aside a part of the total collective farm income for contributions to a state fund for poor harvest and natural calamities, a portion to maintain the central Union of Collective Farms, and another for other funds of the collective itself, and after appropriate deductions for insurance fees, what was left

was to be distributed (minus income tax) among the collective
farm members according to their "participation in work." Thus, the
farmer was still a residual claimant on the income of the collective
as a whole; but still the new system removed many of the uncer-
tainties and inequalities of the old. The annual advanced pay per
production unit (see below) was fixed at up to 80 per cent of the
planned total amount of labor remuneration and, when the production results were known, extra payment could be given to bring
the wages up to 90 per cent of the planned total. The new statutes
also allowed each farm greater flexibility to devise, with the approval of its general assembly, various methods of tying the remuneration of the farmers to the final results achieved. It is too early
to say how this change has affected incomes. Collective farm incomes had been rising steadily in any case in the early 1960's, and
in 1965 the average earnings amounted to 185 leva.[32] Much, of
course, still depended on the harvests; but generally the Bulgarian
collective farm, through these measures, moved toward a higher
and more stable standard of living. This impression was strengthened the following June by new regulations that increased the basic
old-age pension from ten to twenty (new) leva per month, and
added five leva monthly to invalid pensions for collective farm
workers.

The new statutes contained intriguing provisions for organization of work on the collectives. The basic form of labor organization was to be the production brigade, to which farmers were
assigned permanently. The brigade was to be given permanent use
of fixed sections of land and other basic means of production; it
was organized on an internally self-supporting basis. The size and
composition of each brigade was to be determined by the administrative council of the collective farm. The brigades themselves and
their ruling council were then elected by the farm membership.

Work brigades, of course, were not new in the collective system
of Bulgaria or other Eastern European countries. The old Bulgarian
statute referred to brigades, but did not say that they were to be
the basic form of work organization. And what *was* new—and quite
an original departure—were the references to the "internal, self-
supporting basis" of the brigade and the fact that the brigades and
the brigade council were to be elected by the total farm membership. This was designed both to increase incentives and to break
down the highly impersonal character of the collectives. The

[32] "The Spectrum of Wage Payments to Collective Farmers," *Radio Free
Europe Research*, July 13, 1966.

members, instead of feeling themselves to be very small parts of a vast organization, would be directly responsible for a much smaller part of the great undertaking. It was an effort to solve one of collectivization's great problems. As evidence of the regime's flexibility and willingness to experiment in this regard, the new statutes contained a provision allowing for other kinds of work organization to be adopted as the collectives thought fit.

This system of work incorporated some of the features of an earlier incentive scheme which, again, bore the hallmarks of originality. This was the "accord" system, a form of payment by results. This system allowed individuals, families, or groups to farm specific areas of cropland. As remuneration, the individual or family got 50 per cent of the crop over the planned output. The family or group was allowed a great deal of independence by the farm's central management in organizing its own work.

In further efforts to stimulate "internal democracy" on the collectives, the statutes strongly underlined the importance of the farm's general assembly as its supreme legislative organ. More specifically, they provided for secret and direct balloting in the election of the management. This was an important innovation that had already been introduced on some collectives in 1966. More than one candidate could now be proposed for an office and a minimum of half the votes cast was necessary for election. The general assembly of the collective was to meet not less than four times a year and, along the lines of production committees in industry, which included representatives of both management and workers, a production council was to be established on every collective farm. Its duties were not defined in the statutes but its obvious aim was to create some semblance of joint consultation in these huge agricultural undertakings.

The last important change made by the new statutes in the organization of collective farms related to the different funds managed by them. From now on there were to be three main funds on the collectives, although others could be established if considered necessary. These were:

The Expansion and Technical Improvement Fund, financed by deductions from the total income, by amortization deductions, by income from liquidation of basic funds, etc. This fund is used for the introduction of scientific and technical progress in production, for the expansion and strengthening of the material-production basis of the farm, and for turnover needs.

The Social and Cultural Fund, financed by annual deductions from the total income of the collective farm; it is used to provide assistance to disabled farmers and to finance the cultural and educational activity of the farms.

The Reserve Fund for Remuneration of Labor, financed by annual deductions from the total income of the collective farm, is used to compensate the losses of the individual production units in years of poor harvest or natural calamities and to "consolidate" the annual labor remuneration of the collective farm members.

Under the old statutes, the most important fund had been the Indivisible Fund. This was used for buying the means of production (machinery, equipment, livestock); for financing new planting areas and irrigation work; for the construction of agricultural, administrative, and recreational buildings; and for repaying bank credits. The Indivisible Fund was now abolished and its responsibilities divided between the Expansion and Technical Improvement Fund and the Social and Cultural Improvement Fund.

The other old funds now abolished included:

The Reserve Seed Fund and Reserve Fodder Fund, in which 10 to 15 per cent of the seeds and the fodder necessary for one year were kept and renewed each year;

The Poor Harvest and Calamities Fund, in which a reserve stock of products was kept for use in case of need;

The Cultural Fund, for the upkeep of public nurseries, for the training of cadres, and for assistance to the reading rooms and other cultural undertakings;

The Assistance to Disabled Farmers Fund, for assistance to injured old, and disabled farmers, and for payment of remuneration during maternity leaves, etc.

The new financial organization is much simpler and should make for a more efficient administration than in the past.

Bulgaria as Innovator

Even this brief and rather simplified description of the new statutes reveals one important characteristic of Bulgaria's agricultural legislators: their willingness to initiate and experiment. In their provisions for a guaranteed minimum wage and the responsibilities given to the permanent brigades, the Bulgarian statutes were perhaps more "progressive" than any others in Eastern Europe or the Soviet Union. Indeed, only Hungary, which since the beginning of the 1960's has pioneered new and more imaginative agricultural organization, has shown the same spirit of innovation.[33] These, however, were not the first examples of Bulgarian agricultural initiative. The decision to retain the Bulgarian Agrarian Union as a puppet party showed at least a certain independence of thought which was not evinced in Hungary or Rumania, not to mention the Soviet Union. Moreover, although Bulgaria had opted for the full Soviet-type *kolkhoz* rather than going through an intermediary form of agricultural association as Rumania had, the institution of the land rent *was* a unique feature which, though it did not obviate the necessity for "forceful persuasion" in the collectivization campaigns, did at least sugar the pill for many reluctant peasants. In the late 1950's, the merger campaign and the creation of the biggest collectives in Eastern Europe outside the Soviet Union again showed independence of thinking, if not soundness of judgment. Finally, the new statutes of 1967 reflected a boldness and willingness to experiment that was quite remarkable, and some of the innovations they contained had been in operation well before the statutes were published. In many respects, the Bulgarian regime can indeed be faulted as an unimaginative copier of the Soviet Union. But since it adopted the conventional basis of collectivization, it has sometimes shown itself more pioneer than imitator in agrarian policy.

[33] On Hungary, see Fred E. Dohrs, "Incentives in Communist Agriculture: The Hungarian Models," *Slavic Review* (Baltimore), Vol. XXVII, No. 1, March, 1968, pp. 23–38. See also, J. F. Brown, *The New Eastern Europe: The Khrushchev Era and After* (New York, 1966), pp. 140–42.

10

Educational Policy and the Problems of Youth

I. EDUCATIONAL POLICY

IMMEDIATELY AFTER her liberation in 1878, Bulgaria instituted an energetic educational program to catch up on what had been missed during five centuries of Ottoman rule. The 1879 Tirnovo Constitution provided for free and obligatory elementary and first-level secondary education.

The educational system in Bulgaria until 1944 followed the basic European educational pattern. The elementary schools were attended by children from seven to ten years of age. The first-level secondary schools (pro-gymnasia) admitted children from the age of eleven to thirteen for three years of study after graduation from the elementary school. The second-level secondary school (gymnasium) had a course of five years of study.

Children completing the primary (elementary) school could attend a three-year professional school and could either learn a trade or take practical courses in agriculture. Graduates of the first level secondary school (pro-gymnasium) could attend professional or vocational schools, which offered studies in engineering, agronomy, commerce, theology, music, etc. Graduates of the gymnasium (second-level secondary school) were admitted to universities or other institutions of higher education on the basis of grades and a competitive examination.

Besides these schools, which were public, there existed a number of foreign private schools with a curriculum similar to the secondary public schools (gymnasia). In these schools, the teaching was carried out in west European languages and represented an important link between Western civilization and Bulgaria. These private schools, and especially the American College at Simeonovo (near Sofia), enjoyed a special esteem.

One of the most important achievements of Bulgarian education was the reduction in the rate of illiteracy. At the time of liberation (1878) over 90 per cent of the population of school age and over was illiterate, and only 30 per cent of the children of school age (seven to 14 years) were enrolled in schools. At the beginning of World War II, the proportion of illiterates amounted to between 20 and 25 per cent.[1] Illiteracy would have been lower but for the presence of the older generation, which had received no education immediately after the liberation, and for the presence of the Turkish and gypsy elements whose opposition to compulsory school attendance proved a considerable stumbling block.

First Measures Under the Communists

In education, perhaps even more than in any other sphere, the Bulgarian Communists do hold themselves open to the charge of slavishly imitating the Soviet example, and this policy of imitation has continued right up to the present day.

Before setting up their own educational edifice, however, the Communists had first to destroy all traces of the old one. This was done by a series of measures between 1944 and 1948. First, practically all textbooks published before World War II were gradually replaced. Then all school and university teachers with a "record of fascist and reactionary activities"[2] were replaced by persons loyal to the Fatherland Front. The list of unreliables was a large one, and the interpretation of "fascist and reactionary activities" was very broad. Not all teachers in old Bulgaria were qualified to give their students a good, liberal education in the Western sense of the term. But the ranks of those purged included many distinguished and qualified educators and the ranks

[1] L. A. D. Dellin (ed.), *Bulgaria* (New York, 1957), p. 197.
[2] *Darzhaven Vestnik* (Sofia), November 3, 1944.

of those replacing them were dominated by ignorant hacks who were hardly qualified even to teach Marxism-Leninism properly. As with the staff, so with the students: the higher educational institutions were to be open to "working people and the sons and daughters of working people."[3] Persons guilty of "fascist and anti-popular manifestations" were barred.

According to the new "Dimitrov" Constitution of 1947, all schools were taken over by the state. Private schools were not officially forbidden but special permission was needed for their establishment and, if granted, state supervision was still enforced. In practice, all private schools, which had mostly been of a professional nature, were nationalized. All foreign schools were closed for the academic year 1948–49. Foreign diplomatic missions could maintain schools but only the huge Soviet embassy ever made use of this provision. After 1949, no religious denomination was allowed to maintain a school of any kind except theological seminaries for the training of priests, and these were allowed only after special ministerial permission.

The Dimitrov Constitution stipulated that education should be carried out in a "democratic and progressive spirit." This injunction was later amplified by a joint resolution of the Party Central Committee and the Council of Ministers in August, 1949. Education was now to be carried out in the spirit of socialism, based on Marxist-Leninist teaching and the indissoluble brotherly friendship with the Soviet Union. Bulgarian educational policy should use "the rich experience of the Soviet Union."[4]

This resolution was adopted at a time when political power in Bulgaria was clearly passing into the hands of Vulko Chervenkov. Traicho Kostov had been expelled from the Party the previous June and was to be executed the following December. Georgi Dimitrov had died in Moscow the previous month and Vassil Kolarov, who had succeeded Dimitrov as Prime Minister, was old and ailing and died a few months afterwards. In Eastern Europe as a whole, all states were under the *Gleichschaltung* foreshadowed by the establishment of the Cominform and the expulsion of Tito from it. One of the worst-hit victims of this process in Bulgaria was to be the educational system.

Marxist-Leninist courses—involving dialectical materialism, the

[3] *Ibid.*, September 24, 1948.
[4] *Ibid.*, August 24, 1949.

fundamentals of Marxism-Leninism and the history of the CPSU as well as the BCP—became obligatory for all students after the kindergarten stage.[5] No religious instruction was allowed in schools. The study of the Russian language was given emphatic priority over west European languages. The universities and higher educational establishments completely lost their autonomy, as did the Academy of Sciences, which was brought completely under the control of the Ministry of Education. In future, the Council of Ministers was to approve all the work plans of the Academy and the Academy was held responsible to the Council of Ministers for fulfilling them.[6] Needless to say, all "suspicious" elements, including many distinguished scholars, were excluded from the academy. The most important early change in the schools was the reduction of schooling in the gymnasium (medium school) from five to four years, which reduced the total educational period of the new general schools of education from twelve to eleven years. This innovation, on the Soviet model, was introduced in August, 1949.

The practical aim behind the whole of the regime's educational policy had been well put by Minister of Education Kiril Dramaliev in August, 1948, when introducing a new law on education in the National Assembly. It was to bring general education closer to the practice of production in the national economy, to secure a faster rate of vocational training ("polytechnizitation") so that the professional schools might turn out cadres with broad scientific, technical, and political qualifications.[7]

In the years that followed, an average of 16,000 to 17,000 students graduated annually from the gymnasia, but their quality and the use made of them left much to be desired. By 1957, it was time to amend the system. A Party and government decree issued

[5] A decree of November 9, 1954, even extended Communist indoctrination to kindergartens. After saying that kindergartens would be opened for children between three and seven, the decree stated that their purpose, *inter alia*, was "to lay the foundation to their Communist education." *Izvestia na Presidiuma na Narodnoto Subranie* (Sofia), No. 90, 1954. (At the end of 1950, *Darzhaven Vestnik*, the Official Gazette, became *Izvestia na Presidiuma na Narodnoto Subranie*. At the beginning of 1963, it once again became *Darzhaven Vestnik*.)

[6] Law on the Academy of Sciences, October 11, 1949, *Darzhaven Vestnik*, No. 235, 1949.

[7] *Otechestven Front* (Sofia), August 27, 1948.

in July of that year was very frank about the deficiencies that had accumulated:

> Serious mistakes have been made that handicapped the development of the schools of general education. Certain questions on education were decided hastily. No mature consideration on different school reorganizations was at hand. The transplanting of the Soviet school experience was done mechanically. The pedagogical science was inadequately applied in schools. . . . The inheritance of the positive values from the past school system was underrated.
>
> In the professional as well as in higher education there are also serious shortcomings. . . . The practical preparedness of the young specialists with university education is inadequate. Scientific research in the high educational institutes is lagging.[8]

The decree restored the pre-Communist five-year schooling period in the gymnasia, thereby reviving the original twelve-year period of general education. But its main emphasis was on trying to improve the link between education and the requirements of the economy. Thus, experimental vocational training was to be directly introduced into the curricula of some gymnasia in the school year 1957–58, while some gymnasia in rural areas were now required to undergo some form of vocational training connected with economic tasks. The network of professional schools was also to be expanded and their staffs were to spend part of their vacations in productive work in industry. This emphasis on vocational training was accompanied by stern warnings that Communist education was not to be neglected.

The Structure of Education After 1957

As a result of the changes introduced in 1957, the structure of Bulgarian education was as follows:

Pre-School Education: Kindergartens. Children from three to seven years of age could attend kindergartens if such were available. Attendance was not compulsory, but was an absolute necessity if both parents worked. In the school year 1956–57, there were 6,219 kindergartens attended by over 270,000 children.[9]

---

[8] *Izvestia na Presidiuma na Narodnoto Subranie*, No. 59, July 5, 1957.

[9] The statistics for numbers of various kinds of educational establishments and their attendance are taken from the *Bulgarian Statistical Yearbook, 1956*, pp. 114–15.

Schools for General Education. The schools for general education again provided a twelve-year course (twelve classes or grades), divided into basic and medium schools. The basic schools contained the first seven classes. The first to fourth classes provided elementary education; the fifth to seventh classes provided pro-gymnasium or "first level" secondary school. The medium schools went from eighth to twelfth class; the medium school or gymnasium was also known as a "second level" secondary school.

The basic schools were free of charge and compulsory for all children of Bulgarian citizens from seven to fifteen years of age. For the ethnic minorities, state schools were available, with teaching carried in the native language of the pupils, although Bulgarian was an obligatory subject.

The general educational schools were coeducational. An extensive system of evening classes was provided at the general educational school level, to give workers a chance to catch up on their education and improve their qualifications. To graduate from the gymnasium (at the twelfth grade), students took an examination and, if successful, were awarded a diploma which was necessary for entering an institution of university status. In 1956, there were 6,803 schools for general education with over 1,100,000 students. In the gymnasia alone, there were 165,363 students.

Teachers' Training (Pedagogical) Schools. These schools were at the same level as medium schools or gymnasia. Their main purpose was to prepare the future teachers for the first to fourth grade level as well as the organizers of the children's pioneer organizations. Students wishing to enter the pedagogical schools had to have completed the first seven grades of general education. In 1956, there were 22 pedagogical schools with almost 8,989 students.

In addition, there were also pedagogical institutes for the future fifth- to seventh-grade (or pro-gymnasium) teachers. These institutes gave two-year courses of a "semi-university" standard.

Medium Professional Schools (Technical Colleges, and Vocational Schools). All students of the professional schools had to have completed at least seven grades of basic education and, for some schools, as many as all twelve grades. There were day and evening professional schools and the student-workers attending the latter had to have at least two years of practical work experience.

There were twenty-five different professional schools (technical colleges) in Bulgaria in 1958, covering different branches of industry and agriculture. A graduate of any one of them could become a candidate for a place in a university department corresponding to his specialty. For example, a graduate of a technical college for industrial chemistry could continue to study chemistry at the university. In the academic year 1957–58 there were 154 professional schools with nearly 64,000 students.

In addition to these professional schools, some of the bigger factories and mining centers held one- to two-year courses for direct vocational training. Here the purpose was to train skilled workers. There were, for example, two-year courses in the metallurgical industry, the mining industry and the sea and river transport services, and a two-year course for training skilled railroad workers. These courses, introduced in 1951, had begun to lose their importance by 1957.

Higher Educational Institutes (Universities, etc.). In February, 1958, the National Assembly passed a new law on university education.[10] Students who had completed their medium or gymnasium education (eleven or twelve grades) and graduates of the pedagogical institutes and professional schools (technical colleges) could compete for places in the higher educational establishments, provided, in the case of men, they had completed their military service—usually two years. The length of university-type education was from four to six years (up to seven if tuition was by correspondence), depending on the course taken. Graduates of higher technical and agricultural institutions had to do one year of practical work before graduating.[11]

The task of the higher educational institutions, as laid down in the new law, was to train highly qualified specialists—educated in the Communist spirit—for the national economy and the various administrative positions of the state. They were also to develop science and culture on the basis of Marxist-Leninist teaching.[12]

Each higher educational institution was presided over by a rector. He and the deputy rectors were elected for two years from among the professors and faculty members by secret ballot. Actually, these elections were strongly influenced by the Communist Party, since the Party secretaries of these institutions took part in the electoral meetings and the candidates for office were recommended by the Academic Council, the Party organization, and the trade union in the respective institute.

[10] *Izvestia na Presidiuma na Narodnoto Subranie*, February 6, 1958.
[11] *Ibid.*, July 22, 1958.
[12] *Ibid.*, February 6, 1958.

The following is a list of the higher educational institutions existing in Bulgaria:[13]

The State University in Sofia

The "Georgi Dimitrov" Higher Institute of Rural Economy in Sofia

The "Vassil Kolarov" Higher Institute of Rural Economy in Plovdiv

The Higher Institute of Medicine in Sofia

The Higher Institute of Medicine in Plovdiv

The Higher Institute of Forestry

The "Karl Marx" Higher Institute of Economics in Sofia

The Higher Institute of National Economy in Varna

The Higher Institute of Finance in Svishtov

The Higher Institute of the Food Industry in Plovdiv

The Higher Institute of Machine-Electro-Technics in Sofia

The Higher Institute of Chemical Technology in Sofia

The Higher Institute of Mining and Geology in Sofia

The Higher Institute of Building Engineering in Sofia

The Higher Institute of Mechanization of the Rural Economy in Russe

The Higher Institute of Fine Arts in Sofia

The Higher Institute of Theatrical Art in Sofia

The Higher Institute of Physical Culture in Sofia

The State Conservatory in Sofia

There were, in addition, the Superior School for the training of clergy, the military academies, and the higher Party schools, all of which had a status similar to that of the institutions mentioned above.

Scholarships and Stipends

The Bulgarian Communist government, from its inception, has always spent an impressive sum on financial assistance to students. For the academic year 1957–58, it spent 9.329 million old leva and claimed that 46 per cent of all students at the higher educational establishments were on stipends of some kind.[14]

Since 1954, scholarships have not usually been granted for

[13] Taken from Dellin, *op. cit.*, p. 203.

[14] *Otechestven Front*, August 3, 1956. 6.8 old leva then equalled one dollar at the official exchange rate.

students in the gymnasia except to members of the Turkish minority. This exception is presumably designed to stimulate the desire for education in this group of citizens that, educationally at least, is the most backward element in the Bulgarian community. Many scholarships, however, have been given to students in the professional schools and technical colleges. Priority has generally been given to the children of former Communist resistance fighters and political prisoners, but this has not prevented a large number of academically gifted children from being beneficiaries. Consistently excellent students qualify for increments in the amount of their scholarships. A scholarship holder at the professional schools signs a declaration that, after graduation, he will go to a job assigned to him by the government for a period corresponding to the number of years he has held the scholarship.

Many different types of scholarships are available at the higher educational institutes of university status. Most of them are for students working toward scientific and technological degrees. Again, preference is given on political grounds to resistance fighters, etc., or their children, or to young people already distinguished in industry or agriculture—shock workers, innovators, and the like. But, clearly, these could not amount to more than a small proportion of the total number of university students who receive financial aid.

The Reforms of 1959

The changes made in the educational system in 1957, while not very extensive, did at least show some willingness to think in Bulgarian terms rather than simply in terms of the mechanical transplantation of the Soviet experience. But this new departure was to be cut short quickly.

In November, 1958, Khrushchev's theses on "Strengthening the Ties between School and Life" were published, calling for a closer integration of education and the material production of the economy. The very next month Zhivkov, taking his cue, told a Komsomol congress that the changes introduced in 1957 were inadequate and "only a small step" toward overcoming "the separation of school from life." The problem facing the Party, therefore, was "not a mere correction of the educational system in Bulgaria but its basic reorganization."[15]

[15] *Narodna Mladezh* (Sofia), December 2, 1958.

This basic reorganization in the law was approved by the National Assembly in July, 1959.[16] Its most important provision was the introduction of a *unified* twelve-year secondary school called the "Medium Polytechnical School" to replace the existing basic school and medium school (gymnasium).

Secondary education was now divided, therefore, into two phases. The first was the eight-year basic school, which was compulsory (previously, the seven-year basic education had been compulsory). The purpose of this school was to give its pupils general education plus polytechnical knowledge. The second phase was now the upper course, consisting of the four grades from ninth to twelfth grade.

After graduating from the eight-year basic school, four possibilities now existed for the students. They could enter:

1) *The Upper Course of the Medium Polytechnical School,* with four grades: ninth to twelfth. The curriculum for these four years of study provided for about 1,600 hours of work in industrial production. The graduates of these schools would have medium education plus some specialization in production and could enter any faculty of all the higher educational institutes (universities) in the country.

2) *The Medium Professional Schools (Technicums).* The course was four to five years after basic education or one to three years after medium education. The medium professional schools would prepare qualified specialists for the needs of industry, agriculture, trade, building, transport, public health, etc. The graduates of the technicums could continue their education at any higher educational institute.

3) *Professional Technical Colleges,* with courses of from one to three years. These schools were attached to plants, enterprises, state farms, or technicums; they did not provide a medium education. Their main purpose was to prepare their pupils for material production in the economy. If the graduates of these schools later wanted to obtain medium education, their studies during this course would be taken into consideration.

4) *Miscellaneous Training.* Young people who did not continue their education after the eight-year compulsory basic school were admitted to special courses or other forms of training organized by factories, plants, enterprises, etc., in order to enhance their qualifications as workers. One significant innovation was the in-

[16] *Rabotnichesko Delo* (Sofia), July 4, 1959.

troduction of boarding schools into Communist Bulgaria on the Soviet pattern, at first experimentally and then as an established feature. They were to become model schools for training the future Communist elite.

The new law laid commendable stress on improving the quality and qualifications of the teachers at all levels—by 1962, they numbered nearly 80,000.[17] All teachers in the fifth grade and above were now required to have a university education or its equivalent. Future teachers in kindergartens and in schools from the first to the fourth grade would have to be graduates of a three-year special course taken on completion of their twelve years of schooling.

This law of July, 1959, introduced the full-scale "polytechnization" of Bulgarian education on the Soviet model (which was soon applied in most other Eastern European states also).[18] The rationale of the new system was obvious: the need for technologists and highly-skilled workers at all levels in the industrial and agricultural hierarchy. From this point of view, it had a good deal to recommend it. But it had other, more socio-political aims: to break down the exclusiveness that an educated class, in any system, inevitably tends to acquire it by directly harnessing it to economic tasks; and to socialize the mentality of the growing generation.

The Effects of the Reform

It is difficult to give a balanced assessment of the success of this new system of education because the impression gained from the Bulgarian press was more of complaints and criticism than satisfaction. The fact that so much criticism was reflected in the official press, even if it was always followed by (not very convincing) attempts to counter it, indicates the widespread unpopularity of the new programs and the frustrations they caused.

The main point of dissension was undoubtedly the practical work in the economy which all students now had to do. In the first two years of the new system, part of the difficulty was caused by inadequate preparation. In 1960, a deputy minister of educa-

[17] As against 28,236 in 1944: Nacho Papazov, Minister of Education, in a speech to a teachers' congress in April, 1962; *Otechestven Front*, April 7, 1962.

[18] For the general Eastern European scene, see Marin V. Pundeff, "Education for Communism" in Stephen Fischer-Galati (ed.), *Eastern Europe in the Sixties* (New York, 1963), pp. 26–51.

tion admitted that "instead of having their prescribed places in the plants and factories, the pupils, like any visitor, were mere observers of the work being done or were assigned to work which had nothing to do with their field of specialization."[19] The organization subsequently improved, but the attitude of the participants evidently did not.

The managers and the workers who were supposed to receive and train the students obviously thought the whole thing was a waste of time. Open hostility or unfriendly indifference was their general reaction.[20] Their attitude was reciprocated by many of the students, who would often do anything to get out of their practical training assignments. In some areas there was a particular aversion to specializing in rural production.[21] The students were often encouraged in their obstinacy by their parents.

The truth was that, in its new policy, the regime was flying in the face of the educational tradition, not only of Bulgaria, but of practically the whole of Eastern Europe as well. Higher education —the gymnasium and the university—was an avenue into the ranks of the intellectuals, for whom any direct connection with the economy had always been something devoutly to be avoided. The best brains of the pre-Communist era went into law, the administration (often with a law degree), politics, or journalism. The thought of going into industry or agriculture was both revolutionary and revolting. This attitude died hard; it was still alive and kicking in 1959, when the polytechnic system was introduced. It was certainly not an attitude to be praised; Bulgarian society might have been more advanced before the war had this prejudice not existed so strongly. But it was there, and the Communists' drastic attempt to change it and their thoroughly inadequate preparations for the implementation of the new policy did not improve matters.

The new system had its logic and merits, of course. Economic advancement, especially on the scale envisaged by the regime, depended on an ever-increasing number of highly-trained cadres at all levels. But one of the characteristics of the Bulgarian Communist Party, in power as well as out, has been its lack of moderation; it was certainly shown here. Technical specialization was stressed to the almost complete neglect of the humanities and liberal arts. The combination of specialized study, practical training, and

[19] Marin Geshkov, *Otechestven Front*, March 2, 1960.
[20] See, for example, *Vecherni Novini* (Sofia), May 16, 1960.
[21] *Otechestven Front*, February 4, 1961.

compulsory ideological courses resulted in constant complaints that the students were physically overburdened.[22]

In view of all these factors, the new policy's general lack of success is hardly surprising. Almost four years after the introduction of the reform, the Minister of Education was complaining that "our educational worth lags, it has no way satisfied us—we are not satisfied with its results."[23] Various attempts were made to improve the system but it was becoming increasingly obvious that its whole character would have to be revised.

Finally, in the summer of 1967, when other Eastern European countries were also extricating their educational systems from the polytechnical strait jacket, Bulgaria undertook important revisions in her school curriculum. On June 20, 1967, the official teachers' newspaper, *Uchitelsko Delo*, published a draft study plan and a draft curriculum for the medium schools (not, however, for the professional schools or technical colleges). The drafts were submitted for public discussion and the same paper carried numerous comments on them for over two months. The most important innovation in the drafts was the provision for a differentiation of studies in the last three grades of school (grades nine to twelve). These grades would now be divided into a natural sciences-mathematics branch and a humanities branch. Pupils in either of the two branches would also have the possibility of choosing an optional subject (including Latin), to be studied for two hours a week. In October, a new draft was published which obviously incorporated some of the suggestions made about the original draft.[24]

Rather unpromisingly, this draft stated that the importance of practical training would be increased. But its other main points showed that the regime was anxious to mitigate some of the excesses of polytechnization. The number of hours devoted to practical work and vocational training would actually be reduced; the number of subjects of a general educational nature would be increased; more attention would be given to the study of foreign languages and the social sciences. It was also confirmed that two branches of study would be provided for the three senior grades. The new draft plan, which had already been tested experimentally,

---

[22] See speech by Papazov to a teachers' congress in May, 1962: *Literaturen Front* (Sofia), May 24, 1962.

[23] Gancho Ganev (he replaced Papazov in September, 1962) in a speech to the Central Committee of the Union of Teachers, *Uchitelsko Delo* (Sofia), July 7, 1963.

[24] Bulgarian Telegraphic Agency, October 2, 1967.

would be implemented more broadly in the 1967–68 and the 1968–69 school years.

After nine years of much trial and error, the polytechnical system, in the extreme form in which it had been introduced, had been given up as a failure. The "old humanistic gymnasium—detached from real life" had at least been partly revived. Bulgarian education seemed now to be back on a more even keel.

II. THE PROBLEMS OF YOUTH

We, the young people, are the rulers of the present. The old times are passing into history, and do us the favor of not reminding us about them over and over again. You did nothing but lose our confidence. . . .

This is an extract of a letter sent to the editor of *Narodna Mladezh* (People's Youth) by an eighteen-year-old boy from Russe. It was published in the June 19, 1967, edition of the paper. It would be a mistake to dramatize this letter, to consider it as voicing the exact opinions of the overwhelming mass of Bulgaria's young people. Nor are its sentiments peculiar to the youth of Communist countries, as the contemporary ferment in the West signifies only too clearly. But the letter does point to a dissatisfaction and frustration felt, in varying degrees, by very large numbers of young people in Bulgaria as well as other parts of Eastern Europe and the Soviet Union.

The "revolt of youth" is a universal phenomenon about which little is really known except for its outward manifestations. Serious studies will doubtless appear scientifically analyzing and explaining it, comparing its Eastern and Western varieties, and describing the more positive aims and motivations of the younger generation. The following discussion does not attempt such an analysis. It simply describes the Bulgarian regime's attempts to harness youth to the cause of Communism, and the recent signs suggesting that these attempts have been far from successful.

Structure of Youth Organizations

There are several official bodies in Bulgaria responsible for "organizing" youth; they correspond closely with those established in the Soviet Union.

An organization called *Chavdarche* caters for children between seven and nine, i.e., in their first two years at school. It was set up immediately after the Communist takeover in September, 1944, but was discontinued for a time in the middle 1950's. After the Ninth Komsomol Congress in 1958, however, it was gradually revived. By the middle of 1962, its membership stood at 300,000.[25] The aim of *Chavdarche* is to prepare its members for the Pioneer organization.

In Bulgaria this is called the *Septemvriiche*, recalling, of course, the Communists' favorite month. It was also founded in September, 1944, and though it is under the general control of the Communist Party itself, the Komsomol directs its everyday activities. In recent years its membership has been about 700,000.[26]

The first Marxist-oriented youth organization in Bulgaria was set up in 1912 under the name of The Social Democratic Workers' Youth Union. In 1919, the BCP created its youth branch—an organization which was named the Bulgarian Communist Youth Union. Later, following the outlawing of all Communist-sponsored organizations in the country, the Communist Party set up, in 1928, the Workers' Youth Union (RMS) to serve as a legal organization for Communist-oriented youth. The RMS, which was reinforced in 1938 with the members of the underground Bulgarian Communist Youth Union, existed until 1947, when it was transformed into the Union of People's Youth. At its Ninth Congress (November, 1958), the union became Dimitrov's Communist Youth Union, or simply the Komsomol, as it is most often called.

The Komsomol was designed to be "the Party's main assistant in its work for the Communist education of the younger generation, its reserve, and an active participant in socialist construction."[27] According to its old statute, the Komsomol was not a political, but rather a mass, organization of Bulgarian youth, all of whose social, sporting, and extracurricular educational activities were supposed to be under its wing. However, its new statute, approved in January, 1960, laid increased emphasis on the political aspect of the organization.[28] This political context probably explains the recent efforts, at the end of 1967 and in early 1968, to

[25] *Rabotnichesko Delo*, June 18, 1962.
[26] *Ibid.*
[27] *Ibid.*, October 2, 1962.
[28] According to its new statute, the Komsomol is a mass "social-political" organization of Bulgarian youth. See former First Secretary Atanasov's report to the Eleventh Komsomol Congress; *Narodna Mladezh*, January 11, 1968.

improve the selection of would-be Komsomol members and to decrease the total membership. Persons between fourteen and twenty-eight years of age are eligible for membership in the Komsomol.[29] Its membership is well over a million.[30] There are hardly any figures to indicate how many Komsomol members are Community Party members, but it is of some interest to note that 32.6 per cent of all secretaries of Komsomol organizations throughout the country were members of the BCP in 1965.[31]

The Reflections of Alienation

The Communist government has done much for youth in Bulgaria. It has made higher education available for the vast majority and has lavished on them many benefits of a social and recreational nature which were undreamed of twenty years earlier. Like their counterparts in all Communist countries, Bulgaria's youth have in many ways been spoilt. Yet the attitude of this favored youth has given increasing cause for concern. Instead of gratitude there has been dissatisfaction; instead of identification with the system, a growing alienation from it. Here one must enter a note of caution. Many Bulgarian young people, if not exemplary from the Communist point of view, generally support the system and cause no trouble and little concern. (The situation is no different in the West.) But the attitudes against which the regime complains so loudly have undoubtedly spread over the last few years among a generation that is Communist born and bred, the children of parents who, for the most part, have little reason to be nostalgic for the old regime.

There are many reasons for this; they can roughly be divided into the materialistic and idealistic. Many of the former are due to the frustration of rising expectations: inadequacy of housing and consumer goods, inability to find appropriate employment in the place of one's choice, etc. These, however, the Communist regimes can both understand and, up to a point, sympathize with. Far more serious are the idealistic reasons. The contrast between the professed and the practiced, the gap between promise and achievement—these are the factors causing apathy and cynicism among youth. The exposition, beginning in 1956, of the crimes of

[29] Until 1963, the upper age limit was twenty-six.
[30] *Narodna Mladezh*, January 13, 1968.
[31] *Rabotnichesko Delo*, July 9, 1965.

the Stalinist period, the constant purges, and the blasting of once-hallowed reputations, the discouragement of the spirit of inquiry, the mechanical indoctrination of an ossified version of Marxism-Leninism, the subservience to the Soviet Union, the growth of bureaucracy, and various kinds of corruption—these are just a few of the many (legitimate) reasons why Bulgarian and Eastern European youth should have become increasingly resentful of the system or apathetic toward it. As in the West, there is a strong feeling among Bulgarian youth that their elders have made an unholy mess of things. The enthusiasm that was current in the late 1940's had turned to disillusionment by the early 1960's.

Narodna Mladezh, the daily paper of the Komsomol, conducted a poll of youth attitudes in 1964 that revealed some of this negativism. The negative responses were few in number (said *Narodna Mladezh*), but that any at all were published was remarkable enough. One twenty-two-year-old student admitted: "I have no aim in life. Why should I cherish illusions and dream of things that will probably never happen?" Another, more poetic, replied: "Before, I had aims and dreams, but now I follow the coffin in which I am burying them."[32]

One familiar form of escapism resorted to by Eastern European youth has been the aping of all things Western. Judging from the outraged cries of the official press, the Bulgarian youth are no exception—and with the huge increase in Western tourism in recent years the problem has become more acute.

"We have met," complained *Narodna Mladezh*, "these admirers of the foreign. They crowd around a car with a foreign license plate, crane their necks in front of the bright windows of foreign legations. . . . They like nothing at home. According to them we have nothing, neither industry, nor literature, nor art, nor culture. While in the West . . . ! And they twist around to shrill sounds from tape-recorders. . . . They, the worshippers of all that is foreign."[33]

Such outward manifestations of the problem have long been combatted by the imposition of (often unconsciously comic) measures to "take care of behavior inappropriate for a socialist society." There have been numerous instances in which certain types of fashion, music, and dancing were declared to be bourgeois and ridiculed. The "pony-tail" hairdo was described as an attribute of the hooligan, jazz as a decadent phenomenon, manicures as an

[32] *Narodna Mladezh*, January 24 and 25, 1964.
[33] *Ibid.*, January 25, 1964.

aristocratic bourgeois sign, tight trousers, modern dances, etc., as bourgeois in class. And official opposition was not confined solely to words; it has occasionally been unofficially reported that raids were carried out in Sofia's cafes and restaurants by the militia and voluntary "vigilante" units in search of long hair and Western dress. This kind of repression became less prevalent after 1966, but did not cease altogether. The fact that it continued into 1967 was shown by an article in September of that year which appealed for more sophisticated measures in dealing with the problem. "Don't we risk becoming ridiculous," the article asked, "if we cut the hair and shave the beards and ignore the minds they adorn? Are we cutting away the bourgeois influence or our own?"[34]

The Patriotic Campaign

As a somewhat less brutal method to counter this fascination for the West, or "national nihilism," as it was often called, the regime embarked upon a propaganda campaign of "patriotic" education, to make the youth aware of the glories of Bulgaria's past and rid them of the "scornful attitude toward everything that is ours, that is native Bulgarian."[35] This patriotic campaign became one of the paramount features of youth policy, although most Bulgarian youth can hardly have been impressed with the authenticity of a patriotism "inseparable from our love and respect for the Soviet Union and its great Communist Party."[36] Nor could they have appreciated being told that love for the Soviet Union was the "most characteristic and significant point" of that patriotism.[37]

The patriotic campaign has made much of important anniversaries of great personalities and events in modern Bulgarian history. Some of the celebrations of these anniversaries have been relatively free of Communist and pro-Russian bias while others have been positively loaded with it.

An example of the former was the centenary of Pencho Slaveikov (1866–12), perhaps the greatest of Bulgarian poets and a writer of European standing. Slaveikov was considered for the Nobel Prize for literature, mainly in recognition of his epic

[34] *Pogled* (Sofia), September 25, 1967.

[35] Todor Zhivkov, *Rabotnichesko Delo*, April 24, 1963.

[36] Todor Zhivkov at the Ninth BCP Congress: *Rabotnichesko Delo*, November 15, 1966.

[37] Boyan Bulgaranov, *Rabotnichesko Delo*, July 9, 1967.

"Bloody Song" evoking the April, 1876, uprising against the Turks; he might well have won the award but for his untimely death. He was undoubtedly a Russophile and was influenced by writers like Pushkin and Tolstoy. But the Western influences on him were the stronger, especially the German. He had studied in Leipzig, and Heine and Nietzsche were the influences that had most shaped the quality of his poetry. The official campaign marking his centenary, though it exaggerated the Russian orientation of Slaveikov,[38] had to admit these Western influences and, on the whole, was balanced and fair.

An unfortunate example of the distortion of Bulgarian history was in the treatment of the April, 1876, uprising. This event is regarded by most Bulgarians as the most stirring episode in the nation's history; and, unlike the liberation of 1878, which was undoubtedly due to Russian assistance, it was a purely Bulgarian affair. The regime, however, not content to leave well enough alone, attributed to the uprising two characteristics it did not historically have: it insisted on the huge inspirational and material Russian support for it and sought to endow it retroactively with vast social and "progressive" objectives. At the climax of the celebrations, a rally was held in Panagyurishte, a town east of Sofia where the uprising started. Here Zhivkov, in the presence of Nikolai Organov, the Soviet Ambassador (who, like his predecessor, Georgi Denisov, played an ostentatiously important role in Bulgarian affairs), gave a speech so sycophantic to Russia and the Soviet Union that it must have humiliated even many Communists in the audience.[39]

Incidents such as this were hardly likely to appeal to Bulgarian youth, since it is the young, always skeptical of indoctrination, who have reacted most strongly against the incessant pro-Soviet propaganda. Thus, it is not surprising that the Komsomol failed to have the impact desired when its First Secretary could inform its members that "the patriotism of the Bulgarian youth is inseparable from the friendship for, and unity with, the Soviet Union and its glorious youth."[40]

[38] See, for example, the article entitled "Russia—Close and Beloved" in *Rabotnichesko Delo*, April 26, 1966.

[39] Radio Sofia, May 3, 1966. This speech is worth contrasting with that given by Anton Yugov, then Premier, at the eightieth anniversary of the uprising in 1956. Yugov's speech was much more "Bulgarian" and there was much less fawning on "Grandfather Ivan." *Rabotnichesko Delo*, May 4, 1956.

[40] Georgi Atanasov, speech to fourteenth plenum of the Komsomol Central Committee; *Narodna Mladezh*, December 21, 1966.

The Attempts at Reform

What the regime lacked in its dealings with Bulgaria's youth—
its own offspring, since this was the post-1944 generation—was
any semblance of sophistication. It was certainly aware of youthful
apathy and skepticism and grasped at least some of its causes. But
it was psychologically unable to do anything about removing
those causes since, if it did so properly, it would proceed to undermine its own legitimacy. It would, in fact, begin to repudiate
itself, so great was the distance separating it from many of its
youthful subjects.

But, by 1967, some voices had begun to be raised in the press
urging a basic reappraisal of the problems of youth. In July of that
year, Radoslav Radev, the deputy editor-in-chief of *Narodna
Mladezh,* posed the question: "Why, despite all the efforts to
create a Marxist-Leninist outlook among our youth, are the results
quite far from what they should be?" The answer, he thought, was
not to be sought in the failings of youth or in the terrors of bourgeois influence, but rather in the *system:* "I question some aspects
of the system, by means of which for years we have been trying
to stimulate the interest of young people in ideological problems."
Radev was diplomatically vague on what these aspects were but
he had at least raised the key question.[41] Another writer called for
an end to the crude methods of fighting bourgeois influence: "It
should be clearly understood," he urged, "that the scope and size
of the adverse influence of foreign factors depend, to a great
extent, on a number of domestic conditions and factors . . . "[42]

The extent of the official concern over the condition of youth
can be measured by the regime's preoccupation with the subject
at the end of 1967 and the beginning of 1968. In December, a
major analysis was published under the title of the "Zhivkov
Theses" on youth;[43] at the end of December, a Party Central
Committee plenum discussed the situation of youth; and in January, the Eleventh Komsomol Congress was held. These events
were accompanied by a large number of articles in the press devoted to the same subject.

Emerging from this welter of activity was a new official pro-

[41] *Uchitelsko Delo,* July 25, 1967.
[42] Gergin Gerginov in *Politicheska Prosveta* (Sofia), October, 1967.
[43] Published in *Rabotnichesko Delo* and all major Bulgarian papers on December 1, 1967.

gram for the youth of Bulgaria, which can be divided roughly into four parts: Komsomol reform and the increased involvement of youth in society; intensified Marxist-Leninist education, especially as it affected the struggle against the "bourgeois ideology"; increased emphasis on patriotic education; and improvement of the Party's work with the Komsomol and with youth generally.

The Komsomol was an obvious scapegoat for past failures. In his theses, Zhivkov made it clear that only radical reform could make this organization meaningful. It was attacked as being a "copy of the Party," "void of content," detached from "the socio-political, economic, state, and cultural life," unrepresentative of youths' interests. A great variety of youthful activities, said Zhivkov, was taking place outside, rather than inside, the Komsomol. The regime's answer was to try to make the Komsomol "a true representative of the all-round interests and aspirations of Bulgarian young people." Henceforward it was to be the *only* representative of youth: all those organizations and activities, such as sports and tourist unions, pre-military training, and various cultural activities that were outside the Komsomol should be brought under its umbrella and it should have the right of control over all public and state organizations which worked with youth. Regarding the involvement of youth in society, Zhivkov in his theses made the remarkable confession that "the older generation today is a symbol of conservatism, bureaucracy and fossilization." But, despite this, it had not "made way for the young people and does not let them into the leadership of the Party, state, economic and public life."[44]

Zhivkov here was indeed touching on one of the great frustrations of Bulgarian and Eastern European youth. He was also touching on a very sensitive political issue which, since his capture of supremacy in the Party in 1962, had presented problems he had not entirely mastered. In his fumbling, uncertain way, Zhivkov evidently grasped the fact that a modern, economically efficient Bulgaria needed a new "establishment" of younger, trained officials taking the place of the older, relatively untrained Party hands. The implementation of the economic reform only made this need more urgent. Zhivkov, however, though he had brought some trained younger men to the fore, was still far from achieving complete success. In fact, in 1966, he seems to have suffered a serious reverse when it became clear that the Party's older generation, though not challenging his position, was not

[44] *Rabotnichesko Delo*, December 1, 1967.

prepared to be pushed out peacefully. Unwilling or unable to force the issue and perhaps split the Party again, Zhivkov was forced to accept a compromise at the Ninth Party Congress in November 1966. This compromise was symbolized not only by the retention in the Politburo of veterans like Mihailov and Bulgaranov but by the inclusion of "fossils" like Tsola Dragoicheva and Todor Pavlov, who were dredged up from what had seemed a well-deserved retirement.[45] This was an assurance to the veterans in the Party that they still had "their part to play." Short-term political considerations took precedence over those of a longer-term economic and social nature and this may have been one of the reasons for the sluggishness in implementing the economic reform. Zhivkov, in trying to mitigate a serious dissatisfaction on the part of Bulgaria's youth, was also probably seeking to overcome an obstacle that had defied his more direct attacks. A constant theme throughout his theses and in many speeches at the Central Committee plenum that followed was the need for economic expertise to make Bulgaria a really modern state.

The second main plank in the new program for youth warrants little discussion because it was hardly new. The regime simply launched another ideological and educational offensive. What was noticeable, however, was its intensity and the fury of the attacks on Western, bourgeois ideology and its baleful influence. The remedy, however, was the old medicine, but more of it. As Zhivkov put it: "The main and safest barrier against the infiltration of foreign ideological influence among youth is to build a Communist outlook on life and a Communist attitude toward all facts and events, all questions and problems that are generated by reality."[46] Clearly the Party meant business but, unless its rigid concept of ideology changed, it was hard to predict any more success in the future than in the past. This is not to assume that Bulgaria's youth rejects ideology as such. Events in 1967 and 1968 suggest that young people throughout the world have profound interest in ideological questions and motivations. They were rejecting the ossified, ritualized ideologies of the ruling circles in the countries in which they lived. In their reaction, they sought refuge in the young Marx, the old Marcuse, Mao, Che Guevara, and others. To those who would argue that this was a phenomenon of the West rather than the East, the enthusiasm of some Belgrade stu-

[45] See Chapter 8.
[46] "The Zhivkov Theses," *Rabotnichesko Delo*, December 1, 1967.

dents for Mao and Che, shown during the summer of 1968, could be mentioned in reply, and it would seem hardly possible that Bulgarian and other Eastern European young people have remained immune from the "virus." They are certainly tired of the Marxism-Leninism which they have been fed for twenty years, but the Bulgarian regime shows no inclination whatever to alter this basic diet.

Of greater interest is the new approach toward patriotic education. The need for more of this was stressed by Zhivkov in his theses. "Not only do we not use it (i.e., patriotic education—ed.) but there is hardly any other state that allows such an underestimation and even belittling of its historic past."[47] This call was echoed in equally strong terms at the Central Committee plenum in December, 1967.[48] It was universally emphasized that it was not intended to create young chauvinists in Bulgaria, or to downplay the need for a correct spirit of internationalism. On the contrary, in Zhivkov's words, "socialist patriotism" and internationalism were in "dialectical unity."

The stress on patriotism was, of course, not new; As mentioned earlier, it had been introduced some years previously.[49] What was possibly new, however, in the formulations of the Zhivkov Theses and the subsequent debates, was the apparent attempt to give patriotism a more "nationalistic" basis. It was no longer said that internationalism was the essence of patriotism but that they were two parts of a "dialectical unity." Although love for the Soviet Union was constantly expressed throughout the discussions, this love was not specifically linked with patriotism as it had so often been previously. The regime now seemed to be realizing that the automatic equation of love for the homeland with love for Moscow was helping to engender precisely that "national nihilism" against which it constantly railed. If, in the future, it acts consistently on that realization, it will remove one of the obstacles between it and many young Bulgarians. But "independence" in this sphere alone is hardly enough: for Bulgarian youth to be really convinced, it must be evident in other aspects of the regime's domestic and foreign policy.

The regime had great hopes that the reorganization of the

[47] *Ibid.*

[48] See, for example, speech by Venelin Kotsev, CC Secretary: *Rabotnichesko Delo*, December 28, 1967.

[49] It might be noted that, in 1966, the subject had received particular attention in discussions of the preparation of new historical textbooks.

Komsomol would break the *impasse* in its relations with the country's youth. While castigating its previous failings, the Party now sought to rejuvenate the Komsomol by giving it more status and authority. As the Zhivkov Theses stated: "The basic problem is further to raise and develop the freedom of action of the Komsomol . . . to raise [its] role and authority in the overall economic, political, social, and cultural life of the country."[50] This immediately raised the problem of the relationship between the Komsomol and the Party, and here the regime, in spite of all its good intentions, remained as orthodox as ever. In one part of the Zhivkov Theses, Party officials were criticized for "crudely" interfering in the work of the Komsomol; but even after the Komsomol had been raised to its more dignified status, "it is nec- essary directly to lead the Komsomol" and to ensure "the direct participation of a considerable number of Communists in the Komsomol and youth activity."

What emerges on this point from the seemingly confusing verbiage is that, since the Komsomol was to acquire increased powers, including some of an (ill-defined) political nature, it was to be more under the control of the Party than ever before. The control might be exercised more tactfully, but it was still to be increased and Communists within the Komsomol would occupy most of the key positions. Hence this was an example of the essential conservatism of the Bulgarian regime on what, by 1968, had become the key question in Eastern Europe's internal politics: the role of the Party. Whereas the Yugoslav and the (pre-August 1968) Czechoslovak societies—and even, to some ex- tent, the Hungarian—were becoming pluralistic, with the Party less universally dominant than before, Bulgaria clung to the mono- lithic theory of the state and society in which the power of the Party should not only be maintained but increased. This hardly augured well for the Komsomol, or for the attitude of Bulgaria's youth toward it and the higher power whose puppet it was.

In its major attempt to build a bridge to its own youth, the Bulgarian regime has shown a mixture of good intentions and a rigidity caused mainly by the limits of its own political philos- ophy. If the bridge is to be built it will not be the young who will have to change so much as the environment in which they live. And for this to be brought about requires more boldness than Zhivkov, for all his good intentions, has been prepared to show.

[50] *Rabotnichesko Delo*, December 1, 1967.

What is required above all is a closer harmony between precept and practice. The Party Central Committee resolution, at the end of the plenum in December, 1967, noted, with refreshing frankness, that the youth "have a natural sense of reaction against discrepancies between words and deeds."[51] This is the *real* problem. To solve it requires not just a few procedural and institutional changes, but a rejuvenation of the whole society.

[51] *Rabotnichesko Delo*, December 28, 1967.

II

Frost and Thaw in Bulgarian Culture

THE DECISIVE CONTRIBUTION made by writers, most of them Communist, to the relaxation in Eastern Europe during the mid-1950's is recognized by all observers. Adam Wazyk's "Poem for Adults" in 1955 was one of the important avisos of the Polish October. In Hungary, the work of men like Tibor Dery, Peter Veres, and Gyula Illyes both generated and reflected the mood of society, and played a significant role in demolishing the Stalinist edifice. In Bulgaria, the situation could not compare with that in Poland or Hungary, and in any event there was no literary tradition similar to that in other parts of Eastern Europe. Although literature had played an important role in the national awakening of Bulgaria in the nineteenth century, and some of the great revolutionaries themselves had been important writers,[1] the idea that writers were the "conscience of the nation" was nowhere near as prevalent in Bulgaria as in East-Central Europe. Having made this caution against exaggeration, however, one can say that between 1956 and 1958 there *was* a literary ferment in Bulgaria, exceeded only by those in Poland and Hungary,[2] which caused serious concern to the Communist authorities and was dispelled only with some difficulty.

After the Communist takeover, literature and the arts in Bulgaria had suffered the same *Gleichschaltung* process as in other

[1] The most outstanding were Petko Slaveikov (1827–95), father of Pencho Slaveikov; Liuben Karavelov (1827–95); and Christo Botev (1848–76).
[2] One refers here only to Soviet-dominated countries, thereby excluding Yugoslavia.

Eastern European countries. Under the aegis of the Ministry of Culture, the various creative artists—writers, artists, musicians, etc.—were organized into different unions or associations which assigned the subjects to be treated. These bodies, together with the Ministry of Culture, arranged the production of the different creative works and fixed the scale of the material rewards for the deserving artists. They were also responsible for the disciplining of those judged to have strayed from the straight and narrow path mapped out by the regime. Artistic freedom was thus severely limited, but there was great encouragement for those who were prepared to cooperate and the material rewards were handsome indeed.

All the Communist regimes placed great importance on the role of the intellectuals and artists as propagators of the ideology and the new way of life. They spared no effort to persuade prominent writers of the old bourgeois regime to throw in their lot with them, to encourage promising young artists to develop and mature. The result was the very swift creation of a new, privileged, even pampered class, many members of which could not have made the grade in a society where the law of supply and demand operated in the cultural realm. At a time when the general standard of living in Bulgaria and throughout Eastern Europe was very low, this new cultural elite lived off the fat of the land. They had their duties to perform and were closely watched, but most of them were content with the conditions created for them. Not all, of course, were opportunists. Many, at the beginning of Communist rule in Bulgaria, sincerely believed in the new order and in the socialist realism which it was their job to purvey in their works. Some also had real talent, and these went on to demonstrate that socialist realism, severely restrictive though it was, was not an insuperable obstacle to the production of meritorious works. However, a growing number of artists, mostly writers, became increasingly impatient of the restrictions placed upon them and more and more disillusioned over the disparity between Communist ideals and practice. Many of these, as we shall see, had the courage to risk losing the material privileges they enjoyed by asserting the honesty and integrity which are the prime necessities of their profession. In these cases, the regime often found itself the victim of its own policy: having insisted on the importance of this class in the society it was creating, it now found this class using its importance against its own policy. But this was not to become a problem till later.

Under Communism, easily the most important of the creative arts is literature. This, therefore, is the subject to which almost exclusive attention will be given in this chapter and, since literature under Communism is essentially political, it is the political relevance of the literature which will be stressed.

The Stalinist Period and the New Course

Realism had always been the dominant strain in the pre-Communist literature of Bulgaria and it was onto this realist tradition that the Communists sought to graft the new bud of socialist realism. Soon after 1944, a large number of novels began to appear on a small number of themes: historical novels on the exploitation of the Bulgarian peasantry by the Turks, on the revolutionary era of the 1860's and 1870's (designed to prove the link between revolutionary nationalism and Communism), on the growth of the labor movement, and on Communist partisan resistance in World War II. More current novels glorified socialist construction, shock workers in industry, collective farms, MTS's and the like, the wonders of the Soviet Union,[3] and the evils of the capitalist world. Poetry and short stories presented the same themes.

Most of this production was not worth the paper is was written on, but some of it had quality. Able writers of the prewar period—the poetess Elisaveta Bagriana, Ludmil Stoianov, Mladen Isaev, Lamar, even the fanatical Communist Georgi Karaslavov—could not entirely hide their talent behind the often-mediocre themes they now wrote on. Newer writers like Dimitur Talev, Bogumil Rainov, Stefan Bichev, and Dimitur Angelov also showed themselves worthy of better material. Generally, the standard of the novels was higher than that in any other literary form. In drama, only Orlin Vassilev's "Love and Fortune" had made any kind of real impact. As might be expected, genuine literary criticism was practically non-existent because of the crude yardsticks by which all creations had to be judged.

By far the best literary work of this period was the novel "Tobacco" by Dimitur Dimov. This had as its theme the revolutionary movement among Bulgarian tobacco workers before and during World War II. When this novel was published in 1951,

[3] A large number of Russian, particularly Soviet, classics were translated into Bulgarian. Between 1944 and 1951, 2,702 Soviet books were translated and published in 21,104 copies; *Vecherni Novini* (Sofia), September 22, 1952.

it was officially condemned because the heroes were not positive enough and the workers not revolutionary enough. The following year, however, it began to be realized by those framing cultural policy (particularly by Chervenkov, who kept a particularly close eye on culture and ideology), that a less rigid approach might put more life into the new culture and make it more effective. "Tobacco" was now hailed as the finest Bulgarian novel since "Under the Yoke."[4]

This reappraisal of Dimov's work was part of slight but general relaxation in cultural policy. Past writers previously condemned were rehabilitated, republished, and made to form part of the arsenal of Communist indoctrination. These men, such as Botev, Iordon Iovkov, and the great epic poet Pencho Slaveikov, had previously been banned as relics of a shameful past. One provincial library had even burnt every book published before September 9, 1944.[5] Now a somewhat more realistic attitude started to prevail, particularly with the beginning of the new course in 1953. Perhaps the most conspicuous example of this was the exhortation by Chervenkov himself in a letter to Elizaveta in Bagriana in November, 1953: "Do not limit yourself! Socialist realism does not do away with personal experiences, personal emotions, and individual feelings."[6] This new attitude was, of course, not a uniquely Bulgarian phenomenon. It was no coincidence that the thaw in Soviet literature had begun a little earlier, and during this period some of the language used to indicate that the strait jacket of socialist realism was now being loosened appeared to be direct Bulgarian translations from the Soviet originals.

But before 1956, the relaxation was only marginal. The Party was not prepared to allow anything that savored of real spontaneity in literature and the arts although it was quite obvious, even before the Twentieth CPSU Congress and the BCP's April plenum, that some writers were chafing at the discipline forced on them. Addressing the Communist members of the Writers' Union at the end of 1955, Chervenkov attacked those writers who "concentrated their fire against the present leadership of the Writers' Union. They seek to prove that this leadership is despotic . . .

[4] By Ivan Vazov (1850–1921), perhaps Bulgaria's greatest novelist. It deals with life in a Balkan town and the struggle for independence against the Turks.

[5] In the town of Lom; L. A. D. Dellin, *Bulgaria* (New York, 1956), p. 216.

[6] Letter of November 20, 1953 on the occasion of her sixtieth birthday. Published in *Literaturen Front* (Sofia), November 26, 1953.

and they aim against the interference of the Central Committee in literary affairs." Such "freedom of criticism" would not be tolerated, said Chervenkov, and "the hearts of the writers must belong to the Party."[7]

An article in the Yugoslav *Borba* as late as October, 1956, gives a good account of the poor progress Bulgarian literature had made under the conditions set by Chervenkov. *Borba* quoted an unnamed Bulgarian writer as saying that the level of excellence was lower than before the war despite the much better material conditions for the writers now. His description of the contemporary scene is worth quoting:

> Novels with contemporary themes are being written very frequently, but all are similar to each other. Everybody knows that this is not good but everybody does it. Dogmatism and meretriciousness are the most important components of such novels. Our writers are living in contemporary times but they do not know how to describe these times. Usually they write about something unimportant or about something that is too old and without interest. Nevertheless I understand them. What sounds strange to me is that some Bulgarian writers write only for money. It is much better and easier for them to write a bad work in six months than to try hard over a period two or three years to produce a good novel. In any case, both the bad and the good novels would get published and the fees for each would be about the same.[8]

The Ferment of 1956–58

This situation, produced by the regime's cultural policy, drove some of the writers gradually to rebel, and in the turmoil in 1956 they saw their opportunity. The April plenum was the signal for the ferment to begin. Many articles appeared in the literary press, castigating the dullness of literature and blaming the government for clinging to the cult of personality and stifling freedom of expression. For the rest of 1956 and the first few months of 1957, the dissident writers, philosophers, artists, and musicians had something of a field day. A new *avant garde* literary magazine called *Plamuk* was added to the literary press in January, 1957, to help publish the flood of new works that began to appear. Bulgarian literature was freer than it had been for twenty years. Most of the

[7] *Rabotnichesko Delo* (Sofia), February 3, 1956.
[8] *Borba* (Belgrade), October 7, 1956.

interesting works appearing during this short period, like Emil Manov's novel, "An Unauthentic Case," and Todor Genov's play, "Fear," were written by Communists and from a Communist viewpoint. But their rebelliousness against the old dogmatism and their kinship with the literature that had wreaked such havoc in Hungary and Poland were plain and deliberate. And for this reason the ferment could not last.

The process of hardening in the political sphere after the 1956 upheavals in Hungary and Poland has been described in Chapter 4. This inevitably had its effect on literature and the arts. Indeed, since the ferment in Bulgaria was stronger in literature than any other sphere, it was here that the regime's most powerful counterattack was aimed, and a big gun indeed was brought in to lead the assault. Vulko Chervenkov, the man who had symbolized the dogmatism many writers now rejected and whose demotion in April, 1956, had seemed to signal their emancipation, was made Minister of Education and Culture in February, 1957. It was a shrewd choice, not only because of Chervenkov's continuing authority but also because of his intelligence and interest in culture. He was able to grasp nuances in literature which another man might not have detected. Chervenkov received valuable assistance in his task from the like-minded Todor Pavlov, President of the Bulgarian Academy of Sciences, who took upon himself the task of exercising the influence of Hungarian, Polish, and particularly Yugoslav revisionists in Bulgaria.[9]

The Counterattack

At a meeting of the Writers' Union held in July, 1957, "revisionism," of which some writers were said to be guilty, was sharply condemned, as was "exaggeration" of the errors made during the period of the personality cult. To this attack and many others which followed it in the press, some writers answered with a "silence strike" similar to that being used by various Hungarian writers at the time. For this they were severely attacked, particularly Manov and Genov who had replied strongly to criticisms of their works mentioned above. These writers and others were re-

[9] Pavlov was an old enemy of the Yugoslavs, who were highly critical of his part in the campaign against the writers: See, for example, *Politika* (Belgrade), April 28, 1957.

minded that "the Party is free to expel Party members who use the Party label to preach anti-Party views."[10]

Further attacks followed and they became more comprehensive. At a meeting of the Party organization of the Writers' Union at the end of November, 1957, ten leading writers, including Manov and Genov, were accused of opposing the Party line. It was admitted that these dissidents had found support among younger intellectuals and that they had also been aided by the passivity of many of the other Communist writers. Some of the rebels were even accused of supporting the Polish October and the Hungarian Revolution and even of being opposed to the collectivization of agriculture.[11]

In 1958, the cultural authorities not only continued criticizing but also began purging. At the beginning of the year, Vladimir Topencharov, who had spearheaded the political opposition after the April plenum, finally lost his presidency of the Bulgarian Union of Journalists.[12] In February, a number of Communist members of the Academy of Sciences and the whole editorial board of the leading philosophical monthly, *Filosofska Misl*, were criticized either for "revisionism" or a "non-Marxist approach." Here the hand of Pavlov was clearly at work.

But the most important change was made at the general meeting of the Union of Writers in April, 1958, when a wholesale clean-out of officials occurred. Manov and the dramatist Orlin Vassilev were among the eight who lost their places on the board while, in the Secretariat, five of the previous six were not re-elected, among them again Manov, and Lamar, a well-known satirist who had also been very outspoken in the ferment. The most important change, however, affected the position of First Secretary, the effective controller of the Writers' Union. Hristo Radevski was replaced by Georgi Karaslasov, a writer of real ability but a fanatical Communist, a Central Committee member, and a strong

[10] *Otechestven Front* (Sofia), October 17, 1957.

[11] *Rabotnichesko Delo*, November 23, 1957. The man chosen as accuser at this meeting was Andrei Gulyashki who, as chief editor of *Plamuk*, had been responsible for publishing the works of some of the writers he was condemning. Forcing a man like him to do such a task was a device used fairly often by the regime in cultural and political practice. Shortly afterwards, *Plamuk* was purged of six of its editors.

[12] He was also dismissed from the staff of *Otechestven Front*. (He had been dismissed as chief editor of this paper as early as the summer of 1956.) Shortly afterward he became Bulgarian Telegraphic Agency correspondent in Cairo.

exponent of socialist realism. Radevski, an elderly poet of note, was certainly no liberal, but he was evidently not considered strong enough to deal with the situation that had arisen. These changes were largely the work of Chervenkov. They climaxed the policy of repression he had carried out since his appointment to the Ministry of Education and Culture in February, 1957. Chervenkov must also have viewed with satisfaction the number of self-criticisms that were made during the April meeting of the Writers' Union. Genov, for example, capitulated in a rather abject fashion and virtually begged the Party for forgiveness.[13] But the regime's biggest prize was to come the following month when Emil Manov, in the face of mounting criticism, at last broke his silence and made a mild and dignified apology for the uproar his novel, "An Unauthentic Case," had caused.[14]

Chervenkov left the Ministry of Education and Culture immediately after the Seventh Party Congress in June, 1958. The Party leadership had every reason to congratulate him. The ferment had died away and calm had returned to the cultural sphere. Still, the situation was not as it was before the April plenum. The ferment had left its mark and had encouraged a spirit of challenge that could not be completely stifled, especially among the young writers. Even at the fateful Writers' Union meeting in April, where any expression of independence needed considerable nerve, several young writers demanded more latitude in discussing the problems of the day. The statement of one writer, Georgi Dzhagarov, is worthy of note, since Dzhagarov later was to become the regime's top literary official. "Some comrades have the impression," he said, "that socialist realism is like the tablets of Moses's Ten Commandments—everlasting and unchangeable. But this is not true . . . "[15] He was savagely repudiated for his temerity.

The Seventh Party Congress levied three general demands on the country's intellectuals: to associate themselves more directly with the economic, political, and cultural tasks of the country; to raise further the ideological, political, and artistic level of their work and to struggle against "hostile ideology."[16] Later, when the "great leap forward"[17] had begun its headlong course in 1959, the writers were pressed into service as its propagandists. Many com-

---

[13] *Literaturen Front*, April 17, 1958.
[14] Statement to the Bulgarian Telegraphic Agency, May 17, 1958.
[15] *Literaturen Front*, April 17, 1958.
[16] *Trud* (Sofia), June 15, 1958.
[17] See Chapter 5.

plied, but others seemed less interested in the fantasy that characterized the "leap forward" than in the harsh reality of everyday
life. In the summer of 1959, two literary works appeared that
aroused official criticism reminiscent of the worst days of the cult
of personality. The first was the play, "The Buried Sun," by the
veteran Orlin Vassilev. The author was accused of distorting the
image of the Bulgarian Communist and of presenting socialist
reality as "murky, lacking in faith, in a helpless situation with
no outlet." Vassilev stood on "unhealthy positions," a fact he had
shown "openly during the time of the April plenum of the Central
Committee and [had] still not abandoned these positions in his
deeds." Vassilev was accused of looking at life from a "heap of
rubbish." He had tried "to show how people, put into leading
posts and having rich and pure revolutionary pasts, have now become petty bourgeois, spiritually and morally impoverished
souls."[18] "The Buried Sun" certainly caused a furor; the many and
bitter attacks on it showed the regime's sensitivity toward criticisms of this sort at a time when it was trying to harness all the
forces of society for the "leap forward."

Yet there hardly seems much difference between the criticisms
of some Communists attributed to Vassilev and the following,
from the Central Committee's most important monthly, *Novo
Vreme:*

> Unfortunately there are cases (though individual) in our Party
> where tested cadres, fearless revolutionaries who have overcome
> great difficulties and dangers in the past and have a hundred times
> a day exposed their life for the Party cause, are now afraid of diffi-
> culties, lag behind life, pull backward. Such people look upon the
> development of our country . . . from the positions of their own
> welfare and happiness. They look upon everything with doubt.[19]

This passage was written in a purely political vein, but it is
worth quoting in this context because it shows an essential inconsistency in official attitudes that has occurred innumerable times in the
Communist states. Officially sponsored—controlled—criticism to
achieve a definite purpose can be as violent as is needed; the same
criticism rising spontaneously from an unauthorized source, is
branded not only as false but as viciously motivated.

The dust had barely settled on Vassilev's play when a similar
hubbub was aroused by a novel, "The Roads Bypass One An-

[18] *Rabotnichesko Delo,* July 7, 1959.
[19] *Novo Vreme* (Sofia), June, 1959.

other," by Dragomir Assenov. The objections were essentially the same as those about "The Buried Sun," for the subject was the same: the spiritual decline of certain Communists and of Communist reality in general. Assenov's novel touched off a row among the critics that is worth quoting at some length because it shows that the critical Communist spirit unleashed by the April plenum was still alive. One critic defended the approach used by Assenov—and, by implication, Vassilev, Manov, and all the rebels—in the following way:

> It would be naive in the extreme to believe that negative types and negative occurrences have disappeared from our present times, or that they are to be found only outside Party circles. Unfortunately life disproves such naive thoughts. It is a completely normal process in any Communist Party for its members to be carefully selected, for it to be cleansed of undesirables. It is for these reasons that the sanctions exist in the Party statute. But certain hypocrites exist, who kick up a fuss when any mention is made in an artistic work of such occurrences or such types. Why should such occurrences take place in life and yet be excluded from literature? Why is it considered to be a blow to Party prestige when literary works mention the existence of such types? On the contrary, it is stated in many Party documents, that the Party is, in fact, strengthened, becomes stauncher, when purged of unworthy members who have accidentally found their way into its ranks. I have never felt that the image of a Communist should be that of an icon, the image of a saint, or that our faith in it would suffer any if literature were to draw some of its faults to our attention.

There are obvious contradictions between the ideal and the actual. What should be done about such contradictions?

> Should we fight them, or shout hypocritically: "No such thing exists in real life, we are all perfect, why then should we burrow in the seamy and dark sides of life?" No, I cannot agree with such hypocritical bawling. Throughout the ages, literature and art, whenever they have been in contact with the people, have fought for a more perfect society, for a man of higher moral standards. There is no reason why our contemporary socialist literature and art should give up this sacred tradition and struggle.[20]

The inevitable regime riposte came a week later. Assenov had degraded the ideal, the image, of Communist manhood. The "life-blood of the novel" was that Communism had lost its values. Assenov was arguing that a good Communist could be

[20] Yanko Molhov, *Literaturen Front*, August 6, 1959.

"just as much a rogue as anyone else." Then came both a warning and an exhortation:

> Not infrequently, similar theories have been put forward by various critics in the U.S.S.R., but both in theory and in practice they have always suffered total defeat. They might serve to justify certain feeble, pessimistic works, but can never meet with success in our country, because they are contrary to life itself, because they divert the writer's attention from the basic task which the Party has laid down to him, so clearly stated in the BCP Central Committee's message of greeting to the Writers Union gathering in April. "The BCP," it said, "appeals to the writers to create images of heroes, fighters, and builders, who shine with the most striking features of the Bulgarian nation, its revolutionary character, manliness, and hard work, its sense of purpose and loyalty to the cause of Communism, images which can serve as an example to the workers, mobilize the forces, call them to exploits in the name of the people's happiness.[21]

In other words, the Party still wanted the Communist angel, not the fallen angel. This was the voice of dogmatism attacking the protest of those Communists who wished to face boldly up to the imperfections and inconsistencies of the new society. The struggle between the two has been going on unabated since 1956, and nowhere has it been fiercer than in literature.

The Vassilev and Assenov incidents were the last that can be said to have emanated from the April plenum. They were followed by a period of calm in which some writers sought to avoid trouble by avoiding contemporary themes and "digging in the past," seeking ideas in Bulgarian history where controversy could be avoided. This was openly lamented by Karaslavov at the annual meeting of the Writers' Union in July, 1960,[22] one of the quietest writers' meetings for several years and notable chiefly for some conciliatory gestures by the authorities. Emil Manov and Kamen Zidarov, a former director of the National Theater under fire after the April plenum, were re-elected to the Presidium of the union and two non-Communist writers, Dimitur Talev and Dimitur Dimov (the author of "Tobacco") were elected to this body for the first time, underscoring the regime's new policy of appealing to non-Communist writers. Significantly, Veselin Andreev, one of the "angry young men" of the 1958 meeting, was also elected. These gestures were important because they were the beginnings of a new policy

[21] Vassil Kolevsky, *Literaturen Front*, August 13, 1959.
[22] *Literaturen Front*, July 8, 1960.

of courtship by the regime, an attempt to control the writers by reasonableness rather than repression and to bring them into the Writers' Union rather than drive them away from it. For their part, the writers showed themselves ready to compromise. The truce was to last for about two years.

The Second Thaw

At the Twenty-second CPSU Congress in October, 1961, Khrushchev began his second bout of destalinization. Its effect on Eastern Europe, though less shattering than the first, still produced more change and movement than at any time since 1956. On Bulgaria, its effect was perhaps greater than in 1956, and nowhere was this more evident than on the cultural scene.

Taking his cue from the Soviet congress, Zhivkov finally felt able to purge Chervenkov from both the Politburo and his deputy-premiership. The former dictator was now accused in detail of all those cult-of-personality failings of which he should have been accused in 1956 (and which he had then escaped because he was still too powerful). Now, five years later, none rounded on him more sharply than the literary periodicals that, at the height of his power, he had ruled with such an iron hand. The freedom to make these criticisms of Chervenkov, not only in literature but in all walks of public life, must have led many writers to believe in the renewed possibilities of greater freedom of expression. *Literaturen Front*, the organ of the Writers' Union, expressed the general hope:

> The liquidation of the personality cult of Comrade Vulko Chervenkov opens up creative possibilities to all people working in the arts and sciences. It extends their horizon, introduces a breath to their activities, and allows a true reflection of reality in life.[23]

More important, *Novo Vreme*, the authoritative voice of the Central Committee itself, attacked those watchdogs of culture who had ruled so long:

> The cult of personality of Comrade Vulko Chervenkov inflicted serious damage also on our cultural front. The evaluations made by Comrade Chervenkov overpraised and favored some, while the devastating criticisms of other workers in the ideological sector produced a freeze in this sphere. It caused unhealthy manifestations

---

[23] *Literaturen Front*, December 7, 1961.

among the cultural workers and caused in many of them the tendency or the desire to accommodate to his conceptions.[24]

No one, under Chervenkov, had been more responsible for this situation than Radevski and Karaslavov, and they were violently attacked for their sins at a meeting of the Union's Party organization in January, 1962.[25] Some writers during this period were almost masochistic in their self-criticism. Others, however, more conservative and with stronger backing in the Party, sought to keep the new ferment in bounds and warned against any return to "the well-known confusion after the April plenum."[26] But an exhilaration was in the air that had not been known since the Communist takeover.

One of the most important benefits of the new freedom was a greater permissiveness toward Western—especially American—cultural developments. These appealed particularly to the younger writers, who had often been denounced for this inclination. One of them now defended this inclination as follows:

> The works of Hemingway, Steinbeck and Faulkner, for instance, may be foreign to us, but under no circumstances are they hostile, because fundamentally they are realistic works, with a more or less conscious critical attitude toward reality. Although we do not hold to their philosophical attitude to life—a neo-realistic trend in literature —we do not find that this attitude is hostile to us—because at its foundations lies the principle which, although lacking in perspective, unmasks and criticizes reality.[27]

In line with this more flexible attitude, a limited number of Western films and plays began to be shown and more Western writers began appearing in translation, among them Graham Greene, O'Casey, and Lorca. The supply and the variety was still very small by the standards of countries like Poland and Hungary, but it was much better than ever before and it whetted the appetite for more.

Perhaps the most brilliant Bulgarian creation of this second thaw was a theatrical performance called *Improvisations*, a series of loosely knit satirical sketches that was largely the work of Radoy Ralin, one of Bulgaria's wittiest writers. It poked gentle and good-humored fun at authority in general, but it proved too toxic for a

[24] *Novo Vreme*, January, 1962.
[25] *Literaturen Front*, February 8, 1962.
[26] Dimitur Metodiev, member of the Presidium and Party organization of the Writers' Union, *Literaturen Front*, February 8, 1962.
[27] Andrey Gulyashki, *Literaturen Front*, May 31, 1962.

sensitive regime and after only five performances in October, 1962, had to be amended. It was later severely criticized, along with its author, by Zhivkov.[28] Ralin had long been a thorn in the side of the regime because of his wit and irreverence, and in 1960 a book of his called "Safety Pins" was removed from all the libraries in the country because it evidently presented a threat to socialist Bulgaria.

Even more important politically was the brief appearance of the literature of destalinization. The most famous example of this, Solzhenytsin's "One Day in the Life of Ivan Denisovich," was published in installments in the literary press.[29] But Bulgaria produced its own Solzhenytsin in the person of Nikola Lankov. A sixty-year-old Communist (he died in 1965), Lankov had suffered imprisonment in the early years of the regime. Never considered a more than second-rate writer, he now produced a long poem of pathos and power, entitled "The Recollection." This poem was the first, and so far remains the only, direct and outspoken account of the brutality and suffering under the first years of Communist rule.[30] Lankov wrote of his own prison experiences. The following passage, with its evident reference to Chervenkov, was by no means atypical:

> Did I live through this night
> of cult oppression?
> Did I live?
> Oh, no!
>
> I dare not admit that
> a certain person, called someone who is "9,"
> in a disgusting epoch
> shot Communists
> to clear his own path
> to a throne and personal power.

Nor was this passage, dealing with Lankov's experience in prison:

> The door opens,
> the investigator enters
> and begins to rail:

[28] See *Rabotnichesko Delo*, April 24, 1963.

[29] *Literaturen Front*, December 6, 1962.

[30] See Christo Ognjanoff, "A New Bulgarian Poetry," March 14, 1963 in *East Europe* (New York), September, 1966.

—What are you talking to?

My head shakes
My sleep is broken
and on this late evening
I hear again:

—To interrogation,
to interrogation![31]

The dominant theme of the 1961–62 period, running through most of the literature and literary criticism, was a cathartic one. By bringing to consciousness and expression thoughts and emotions long suppressed, the writers sought to purge themselves of this heavy psychological burden and turn it into artistically-meaningful works at last having the ring of truth. The following semi-official statement sums up this feeling:

> We know from the history of literature that when a writer, no matter how gifted, betrays truth, he not only fails to justify his high calling but destroys his talent. Because no talent is capable of turning a lie into truth. We have no reason to fear the truth. . . . But it often brings bitterness, because life has many dark, unpleasant sides and the writer must have the courage to reveal them.[32]

The political background for these exciting literary developments was the tense period of preparation for the Eighth BCP Congress, scheduled for November, 1962. The Twenty-second CPSU Congress, and the BCP's own November plenum following it, had set the stage for the culminating power struggle between Zhivkov and Premier Yugov, who was now the rallying point for the conservatives.[33] With Khrushchev's support, Zhivkov used the issue of reform against the conservatives. He found the writers were useful allies, while the writers, for their part, took advantage of the unsettled situation and seized the chance to shake off the burdens of the past. In doing so, many went further than Zhivkov, always a timid reformer, really wanted them to go. But until he finally sealed his supremacy, he could not afford to check them.

[31] The poem was published in *Narodna Kultura* (Sofia), November 10, 1962 and February 19, 1963; see also J. F. Brown, *The New Eastern Europe: the Khrushchev Era and After* (New York, 1966), p. 147.

[32] *Septemvri* (Sofia), June, 1962.

[33] See Chapter 6.

Counterattack and Courtship

It was only a matter of time, however. Zhivkov's victory came at the Eighth Congress with the removal of Yugov from all his Party and state positions, along with Politburo member Georgi Tsankov, deputy premier and former Minister of the Interior, and several others. These purges were carried out under the banner of the final destruction of the personality cult, and implied a program of greater liberalization. But for the writers, the period of freedom was approaching its end. Once he was firmly in control of the political situation, Zhivkov sought to suppress that spontaneity in the cultural sphere that he had previously found useful and now considered a threat. He received great encouragement in March, 1963, from his mentor, Khrushchev, who strongly attacked "abstractionism" and "formalism" in literature and art, urged the strict observance of "socialist realism" and *Partiinost* (the "Party spirit") in all creative works and, an inevitable concomitant, called for the extirpation of the allegedly burgeoning bourgeois influence.

The effect of Khrushchev's speech in Bulgaria was immediate. Some liberal writers tried to head off the coming assault by boldly asserting the spirit of the Twentieth and Twenty-second Soviet Congresses and denying the right of the dogmatists to pre-empt Khrushchev's speech for their own ends. But that was precisely what the dogmatists did, with the decisive backing of Zhivkov himself. In a speech given in April, which he openly admitted had been inspired by Khrushchev's, Zhivkov showed that what applied in the Soviet Union also applied in Bulgaria. The weight of his remarks rested on three main considerations. The first was his highly critical and defensive admission of increasing Western influence in the daily and cultural life of the people. He attacked trends in literature and art which he described as "pseudo-innovational" and "bourgeois national," criticizing a whole range of cultural activities, ranging from an art exhibition in November, 1962, in honor of the Eighth Party Congress to the decorations adorning Bulgarian stands at various exhibitions and fairs. Zhivkov's second main concern was the nation's youth, which he subjected to a detailed and frank analysis. Here he attacked not only the pervasive influence of Western-style dance and dress among the students, but also the prevalence of "decadent and pessimistic" verse by young Bulgarian poets. (Among those he reproached, though without the severity he reserved for others, was Georgi Dzhagarov.) The third main point of his speech was a condemnation of specific writers, poets, and critics who allegedly personified different reprehensible Western tendencies. At the same time, he defended the well-known dogmatists, Radevski and Karaslavov, both of whom had been criticized heavily since the Twenty-second Soviet Congress—particularly Karaslavov, who had been forced out of the first secretaryship of the Writers' Union the previous year.[34]

Zhivkov's speech marked the end of the second thaw in culture during Communist rule in Bulgaria. The writers had received their warning and, mindful of the previous crackdown by Chervenkov, headed the implied lesson. But the advances they had made since the Twenty-second CPSU Congress were not subsequently wiped out. Literature did not return to the dark ages; instead it reverted to its apolitical character, thus seeking to avoid a direct confrontation with the authorities. There began a considerable flowering of naturalistic poetry, for example, and of many literary works dealing with purely human problems, avoiding anything that could be construed as directly subversive. This, of course, was not what the Party wanted; it had little relation to socialist realism or *Partiinost*. But now it appeared that Zhivkov, having made his point and nipped in the bud what might have become another rebellion, was content to let the matter rest and not pursue the writers any further. He had told them what *not* to do, but he made no effort to force them to produce what he actually did want. The writers, for their part, accepted this as the best solution in the circumstances.

But this was hardly a situation that any Communist government could accept for long without abdicating responsibility in a sphere considered vital. Gradually, therefore, the Party sought to re-establish the positive role it had always played; but its method of doing so was novel for Bulgaria. Having seen that repression brought few results, the Party now began fully to implement the courtship of the writers, tentatively begun in 1958, seeking a compromise in which, without sacrificing its dogmas of socialist realism and *Partiinost*, it could establish more flexible guidelines for all creative artists. The basis for this new approach was the friendship and confidence that steadily developed between Zhivkov and Georgi Dzhagarov.

Dzhagarov, a poet and dramatist, had previously been known as a young rebel. As mentioned above, he was prominent in the first thaw and the second. Born in 1925, he was a Komsomol member before 1944 and had been sentenced to a long term of imprison-

---

[34] *Rabotnichesko Delo*, April 24, 1963.

ment shortly before the September liberation brought him freedom. In 1947, he studied at the Maxim Gorky institute in Moscow, and in the early 1950's he won recognition in Bulgaria as a promising young poet. Until 1963, he seemed destined for a lifetime of trouble with the authorities for his courage and independence. By 1967, however, he was one of the most important men in Bulgaria, a member of the Party Central Committee and real power at court.

As we have seen, Zhivkov mildly reproached Dzhagarov for his pessimism in his April, 1963, speech. He said the Party must try to help Dzhagarov, and Dzhagarov, for his part, showed himself almost indecently ready to be helped. Only two days after Zhivkov's speech, he published an article describing that speech as "comparable with the greatest aspects of the construction of socialism in Bulgaria."[35] There was a strong suspicion of connivance about this transformation. Dzhagarov saw the light instantly; many of his fellow writers must have believed that he sold his conscience rather too easily. It is impossible for an outsider to say how much sincerity and how much opportunism went into his decision. Just as several Hungarian writers, silent and hostile between 1956 and the beginning of the new course in 1961, later began to support Kadar, so Dzhagarov might have genuinely thought that cooperation and compromise were possible with Zhivkov. At any rate, the cooperation that ensued did not turn out to be entirely disadvantageous to the great majority of writers. Nor did Dzhagarov himself change overnight from young rebel to old hack. His play *The Prosecutor*, an attack on the Stalinist period produced in 1965, was hardly the work of a dogmatist like Karaslavov.[36] If Zhivkov and his power of patronage influenced him, then he certainly influenced Zhivkov, perhaps over those draughts of wine they occasionally imbibed together at a well-known hostelry on the outskirts of Sofia.[37]

Dzhagarov was elected Secretary of the Party Bureau of the Writers' Union in December, 1964, at a meeting which saw the influx of many young writers into official positions in the Union. His election took place only two months after the fall of Khrushchev, an event which had severely shaken Zhivkov and evidently

[35] *Kooperativno Selo* (Sofia), April 26, 1963.

[36] This play was produced at the Hampstead Theater Club in London in the fall of 1967 and was received with some condescension by the London critics.

[37] He also frequently traveled with Zhivkov on official visits round the country. In November, 1965, Zhivkov took him with him on an official visit to the U.A.R. and Ethiopia.

prompted him, now that his protector was gone, to try to broaden his own base at home, a determination only hardened by the April conspiracy in 1965.[38] Once again, therefore, political considerations directly affected the cultural sphere: the official mood was one of compromise. Dzhagarov was the spearhead of the regime's attempt to win over the dissident writers and forge some unity in the Writers' Union. Aided mainly by Dimitur Dimov, the respected author of "Tobacco" and now Chairman of the Writers' Union, he achieved considerable success. His work, and his own personal success, were crowned by April, 1966, when, shortly after the death of Dimov, he was elected chairman of a Writers' Union more united than at any time since 1956.[39] It was so united mainly because Emil Manov had agreed to be elected vice-chairman of the Union, thus bringing into line the large number of writers who looked to him as their leader.

Manov has been an outstanding figure in Bulgarian literature since 1956, and he typifies the writer of integrity under Communism. Forty-eight years old in 1966, he had been a Communist since the liberation. Up to 1957, he gave no indication of his later rebelliousness. First a political officer in the army, he then held various posts typical for the cultural apparatchik. From about 1952 to 1954 he was deputy chairman of the Committee for Science, Art and Culture; then he was deputy chief editor at the *Bulgarski Pisatel* state publishing house and from 1956 to 1958 a secretary of the Writers' Union. In 1958, he was strongly criticized for his novel, "An Unauthentic Case," and for his stubborn refusal to bow before official pressure. In 1960, in the calm that followed the Chervenkov counter-offensive, he was elected to the Presidium of the Writers' Union. He published several works after 1960, some of which were favorably received (as, for example, the play "Conscience")[40] while others were criticized. His novel, "The Flight of Galatea" (1963) was attacked for "reflecting decadent views and moods"[41] and his play "Abel's Mistake" was condemned for being deficient in socialist realism and for having serious political and artistic shortcomings.[42]

For a man like Manov to agree to resume a senior post in the Writers' Union, the regime must have made important conces-

[38] See Chapter 8.

[39] Dzhagarov was now both Chairman of the Writers' Union and Secretary of its Party Bureau, the first man ever to hold both positions.

[40] See the article by Venelin Kotsev, then head of the CC's Culture and Art Department, in *Novo Vreme*, August, 1964.

[41] *Narodna Kultura*, April 4, 1964.

sions. Judging from an important speech by Dzhagarov shortly before Manov's election, it seems that these concessions were in approach rather than in essential principle. While there was considerably less harping than usual on socialist realism, the principle of *Partiinost* was expounded with great vigor. But *Partiinost* can be a broad term and, since Dzhagarov implied that there would be less official interference in literature, it now seemed to give the writers considerably more leeway than before. Dzhagarov also extended a hand of forgiveness, even sympathy, for those writers who had "erred" in the past and, in general, his speech promised a more understanding atmosphere than had ever been offered in the past.[43] That Dzhagarov spoke with Zhivkov's full backing was evident from his constant references to the First Party Secretary in his speech.

Following this reassurance to the writers, the climate certainly improved. The year 1966 saw a series of important changes in the editorial staffs of the leading literary periodicals. It would be pointless to enumerate these changes here but, in general, they involved the pushing aside of older, more conservative cultural officials and their replacement by younger, more liberal men. There was also positive encouragement for writers to expose all the faults in Bulgarian society and to act as a purifying agent in the interests of a more honest and efficient way of life. This was thoroughly in keeping with Zhivkov's new policy after the fall of Khrushchev and particularly after the April conspiracy in 1965. Seeking more popularity and more props for his power than a majority in the Central Committee and support from Moscow, he appeared at last to be shaking off his timidity and embarking on a program which would, in some ways, be called national. In this he sought the support of the writers, who could become allies in this new venture under Dzhagarov's care and enlightened leadership. There is a close parallel between this policy and that pursued with considerable success by Janos Kadar in Hungary. The Kadar government kept a firm but far from severe control over its writers, encouraging them to criticize and expose mercilessly the faults in the construction of Hungarian socialism.

But Zhivkov always lacked both Kadar's confidence and his ability, and there was no guarantee that some Bulgarian writers, in their exposure of socialist weakness, would not fall back into that gloom and pessimism which had been found unacceptable before. The following *cri du coeur* from the well-known writer,

[42] *Vecherni Novini*, July 12, 1964.
[43] *Literaturen Front*, March 31, 1966.

Mladen Isaev, for example, must have come pretty close to the limit of what was acceptable:

> All over our blessed Bulgarian land, egoism, careerism, bureaucracy, narrow-mindedness, and callousness toward the people's destiny still exists. There are even more dangerous phenomena: perfidy, slander, cruelty. All these elements poison the atmosphere, stand in the way of our development. We have no right to watch this "second reality" in silence, to play down its negative influence. . . . To imagine it is possible to rid ourselves of all these phenomena by waving a magic wand would make us look silly and utterly unrealistic. They have widespread roots . . .[44]

This was worrying enough, but even less acceptable were certain voices which took advantage of the more permissive atmosphere to question the practice of Party control over culture and to urge a new concept of socialist humanism. Once again Manov was in the van. In a contribution to a discussion of the "contemporary hero" in *Literaturen Front*, Manov referred to his ideal of "Communist-democrat":

> In my opinion, the contemporary Communist who encompasses the ideas of progressive development—both of Communism and the world—is the Communist-democrat. This is, I surmise, the hero of our times, this is my hero. . . . The most characteristic feature of this hero is his affinity with the people as well as his humanism.[45]

Manov was criticized for this concept on the grounds that his hero was more of a Western social-democrat than a Communist. He was, however, treated with greater decency than he had been in 1958 and this was in itself a sign of the times, of the more civilized mode of government that now characterized Bulgaria. But Manov's article was the parting of the ways between him and cultural officialdom. After almost a year's silence, it was quietly announced in July, 1967, that he had been released from the management of the Writers' Union at his own request, "for reasons of health." A sincere attempt—on both sides—had failed after a year of effort.

The attempt had failed because it was not possible to give the degree of freedom which some writers, like Manov, wanted and to preserve unity at the same time. This was put very well by

[44] *Literaturen Front*, February 16, 1967; see also Emil Popoff, "Bulgaria's Literary 'Mini-Thaw,'" *East Europe*, February, 1968.
[45] *Literaturen Front*, September 29, 1966.

Bogumil Rainov, who had been appointed chief editor of *Literaturen Front* in 1966:

> On the one hand we speak of a complete unification and consolidation of the creative forces while, on the other, we stress the need for free discussions. It is well known, however, that with the present relations among our writers, polemics will not help unity but, on the contrary, will speed up centrifugal tendencies. We have arrived at the point where we must renounce unity if we want discussions. If we want unity we must give up the thought of discussions.[46]

The New Gleichschaltung

The regime had already come to a similar conclusion. This was one of the reasons for the decision to reorganize the Committee for Culture and Art in September, 1966, and to hold the first-ever Congress of Culture in May, 1967. The Committee for Culture and Art had been formed in 1962 when education and culture had been separated, with culture coming under the new committee and education under a separate Ministry of Education. Under the new reorganization, the control of the Committee for Culture and Art over the various creative unions—the Writers' Union, the Artists' Union, etc.—was greatly strengthened. The Committee was now termed a "public-state" agency, to connote the fact that it was now to be considered an organization belonging to all the people, and was to have branches in all Bulgarian towns and large villages.

Clearly, the need to control the writers was not the only reason for such a massive undertaking—a veritable Bulgarian "first" in Communist cultural policy and a move characterized by an almost "Chinese" comprehensiveness. The regime felt the need to launch a full-scale counter-offensive against what it considered the dangerous inroads of Western bourgeois influence, the so-called increasing aggressiveness of imperialist ideological subversion, and the political apathy of large sections of the population, particularly among the young. There was, indeed, some cause for concern. Bulgaria was no longer an unknown and ignored corner of the Balkans. It had become a tourist attraction for well over a million visitors every year, about half of whom came from the West. These guests were welcomed sincerely by a hospitable people, but welcomed by the regime only for the hard currency they brought.

[46] *Literaturen Front*, March 2, 1967; Popoff, *loc. cit.*

These, plus Western radio stations, books (although still very few), music, and dress fashions were the exemplars of the bourgeois culture that startled the regime while it tempted many Bulgarians.

The important shift in cultural policy, announced in the second half of 1966, stemmed from the regime's fears about these Western influences. Another sign of this was the election of Todor Pavlov to the Politburo at the Ninth BCP Congress in November, 1966. Prematurely dismissed by everyone as a relic of the Stalinist era, Pavlov was seventy-six when called to the highest Party body. His election, along with that of the veteran Tsola Dragoicheva, may have been partly designed as a gesture to the old guard of the Party. But Pavlov was not the man to treat his new post as a sinecure and his influence can be detected behind what might be called the "cultural revolution"—Bulgarian style.

The following quotation will give some idea of what a colossus the Committee for Culture and Art became:

> Approximately 900 village municipal councils for Culture and Art, 28 district, 215 city, and six Sofia city rayons were elected on the eve of the Congress [of Culture]. About 1,254 people were elected to the district councils, 3,000 to the city councils, and more than 9,000 to the village municipal councils. Thus, some 14,000 creative and cultural workers, scientists, public workers, and cooperative farm members became directly involved in, and responsible for the fate of, our present culture and the education of the Bulgarian people.[47]

Only the future will tell whether this new creation will turn out to be a white elephant or an effective instrument of coordination. As for the writers, it may have the effect for a time of diverting them from the polemical activities which the authorities found so distasteful. Moreover, in some ways excellent conditions were now offered: many new jobs were open in the Committee for Culture and Art and assurances continued to be given about creative freedom and artistic initiative. But writers of merit and integrity were not likely to be diverted for long, and those who thought only of place and privilege might find the new spoils system simply a bigger excuse for falling out among themselves. As for the future of Bulgarian culture, one could not help feeling that this massive new superstructure would be even more irrelevant to its real development than were the previous attempts at control and regimentation.

[47] Penyu Astardzhiev in *Narodna Kultura*, October 28, 1967.

12

Aspects of Bulgarian Foreign Policy

SOME WOULD argue that, in a relatively brief survey of Communist rule in Bulgaria, a chapter on foreign policy is superfluous, since Bulgarian foreign policy has simply been a mirror of Soviet policy. Look at what Moscow has done and then see how quickly Sofia has done likewise!

There is much truth in this contention. Ever since Stalin, early in 1948, crudely repudiated Georgi Dimitrov's suggestions for a federation of the Balkan Communist states, Bulgaria has seldom ventured into the foreign field without an anxious, eastward look over her shoulder. On occasion, she has shown an inclination to act in her best interests but, if this was not in conformity with Soviet desires, she has desisted. She has been the Soviet Union's most loyal ally, supporting her on every issue, large and small, both in intra-bloc Party affairs and in relations with the non-Communist world. Whether through choice or circumstance, she ostentatiously turned her back on the centrifugal forces at work in Eastern Europe in the late 1950's and throughout the 1960's; in fact, her only response to them was to bind herself even more closely to the authority of Moscow.

Yet it is worth discussing the motives for this policy, as well as those areas where Bulgaria has played an active rather than passive role and, finally, the recent signs of Bulgaria's will to play a positive role in foreign affairs, although still under the Soviet aegis.

263

The Possible Motives

There are three possible explanations why Bulgaria did not take advantage of the opportunities in the late 1950's, and especially the early 1960's, to shake off some of her dependence on the Soviet Union:

The first is that the Zhivkov regime deliberately chose to spurn all opportunities for more autonomy because, in the classical Communist tradition, it regarded Soviet interests as having exclusive priority, or because it considered Soviet and Bulgarian interests as so indissolubly linked that any threat to the one would have disastrous effects on the other. Thus, even if the Zhivkov regime had been strongly entrenched and had ruled efficiently and successfully, this would have meant no change in its policy and attitude toward the Soviet Union. To reinforce this explanation, some observers point to the traditional affinity of Bulgaria and Russia, and argue that Zhivkov's policy toward Moscow was only the reflection, or the fulfillment, of a traditional Bulgarian orientation.

The second possible reason is that Zhivkov's pro-Soviet policy stemmed, not from an abject dependence, but from a calculated assessment of how Bulgaria's interests might best be served. Take the case of the Sino-Soviet dispute. This dispute presented three possible courses of action to the Eastern European states: to support China to the point of openly breaking with Moscow; to gain maneuverability and material advantage by playing the two antagonists against each other; or to give the Soviet Union complete loyalty and thereby gain various rewards and concessions. Albania is the example of the first course of action, Rumania of the second. Bulgaria, it might be argued, is an example of the third. Certainly no state has been more loyal to the Soviet Union and none has received more favorable treatment. Bulgaria, unlike Rumania, was allowed to continue her ambitious industrialization program without let or hindrance and Bulgaria has received more Soviet credits in recent years than any other Eastern European state.

The third possible explanation is that, because of its own weakness, incompetence, and failure, the Zhivkov regime had no alternative but to lean more and more heavily on the Soviet crutch. Zhivkov himself, though First Party Secretary since 1954, was so beset by rival factions in his early years of power that, without the support of Khrushchev, he could hardly have survived. Certainly, only the help of the Soviet leader enabled him to get rid of his two most powerful rivals: first Vulko Chervenkov in November, 1961, and then Premier Yugov exactly one year later. As for incompetence, while Zhivkov has shown a fair measure of political skill in intra-Party politics and has worked some improvements in the economy, no one can claim that his stewardship has been a successful one. It has been this lack of success that has made dependence on the Soviet Union all the greater and more essential.

Of these three possible reasons, it is safe to consider the third—weakness and dependence—as the most convincing single explanation. The second—the calculating assessment of Bulgaria's best interests—would presuppose, not only an uncharacteristic political aplomb on the part of the Bulgarian leadership, but also a certain stability and strength enabling a rational choice between alternatives. Therefore, it is very difficult indeed to imagine that in the relationship between Zhivkov and Khrushchev there was any real element of *quid pro quo*. As for the first possibility—simple Communist devotion to the U.S.S.R. reinforced by simple Bulgarian devotion to Russia—this would indeed appear the most convincing of the three, to judge from Sofia's official pronouncements on relations with Moscow. It could, moreover, have some degree of validity. The BCP has a long record of almost feudalistic devotion to the CPSU and Georgi Dimitrov's dictum of over thirty years ago, that the true test of a Communist was his attitude toward the Soviet Union, has remained a hallowed *agitprop* shibboleth down to the present day. But this devotion, undoubted though it has been, seems insufficient in itself to explain the closeness of the attachment to Moscow since the death of Stalin or, more correctly, since 1956. It was more likely the harsh realities of his position that caused Zhivkov to cling to Khrushchev when other Eastern European leaders were distancing or even detaching themselves from him.

It is worth pausing here briefly to review the very widespread notion that Sofia's devotion to Moscow has in part been a reflection of the traditional Bulgarian pro-Russian sentiment and, therefore, has had strong popular support. This is a point on which the Bulgarian regime and most Western journalists who visit Bulgaria seem to be in agreement. It is impossible, of course, to get a really scientific assessment of whether this contention is true or not. Some public opinion polls—of rather a crude kind—began to be conducted in Bulgaria in 1967, but this was hardly one of the questions that was, or ever will be, asked. There are strong ethnic, linguistic, religious, and cultural affinities between Russians and

Bulgarians. Historically, Bulgarians looked to Russia for deliverance or succor in the same way that Serbians and Montenegrins did. Russia did liberate Bulgaria from the Turks in 1878 and, over sixty years later, even the pro-German government in Sofia did not declare war on the Soviet Union despite considerable pressure from Berlin to do so. (In World War I, however, Bulgaria *did* declare war on Russia, although this was a highly unpopular move.) But the impression gained over the last few years is that the pro-Soviet policy of the Bulgarian government has become increasingly unpopular, especially among the young and the educated. Sofia's subservience has been contrasted with the greater independence or dignity of other Eastern European states and Moscow's domination has been more and more resented. One is reminded of the words of Liuben Karavelov, one of Bulgaria's founding fathers, ninety years ago: "If Russia comes to liberate, she will be met with great sympathy; but if she comes to rule, she will find many enemies." This is truer now than ever it was and it would seem high time that the notion of Bulgarians' *unconditional* affection for Russia, like that of the Bulgarian peasant's readiness for collectivization, should be relegated to the closet of old misconceptions.

The Bulgarian Inferiority Complex

In insisting that it was weakness and lack of success that has mainly accounted for Zhivkov's relationship with Moscow, one need not, of course, jettison every other explanation completely. As pointed out, the BCP's traditional devotion to Moscow may also have been a contributory factor. Moreover, while rejecting the idea that Zhivkov weighed his loyalty in terms of the political and economic rewards he would get for it, it is reasonable to suppose that these rewards only strengthened Zhivkov's resolve to continue his policy, and the Soviets, for their part, may have wished to use Bulgaria as an example of the benefits that loyalty could bring. In trying to account for this, or any other, policy, one can only try to pinpoint the main reason, leaving open the possibility that other reasons played their part in initiating or continuing the policy.

An inevitable consequence of failure is lack of confidence; this encourages dependence which, in turn, only increases the lack of confidence. But failure implies that something has, at least, been attempted, and the history of the Bulgarian Communist Party is studded with quite spectacular ventures whose subsequent failure has led to periods of depression, unsureness, and doubt; in short, to what everybody nowadays calls an inferiority complex. The BCP's loyalty to Moscow has not prevented it on occasion from taking its own initiatives—never in defiance of Moscow, but sometimes not in full concert with it. The trouble has been that these initiatives have failed, and been followed by periods of passivity amounting almost to paralysis. Three examples will suffice. In 1923, the Bulgarian Communists staged their disastrous September Uprising following the fall some months earlier of the Agrarian leader, Stamboliski. For their failure, they were roundly criticized by the Comintern, whose criticism turned to utter scorn two years later after the unsuccessful attempt to murder Czar Boris by blowing up the Sveta Nedelia Cathedral in Sofia. The Party never quite recovered from this failure throughout the inter-war period. The partisan exploits of World War II, limited but creditable, and the seizure of power immediately after it, produced a new flush of self-confidence, bolstered by the international fame of such leaders as Georgi Dimitrov and Vassil Kolarov. Once more, however, this was soon to be undermined. First the aging and ailing Dimitrov was humiliated by Stalin over his plans for a Balkan Federation; one year later Dimitrov died in Moscow. The suspicions that he did not die from natural causes cannot be proved but, in the terror-ridden atmosphere of Stalin's court in his last years, anything could have happened. In the meantime Stalin, in the course of his ruthless *Gleichschaltung*, removed Traicho Kostov, Bulgaria's foremost home Communist and a man widely known for defending what he considered his country's best interests. In 1950, the prestigious Kolarov died. There followed the six years of Chervenkov's role, which paralyzed much of the initiative and ability inside the Bulgarian Party and spent its energies in strenuous attempts to model Bulgaria entirely in the Soviet image.

A third example of a quite spectacular Bulgarian initiative is found in the Zhivkov era. This was the "great leap forward" of 1959 and 1960. This episode has been described in some detail in Chapter 5. There can be little doubt that, in part, this was an initiative on which Moscow was not fully consulted. The original enthusiasm for the communes, soon to evaporate under Moscow's frown, seems to confirm that in the latter part of 1958 Sofia was prepared to take initiatives without first consulting the Soviet

Union, but immediately abandoned them when the Soviet's displeasure became known. The point here, however, is that the "great leap forward" was a failure with serious economic, political, and psychological consequences. The result was that the BCP lapsed into another cycle of depression, its confidence further undermined, its dependence on the CPSU reconfirmed. Though the failure of the "great leap forward" was not the sole cause of Zhivkov's submissiveness to Khrushchev in the early 1960's, it was certainly a contributory factor to it.

To this lack of confidence on the part of the BCP one should add a general lack of self-confidence in the Bulgarian nation as a whole. This observation applies to post-1878 Bulgaria, of course, and not to the historical Bulgarian empires of the Middle Ages, which lacked nothing in confidence and optimism. For modern Bulgaria, the joy at being liberated from the Turks and the historical fulfillment reflected in the Treaty of San Stefano in March, 1878, were quickly soured by the humiliations of the Treaty of Berlin the following July, which deprived the new state of territories—especially large parts of Macedonia—which every Bulgarian passionately claimed as essential parts of his country. The subsequent history of Bulgaria was often dominated by disastrous attempts to recover all or parts of the San Stefano territories, attempts which cost the country dear in lives, resources, and reputation. All this sapped the confidence of the nation. The victorious Western powers of the twentieth century considered Bulgaria, when they considered it at all, as a constant enemy deserving short shrift either in the conference room or outside it. This only increased the Bulgarian inferiority complex—and the situation was all the more humiliating because her two neighboring enemies, Greece and Serbia, were the darlings of the West, enjoying a prestige and even a glamor in sharp contrast to the sorry figure cut by Bulgaria. Serbia, through sheer circumstance, always found herself on the "right" side and always acquitted herself heroically; Greece, too, was always on the winning side and profited from an almost universal philhellenism. Bulgaria, the pariah, had no powerful friend, usually no friend at all. Her "allies" since liberation, Germany and Russia, have seen her as an object to be used and exploited rather than respected and valued. It will not do simply to say that the Bulgarians had no one to blame but themselves. No one can claim that the face Bulgaria has presented to the world has always been an attractive one: her public relations have been disastrous indeed. But that is hardly the fault of the nation as a whole, which has great virtues and talents all too often ignored, and has had justified grievances against the way history has used it.

The Balkan Stage

Bulgaria's foreign policy initiatives have been almost exclusively confined to the Balkans. Here Bulgaria, a loyal member of the Warsaw Pact facing two relatively weak and unstable members of NATO, Greece and Turkey, has been a valuable agent of the Soviet Union in her constant probings for openings and opportunities.

Diplomatic activity in the Balkans had been virtually frozen since the failure of the Communists in the Greek civil war and the decisions of both the Greek and Turkish governments to join NATO and accept American help under the Truman Doctrine. As part of the "new course" after Stalin's death, the Bulgarian government did seek to improve relations with Greece; but despite the agreement to establish diplomatic relations in 1953 and the conclusion of trade agreements, neither side showed a real disposition to improve relations. In 1957, however, the Warsaw Pact states, under the leadership of the Soviet Union, initiated their proposals for European security based on a number of regional nuclear-free-zone agreements. The most notable of these was the Rapacki Plan (named after the Polish Foreign Minister) affecting central Europe. In the Balkans, however, a number of proposals were made—first for *détente* and then for an atom-free zone—and it was in these that Rumania and Bulgaria (and, to a lesser degree, Albania while she was still a Soviet ally) played an important role.

Rumania made the first gesture. In September, 1957, the then Rumanian Premier, Chivu Stoica, circulated notes to Bulgaria, Albania, Greece, Turkey, and Yugoslavia urging a summit meeting of these states to discuss their differences and pave the way for a general *détente* in the area.[1] Bulgaria and Albania—there was clear collusion with the Soviet Union—accepted immediately. Yugoslavia accepted in principle but was evasive on the question of an actual conference. Both Greece and Turkey rejected the proposal, the Greeks cautioning that it was inopportune for the time being.

[1] Radio Bucharest, September 10, 1957.

This setback, however, did not daunt the Rumanian government, still outwardly a loyal Soviet ally. A strong propaganda barrage, a veritable "peace offensive," was launched by the three Balkan Communist allies. It was obviously aimed at appealing to the Greek and Turkish populations over the heads of their governments. But not long afterwards, bloc relations with Yugoslavia took a serious turn for the worse when the Seventh Yugoslav Party Congress met at Ljubljana in April, 1958, and approved its highly controversial "revisionist" program. Relations with Greece and Turkey also became increasingly acrimonious by 1958 because of the decisions of the Athens and Ankara governments to install NATO rocket bases on their territories.

It was probably this decision that prompted Bucharest's next move in the Balkans. On June 9, 1959, Stoica again called for a Balkan summit conference to discuss the establishment of a zone of peace and a ban on rocket bases and nuclear weapons in the area.[2] This new proposal was obviously the result of Khrushchev's visit to Albania in May and early June, 1959, where he delivered a series of broadsides against the Greeks and the Turks for their rocket-base decisions. Khrushchev promptly (and naturally) welcomed the renewed Rumanian initiative and Albania and Bulgaria once again warmly greeted it. Marshal Tito repeated his acceptance of the proposal in principle although he declared that such a meeting in itself would not remove the danger of nuclear warfare in the area. Greece rejected the proposal and Turkey ignored it.

The Greek and Turkish refusals produced a renewed propaganda barrage, which was opened on June 25, 1959, by a Soviet call for the creation of an atom-free zone in the Balkans and in the Adriatic area,[3] the inclusion of the Adriatic obviously being aimed against rocket installations in Italy.

The Bulgarian, Rumanian, and Albanian governments promptly came out in strong support of the Soviet declaration. The peace offensive became more and more focused on Greece; in August, the Bulgarian government renewed its offer to sign a treaty of non-aggression with its southern neighbor.[4] The overture was immediately rejected by the Greeks, causing a howl of resentment in Tirana and Bucharest as well as in Sofia. (At this stage the Albanians were supporting the Bulgarian and Rumanian proposals.)

[2] *Scînteia* (Bucharest), June 10, 1959.
[3] *Pravda* (Moscow), June 25, 1959.
[4] Radio Sofia, July 22, 1959.

Premier Mehmet Shehu of Albania stated that he "highly esteemed the endeavors of the Bulgarian government," and considered the proposal as "realistic."[5] The barrage was now clearly directed against Greek public opinion. In an interview given to the Greek Communist paper *Avgi* in December, 1959, Zhivkov stated that "Greek public opinion more and more reflects sober and persistent voices urging that Greek foreign policy keep in harmony with changes made in the international situation in favor of peace and understanding." In the same interview, Zhivkov made an ominous remark on the question of rocket bases. "We have declared on other occasions," he said, "that rocket installations do not exist on Bulgarian territory. We can say the same again today. If, however, such installations are constructed in neighboring countries, we shall, of course, be obliged to draw the necessary conclusions from such action."[6]

But the tone applied to the Greeks was usually not threatening at all. In fact shortly after he gave this interview to *Avgi*, Zhivkov made his most alluring proposal. Addressing the Bulgarian National Assembly on December 25, 1959, he proposed to Greece that both countries should reduce their forces to the minimum needed for border guards.[7] This he offered as an earnest of Bulgaria's good intentions and of her desire to implement Khrushchev's worldwide disarmament proposal made earlier that year. It was a remarkable offer and went much further than anything previously proposed. Neither Rumania nor Albania, or the Soviet Union, had gone so far. The Greeks did not respond, however, and the Bulgarians allowed the proposal to drop.

It was brought up again in September, 1960, at the session of the General Assembly of the United Nations that Khrushchev and all the Party leaders of the Eastern European states attended.[8] In his address to the U.N., Zhivkov repeated his offer. Bulgaria had proposed, he said, "the conclusion of a non-aggression treaty among the Balkan states, agreement on a considerable cut in the armed forces of the Balkan countries, reduction of these forces to a point needed only to guard the borders, and the transforma-

[5] *Rabotnichesko Delo* (Sofia), August 10, 1959.

[6] There was much speculation in the West at that time on whether the Soviets already had rocket bases on Bulgarian territory. Most expert sources concluded that they did not.

[7] *Rabotnichesko Delo*, December 26, 1959.

[8] Except, of course, Ulbricht, because the G.D.R. was not a member of the U.N. Albania was represented by Premier Shehu and not by First Party Secretary Hoxha.

tion of the Balkans into the first region to implement the idea of general and complete disarmament."[9]

What Zhivkov presumably meant was not that Bulgaria would agree to complete disarmament in the Balkans alone, but that, once worldwide disarmament had been agreed upon, Bulgaria would agree to the Balkans being the first area where the decisions should be implemented. It is unlikely he was suggesting that the Balkans should set the example in the hope that the rest of the world should follow. But even accepting the minimum interpretation it was a radical proposal. Gheorghiu-Dej's speech to the U.N. assembly contained no such proposal, nor had the Soviet Union suggested anything like it. But it was hardly likely that Zhivkov would make a move like this without clearing it with Khrushchev and, if Moscow had objected to the idea, it could have scotched it when Zhivkov first aired it in December, 1959.

One Balkan ally—Albania—repudiated the idea completely. It was becoming clear that the Hoxha regime was drifting further away from the Soviet Union in the direction of Peking,[10] but her attack on Zhivkov's proposal was the first example of open polemics between herself and one of her allies. Addressing the Albanian parliament in October, 1960, Shehu said his government "could never accept the idea of local and complete disarmament, which may have been conceived in the mind of someone in the Balkans" (i.e., Zhivkov). Such an idea, with NATO bases in Italy and the American Sixth Fleet cruising about "like an open-mouthed dragon" was "absurd and dangerous for every socialist state in the Balkans."[11]

Zhivkov's proposal received no positive response from either Greece or Turkey and was once again shelved. It may simply have been a trial balloon, supported or even prompted by Moscow. But it certainly broke the unity of approach that had existed among the three Warsaw Pact states of the area. Henceforward, with Albania a pro-Chinese dropout and Rumania taking a progressively more independent course, Communist initiatives in the Balkans

[9] Radio Sofia, September 28, 1960.

[10] See William E. Griffith, *Albania and the Sino-Soviet Rift* (Cambridge, Mass., 1963); J. F. Brown, "Albania, Mirror of Conflict," *Survey* (London), No. 40, January, 1962.

[11] *Zeri i Popullit* (Tirana), October 26, 1960. Shehu also attacked a proposal Gomulka made at the U.N. session that no *new* military bases be built on the territories of either the Warsaw Pact or the NATO countries. This, said Shehu, implied the acceptance of all the existing bases on NATO territory that were threatening the socialist camp.

took on a different character. The period of cohesion was definitely over. It was to be four years before serious diplomacy was revived in the Balkans.

Relations with Greece

Perhaps the best explanation for the renewal of Zhivkov's offer on disarmament was that, in the second half of 1960, there appeared to be real prospects for meaningful talks with Greece on the settlement of what were generally referred to as "outstanding problems." Hence the timeliness of a grand gesture as an earnest of good faith and reasonableness.

The Bulgarian-Greek negotiations over these "outstanding problems" always had about them a certain Levantine character—the haggling, the appeal to principle, the statement followed by its denial or strong modification and then finally, in 1964, the rapid agreement achieved with such apparent ease as to make the previous difficulties seem almost inexplicable. The "outstanding problem" was undoubtedly the payment of Bulgaria's war reparations debt to Greece, fixed by the Paris peace treaties of 1947 at 45 million dollars, of which not one cent had been handed over. Other problems to which the Greeks constantly referred were compensation for Greek property nationalized in Bulgaria after the Communist takeover, the inflated size of the Bulgarian army compared to the limits set by the Paris treaty,[12] and the regular flow of Bulgarian spies and saboteurs into Greece which had been a continuing source of friction between the two countries in the early 1950's.

Since 1953, the Bulgarian government had offered to open talks on several occasions, but the successive Greek governments had had a constant answer to such blandishments: Bulgaria must pay her war debt which, it was later maintained, had now risen to 65 million dollars through postwar inflation. And before negotiations could begin, Bulgaria must make a down payment on her debt as a proof of her good intentions. This had proved the stumbling block. The Bulgarians, in a gambit worthy of the bazaar, had produced a counter-claim of their own. This was that, under a treaty signed between the two countries in 1927, Greece should have—

[12] The size of the Bulgarian army was fixed at 65,000 men by the treaty. Its first-line strength, however, was estimated at between 150,000 and 200,000.

but had not—paid Bulgaria the equivalent of 3.5 million old German Reichmarks as compensation for the repatriation of Bulgarians from Greek territory after World War I. This hoary bourgeois relic was probably not taken seriously by either side but it was a useful stalling device for Sofia. Meanwhile, the Greeks stubbornly pressed their claim for initial down payment. In 1954, they are reported to have asked for 8 million dollars as a guarantee. This was probably more than the Bulgarians had envisaged paying altogether. In February, 1956, Sofia offered a down payment of 2 million but the Greeks rejected this as insufficient. After that the matter had comfortably bogged down in complete impasse.

The result of this deadlock had been an iron curtain between Greece and Bulgaria much less penetrable than that between any other two European countries. Rail and road communications between these two neighbors were almost completely cut off and telephone and telegraphic contacts were such as to defy all but the most tortuous imaginations. A telephone call from Athens to Sofia had to go through Edirne in Turkish Thrace. Trade, it is true, had slowly increased, but the turnover envisaged for as late as 1960 was only valued at 8 million dollars. Cultural relations increased, but again the contacts were almost negligible. As mentioned earlier, diplomatic relations were agreed to as early as 1953, but because of Greek persistence on the reparations issue they are still only at the chargé d'affaires level. The only real progress made was on the problem of the exact demarcation of certain parts of the border. In July, 1953, there was a meeting between border officials of the two countries and since then a joint border commission had met fairly regularly and with some success. But this had not prevented the Bulgarians from sending their agents into Greece, thereby arousing the suspicions of Athens even further.

In July, 1960, two months before Zhivkov made his dramatic proposal at the U.N. Sofia suggested talks between the two governments on the mutual exploitation of two rivers on the Greek-Bulgarian frontier. The Greeks countered by demanding that any talks include the reparations issue; the Bulgarians agreed and it was decided to begin talks in Athens in December. Although the Greek government officially denied that it had withdrawn any of its former preconditions for talks, it was evident that it had, in fact, dropped its demand for a downpayment. Thus, though the talks which began in December, 1960, stalled and were subsequently shelved, Bulgarian persistence had won an important point.

Once this point had been surrendered by the Greeks it was only a matter of time before agreement was reached. That time came in the middle of 1964. Bulgarian persistence was aided by the presence in power in Athens of the Papandreou government, whose leader had been pressing for normalization of relations with Sofia, and by the sharp increase of anti-Western sentiment in Greece over Cyprus. It was clearly the occasion for another Bulgarian approach. It was made with unaccustomed skill and met with swifter success than the Bulgarians ever dared expect. In July, 1964, a number of agreements were signed in Athens. Bulgaria agreed to pay Greece a sum of 7 million dollars in goods against her war reparation obligations—a far lower sum than the Greeks had ever mentioned. In addition, a number of other agreements were signed involving trade, improvement of communications between the two countries, cultural cooperation, and tourism.[13] Bulgaria's Foreign Minister, Ivan Bashev, visited Athens to sign the agreements in an atmosphere of cordiality unthinkable only two years before. The 1964 agreements did not suddenly make friends out of enemies, but the formal groundwork for better relations were laid. Bulgaria's approach to the south, long a dead end, had at least become a through road again.

Balkan Cooperation

The successful conclusion of the agreements with Greece occurred *before* the fall of Khrushchev in October, 1964. This fact shows the danger of too schematic a view, which would make the "event of October 14" the neat dividing line between paralysis and movement on the part of the Bulgarian government in foreign affairs. But from what happened after October, 1964, the generalization can be made that Khrushchev's fall spurred the Zhivkov regime to more "individual" action abroad, as at home—a change which the April conspiracy in 1965 only accelerated. This more active diplomatic engagement hardly involved any distancing of Bulgaria from Moscow. As we have seen, no matter what the Sofia leadership may have felt about Khrushchev's fall, it renewed

[13] *Rabotnichesko Delo*, July 10, 1964, published a complete list of the agreements.

its fealty to the Soviet Union without even a word about the dismissed leader's merits,[14] and the April conspiracy only caused almost embarrassing outbursts of fealty to Moscow. But once the shock of both these events had passed, Sofia may have felt less restraint than in the past in pursuing foreign policy objectives which it considered both necessary and advantageous.

The Balkans once again became the scene of considerable diplomatic activity. As in the period from 1957 to 1960, the initiatives usually came from the Communist states, but they were now quite different in character. The initiatives were more individual than concerted, and where there was concerted action, it originated with the Balkan states themselves rather than being prompted by, or closely coordinated with, Moscow. They were much more Balkan, and less Soviet-directed, than before. Now that the dominant Khrushchev had been replaced by the colorless Brezhnev and Kosygin, who were primarily concerned with consolidating their domestic position and could pay little attention to Balkan problems, the Communist Balkan states had a freer hand. Moreover, of those states, only Bulgaria now remained a loyal ally of the Soviet Union. Rumania was pursuing her own line; Albania was a pro-Peking outcast, and Yugoslavia, despite the improvement in her relations with Moscow, was still very much a free agent. The scene had changed completely. There was now a greater chance of genuine Balkan cooperation than at any time since World War II.

The attempts to achieve Balkan cooperation have a long history of failure dating back to the early part of this century. To provide the necessary background for the diplomacy of the 1960's however, one need only cite the Balkan Entente of 1934 between Yugoslavia, Rumania, Greece, and Turkey. This grouping had an integral connection with the Little Entente, of which Yugoslavia and Rumania were also members. But the Balkan Entente, by its exclusion of Bulgaria, reflected an atmosphere of tension as much as a spirit of cooperation, since one of the main reasons for its foundation was precisely the fear of Bulgaria, whose irredentism was encouraged first by Italy and then Germany.

After World War II the Balkan states, with the exception of Turkey and (narrowly) of Greece, found themselves once more in the grip of a great imperial power, one with whom they were

[14] See Central Committee Declaration, *Rabotnichesko Delo*, October 21, 1964.

by no means unfamiliar. The diplomatic history of these states since the war must be viewed in the light of this cardinal fact. Russia returned to the Balkans, more powerful and in greater control than ever before. The events of the last two decades have been largely dominated either by Soviet efforts to extend that control or by the efforts of others to check it or to struggle free from it. This, therefore, has been the essential framework for the post-war efforts aimed at reviving the idea of Balkan cooperation.

The first such effort was made at the beginning of 1947 by Tito and Dimitrov. In February of that year, when Dimitrov was on a visit to Bled in Slovenia, the two leaders announced the conclusion of an agreement ending frontier travel barriers between the two countries and arranging for a later customs union. The following August, Tito visited Sofia, signed the Yugoslav-Bulgarian treaty of friendship, and predicted a cooperation so close that federation would become "a mere formality." What Tito and Dimitrov had specifically in mind was a South Slav rather than a Balkan Federation, a union between Yugoslavia and Bulgaria. Albania, a non-Slav nation, would probably have been thrown in but it was a Yugoslav fief anyway at the time. Dimitrov, however, seems to have had the notion of a broader association which would embrace all the Balkan Communist states, including Rumania and even Greece; he was evidently confident that the latter would soon fall under Communist control. All these schemes were struck down by Stalin at the beginning of 1948, mainly because of his growing distrust of Yugoslavia and his suspicion that a Balkan association would dilute Soviet control. Yugoslavia's subsequent expulsion from the Cominform and the Communist defeat in Greece completed the destruction of the immediate postwar efforts toward Balkan unity.

The Balkans soon reverted to its unfortunate role of an international cockpit. It became an important front in the Cold War. Albania, Bulgaria, and Rumania were the clients of the Soviet Union. Turkey and especially Greece became dependent, even for their survival, on the United States, who had assumed Western obligations in the area because of the decline of Britain. Though the struggle was now labeled as one between ideologies, the old national resentments of Albania and Bulgaria against Greece added a sharpness and a relish to the conflict.

The situation was further complicated by the transformation of Yugoslavia into a Communist outcast in great danger of subversion by her former allies. Here again, under the cloak of a struggle between dogma and heresy, time-worn feuds took on a fresh virulence, with Tirana and Sofia pressing their grievances against the Belgrade government. The danger to Yugoslavia from her erstwhile friends was such that she had to draw closer to her erstwhile enemies, Greece and Turkey. This gravitation was skillfully encouraged by American diplomacy, in an effort to bring Yugoslavia into a defensive system covering the eastern Mediterranean. In 1951, Greece and Turkey had been asked to join NATO. Yugoslavia was needed to complete the chain beginning with Italy and ending with Turkey (and later to extend through the Near East to Pakistan). Tito proved amenable, and in February, 1953, a treaty of friendship and cooperation between Yugoslavia, Greece, and Turkey was signed, followed in 1954 by a military alliance. This alliance had, *mutatis mutandis*, certain similarities with the Balkan Entente of twenty years before. All three signatories agreed that they would regard an act of aggression against any one of them as an act of aggression against all of them. A permanent council and secretariat were set up and regular consultations at various levels were agreed upon. It might be added that American diplomacy achieved its crowning triumph in this field by the agreement reached in October, 1954, between Yugoslavia and Italy over Trieste. The chain was complete and it looked secure.

That it was, in fact, not secure was shown by the Soviet-Yugoslav *rapprochement* of 1955. In his courtship with Yugoslavia, Khrushchev was no doubt mainly motivated by the need to mend socialist fences, but one of his important subsidiary aims was to break the Western chain of alliance in the Eastern Mediterranean at its weakest point. In this he succeeded: from the first moment of the Soviet-Yugoslav *rapprochement*, the infant Balkan Alliance became only a museum piece, occasionally polished but never used.

The Soviet-directed peace offensive in the Balkans between 1957 and 1960, spearheaded by Rumania and Bulgaria, was further designed to weaken that chain. But the Soviet drive backfired because of the defection of Albania and, partially, of Rumania. The diplomatic initiative now came from the Balkan states themselves.

After the Bulgarian success with Greece in 1964, Rumania took up most of the running in 1965. Premier Maurer visited Ankara in July and Athens in September. The result of these visits was the settlement of outstanding problems and an improvement of general relations. But such was the condition of Communist unity on the Balkan peninsula that the most significant of Rumania's overtures in 1965 and 1966 were to Bulgaria, her "ally" in the Warsaw Pact.

Rumanian-Bulgarian relations had almost always left much to be desired. The two states, though bound to each other not only by geography but also in recent years by a common ideology and a system of economic and military alliances, have seldom been examples of the neighborly spirit. Relations became particularly strained when Rumania embarked on her policy of "nationalist deviation" to which Bulgaria's only response was to draw even more closely to the Soviet Union. Certainly, there was no love lost between Gheorghiu-Dej and Todor Zhivkov and, from what has happened since his death, it is evident that the old Rumanian leader's attitude was, in itself, a hindrance to the improvement of relations between Bucharest and Sofia.

Scarcely had Gheorghiu-Dej been laid to rest in March, 1965, however, when attempts at a *rapprochement* began in earnest. At whose initiative they began is difficult to say, but both sides were obviously ready for them. Zhivkov visited Bucharest for Gheorghiu-Dej's funeral in March, 1965, and returned the following July for the Ninth Rumanian Party Congress. Thereafter, however, it was Ceausescu who did the traveling. Gheorghiu-Dej did not visit Bulgaria once after 1957; Ceausescu, between August, 1965 and August, 1966, visited Bulgaria four times for talks with Zhivkov and other Sofia leaders.

That both leaders were anxious to establish closer relations is obvious enough. Their motives are not so clear. It is unlikely that Ceausescu sought to infect Zhivkov with the virus of nationalism and persuade him to adopt a less loyal policy to Moscow. It is more probable that the courtship of Zhivkov was considered an essential part of a Rumanian initiative for *détente* in the Balkans and for more active cooperation in the area, perhaps eventually in the framework of a specifically Balkan regional concept.[15] Zhivkov's motives are more difficult to determine. Moscow must have taken more than a passing interest in his frequent meetings with Ceausescu. The Soviets may possibly have encouraged him

[15] Note that while these initiatives were taking place in the Balkans, Hungary was making initiatives for a grouping of states in the Danubian region of Central Europe. See Charles Andras: "Neighbors on the Danube; New Variations on the Old Theme of Regional Cooperation," *Radio Free Europe Research* (Munich), December, 1967.

in the hope that he could be a restraining influence on Rumania. But it is easier to imagine Zhivkov reassuring the Soviets that his cooperation with Bucharest did not at all impinge on his loyalty to them, and that it might indeed have beneficial results in restraining Ceausescu. It may also be assumed that he, too, like Ceausescu, genuinely believed in Balkan cooperation and had little difficulty in persuading the Soviets that it was in their interests too.

But if real Balkan cooperation demanded a *rapprochement* between Bulgaria and Rumania, it also demanded one between Bulgaria and Yugoslavia. Here the problems were far greater. The differences of ideology after 1948 only added a new element to the old historical differences. It is not possible here to discuss the background of the age old problem of Macedonia[16] but a brief allusion to the core of the problem is necessary.

The "Greater Bulgaria" established by the Treaty of San Stefano in March, 1878, included most of Macedonia, but this was quickly lost at the Congress of Berlin the same year. It was never to be part of Bulgaria again except temporarily in the Balkan Wars and in the first and second World Wars. At the end of World War I, Macedonia was divided among four Balkan states: of its approximately 26,150 square miles, about half went to Greece (13,300 square miles); Yugoslavia got over 10,000 square miles, Bulgaria 2,600 square miles, and Albania occupied a tiny strip on her eastern border. The Bulgarian claim to Macedonia was based on history, race, and language. The historical claim was based on the grounds of their medieval empires, particularly that of Czar Simeon (893–927) and the Treaty of San Stefano. The Bulgarians also insisted that the Macedonians were ethnic Bulgarians in terms of language and custom. Until World War II, Bulgaria maintained that Macedonia was an integral unit, that all Macedonians were Bulgarians, and hence that all Macedonia should be part of Bulgaria.

The Serbs had also used language and custom as a proof that Macedonians were closer to the Serbs than anyone else and also made historical claims based on the medieval empire of Stephan Dusan in the fourteenth century. The Greek case was based on the historical claims to Macedonia dating back to Alexander of Macedon and to the long period of Byzantine rule. They also pointed out that, under the Turkish Empire, the people of Macedonia were members of the Greek Orthodox Church until

[16] See Elisabeth Barker: *Macedonia, Its Place in Balkan Power Politics,* (London, 1950).

the creation of the Serbian and Bulgarian churches in the nineteenth century. To the Greeks, the people of Macedonia had no real national consciousness: they referred to them as "Slavophones" who were really "Greek at heart."

After World War I, the Greek part of Macedonia became thoroughly hellenized as a result of the exchange of minorities between Greece and Turkey and Greece and Bulgaria and the settlement of a large number of Greeks in Greek Macedonia. The Slav Macedonians became a distinct minority and, though Bulgarian sources have continued to claim the presence of a much larger number of Slavs in Greek Macedonia than there probably are and have not formally dropped their territorial claims, the matter has generally been allowed quietly to drop. Though occasional polemics between Athens and Sofia flare up on the question, it is now not considered an "outstanding problem" between the two countries.

In 1944, a completely new dimension was given to the Macedonian problem when the "People's Republic of Macedonia" was established as one of the federal units of Yugoslavia. The Macedonians were recognized as a separate group of the Slavic race, having their own official language. This new conception was utterly at variance not only with the Bulgarian and Greek attitudes but with the previous contentions of the Serbs. None—including even many Serbs—have ever accepted it.[17]

Yet, in the early postwar friendship between Tito and Dimitrov, it seemed possible that all this hostility might be overcome through a federal union between Yugoslavia and Bulgaria, with Yugoslav and Bulgarian (Pirin) Macedonia forming a single republic within the greater union. Such hopes finally came to an end when Yugoslavia was expelled from the Cominform in 1948. Since then, polemics over Macedonia have been a recurring irritant in relations between the two countries, abating only during periods of Soviet-Yugoslav *rapprochement*. They were at their most vitriolic between 1948 and 1953, then slackened during the "new course" and particularly after the Khrushchev-Tito reconciliation in 1955. After the Hungarian Revolution they picked up again and became quite intense between 1958 and 1961, when Yugoslavia's relations with the Soviet camp cooled largely because

[17] This very brief summary has drawn heavily on an excellent resumé of political problems in the Balkans by Huey Louis Kostanick, "The Geopolitics of the Balkans" in Charles and Barbara Jelavich (eds.), *The Balkans in Transition* (Berkeley and Los Angeles, 1963), pp. 1–55.

of her adoption of the "revisionist" Party program at Ljubljana in 1958. After the second *rapprochement* between Moscow and Belgrade at the end of 1960, relations eased again, though between 1960 and 1965 they continued only intermittently. Indeed the heat of the Macedonian dispute between Bulgaria and Yugoslavia was usually a good indication of relations between Yugoslavia and the Soviet bloc as a whole. When the polemics began to gather momentum, this was a sign that things were not going well between Belgrade and Moscow.

Macedonia was the most fundamental but not the only cause of ill will between the Bulgarian and Yugoslav regimes. In the Bulgarian Party, the conservative elements regarded Tito as their mortal enemy not only because of their distrust and fear of his revisionism, but also because they could not forget that the Yugoslav had played an important part in the fall of their leader Chervenkov in 1956. These elements steadily opposed reconciliation with Yugoslavia, and it will be recalled that one of the reasons for Khrushchev's visit to Bulgaria in 1962 was to support Zhivkov in the policy of closer relations with Belgrade.

Relations, however, did improve steadily after 1962. In January, 1963, Todor Zhivkov himself called on Tito in Belgrade on his way back from an East German Party congress in Pankow. But, despite this and other signs of improvement, the Bulgarian-Yugoslav *rapprochement* was noticeably more hesitant and less warm than that between Yugoslavia and other socialist countries, for example with the Soviet Union, Rumania, or Hungary. The initiative for acceleration seems to have come from the Bulgarian side and, again, it came after the fall of Khrushchev. In January, 1965, the then Yugoslav Foreign Minister, Koca Popovic, paid an official visit to Sofia and it was probably he who made preparations for a Tito visit. One of the most important factors prompting Tito to go to Sofia was his apparent conviction that this recent Bulgarian initiative was not so much an extension of Soviet policy but was more genuinely Bulgarian—something new on the Balkan scene. He went in September, 1965, his first official visit to the Bulgarian capital in eighteen years. The communiqué issued at the end of his visit was a routine, bland document covering bilateral relations, the need for closer collaboration in the Balkans, the international situation, and the situation in the international Communist movement.[18] It gave little indication of agreement, or

[18] *Rabotnichesko Delo*, September 28, 1965.

even discussion, about the real problems between the two coun-tries. It was Tito himself who gave some indication that these had, in fact, been discussed as he returned to Yugoslav soil:

> After our talks, which we conducted there, everything which had earlier made it impossible to maintain good relations was dropped away. All this is now overcome. . . . We have to take from the past only positive things. We do not need the negative ones. Look now, we have, together with our Bulgarian comrades, abandoned everything which in the past was negative and we shall stick to this firmly. . . . We found very easily a common language in discussing many prob-lems of our bilateral cooperation and international politics. I can say that there were almost no important issues about which we did not reach mutual understanding and over which we did not agree. . . . Together with our Bulgarian comrades, we have to fight all phenomena which might inflame mutual mistrust or might revive some old passions, as for instance when some historians write and interpret the history of our peoples according to their own will.[19]

Although Tito did not mention Macedonia—and it was not mentioned at all during his visit—he clearly had the subject in mind in the last sentence of the above passage. He was referring to the work of certain Bulgarian historians whose nationalist com-ments on Macedonia drew an immediate response from the Yugo-slav side, and he was appealing for calm. For a time he was successful and, though polemics did not cease entirely, it did seem possible that Yugoslavia and Bulgaria would enter their most fruitful period of cooperation since the years immediately after World War II.

The Wider Stage

While rightly concentrating on improving relations and refur-bishing her image with her Balkan neighbors, Communist and non-Communist, Bulgaria made serious efforts in 1965 and 1966 to improve her relations with the Western states.

By Western is meant mainly European. Bulgarian relations with the United States have never progressed to an extent that prom-ised any real improvement. In February, 1950, relations between the two states had been completely broken off after the U.S. Minister in Sofia, Donald Heath, was accused of complicity with

[19] Speech at Pirot: *Tanjug* (Belgrade), September 28, 1965.

Traicho Kostov, executed the previous December. Kostov was partially rehabilitated in 1956 and the Bulgarian government subsequently informed Washington that, since the charges against Kostov had been annulled, those against Mr. Heath were also groundless. It was not, however, until March, 1959, that it was announced that the U.S. and Bulgaria would resume diplomatic relations, a State Department spokesman announcing that "previously existing obstacles" had been successfully overcome.[20] Relations since then have improved slightly but there have been periods of tension, as in December, 1963, when a Bulgarian diplomat, Assen Georgiev, was sentenced to death on charges of spying for the U.S., his trial being celebrated by a violent demonstration outside the American Legation. Subsequent efforts on the part of Washington to improve relations with Bulgaria, and with the rest of Eastern Europe, were vitiated by the Vietnam conflict. The *détente* that slowly developed after the Cuban crisis of 1962 was largely an affair between the two parts of Europe.

In this the Bulgarian role was by no means negligible. High level visits were exchanged with every country of Western Europe except West Germany and, of course, Spain and Portugal. Because of President deGaulle's anti-American policy, the most spectacular developments were with France. A visit by Foreign Minister Couve de Murville early in 1966 paved the way for a visit to France by Zhivkov himself in October of that year which resulted in a series of economic, technical, and cultural agreements. One of the most intriguing economic agreements between the two countries had been signed shortly before Zhivkov's visit. This was between the Renault motor company and the Bulgarian government for the assembly of Renault automobiles in Bulgaria.[21] The assembly plant would be at Kazanlik (the center of the rose region). It was to have an annual capacity of 3,000 automobiles at first, and 10,000 eventually.

More significant, however, was the movement in Bulgarian relations with the Federal Republic of Germany. Trade relations had existed between the two countries since 1954 and commerce had grown steadily. But Bulgaria had participated fully in the violent anti-Bonn campaign that the Warsaw Pact states had waged. However, when the Bonn government began its slowly-unfolding policy of reconciliation with the Eastern European states, Bulgaria showed a ready response. In March, 1964, she signed an agreement

[20] Associated Press (Washington), March 27, 1959.
[21] Reuters (Vienna), September 17, 1966.

with the West German government for the exchange of trade missions and for a long-term trade treaty till the end of 1966.[22] The treaty provided for a total annual exchange of 460 million marks, an increase of some 65 per cent compared with the previous trade agreement of 1959.[23] Later, when the approaches of Chancellor Erhard and his Foreign Minister, Gerhard Schroeder, began to assume a more political character, the Bulgarian response was more cautious. But it was still not negative, as were those from Poland, Czechoslovakia, and the Soviet Union. The best example of the contrast was in the responses to Erhard's "peace-note" of March, 1966, to Eastern European governments, urging a new beginning in relations between them and Bonn. The replies of the Soviet, Polish, and Czechoslovak governments were decidedly negative, that of the Hungarian rather less so. Bulgaria, however, like Rumania, published no reply. In view of the rather promising atmosphere prevailing between Bonn and Sofia at the time this silence can best be construed as an act of tactful sympathy toward the West German overture. Had Sofia publicly replied, the answer would have had to have been negative because of the Soviet attitude; it would thus have ruffled feathers in Bonn. The best way out of the dilemma, therefore, was not to reply officially at all—hardly a course of great courage, but still a marked change from the usual habit of immediately parroting Moscow on every issue. Propaganda attacks against West Germany continued, of course, but they were not allowed to interfere with the quietly promising developments that were taking place. The promise continued in September, 1966, with the visit of State Secretary Rolf Lahr to the Plovdiv Fair, where he had informal talks with Foreign Minister Bashev and other senior Bulgarian officials. It was advanced by the conclusion of a new trade treaty in November.

Sofia's main interest in a *rapprochement* with Bonn was, of course, economic. Though prepared to be heavily dependent on the Soviet Union, the Bulgarian government was not blind to the advantages for its industry of the advanced technology West Germany could supply. There was also an element of rivalry with the other Eastern European states. All were seeking closer economic relations with Bonn; why should Bulgaria be left out? But

[22] In this period, Bonn signed similar agreements on the exchange of trade missions with Poland, Hungary, and Rumania. A semi-official Bulgarian trade agency already existed in Frankfurt and this now became an official government mission.

[23] DPA (West German News Agency), March 6, 1964.

behind this, the forces of history were probably working also. Bulgaria, like Rumania and Hungary, was not traditionally anti-German as were Poland, Czechoslovakia, and the Soviet Union. She had fought with, not against, Germany in two world wars; there were no "outstanding problems" between the two countries. Germany again showed herself to be a divisive force in Eastern Europe and the division was down the line drawn by history.

This vigor in foreign policy coincided with the return to reform on the internal scene (discussed in Chapter 6) and produced an atmosphere of buoyancy and confidence in the nation as a whole. Contributing to the national uplift was the astonishing success Bulgaria was having with her tourist industry. Eight hundred thousand foreigners visited Bulgaria in 1964, over 1 million in 1965, and over 1.5 million in 1966.[24] This long-forgotten corner of the Balkans was now on the world's vacation circuit and, though tourism caused superficial grumbles, it was basically a source of gratification to most Bulgarians.

The Brake on the Process

This sense of invigoration, the feeling that at last Bulgaria was going somewhere, was not to last long, however. Having stepped out of her shell in 1965 and 1966, Bulgaria retreated back into it in 1967.

There were several reasons for this. The period during which the Bulgarian government showed its unwonted confidence in foreign fields was one of relative calm in international politics. There was, of course, Vietnam; but this hardly affected Bulgarian foreign policy in the immediate sense, except in relations with the United States. There were no abrasive issues on which the Soviet Union would demand a show of solidarity that could inhibit Sofia's freedom of action. In any case, the Soviet Union, under new management since October, 1964, showed her allies no really positive leadership; the reins, therefore, slackened and her Eastern European allies, loyal or less loyal, could take initiatives which otherwise they might not have attempted. Not that there was much in Bulgaria's policy—for example, in the Balkans—to which Moscow might object. This policy dovetailed with Russia's

[24] See J. V. Storojev; "Vacationland Bulgaria: The Tourist Boom," *Radio Free Europe Research*, February 24, 1966.

in that area, especially as it affected Greece and Turkey. Anything that tended to weaken the solidarity of these two states with the NATO alliance was fulfilling the broader aim of Soviet policy. Only in the Bulgarian attitude to West Germany was there an element of uncertainty that might have caused Moscow a little concern. But, still, the atmosphere in 1965 and 1966 certainly encouraged Moscow's allies to act on their own with more confidence.

But toward the end of 1966, this began to change. First, the Kremlin began to feel more sure of itself, and then in 1967, important international issues came to the fore which caused a certain repolarization in world politics.

After a period of attempted reconciliation with China, Moscow at last resumed the polemics that had been interrupted by the fall of Khrushchev. The Soviets also concluded that organizational steps against Peking were after all necessary and revived Khrushchev's idea of a new world conference of Communist Parties. Little need be written about Bulgaria's official stand in the course of the Sino-Soviet dispute because it was simply a carbon copy of the Soviet stand. Every initiative taken by the CPSU had been immediately supported in Sofia (by the Party leadership, that is; the dissension which this caused in the rank and file of the Party has been described). Thus, Khrushchev's abortive efforts to organize a new conference shortly before his fall had been fully endorsed by Sofia.[25] The Bulgarian Party leadership may have shared the reservations of some of the other Parties about the wisdom of such a conference and was perhaps relieved when the idea seemed to have been indefinitely shelved after March, 1965. Yet, when Brezhnev chose to revive the subject and made it an issue of loyalty, the Bulgarian leadership immediately fell into line. In fact, it fired the opening shot in the campaign for a new world conference. In his speech to Ninth BCP Congress on November 14, 1966, Zhivkov, with Brezhnev present, was the first to express publicly the now-celebrated opinion that "conditions are ripening more and more for the convening of an international conference

[25] For example, two days after *Pravda* published Suslov's speech to the Soviet CC plenum in February, 1964, first proposing a conference, the BCP declared its "ardent approval and unanimous support" for the idea; *Rabotnichesko Delo*, April 5, 1964. The CPSU's subsequent proposal for a twenty-six Party preparatory conference in December, 1964, was also immediately approved; *Rabotnichesko Delo*, August 14, 1964.

of the Communist and Workers' Parties."[26] Subsequently the BCP supported every Soviet move to get the conference organized.

This stand by the Bulgarian leadership was by no means inconsistent with its previous stand on inter-Party problems nor, by itself, did it affect Bulgarian foreign policy in the Balkans or in the rest of Europe. But the fact that Bulgaria was first to kick the Soviet football was a depressing symbol of her continued fealty. And this action of steadfastness was to be followed by others which did affect her foreign policy and her national interest as well.

In December, 1966, the new Kiesinger government in Bonn launched its new *Ostpolitik*, which actually was an intensification and acceleration of the policy previously pursued by Erhard and Schroeder. Kiesinger offered to discuss a "normalization" of relations with the Eastern European states and to establish diplomatic relations with all who were willing. This move created a divisiveness amounting almost to polarization among the Eastern European states. The G.D.R. and Poland responded with an almost hysterical rejection; in Czechoslovakia, there was obviously a division of opinion in the leadership though the overall impression was of a distinct interest; Rumania responded with alacrity, while it seemed that Bulgaria and Hungary, though far more cautious, were again showing a genuine receptiveness to the West German initiative. Moscow at first seemed hesitant. But, prodded by alarmed Ulbricht and Gomulka, and concerned over the danger of a chain reaction once Rumania had decided to establish diplomatic relations with Bonn in January, 1967, Moscow finally made a rejection of the West German overtures a condition of loyalty. However reluctantly, Bulgaria and Hungary immediately complied. A year later, when Yugoslavia had re-established diplomatic relations with Bonn, Bulgaria was to find that both her Communist neighbors had successfully taken the step which she had also wished to take but was prevented from doing by "higher considerations."

Loyalty to the alliance was also to have an adverse effect on Bulgaria's Balkan policy by causing a cooling off in relations with Rumania. In 1967, Bucharest's apostasy took on a new dimension in that it was carried outside the socialist family into the arena of international politics. The Soviet Union had become accustomed, perhaps even inured, to the Rumanian independence in inter-

[26] *Rabotnichesko Delo*, November 15, 1966. Brezhnev repeated the call the next day.

Party affairs; but now Rumania was defying the Soviets on world issues crucial to their interests. First, it was the German question, already discussed: in June came perhaps the most blatant defiance of all—on the Arab-Israeli War (here, Bulgaria was 100 per cent loyal to Soviet policy); in addition, the Rumanians had reservations about the nuclear non-proliferation treaty. This behavior on the part of the Rumanians caused relations with Bucharest to enter their most strained period since the Rumanian deviation began. Hence it was hardly politic for Bulgaria to continue the very close relations with Rumania that had existed in 1965 and 1966 and that had seemed so promising for the future of Balkan cooperation. Relations did not sink into the deep freeze that had characterized them in Gheorghiu-Dej's time, but they cooled considerably and the personal intimacy between Ceausescu and Zhivkov came to a close.

Nor was this the only blow to hopes that Bulgaria would take a lead in promoting Balkan *détente*. Indeed, in 1967, the Balkans reverted to its traditional pattern of disunity. First, in April, the military coup in Greece seriously damaged the results of the patient diplomacy that had gone before. Far more serious, both from the short and long view, was the acrimony that developed between Yugoslavia and Bulgaria. The issue, once again, was Macedonia.

Tito's appeal for an end to the polemics (quoted above) was not long successful. The polemics had not ceased altogether, but they had been kept at a level which did not jar the harmony both governments were trying to create. But in the fall of 1966, their volume and tempo increased sharply. A serious incident occurred in October when a delegation from the Republic of Macedonia's Writers' Union visited Sofia. This first seemed an important step on the path to better understanding. It later proved just the opposite when, at the end of their visit, the Macedonian delegation insisted that the communiqué be drawn up in both the Bulgarian *and* the Macedonian languages. This the Bulgarians refused to do, declaring that they did not recognize the existence of a Macedonian language. From then on, polemics rained thick and fast. Contributing to their proliferation was the occurrence of many Bulgarian historical anniversaries at about this time, recalling incidents or personalities pertaining to Macedonia. Moreover, these coincided with the new "patriotic" propaganda campaign of the Sofia regime, which seized on the anniversaries as an opportunity to glorify the national past. Thus the 1,050th anniversary of St.

Clement of Ochrid fell in December, 1966, and the ninety-fifth anniversary of Gotse Delchev in January. The Bulgarians—quite understandably—celebrated these men as Bulgarians while the Yugoslavs, particularly in the case of Delchev, claimed them as Macedonians.[27] As the ninetieth anniversary of Bulgaria's liberation from the Turks, and as the anniversaries of San Stefano and Berlin approached, the polemics became even fiercer. Every Bulgarian "slur" on the Macedonian nation was angrily rebuffed in the Yugoslav press, especially by *Nova Makedonja*, the Skjoplje organ of the Republic of Macedonia's Communist Party.

Efforts were made to calm down the battle. In May, 1967, Krste Crvenkovski, President of the Central Committee of the Macedonian Communist Party, visited Sofia and met Zhivkov. In the list of problems discussed, Bulgarian media specifically mentioned the "Macedonian question," an item that had never previously been publicly listed on any agenda in talks between Bulgarian and Yugoslav officials.[28] The content of these talks was never divulged, but it can be assumed that attempts were made to find a basis of agreement on which the polemics could be moderated. If so, they were completely unsuccessful. In June, Zhivkov himself, at the head of a strong Party and government delegation, visited Belgrade, but his visit was cut short by the outbreak of the Arab-Israeli war. The polemics continued and even intensified; by 1968, Yugoslav-Bulgarian relations were probably worse than at any time since 1958 and 1959.

What was behind these polemics? It was said earlier that polemics on Macedonia were previously a good indication that strained relations existed between Belgrade and Moscow. This may once again have been the case. The dramatic internal changes in Yugoslavia in the first half of 1966—the fall of Rankovic and the final victory of the "liberals," the "revisionist" concepts about the future weakening of the role of the Party, the schemes of further decentralization on national lines—none of these pleased Moscow. The tension between the two states disappeared briefly in mid-1967 because of Tito's full support for the Arab cause in the Middle East, but the basic division still remained. Hence the bitter revival of the Macedonian issue may not have been coincidental. But a new factor may now have entered the picture: the Bulgarian regime's determination to continue its "patriotic" cam-

[27] A Macedonian writer in *Politika* (Belgrade), January 29, 1967, violently attacked the Bulgarian press for its treatment of Delchev.
[28] Bulgarian Telegraphic Agency, May 20, 1967.

paign regardless of the consequences. This campaign was one of the new cards being played in the effort to legitimize itself in the eyes of the nation and try to break down the "national nihilism" in the younger generation that was causing so much concern. To discontinue it because of the Yugoslav reaction would have only increased the cynicism it was calculated to break down.

This latter explanation, if true, would be even more depressing than the former. It would, no doubt, be a sign that the Bulgarian regime was standing on its own feet for once at least, while the former would suggest that it was still dancing to Moscow's tune. But one of the disconcerting features about Eastern Europe in the 1960's has been the revival of the nationalist-territorial feuds of the "bourgeois" era. Transylvania, Macedonia, the Slovak-Czech relationship, nationalism within Yugoslavia itself—the gloomy pattern was recurring again. This reopening of the old wound between Bulgaria and Yugoslavia, though it may have given many Bulgarians temporary satisfaction, was not in Bulgaria's national interest.

In Bulgaria's situation, the best possibility of asserting her real interest lies in the closest collaboration with Yugoslavia, even with a view eventually to federation—Dimitrov's old idea, and that of many Bulgarians before him. Other Bulgarians fear this on the grounds that their country would be swamped by the stronger Yugoslavia. But that, surely, is to ignore the situation in Yugoslavia itself. If Bulgaria entered the Yugoslav federation as its seventh republic, she would be the most powerful state within it and—to be Machiavellian for a moment—she might well be the master of it if she played her cards wisely, and tactfully used the Serb-Croat rivalry to her advantage. (This, of course, would require a skill in diplomacy which Sofia has not always shown.) Bulgarian nationalist pride would be fulfilled, as their country would become the most important in the Balkans. Sofia would have to accept the existence of a separate Macedonian state, and might even have to surrender Pirin Macedonia—the district of Blagoevgrad—to it. But this would be a small price to pay for the prizes at stake.

The danger inherent in such a grand solution would arise if Croatia and Slovenia should leave the Yugoslav federation or, even if they formally remain, become so estranged from it as to be only passive members. In such an event—and, unfortunately, it is by no means impossible—then Bulgaria and Serbia would be in direct confrontation and the problem of Macedonia, rather than being solved, would only be aggravated. It would, therefore, be very much in Bulgaria's interests if Croatia and Slovenia stayed as active members of the Yugoslav federation. Of course, these two states might object to Bulgaria's joining on the grounds that the Federation would then be too Balkan in character, or Bulgaria's admission, if achieved, might be the ultimate grievance prompting their withdrawal. Conversely, they might welcome Bulgaria's participation as an additional counterweight to Serbia. Of course, none of the Yugoslav republics—not even the political conservatives in Serbia—would have Bulgaria in the federation as the Trojan Horse of the Soviet Union. Therefore, a drastic reappraisal of Sofia's relations with Moscow would be necessary and this, at present, is impossible. But in twenty years it might not be.

All this may seem the fantasy of an unhinged mind. Obviously many conditions, now absent, must be present before such a possibility can even be contemplated. But it seems the best way out for Bulgaria—far better than attempts to foster national pride by a patriotic campaign that is essentially bogus and leads to hostility with the state with which it is in her best interests to cooperate.

The Impact of Crises in the Soviet Alliance

The disappointments of 1967 did not mean that Bulgaria's foreign policy came to a standstill. The good relations with France continued, as did the successful efforts to increase trade with other Western European countries. Despite the enforced rebuff to Bonn's political overtures, trade relations with West Germany prospered. By the end of 1967, 10 per cent of Bulgaria's imports came from West Germany; only the Soviet Union supplied her with more. In terms of total trade—imports and exports—the Federal Republic had moved up to fourth place on Bulgaria's list, preceded only by the U.S.S.R., Czechoslovakia, and East Germany. But the momentum which characterized Bulgarian foreign policy in 1965 and 1966 had gone, as it had from her internal policy. International crises on which Moscow demanded solidarity, an "accident" like the Greek *coup*, and the unfortunate twist in relations with Yugoslavia all conspired to block what had been promising progress. In August, 1968, of course, the Soviet-led invasion of Czechoslovakia, in which Bulgaria participated, caused Bulgarian relations with Yugoslavia (and Rumania) to descend to a new and dangerously low point.

One lesson to be drawn from this is that what Bulgaria requires for the pursuit of an "individual" foreign policy is not international or intra-bloc crises, but calm and stability. In a period of international calm, Bulgaria can ·feel free to attempt initiatives in foreign policy. In doing so, it might be possible for her to inch almost imperceptibly toward greater freedom of action. After a long period of calm, especially if her efforts were successful, this could lead to a confidence and independence of attitude which might be permanent. The same is true for Hungary: what Kadar wants is peace and quiet—to be able to pursue his commercial relations with the West and his schemes for international co-operation in the Danube valley, of which Austria would be an integral part. With their present leadership, one cannot, then, expect Bulgaria and Hungary to respond to the "opportunities" to assert their independence. The Rumanian course is not for them. "Opportunities" such as the Sino-Soviet dispute, the West German *Ostpolitik* and, in 1968, the Czechoslovak crisis, only cause Moscow to assert its authority more strongly; and Bulgaria and Hungary feel constrained to bow to this assertion. It is true that the centrifugal forces working in Eastern Europe might *eventually* bring about a situation where even Bulgaria can openly cast off her inhibitions. But the dramatic manifestations of these forces have only resulted in her (and Hungary) reaffirming their loyalty to Moscow. So far, the crises that were supposed to further the independence of the Eastern European states have, in the case of some, produced only greater demonstrations of dependence.

Relations with Turkey

One country with which the Bulgarian policy of *rapprochement* went on unhindered, and was crowned with considerable success, was Turkey. The reason for this was quite consistent with the foregoing analysis: *rapprochement* with Turkey, far from being unsympathetically viewed in Moscow, had become one of the chief aims of Soviet policy in the eastern Mediterranean and the near East, an aim pursued with persistence and skill. Here was a perfect example of Bulgarian foreign policy complementing that of the Soviet Union.

Rapprochement with Turkey was no easy matter: here too, there were old wounds to heal. Before World War II, there were about 700,000 Turks living in Bulgaria, a residue of the centuries of

Turkish domination. On the whole, they were treated fairly by the Bulgarian government, which had a good record with minorities. Under a 1925 agreement, those Turks who wished to be repatriated to Turkey were free to leave, but an average of only about 10,000 to 12,000 emigrated each year except in the depression years of the mid-1930's, when the number fell to less than a thousand annually.[29]

As a result of the recovery of South Dobruja from Rumania in 1940 by the Treaty of Craiova, Bulgaria acquired another 100,000 Turks, bringing the total number to over 750,000. The treatment of the Turks by the Communist government contrasted sadly with the "oppressive" bourgeois regime it replaced. Turkish minority rights of religion and separate education were revoked and many mosques were simply nationalized. In addition, agricultural collectivization was bitterly resented by the Turks, almost all of whom were peasants. At first the Bulgarian regime had discouraged emigration but, presumably because of lack of cooperation on the part of the Bulgarian Turks, Bulgaria lifted its restrictions in 1950 and several thousand Turks began to leave each month. Then in August, 1950, a mass expulsion of Turks was announced and in the 1950–51 period a total of about 150,000 left for Turkey, most of them taking only what they could carry.[30] In 1951, Sofia again reversed its policy and discouraged emigration. It did, however, improve the treatment of the remaining Turks, re-establishing the privileges of separate schools and desisting from some of the cruder insults to the Moslem religion. However, in 1958, some Turkish schools began to be merged with the Bulgarian schools.[31]

In 1963, there was considerable unrest among a minority that, when left alone, had usually been rather docile. From the official statements, it was difficult to discern just what the trouble was about, but the question of expatriation was certainly involved. In October of that year, Zhivkov himself made a statement denying rumors that the regime was preparing another mass expulsion. Such rumors, he charged, had been spread by people serving for-

[29] Kostanick, *loc. cit.*, p. 40. Professor Kostanick's figures for the Turkish minority seem rather too low.

[30] For a detailed account of this migration, see Robert Lee Wolff, *The Balkans in Our Time* (Cambridge, Mass., 1956), pp. 476–80. According to the official census in 1956, there were 656,000 ethnic Turks in Bulgaria. By 1965, the official figure was 746,755.

[31] See interview with Bistra Avramova in *Zemedelsko Zname* (Sofia), March 21, 1964.

eign interests (presumably Turkish).[32] However, a provincial paper approached the problem from a different angle, saying "some misled people were influenced by the rumors, forgetting the fate of the repatriated Turks in 1951."[33] This was a hint that some Turks were actually pressing for the right to emigrate. In March, 1964, Zhivkov felt compelled to return to the subject. In a letter to the Turkish language periodical, *Yeni Hayat*, Zhivkov praised Communist policy toward the Turkish minority but then strongly attacked "reactionary circles" in Turkey for trying to alienate the minority from the Bulgarian regime. It was these circles that had spread the rumors about mass repatriation, he charged. But Zhivkov then added that some Turks were receptive to these rumors and had succumbed to "moods of expatriation."[34]

There was at the time considerable discontent among Turkish tobacco growers in the Smolyan and Kurdzhali districts of the Rhodope mountains because of the very low remuneration for their crops, and it was quite possible that some of these had expressed a desire to leave.[35] But the "hard core" of would-be emigrants were the 30,000 or so close relatives of those who had been repatriated in 1950 and 1951. They had been the object of concern of successive Turkish governments which, during the 1950's and early 1960's, had pestered Sofia, to no avail, to release them. Some, taking the law into their own hands, had tried to escape to Turkey but relatively few succeeded.

This, then, was the outstanding bilateral problem between Bulgaria and Turkey, just as Sofia's war debt had been the outstanding problem between Bulgaria and Greece; and as late as 1964, judging by Zhivkov's remarks, it was far from being solved.

The first sign of a better atmosphere was the visit of the Bulgarian Minister of Foreign Trade, Ivan Budinov, to Ankara in August, 1965, the first Bulgarian cabinet minister to go to Turkey since World War II. This visit was preceded and followed by a number of minor agreements of an economic and cultural nature and by the establishment of air links between the two countries. Mutual trust between the two governments had sufficiently im-

[32] Bulgarian Telegraphic Agency (in English), October 9, 1963.

[33] *Kolarovgradska Borba* (Kolarovgrad), October 8, 1963. The allusion to the fate of the repatriated Turks was unfair to the Turkish government, which had tried valiantly to accommodate them.

[34] *Rabotnichesko Delo*, March 4, 1964.

[35] Subsequently, however, improvements in remuneration were made; *Rodopski Ustrem* (Smolyan), October 15, 1963.

proved for Foreign Minister Bashev to visit Ankara in August, 1966. Bashev and his hosts agreed on further collaboration in various economic fields, communications, and tourism, and made considerable progress on the most sensitive topic of all. He and the Turkish Foreign Minister, Ishan Sabri Caglayangil, agreed that "the problem of voluntary emigration to Turkey of Bulgarian citizens of Turkish descent whose close relatives had previously emigrated must be solved in the shortest possible time."[36] To achieve this, a commission of experts was appointed.

As in the case of the war debt problem with Greece, progress on this far more human problem was painfully slow. It had hardly progressed at all by the time Mr. Caglayangil visited Sofia in May, 1967, returning the visit paid by Bashev the previous August. At the end of Caglayangil's visit the official communiqué simply stated that the matter was being discussed by experts of both countries whose conclusions would be "brought to the knowledge of those concerned."[37]

The two main obstacles to final agreement were the problem of defining what was a close family relationship to those Turks who left in 1950 and 1951, and Bulgarian stipulations over the amount of the property the departing Turks could take with them. On the latter point, the Bulgarian government objected to the proposal that these Turks should be able to take with them the proceeds of the sale of any property they had held; the Turkish government was naturally anxious that they should arrive as self-sufficient as possible. In the meantime, the delay caused considerable unrest among the Turkish minority as a whole, and there is little doubt that more Bulgarian Turks were pressing to leave than either Sofia or Ankara had ever envisaged.[38]

Finally a compromise agreement was reached in February, 1968. It affected only some 10,000 to 15,000 Bulgarian Turks, who would be alllowed to leave at the rate of about 300 a week between April and November, 1968. They could take with them, free of export duty, their personal and household belongings, as well as the instruments or tools of their profession, provided this was not forbidden by law. They were allowed to sell their real estate and livestock but it was not made clear whether they could take the proceeds with them to Turkey.

It was this agreement that paved the way for a visit to Ankara

[36] Radio Free Europe special report from Ankara, August 22, 1966.
[37] Bulgarian Telegraphic Agency, May 31, 1967.
[38] See *Ludogorska Pravda* (Razgrad), July 29, 1967.

in March, 1968, by Zhivkov himself at the head of an important government delegation. There the agreement was formally signed, together with others indicating that an era of closer relations had dawned. As with Greece in 1964, these agreements were a success for Bulgaria's Balkan diplomacy. But, as with Bulgarian foreign policy generally, whether Bulgarian-Turkish relations had permanently improved would depend, not on the wishes of Sofia, but on the shifts and changes of Moscow's line.

The Soviet Domination

From this relatively brief survey of the most important aspects of Bulgarian foreign policy, the cardinal point of Soviet domination stands out clearly in spite of an evident Bulgarian inclination to pursue a policy which, if not independent, was at least autonomous.

But if the Party leadership has been consistently loyal to the Soviet Union, it has not always been the most reliable. On several occasions it has caused problems for Moscow that the Soviet leadership, harassed by bigger problems, could well have dispensed with. The dislike between Khrushchev and Chervenkov, the persistent factionalism after 1956, the lunacy of the "great leap forward" and the scare over the Bulgarian fascination with China, the apparently strong rank-and-file opposition to Zhivkov's pro-Khrushchev stand in the Sino-Soviet dispute, the April conspiracy —factors such as these have made the BCP an awkward client to handle, certainly the most awkward of the "loyal" Parties until the Czechoslovak crisis of 1968.

Above all, there was Bulgaria's constant economic weakness, which necessitated a steady stream of Soviet loans. It has been estimated that between 1948 and 1962, Soviet loans to Bulgaria totaled the equivalent of one billion dollars.[39]

Economic relations, of course, were not all one-sided. Up to 1954 or 1955, Bulgaria was ruthlessly exploited by the Soviet Union, as all the Eastern European states were. Throughout the period of Communism, Bulgaria has also exported some goods to the Soviet Union at cheaper prices than she has charged elsewhere and imported certain goods from the Soviet Union at higher prices

[39] Marshall G. Goldman, *Soviet Foreign Aid* (New York, 1967), p. 36. Since 1964, Professor Goldman estimates that a further 513 million dollars credit (plus a possible further 72 million) had been agreed to.

than the Soviet Union has charged the West or the developing countries. It is very difficult to come to a safe conclusion as to who exploited whom, but it would appear that, at least since 1959–60, Bulgaria has been more of an economic liability to the Soviet Union than an asset.

There can be little doubt about that, in many ways, Bulgaria has gained economically from the close Soviet connection. Without Soviet assistance it would have been impossible to create an industrial state and to maintain a very high rate of industrial growth, as Bulgaria has. (Whether it has been wise to concentrate on industry to such an extent is, of course, another question. But the Soviet Union can hardly be blamed for this: she would have been only too happy had Bulgaria concentrated on her agricultural produce.) It might be argued that Bulgaria would have industrialized more cheaply, efficiently, and with fewer adverse political consequences had the West been the main supplier. This is probably true but, in the circumstances, unrealistic. Until the late 1950's, there was no "activist" Western policy toward Eastern Europe that would have led to Western trade to the extent required and, if Bulgaria had followed the Yugoslav example in 1948 and broken with Moscow, she would almost certainly have been overrun by Soviet troops. In recent years, the Rumanian example has been more feasible to follow because it did coincide with a new approach to Eastern Europe by the West and the development of more maneuverability within the Soviet alliance itself. The advantages to Rumania have been obvious[40] and the Bulgarian leaders can be criticized for neglecting their country's best interests in rejecting the Rumanian example so firmly. But taking the Sofia view, it could be argued that Bulgaria's natural wealth is much less than Rumania's. Almost 100 per cent of Bulgaria's coal and over 90 per cent of her oil comes from the Soviet Union; in 1965, 60 per cent of her machines had come from the same source. Within the limits of her capacity, it could also be claimed that Bulgaria has made considerable progress in economic relations with the West; the fact that 10 per cent of her entire imports came from West Germany in 1967 could be held out as a proof.

And the Sofia apologists could point to another grave problem

[40] Needless to say, however, up to 1965 and even beyond, the high rate of Rumanian industrial growth was based mainly on Soviet and East European trade. The big imports of Western plant and equipment had not begun to pay off.

of trade with the West: How are the Eastern European states, particularly the Balkans, to trade effectively with the West and pay for the modern technology they sincerely desire? Their traditional agricultural produce and raw materials will always find a market but, due to industrialization, the export lists of the Eastern European countries are now dominated by items of heavy industry. Who in the West wants these? Even if someone did, Eastern Europe is faced by a protectionist Common Market in Europe and an American Congress that, except for an enlightened minority, has been more prone to preach to Eastern Europe than to give it the chance to help itself. Even now, the problem is acute; in 1966, Bulgaria's trade deficit with West Germany amounted to about 250 million marks[41] and by 1975, by which time the Soviet share of total Rumanian trade will have dropped to below 25 per cent, Rumania is expecting a trade deficit of two and a half billion lei. The implications of this situation are political as well as economic. If the Soviet Union remains the only large market for most of the substandard Eastern European exports because of the huge difficulties these exports will face in the West, there could be a strong economic gravitation back to the Soviet Union and the reassertion of a measure of political control even over a country like Rumania. The various measures like joint production and marketing schemes—even long-term credits—are only short-term palliatives. The real answer would probably be the investment of Western capital in Eastern Europe. The Yugoslavs began to allow this, although with many restrictions, in 1966. But, if it is to be effective, it would have to be on a large scale, and this could create serious ideological and nationalistic problems for the Eastern European governments.

This, then, is a looming problem which should militate against undue optimism in the West about economic relations with Eastern Europe and their possible consequences. It also provides the Bulgarian regime with some defense against charges of being too close economically to the Soviet Union.

Where there is less defense, however, is in the political subjection of Bulgaria to the Soviet Union. Sofia could remain a loyal ally of Moscow and continue to gain economic advantage with-

---

[41] See Situation Report: Bulgaria; *Radio Free Europe Research*, October 12, 1967, quoting a West German government business catalogue issued in connection with the F.R.G.'s participation in the 1967 Plovdiv Fair. The introduction to the catalogue is by Herr Heinz Hermann, head of the West German trade mission in Sofia.

out the humiliating deference in word and deed to Soviet wishes and dictates. Even allowing for the weakness of the Zhivkov regime, the point to which this deference is taken is completely unnecessary. Bulgaria, small and weak as she is, is of considerable value to the Soviet Union as an ally. She is strategically located as the Communist outpost in the Balkans, bordering on two NATO allies that have long been targets of Soviet aims. Since 1964, she has been the Soviet Union's only trusted ally in the Balkans and the concern of Moscow to keep her that way was dramatically shown after the April conspiracy in 1965 when Suslov came hurrying down to inspect the situation. Bulgaria, therefore, is not without her bargaining counters in relations with the Soviet Union. If she has used them at all, she has certainly not used them strongly enough.

13

A Summing Up

IN JULY, 1968, the Bulgarian Party leadership announced changes in economic planning, the governmental and administrative structure, education, and cadre policy; these, if thoroughly implemented, will be far-reaching indeed. The changes were evidently designed as the preparatory phase in the introduction of a new Socialist constitution for Bulgaria, to be approved in the course of 1969.[1] This constitution would make Bulgaria a Socialist Republic instead of the People's Republic she had been since the adoption of the "Dimitrov" constitution in 1947. It would reflect the economic, political, social, and ideological changes wrought since then. On September 9, 1969, Bulgaria marks a quarter of a century of Communist rule, a date for triumphant official stocktaking of the achievements of the previous twenty-five years.

Few could deny that it has been a momentous quarter of a century, or that more change has been wrought during it than in any other period in modern Bulgarian history. The very face of the country has been radically altered by the drastic transformation of the agricultural structure and the introduction of heavy industry. An overwhelmingly peasant country has now become an industrial-agrarian state, with steel mills, oil refineries, and chemical plants undreamed of in 1939. Urbanization has proceeded rapidly: in 1934, Sofia was a pleasant town of under

---

[1] During the course of 1969, however, there was very little publicity given to this new constitution, and it began to be more and more doubtful whether it would be officially approved in the course of that year.

300,000; by 1954, it had 600,000 inhabitants; in 1968, it was a cramped city of about one million. The old social structure and many of the old mores that issued from it had been swept aside.

The Communists have certainly done much. They might claim that they have indeed fulfilled Dimitrov's promise in 1948: to achieve in one or two decades what other countries had taken a century to achieve.

But if their achievements are viewed in terms of the advantages they have brought the Bulgarian nation, and of what they promise for it in the future, then the jubilation of September 9, 1969 will need to be tempered by both doubt and foreboding. Some aspects of the progress made must, of course, be thoroughly welcomed. The great strides in public health, in education, the creation of greater opportunity—only a blind opponent of Communism would begrudge the official self-satisfaction over these. Again, in certain areas of economic expansion—electrification, transportation, the astonishing development of the tourist industry in the 1960's—the progress has been beneficial and impressive.

Taking the Communists' record as a whole, however, it can be seriously questioned whether either their policy or performance justifies the claims now being made. Industrial expansion, their greatest visible monument, has been impressive both in speed and dimension, even when allowance is made for the fact that it was begun in a relatively backward country, and for the inefficiency, waste, and human deprivation that have accompanied it. But has this expansion made Bulgaria a more powerful nation economically, more prosperous, more able to compete commercially in either the socialist or the world market? Is her future in the world economy any the more assured because of it? Clearly, the answer is no. Bulgaria is now faced by the great dilemma of how to turn all this effort to account. Her leaders have often enjoyed comparing Bulgaria's socialist economic progress with that of "monarcho-fascist-capitalist" Greece, and, statistically, their case is often a good one. But Greece, for all its turbulence and social short-comings, has made better progress toward economic efficiency and competitiveness than Bulgaria.

There is no real purpose in comparing Bulgaria's political course with that of any country with a different political system or ideology, or even with an independent Communist state like Yugoslavia. It is as a member-state of the Soviet alliance that she must be viewed. As such, she has displayed many of the characteristics common to all or most of her partners: the mass terror dur-

ing the consolidation of Communist rule; the bloody struggle between home Communists and Muscovites; the emergence of a
one-man dictatorship (Chervenkov) sanctioned or imposed by
Moscow; the relaxations after 1953 with their attendant factionalism. But perhaps more than in any other Eastern European state,
the course of Bulgarian internal politics since 1953 has been
impeded by a lack of consistency in developing and enlarging a
program of reform. The brief reform periods of 1955–57, 1961–62
and 1965–66 have been followed by longer periods of immobilism
and even retrogression. In July, 1968, a new period of reform
seemed to be in the offing, with no promise at all, however, that
it would not suffer the fate of the previous three.

These interludes of fitful reform have, of course, left their mark;
despite the ensuing periods of stagnation, Bulgaria has gradually
inched forward toward a better life for the masses of its people.
But the reforms, promising much and giving little, have produced
frustration rather than satisfaction, a treadmill complex rather
than any popular feeling that Bulgaria was getting somewhere.

The main reason for this inconsistency would seem to lie in the
lack of firm leadership after 1953. Todor Zhivkov, who in 1969
was celebrating a decade and a half as Party leader, was first faced
with the problem of asserting control over the warring elements in
his Party. This undoubtedly impeded the implementation of a
consistent program of any kind. But, even after he gained control,
the same kind of hesitancy and vacillation manifested itself. Zhivkov, a modest and well-meaning man, probably believes in the reform sentiments and proposals he has so often expressed. But he
has lacked both the intelligence and the decisiveness to implement
them. Thus reforms in Bulgaria, unlike those in Hungary or more
recently those of Ceausescu in Rumania, have often seemed to be
something incidental, or merely an automatic response to those
begun in Moscow, rather than something indigenously based, an
integral part of the regime's posture.

Nor has this lack of direction from above been compensated for
by any strong stimulus from below. This is not to disparage the
intellectual ferment which has taken place in Bulgaria during
Communist rule, or the pressure for change inside the lower and
middle echelons of the Party itself. But the drive from below
which produced the great changes in Poland and Hungary in
1956 and in Czechoslovakia twelve years later has, for obvious historical reasons, never been evident in Bulgaria. And the Bulgarian
working class, still in its formative stage, could not show the soli-

darity or articulateness of its counterparts in some of the Communist states to the north. Revisionism, therefore, has never been a real danger to the Bulgarian Party. In fact the "deviation" that has presented the greater threat (or, at times, apparently had the stronger influence on policy) has been of the left-sectarian variety. This leftist tradition, strong in the BCP before it assumed power, manifested itself again in the "great leap forward" and in the evident reluctance of many within the Party to endorse the total official support for the CPSU against the Chinese Party. Nowhere in Eastern Europe, except in the special case of Albania, has there been such fascination with China or preoccupation with the problems presented by her.

Bulgaria's unswerving support of the Soviet Union and the benefits this alliance has brought her will, of course, be one of the most prominent features of the quarter-century celebrations. The Soviet Union has, indeed, made Bulgaria's industrialization possible and provided a huge market for her produce. But whether the Bulgarian public is persuaded of the comprehensive merits of the Soviet connection is doubtful indeed. It must seem that since World War II Bulgaria has simply had a new patron, and that this patron, like Italy and then Germany before the war, mainly regards Bulgaria as a means to her own ends. (The thoughtless chauvinists might even consider that this new patron has done much less to fulfill their irredentist dreams than the old ones.) This patronage has denied Bulgaria the chance of working out her own destiny in harmony with the other small Balkan states, something she must eventually do if her dignity is to be restored and her real national interests served. It has kept Bulgaria out of war—a service not to be ignored in view of her turbulent history—but has provided no real framework for her progress as a nation. In fact, the Bulgarian regime's concept of the Soviet alliance—devotion to the point of servility—has offended the self-respect of most Bulgarians, even those who accept the necessity or the inevitability of the alliance itself, even those imbued with the traditional Russophilism of the Bulgarian nation.

This resentment at the foreign policy of the regime—aggravated by comparisons with the sturdy independence of the Yugoslavs, Rumanians, and Albanians—is only one instance of public disenchantment. In many fields the gap between the regime and the public, state and society, is widening rather than narrowing. This is ironical in many ways, because life in Bulgaria has perceptibly improved over the last twenty years; living standards have risen and regime repression has slackened. But the improvements have in no way kept pace with the rising expectations, nor have they compensated, particularly in the minds of the young, for the grievous errors made, the unfulfilled promises, the sins committed and only partly expiated, the hypocrisy and cant, which has lessened in neither volume nor intensity during the whole period of Communist rule. Most basic is the feeling of many—and these include the most talented and energetic of Bulgarians—that, whatever the achievements of Communism in Bulgaria, the country has now reached a stage of development where no further progress is possible without a radical change in the whole ruling system. These dissidents have no blueprint for the future, but it can be assumed that they viewed the Czechoslovak experiment of 1968 with an eager, sympathetic, and envious interest. This was the kind of breakthrough they regard as necessary for Bulgaria. The possibility that Sofia would become another Prague in the foreseeable future were always slim but, had the Czechoslovak experiment succeeded, Bulgaria would not have remained immune from its contagious influence.

The Soviet invasion of Czechoslovakia dashed the hopes of these Bulgarians and of like-minded men throughout Eastern Europe. It brought comfort and a new lease of security to the Party *apparat* which, despite the reforms of the Zhivkov era, is incapable of initiating the kind of reform or mounting an attack on basic problems which would mark a new beginning for Bulgaria. The gap, therefore, between impervious but uneasy rulers and malcontent, frustrated ruled may well grow in the future. The result could be—not only in Bulgaria but in the Soviet Union and other East European states—increased repression rather than reform. In Bulgaria's case it could be accompanied—as a diversion—by an intensified nationalistic policy aimed at her Balkan neighbors. Either course would be disastrous. Both could still be avoided. But the time is short and, since August, 1968, the omens have not been favorable.

Appendix I

Members of the Politburo, Central Committee, and Council of Ministers, *1944–68*

Ivan Abadzhiev   (b. 1930) Politburo candidate-member since 1966.

Racho Angelov   (1873–1956) Communist. Minister of Public Health, 1944–47.

Luchezar Avramov   (b. 1922) Communist. Minister of Foreign Trade, 1962. Minister without Portfolio, 1962–66. Deputy Prime Minister since 1966. CC secretary, 1962–66. Politburo candidate-member since 1966. Minister of Foreign Trade since 1968.

Ruben Avramov   (b. 1900) Communist. CC secretary, 1950–52. Chairman, Committee for Science, Culture, and Art, 1952–54. Minister of Culture, 1954–57.

Boyan Bulgaranov   (b. 1896) Communist. CC secretary, 1956–67. Politburo member since 1957.

Ivan Bashev   (b. 1916) Communist. Minister of Foreign Affairs since 1962.

Dora Belcheva   (b. 1922?) Communist. Minister of Light Industry since 1966.

Yordan Bozhilov   (1883–1955) Communist. Minister of Trade, 1946–47.

Georgi Brankov   (b. 1913) Communist. Professor. Engineer. Chairman, Committee for Construction and Architecture, 1963–66.

Ivan Budinov   (b. 1918) Communist. Minister of Foreign Trade, 1962–1968.

Boris Bumbarov   (?–1959) Agrarian. Minister of Constructions, 1944–45. Joined the opposition, 1945.

Georgi Chankov   (b. 1909) Communist. Politburo member, 1944–

57 (ousted). CC secretary, 1944–54. Chairman, Commission for State Control, 1947–49. Minister of Transport, 1949–50. Deputy Prime Minister, 1950–56. Chairman, State Planning Committee, 1952–56. First Deputy Prime Minister, 1956–57 (ousted).

Titko Chernokolev (1910–1965) Communist. Professor. Academician, 1962. Politburo candidate-member, 1945–49. Politburo member, 1949–51 (ousted). Minister of Agriculture, 1950–51 (ousted and rehabilitated). Minister without Portfolio, 1962–65.

Vulko Chervenkov (b. 1900) Communist. Politburo member, 1944–61 (ousted). CC secretary, 1944–50. Party Secretary-General, 1950–54. Chairman, Committee for Science, Culture, and Art, 1947–49. Deputy Prime Minister, 1949–50. Prime Minister, 1950–56. Deputy Prime Minister, 1956–61 (ousted). Minister of Education and Culture, 1957–58.

Grigor Cheshmedzhiev (1877–1945) Social-Democrat. Minister of Social Policy, 1944–45. Joined the opposition, 1945.

Stancho Cholakov (b. 1900) Zveno Political Group member. Professor. Minister of Education, 1944–45. Minister of Finance, 1945–46.

Mako Dakov (b. 19[?]) Communist. Professor. Minister of Forests and Timber Industry since 1966.

Georgi Damyanov (1892–1958) Communist. General. Politburo member, 1945–58. Minister of National Defense, 1946–50. Chairman, National Assembly Presidium (head of state), 1950–58.

Raiko Damyanov (b. 1903) Communist. Politburo member, 1945–48. Politburo candidate–member, 1948–49. Politburo member, 1949–62. Deputy Premier, 1950–57. Chairman, Committee for Construction and Architecture, 1956–57. Minister of Trade, 1957. First Deputy Premier, 1957–62. Minister of Trade, 1959.

Svetla Daskalova (b. 1921) Agrarian. Minister of Justice since 1966.

Angel Derzhanski (?–1964) Agrarian. Minister of Railways, 1944–45. Joined the opposition, 1945.

Dimo Dichev (b. 1902) Communist. Chairman, Commission for State Control, 1949–57.

Diko Dikov (b. 1910) Communist. General. Minister of Interior, 1962–68.

Atanas Dimitrov (b. 1914) Communist. Minister of Light and Food Industry, 1951–56. Minister of Food Industry, 1956–59. Chairman, Committee for Industry, 1959–62. Minister of Food Industry, 1966–68. Chairman, Committee for Public Services since 1968.

Dancho Dimitrov (b. 1911) Communist. Minister of Transport, 1950–57. CC secretary, 1957–58. Minister of Transport and Communications, 1958–62.

Georgi Dimitrov (1882–1949) Communist. Bureau in Exile member, 1924–44. Politburo member, 1944–49. Party Chairman, 1944–48. Party Secretary-General, 1948–49. Prime Minister, 1946–49.

Dimitur Dimov (1903–1968) Communist Politburo candidate-member, 1945–48, 1949–54. CC secretary, 1949–50. Politburo candidate-member, 1957–68.

Krastyo Dobrev (b. 1903) Communist. Professor. Minister of Trade, 1947–49. Minister of Internal Trade, 1949–50.

Traycho Dobroslavski (1903–1964) Zveno Political Group member. Minister of Public Health, 1947–50.

Georgi Dragnev (1887–1955) Agrarian. Minister of Public Works, 1945–47.

Tsola Dragoicheva (b. 1898) Communist. Politburo member, 1940–48. Minister of Posts, Telegraphs, and Telephones, 1947–57. Politburo member since 1966.

Kiril Dramaliev (1892–1961) Communist. Minister of Education, 1947–52.

Dobri Dzhurov (b. 1916) Communist. General. Minister of National Defense since 1962.

Dimitur Ganev (1898–1964) Communist. Politburo member, 1942–48. Politburo candidate-member, 1949–54. CC secretary, 1958. Politburo member, 1957–64. Minister of Foreign Trade, 1948–52. Chairman, National Assembly Presidium (head of state), 1958–64.

Gancho Ganev (b. 1919) Communist. Minister of Education and Culture, 1962–63. Minister of Education, 1963–68.

Sava Ganovski (b. 1897) Communist. Professor. Academician. Chairman, Committee for Science, Culture, and Art, 1949–52.

Mihail Genovski (b. 1903) Agrarian. Professor. Minister of Agriculture, 1945–46.

Kimon Georgiev (b. 1882) Zveno Political Group Member. Minister of Railways, Posts, and Telegraphs, 1926–28. Prime Minister, 1934–35, 1944–46. Deputy Prime Minister, 1946–50. Minister of Foreign Affairs, 1946–47. Minister of Electrification, 1947–59. Chairman, Committee for Construction and Architecture, 1959. Deputy Prime Minister, 1959–62.

Vulko Gochev (b. 1903) Communist. Minister of Industry, 1949–50.

Marin Grashnov (b. 1919) Communist. Minister of Constructions, 1952–57. Chairman, Committee for Construction and Architecture, 1957–59. Chairman, Committee for Architecture and Public Works, 1959–61. Chairman, Committee for Constructions, 1961–62. Minister of Construction, 1962–68.

Mitko Grigorov (b. 1920) Communist. CC secretary, 1958–66. Politburo member, 1961–66. Minister and Chairman, Commission for Ideological and Cultural Problems, 1962–66.

Gocho Grozev (1900–1966) Communist. Politburo candidate-member, 1945–48.

Kostadin Gyaurov (b. 1924) Communist. Politburo candidate-member since 1966.

Stoyan Gyurov (b. 1915) Communist. Chairman, Committee for Constructions, 1959–61.

Rusi Hristozov (b. 1914) Communist. Minister of Interior, 1949–51. Minister of Supply and Food Industry, 1951–56. Chairman, State Planning Committee, 1956–59. Minister of Internal Trade, 1959–62.

Kiril Ignatov (b. 1913) Communist. Doctor. Minister of Public Health and Social Welfare since 1962.

Blagoi Ivanov (1898–1951) Communist. Lieutenant-General. Minister of Constructions and Roads, 1949–51.

Mariy Ivanov (b. 1919) Communist. Engineer. Chairman, Committee for Machine Building, 1962–66. Minister of Machine Building since 1966.

Petar Kamenov (b. 1896) Agrarian. Minister of Public Works, 1947–51.

Stoyan Karadzhov (b. 1905) Communist. Engineer. Chairman, Committee for Technical Progress, 1959–62.

Dimo Kazasov (b. 1887) "Independent" until 1946, then Communist. Minister of Propaganda, 1944–45. Minister of Information and Arts, 1945–47.

Kiril Klissurski (b. 1906) Agrarian. Minister of Mines, 1948–50.

Lyuben Kolarov (1897–?) Agrarian. Minister of Justice, 1946.

Peter Kolarov (1906–1966) Communist. Doctor. Major-General. Minister of Public Health and Social Welfare, 1950–62.

Vassil Kolarov (1877–1950) Communist. Bureau in Exile member, 1936–45. Politburo member, 1945–50. Chairman, National Assembly, 1945–47. Deputy Prime Minister, 1947–49. Minister of Foreign Affairs, 1947–49. Prime Minister, 1949–50.

Traicho Kostov (1897–1949) Communist. CC secretary, 1944–48. Politburo member, 1945–49 (ousted). Minister of Electrification, 1946. Deputy Prime Minister, 1946–49. Chairman, Committee for Economic and Financial Questions, 1947–49. Executed, 1949.

Stoyan Kosturkov (1866–1949) Radical Party secretary. Minister of Education, 1918–19. Minister of Railways, 1931–34. Minister of Education, 1945–47.

Dimitar Kotev (b. 1909) Communist. Engineer. Chairman, Committee for Architecture and Public Works, 1961–63.

Venelin Kotsev (b. 1922?) Communist. CC secretary since 1966.

Lyubomir Krastanov (b. 1908) Communist. Professor. Academician. Chairman, Bulgarian Academy of Sciences, 1962–68. Minister without Portfolio, 1962–66.

Pencho Kubadinski (b. 1918) Communist. CC secretary, 1958–62. Politburo Candidate-member, 1962–66. Politburo member since 1966. Minister of Transport and Communications, 1962–66. Deputy Prime Minister since 1962. Minister of Construction and Architecture since 1968.

Georgi Kulishev   (b. 1885) Zveno Political Group member. Minister of Foreign Affairs, 1946.

Georgi Kumbiliev   (b. 1915?)   Communist.   Lieutenant-General. Minister of Foreign Trade, 1959–62.

Petko Kunin   (b. 1900) Communist. Professor. Politburo member, 1932–33, 1945–48. Minister of Industry, 1947–49. Minister of Finance, 1949.

Kiril Lazarov   (b. 1895) Communist. Professor. Chairman, State Planning Committee, 1949. Minister of Finance, 1949–62.

Hristo Lilkov   (Birth and death dates unknown.) Zveno Political Group member. General. Minister of Industry, 1946–47.

Karlo Lukanov   (b. 1897) Communist. Minister of Foreign Affairs, 1956–62.

Pavel Matev   (b. 1924) Communist. Chairman, Committee for Art and Culture since 1966.

Ivan Mihailov   (b. 1897) Communist. General. Deputy Prime Minister since 1950. Politburo member since 1954. Minister of Transport and Communications, 1957–58. Minister of National Defense, 1958–62.

Misho Mishev   (b. 1911) Communist. Lieutenant-General. Chairman, Committee for Labor and Wages, 1962–68. Minister of Labor and Social Welfare since 1968.

Zdravko Mitovski   (b. 1908) Communist. Social-Democrat until 1948. Minister of Social Policy, 1946–47. Minister of Labor and Social Welfare, 1947–50.

Radi Naidenov   (b. 1895) Agrarian. Minister of Justice, 1946–62.

Mincho Neichev   (1887–1956) Communist. Doctor. Minister of Justice, 1944–46. Minister of Education, 1946–47. Chairman, National Assembly Presidium, 1947–50. Politburo candidate-member, 1948–49. Politburo member, 1949–54. Minister of Foreign Affairs, 1950–56.

Dimitar Neikov   (1885–1949) Social-Democrat. Minister of Trade, Industry and Labor, 1944–46. Minister of Trade, 1946.

Alexandur Obbov   (b. 1877) Agrarian. Minister without Portfolio, 1945–46. Minister of Agriculture, 1946. Deputy Prime Minister, 1946–47.

Nikola Palagachev   (b. 1917) Communist. Minister of Agriculture, 1966–68.

Petur Panchevski   (b. 1902) Communist. General. Minister of National Defense, 1950–58. Politburo candidate-member, 1954–58.

Nacho Papazov   (b. 1921) Communist. Minister of Education and Culture, 1959–62. Chairman, Committee for Science and Technical Progress, 1962. CC secretary, 1962–66.

Apostol Pashev   (b. 1914) Communist. Professor. Engineer. Chairman, State Planning Committee, 1962–68. Minister of Supply and State Reserves since 1968.

Assen Pavlov (b. 1898) Agrarian. Minister of Agriculture, 1944–45. Joined the opposition, 1945.

Georgi Pavlov (b. 1921) Communist. Chairman, Committee for Chemistry and Metallurgy, 1962–66. Minister of Chemistry and Metallurgy since 1966.

Nikola Pavlov (b. 1906) Communist. CC secretary, 1946–48.

Todor Pavlov (b. 1890) Communist. Academician. Chairman, Bulgarian Academy of Sciences, 1947–62. Politburo member since 1966.

Vassil Pavurdzhiev (1897–1948) Agrarian. Minister of Mines, 1947–48.

Pelo Pelovski (1903–1957) Communist. Minister of Internal Trade, 1950–57.

Nikola Petkov (1889?–1947) Agrarian. Minister without Portfolio, 1944–45. Became head of the opposition, 1945. Executed, 1947.

Dimitur Popov (b. 1912) Communist. Minister of Finance since 1962.

Georgi Popov (b. 1889) Communist. Social-Democrat until 1948. Minister of Social Policy, 1945–46. Deputy Prime Minister, 1946–49. Minister of Forests, 1949–51.

Ivan Popov (b. 1907) Communist. Professor. Engineer. Chairman, Committee for Science and Technical Progress since 1962. Politburo member since 1966.

Konstantin Popov (b. 1917) Communist. Engineer. Chairman, Committee for Power and Fuel, 1962–66. Minister of Power and Fuel since 1966.

Vladimir Poptomov (1890–1952) Communist. Politburo member, 1945–52. Minister of Foreign Affairs, 1949–50. Deputy Prime Minister, 1950–52.

Todor Prahov (b. 1904) Communist. Politburo candidate-member, 1954–62.

Ivan Prumov (b. 1921) Communist. Minister of Agriculture, 1957–62. CC secretary since 1962.

Ivan Raikov (b. 1912) Communist. CC secretary *ca.* 1952–54.

Manol Sakelarov (1890–1955?) Communist. Engineer. Minister of Electrification, 1946–47. Minister of Construction and Roads, 1947–49.

Angel Solakov (b. 1922) Communist. Lieutenant-General. Chairman, Committee for State Security since 1965. Minister of Internal Affairs and State Security since 1968.

Encho Staikov (b. 1901) Communist. CC secretary *ca.* 1952–54 and 1956–57. Politburo member, 1954–66.

Petko Stainov (b. 1890) Zveno Political Group member. Professor. Academician. Minister of Foreign Affairs, 1944–46.

Ivan Stefanov (b. 1899) Communist. Professor. Academician.

Minister of Finance, 1946–49. Sentenced to life imprisonment, 1949 (Kostov trial). Rehabilitated, 1956.

Ninko Stefanov (b. 1911) Communist. Chairman, Committee for State Control, 1959–62 and since 1965.

Nikola Stoilov (b. 1915) Communist. Minister of Agriculture, 1951–52.

Mladen Stoyanov (b. 1896) Communist. Politburo candidate-member, 1957–62.

Petko Stoyanov (b. 1879) "Independent." Former member of the Democratic Party. Professor. Minister of Finance, 1944–45.

Peko Takov (b. 1909) Communist. Minister of Internal Trade since 1962. Politburo candidate-member since 1966.

Petur Tanchev (b. 1920) Agrarian. Minister of Justice, 1962–66. Deputy Prime Minister since 1966.

Boris Taskov (b. 1906) Communist. Chairman Department for Supplies and State Reserves, 1950–52. Minister of Trade, 1957–59. CC secretary, 1954–57. Politburo member, 1957–59 (ousted).

Dobri Terpeshev (1884–1967) Communist. Politburo member, 1943–50. Minister without Portfolio, 1944–46. Chairman, Supreme Economic Council, 1946–47. Chairman, State Planning Committee, 1947–49. Deputy Prime Minister, 1949–50. Minister of Labor and Social Welfare, 1950.

Stanko Todorov (b. 1920) Communist. Minister of Agriculture, 1952–57. CC secretary, 1957–59. Politburo candidate-member, 1959–61. Chairman, State Planning Committee, 1959–62. Deputy Prime Minister, 1959–66. Politburo member since 1961. CC secretary since 1966.

Stefan Tonchev (b. 1899) Agrarian. Minister of Railways, Posts, and Telegraphs, 1945–49.

Stoyan Tonchev (b. 1902) Agrarian. Minister of Municipal Economy, Roads, and Public Works, 1951–59. Chairman of the Committee for Labor and Prices, 1959–62. Minister without Portfolio, 1962–66. Minister of Communications since 1966.

Georgi Traikov (b. 1898) Agrarian. Minister of Agriculture, 1946–50. Deputy Prime Minister, 1947–56. First Deputy Prime Minister, 1956–64. Chairman, National Assembly Presidium, (head of state) since 1964.

Krustyo Trichkov (b. 1923) Communist. Politburo candidate-member since 1966.

Angel Tsanev (b. 1912) Communist. Lieutenant-General. Politburo candidate-member since 1966.

Georgi Tsankov (b. 1913) Communist. Lieutenant-General. CC secretary, 1950–51?. Minister of Interior, 1951–62. Politburo member, 1951–62 (ousted). Deputy Prime Minister, 1962.

Stanka Tsekova (b. 1901) Communist. Minister of Light Industry, 1956–59.

Tano Tsolov (b. 1918) Communist. Minister of Heavy Industry, 1952–59. Chairman, Committee for Industry and Technical Progress, 1959. CC secretary, 1959–62. Politburo candidate-member, 1962–66. Deputy Prime Minister since 1962. Politburo member since 1966. Chairman, State Planning Committee since 1968.

Marin Vachkov (b. 1922) Communist. Minister of Rural Production, 1962–66. Minister of Transport since 1966.

Boris Velchev (b. 1914) Communist. CC secretary since 1959. Politburo member since 1962. Chairman, Committee for Party and State Control, 1962–65.

Damyan Velchev (1883–1954) Colonel-General. Zveno Political Group member. Minister of National Defense, 1944–46. Exiled.

Vladimir Videnov (b. 1921?) Communist. Minister of Architecture and Public Works, 1966–68.

Radenko Vidinski (b. 1899) Communist. Minister of Construction Materials and Timber Industry, 1956–57. Minister of Construction and Construction Materials, 1957–59.

Petur Vutov (b. 1917) Communist. Doctor. Chairman, Committee for Culture and Art, 1963–66.

Demir Yanev (b. 1910) Communist. Minister of Education, 1952–57.

Anton Yugov (b. 1904) Communist. Politburo member, 1937–62 (ousted). Minister of Interior, 1944–49. Deputy Prime Minister, 1949–50. Minister of Industry, 1950–51. Minister of Heavy Industry, 1951–52. Deputy Prime Minister, 1952–56. Chairman, State Committee for Construction and Architecture, 1955–56. Prime Minister, 1956–62 (ousted).

Todor Zhivkov (b. 1911) Communist. CC secretary, 1950–54. Politburo candidate-member, 1950–51. Politburo member since 1951. First Secretary, CC since 1954. Prime Minister since 1962.

Zhivko Zhivkov (b. 1915) Communist. Minister of Foreign Trade, 1952–57. Minister of Education and Culture, 1958–59. Deputy Prime Minister, 1959–62. First Deputy Prime Minister since 1962. Politburo member since 1962. Chairman, Committee for Economic Coordination since 1968.

Appendix II

Bulgarian Communist Party Politburos and Secretariats, 1944–66

I. *Eighth Enlarged Plenum* (*Elected March 1, 1945*)

Politburo Members
1. Georgi Dimitrov
2. Vassil Kolarov
3. Traicho Kostov
4. Georgi Chankov
5. Vulko Chervenkov
6. Dobri Terpeshev
7. Anton Yugov
8. Tsola Dragoicheva
9. Dimitur Ganev
10. Raiko Damyanov
11. Georgi Damyanov
12. Petko Kunin
13. Vladimir Poptomov

Politburo Candidate-Members
1. Dimitur Dimov
2. Gocho Grozev
3. Titko Chernokolev

Chairman of Central Committee
Georgi Dimitrov

First Secretary
Traicho Kostov

Secretaries
Georgi Chankov
Vulko Chervenkov

II. *Fifth Party Congress* (*Elected December 27, 1948*)

Politburo Members
1. Georgi Dimitrov
2. Traicho Kostov
3. Vassil Kolarov
4. Vulko Chervenkov
5. Georgi Chankov
6. Anton Yugov
7. Georgi Damyanov
8. Dobri Terpeshev
9. Vladimir Poptomov

Politburo Candidate-Members
1. Titko Chernokolev
2. Raiko Damyanov
3. Mincho Neichev

Secretary-General
Georgi Dimitrov

Secretaries
Georgi Chankov
Vulko Chervenkov

315

III. *Sixth Party Congress (Elected March 3, 1954)*

Politburo Members
1. Vulko Chervenkov
2. Georgi Damyanov
3. Anton Yugov
4. Georgi Chankov
5. Raiko Damyanov
6. Todor Zhivkov
7. Georgi Tsankov
8. Encho Staikov
9. Ivan Mihailov

Politburo Candidate-Members
1. Todor Prahov
2. Petur Panchevski

First Secretary
Todor Zhivkov

Secretaries
Dimitur Ganev
Boris Taskov

IV. *Seventh Party Congress (Elected June 7, 1958)*

Politburo Members
1. Boyan Bulgaranov
2. Dimitur Ganev
3. Georgi Damyanov
4. Raiko Damyanov
5. Todor Zhivkov
6. Ivan Mihailov
7. Encho Staikov
8. Boris Taskov
9. Georgi Tsankov
10. Vulko Chervenkov
11. Anton Yugov

Politburo Candidate-Members
1. Dimitur Dimov
2. Mladen Stoyanov
3. Todor Prahov

First Secretary
Todor Zhivkov

Secretaries
Dimitur Ganev
Boyan Bulgaranov
Stanko Todorov
Mitko Grigorov
Pencho Kubadinski

V. *Eighth Party Congress (Elected November 14, 1962)*

Politburo Members
1. Boyan Bulgaranov
2. Boris Velchev
3. Dimitur Ganev
4. Mitko Grigorov
5. Zhivko Zhivkov
6. Todor Zhivkov
7. Ivan Mihailov
8. Encho Staikov
9. Stanko Todorov

Politburo Candidate-Members
1. Dimitur Dimov
2. Pencho Kubadinski
3. Tano Tsolov

First Secretary
Todor Zhivkov

Secretaries
Boyan Bulgaranov
Mitko Grigorov
Boris Velchev
Nacho Papazov
Luchezar Avramov

VI. *Ninth Party Congress (Elected November 19, 1966)*

Politburo Members
1. Boyan Bulgaranov
2. Boris Velchev
3. Zhivko Zhivkov
4. Ivan Mihailov
5. Ivan Popov
6. Pencho Kubadinski
7. Stanko Todorov
8. Tano Tsolov
9. Todor Zhivkov
10. Todor Pavlov
11. Tsola Dragoicheva

Politburo Candidate-Members
1. Dimitur Dimov
2. Luchezar Avramov
3. Peko Takov
4. Angel Tsanev
5. Kostadin Gyaurov
6. Krustyo Trichkov
7. Ivan Abadzhiev

First Secretary
Todor Zhivkov

Secretaries
Boyan Bulgaranov
Boris Velchev
Venelin Kotsev
Ivan Prumov
Stanko Todorov

Appendix III

Bulgarian Communist Party Membership

	Total	Full members	Candi-date-members	Per cent of total			
				Workers	Peas-ants	Em-ployees	Others
1922	38,036						
September, 1944	25,000						
February, 1945	250,000						
December, 1948	495,658			26.50	44.74	16.28	12.48
February, 1954	455,251	368,142	87,109	34.06	39.76	17.94	8.24
June, 1958	484,255	467,546	16,709	36.09	34.16	21.72	8.03
November, 1962	528,674	506,261	22,413	37.16	32.09	23.56	7.19
November, 1966	611,179	571,005	40,174	38.41	29.21		

SOURCES: 1922, 1944, and 1945: *Kratka Bulgarska Entsiklopedia*, I, (1963), 410–11. 1948 and 1954: *Rabotnichesko Delo*, February 26, 1954. 1958: *Ibid.*, June 3, 1958. 1962: *Ibid.*, November 6, 1962. 1966: *Ibid.*, November 15, 1966.

Appendix IV

Statistical Tables

TABLE 1
Volume of Foreign Trade (in Millions of Leva)

	Total	Exports	Imports
1939	116.7	63.4	53.3
1950	173.7	118.7	55.0
1955	568.8	276.4	292.4
1957	821.6	433.0	388.6
1960	1,408.7	668.6	740.1
1962	1,822.0	903.9	918.1
1964	2,389.2	1,146.2	1,243.0
1966	3,256.5	1,526.9	1,729.6
1967	3,565.3	1,731.4	1,833.9

SOURCES: 1939, 1950, and 1964: *Vanshna Targovia na NR Bulgaria, 1939, 1945–64*, p. 9. 1955–62: *Statistical Yearbook of PR Bulgaria, 1963*, p. 304. 1966–67: *Statistical Handbook, 1968*, p. 91.

TABLE 2
Structure of Bulgarian Imports (Per Cent)

	1939	1955	1957	1960	1962	1964	1966
Means of production	80.6	94.6	84.9	87.3	87.7	88.1	88.9
Consumer goods	19.4	5.4	15.1	12.7	12.3	11.9	11.1
Vegetable	7.7	1.3	7.7	5.6	5.9	5.5	4.8
Animal	1.3	0.4	0.7	2.0	0.8	1.1	0.8
Industrial	10.4	3.7	6.7	5.1	5.6	5.3	5.5

SOURCES: 1939–57: *Statistical Yearbook of PR Bulgaria, 1963*, p. 304. 1960–62: *Statistical Yearbook of PR Bulgaria, 1964*, p. 301. 1964–66: *Statistical Yearbook of PR Bulgaria, 1967*, p. 300.

TABLE 3

Structure of Bulgarian Exports (Per Cent)

	1939	1955	1957	1960	1962	1964	1966
Industrial products	62.6	84.4	88.9	86.6	88.0	89.5	89.7
nonrural	0.4	26.7	27.0	25.7	35.9	40.1	41.0
rural	62.2	57.7	61.9	60.9	52.1	49.4	48.7
Food products	15.5	19.3	14.0	22.4	22.6	20.0	18.7
Non-food products	46.7	38.4	47.9	38.5	29.5	29.4	30.0
Nonprocessed rural products	37.4	15.6	11.1	13.4	12.0	10.5	10.3

SOURCES: 1939–57: *Statistical Yearbook of PR Bulgaria*, 1963, p. 305. 1960–62: *Statistical Yearbook of PR Bulgaria*, 1964, p. 303. 1964–66: *Statistical Yearbook of PR Bulgaria*, 1967, p. 302.

TABLE 4

Bulgarian Foreign Trade by Groups of Countries (Per Cent)

	Socialist		Non-Socialist	
	Exports	Imports	Exports	Imports
1955	89.7	89.4	10.3	10.6
1960	84.0	83.9	16.0	16.1
1965	79.4	74.2	20.6	25.8
1966	76.4	69.5	23.6	30.5
1967	77.3	73.9	22.7	26.1

SOURCE: *Statistical Handbook*, 1968, p. 95.

TABLE 5
Bulgarian Foreign Trade by Countries (Per Cent of Total
Exports and Imports)

	1952	1955	1960	1965	1966
U.S.S.R.	57.2	50.5	53.8	52.2	50.8
	56.9	47.5	52.4	50.0	47.8
G.D.R.	6.4	13.7	9.8	9.2	8.2
	7.1	9.2	11.1	7.3	7.0
Czechoslovakia	12.5	10.8	9.6	7.7	4.8
	12.6	16.6	9.8	6.5	5.3
West Germany	1.0	2.3	3.5	3.5	3.1
	0.7	2.5	5.9	5.8	8.8
Poland	5.8	3.0	3.6	3.3	3.4
	5.0	4.2	3.4	3.9	2.9
Italy	0.4	0.4	1.7	3.3	4.4
	0.5	0.4	1.1	2.8	3.6
France	0.2	0.7	0.9	0.6	1.1
	0.5	0.5	1.2	2.1	3.2
Austria	4.1	2.2	1.9	1.1	2.4
	4.6	2.2	1.5	2.0	2.1
Britain	1.8	0.9	1.1	1.6	1.6
	1.9	1.8	1.7	1.5	2.1

NOTE: The first line for each country is exports, the second imports.
SOURCES: Percentages are based on figures in leva in *Statistical Yearbook of
PR Bulgaria, 1956*, p. 82; *Statistical Yearbook of PR Bulgaria, 1962*, p. 301;
Statistical Yearbook of PR Bulgaria, 1967, pp. 304–305.

TABLE 6

Rates of Growth of GNP and National Income

(1939 = 100)

	GNP	National income	National income per capita
1939	100	100	100
1948	123	101	89
1952	184	140	121
1954	224	168	143
1956	251	179	149
1958	311	217	177
1960	412	282	226
1962	473	308	242
1964	564	364	282
1966	693	433	330
1967	764	473	359

NOTE: The rates of growth for years up to 1962 were calculated on the basis of 1957 prices. Rates after 1962 have been calculated on the basis of January 1, 1962, prices and have been linked with the rates based on 1957 prices.

SOURCES: 1948–58: *Statistical Yearbook of PR Bulgaria, 1960*, p. 88. 1960–64: *Statistical Yearbook of PR Bulgaria, 1965*, p. 96. 1966–67: *Statistical Handbook, 1968*, p. 27.

TABLE 7
Proportions of Accumulation and Consumption Funds of
National Income

	Accumulation	*Consumption*
1952	23.8	76.2
1953	30.3	69.7
1954	20.3	79.7
1955	20.7	79.3
1956	14.3	85.7
1957	20.1	79.9
1958	19.4	80.6
1959	30.1	69.9
1960	27.5	72.5
1961	22.3	77.7
1962	25.4	74.6
1963	29.0	71.0
1964	31.0	69.0
1965	28.3	71.7
1966	34.2	65.8
1967	33.1	66.9

NOTE: The proportions for years up to 1962 have been calculated at 1957 prices, those for years after 1962 at January 1, 1962, prices.

SOURCES: 1952–59: *Statistical Yearbook of PR Bulgaria*, 1960, p. 88. 1960–62: *Statistical Yearbook of PR Bulgaria*, 1963, p. 106. 1963–65: *Statistical Yearbook of PR Bulgaria*, 1966, p. 88. 1966–67: *Statistical Handbook*, 1968, p. 28.

TABLE 8
Distribution of Capital Investments (Per Cent)

	1949	1952	1956	1960	1962	1964	1965
Heavy industry (Group A)	30.3	34.3	39.5	31.1	40.7	41.4	42.3
Light industry (Group B)	8.2	6.3	4.2	8.0	5.7	7.5	7.2
Rural economy (without collective farms)	11.2	7.9	14.2	11.2	7.0	7.5	7.3
Collective farms	3.4	8.3	11.5	20.7	17.4	14.1	13.5
Forestry	1.0	1.1	1.5	2.1	2.0	0.9	1.0
Transport and communications	22.2	12.9	8.2	6.7	7.7	8.4	7.5
Trade	3.0	5.5	2.3	2.6	3.2	3.2	3.4
Housing and communal economy	5.2	4.2	9.3	7.5	7.1	7.6	8.0
Science, education, culture	3.6	2.3	4.4	5.0	4.4	3.9	4.1
Health and sports	2.7	1.4	2.3	1.7	1.2	1.3	1.4
Other	9.2	15.8	2.6	3.4	3.6	4.2	4.3

SOURCES: 1949–62: *Statistical Yearbook of PR Bulgaria, 1964*, pp. 228–29. 1964–65: *Statistical Yearbook of PR Bulgaria, 1966*, pp. 226–27.

TABLE 9
Growth of Total Industrial Production (1939 = 100)

	Total	Heavy industry (Group A)	Light industry (Group B)
1948	203	329	166
1950	309	522	247
1952	430	821	315
1954	545	×11	381
1956	674	×14	468
1958	899	×18	633
1960	×12	×27	793
1962	×15	×34	×10
1964	×19	×45	×11
1966	×24	—	—
1967	×27	—	—

SOURCES: 1948–58: *Statistical Yearbook of PR Bulgaria, 1960*, p. 93. 1960–62: *Statistical Yearbook of PR Bulgaria, 1964*, p. 106. 1964: *Statistical Yearbook of PR Bulgaria, 1966*, p. 95. 1966–67: *Statistical Handbook, 1968*, p. 29.

TABLE 10
Total Production of Some Important Industrial Goods

	1939	1948	1952	1956	1960	1965	1967
Electric power (million kwh)	266	550	1,352	2,393	4,657	10,244	13,600
Coal (thousand tons)	2,214	4,266	7,410	10,817	17,147	26,254	28,808
Crude oil (thousand tons)				247	200	229	499
Iron ores (iron content, thousand tons)	11	10	54	105	188	585	797
Steel (thousand tons)	6	5	6	130	253	588	1,239
Lead and zinc ores (metal content, thousand tons)	6	23	90	109	173	180	177
Copper ores (metal content, thousand tons)	0.4	1	4	6	11	30	35
Lead (tons)	9	2,131	2,729	6,009	40,406	93,421	94,217
Zinc (tons)				5,838	16,909	65,764	71,698
Internal combustion engines		54	1,059	1,342	10,657	23,073	40,526
Radio sets		2,713	11,279	92,200	157,403	129,858	149,404
Nitrogen fertilizers (in 100 per cent nitrogen, tons)				34,229	83,594	245,834	264,872
Cement (thousand tons)	225	378	672	859	1,586	2,681	3,358
Paper (tons)	14,500	21,991	29,999	44,532	53,909	85,246	150,832
Cotton fabrics (thousand meters)	34,121	58,263	105,939	142,259	218,389	291,310	306,347
Wool fabrics (thousand meters)	5,296	5,418	9,210	12,701	18,724	20,119	21,643
Shoes (thousand pairs)		1,643	4,143	3,983	7,534	10,062	13,881
Butter (tons)	694	550	3,143	4,660	10,987	11,922	13,359
Sugar (tons)	25,000	61,000	54,000	107,000	171,000	315,000	397,000

SOURCE: *Statistical Handbook, 1968*, pp. 34–39.

TABLE 11

Growth of Total Rural Production (1932–38 = 100, 1935 Excluded)

	Total	Plant	Livestock
1939	113.5	123.8	97.5
1948	116.3	123.0	105.9
1950	95.7	103.4	83.8
1951	134.4	159.3	96.0
1952	112.3	118.1	103.4
1953	136.2	156.7	104.5
1954	119.6	128.7	105.7
1955	130.7	142.0	113.2
1956	122.4	129.9	111.0
1957	142.6	159.2	116.9
1958	141.7	149.1	130.3
1959	167.3	187.6	136.1
1960	172.8	190.9	144.8
1961	166.8	173.1	157.0
1962	173.8	188.3	151.2
1963	178.3	197.0	149.5
1964	198.6	217.3	170.0
1965	202.2	214.0	184.1
1966	231.1	254.7	194.8
1967	231.1	246.5	207.5

SOURCES: 1939–59: *Statistical Yearbook of PR Bulgaria, 1960*, p. 156. 1960–62: *Statistical Yearbook of PR Bulgaria, 1963*, p. 182. 1963–65: *Statistical Yearbook of PR Bulgaria, 1966*, p. 172. 1966–67: *Statistical Handbook, 1968*, p. 57.

TABLE 12

Total Production of Some Crops (Thousands of Tons)

	Wheat	Barley	Maize	Oriental tobacco	Sugar beets	Tomatoes	Grapes
1939	2,003	414	1,077	41	234	44	659
1948	1,688	270	802	28	560	95	473
1949	814	134	689	45	498	96	581
1950	1,757	326	654	40	331	95	465
1951	2,499	502	1,279	58	839	200	606
1952	2,041	429	487	41	381	215	394
1953	2,334	505	961	52	782	303	492
1954	1,651	340	975	48	650	210	430
1955	1,921	471	1,477	66	596	221	513
1956	1,717	343	1,056	51	943	372	399
1957	2,395	478	1,492	75	1,434	366	573
1958	2,322	444	882	77	882	464	888
1959	2,426	560	1,506	93	1,450	479	686
1960	2,379	622	1,505	60	1,650	634	589
1961	2,028	612	1,424	53	1,463	726	579
1962	2,081	599	1,556	98	1,121	793	1,000
1963	1,892	618	1,732	97	1,122	704	1,094
1964	2,118	764	2,056	141	2,100	694	826
1965	2,921	876	1,238	116	1,392	775	1,215
1966	3,193	1,064	2,207	125	2,528	751	977
1967	3,241	985	1,977	107	2,040	702	799

SOURCES: 1939–59: *Statistical Yearbook of PR Bulgaria, 1960*, pp. 185–88. 1960–62: *Statistical Yearbook of PR Bulgaria, 1963*, pp. 203–206. 1963–65: *Statistical Yearbook of PR Bulgaria, 1966*, pp. 189–92. 1966–67: *Statistical Handbook, 1968*, p. 64.

TABLE 13
Railroads and Roads (Kilometers)

	Railroads		Roads				
	Lines operated	Station sidings	Total	Main roads	1st class	2nd class	3rd class
1939	3,477	949	19,554				
1948	3,786	1,140	23,486				
1952	4,057	1,333	24,519	2,407	2,753	6,381	12,978
1955	4,091	1,377	25,124	1,948	4,212	3,939	15,025
1957	4,108	1,419	25,719	1,980	4,199	4,033	15,507
1960	4,111	1,509	27,412	2,062	4,128	4,226	16,996
1962	4,125	1,549	27,953	2,342	4,483	4,751	16,377
1964	4,160	1,611	28,550	2,350	4,495	4,855	16,850
1966	4,094	1,694	29,233	2,418	4,572	4,747	17,496

SOURCES: 1939–62: *Statistical Yearbook of PR Bulgaria*, 1964, pp. 253 and 264. 1964–66: *Statistical Yearbook of PR Bulgaria*, 1967, pp. 253 and 264.

TABLE 14
Education (Schools and Institutes)

	Elementary and secondary	Special (blind, deaf, slowly developing children)	Profes- sional- technical	Tech- nicums and art	Semi- high	Univer- sities
1939–40						
Schools	7,455	5	385	36	5	5
Students	1,009,690	376	41,049	10,118	803	10,169
Teachers	28,625	64	2,261	422	64	453
1944–45						
Schools	7,932	4	323	62	9	7
Students	1,052,566	208	28,018	21,212	1,697	26,412
Teachers	29,697	43	1,130	792	100	803
1960–61						
Schools	6,448	66	236	231	18	20
Students	1,212,383	7,080	42,123	93,944	6,187	54,965
Teachers	51,067	881	2,835	5,307	360	3,883
1966–67						
Schools	5,020	106	319	257	16	26
Students	1,231,560	15,756	94,694	172,098	10,234	82,573
Teachers	56,574	1,898	6,422	8,902	491	6,156

SOURCES: 1939–40, 1944–45, and 1966–67: *Statistical Yearbook of PR Bulgaria*, 1967, p. 333. 1960–61: *Statistical Yearbook of PR Bulgaria*, 1963, p. 339.

TABLE 15
Total Population by Age Groups

Age	1920	1934	1946	1956
Up to 9	1,114,488	1,434,245	1,263,776	1,395,521
10–19	1,180,402	1,167,235	1,391,331	1,196,246
20–29	777,690	1,109,690	1,228,167	1,300,753
30–39	611,923	849,680	1,046,159	1,140,028
40–49	416,733	588,745	869,961	977,971
50–59	332,219	454,010	557,100	790,040
60–69	233,067	277,706	435,937	468,936
70–79	120,671	141,953	173,521	272,423
Over 80	57,652	53,473	62,776	71,788
Unknown	2,126	1,202	621	3
TOTAL	4,846,971	6,077,939	7,029,349	7,613,709

NOTE: The figures are obtained through the censuses of 1920, 1934, 1946, and 1956; the 1965 census is not yet available.
SOURCE: *Statistical Yearbook of PR Bulgaria,* 1966, pp. 16–17.

TABLE 16
Growth Rate of Population (Per Thousand Inhabitants)

	Birth	Death	Natural growth
1900	42.2	22.5	19.7
1910	41.7	23.2	18.5
1920	39.9	21.4	18.5
1925	36.9	19.2	17.7
1930	31.4	16.2	15.2
1935	26.4	14.6	11.8
1940	22.2	13.4	8.8
1945	24.0	14.9	9.1
1950	25.2	10.2	15.0
1952	21.2	11.6	9.6
1954	20.2	9.2	11.0
1956	19.5	9.4	10.1
1958	17.9	7.9	10.0
1960	17.8	8.1	9.7
1962	16.7	8.7	8.0
1964	16.1	7.9	8.2
1965	15.3	8.1	7.2
1966	14.9	8.3	6.6
1967	15.0	9.0	6.0

SOURCES: 1900–1966: *Statistical Yearbook of PR Bulgaria,* 1967, p. 18.
1967: *Statistical Handbook,* 1968, p. 10.

TABLE 17
Development of Urbanization (Per Cent of Population)

Inhabitants	1934	1946	1956
Up to 199	2.3	1.8	1.6
200–499	6.7	6.2	5.7
500–999	15.7	15.2	14.0
1,000–1,999	28.5	25.8	21.7
2,000–4,999	23.5	23.7	20.4
5,000–9,999	6.7	7.3	7.0
10,000–24,999	5.3	5.4	7.1
25,000–99,999	6.6	6.6	10.3
100,000–499,999	4.7	8.0	3.7
Over 500,000			8.5

SOURCE: *Statistical Yearbook of PR Bulgaria*, 1967, p. 16.

Bibliography

Most of the material on which this book is based was derived from original Bulgarian Communist sources, mainly newspapers and periodicals, but also certain broadcasts of Radio Sofia as monitored by Radio Free Europe in Munich. As mentioned in the preface, I have also used many of the analyses of Bulgarian events that were published by Radio Free Europe. Bulgaria has not received much attention, either by Western analysts or by journalists, but occasionally articles on Bulgaria and its problems appear in specialist journals like *The Journal of Central European Affairs, The Slavic Review, Survey, East Europe, Problems of Communism, The World Today,* and *Osteuropa.* Of the Western press, the *Neue Zuercher Zeitung, Frankfurter Algemeine Zeitung, Christ und Welt, Die Zeit, Le Monde, Die Presse, The Times, The Guardian, The Economist,* and *The New York Times* have had the best coverage in recent years.

The following are books that I found most helpful. Other books not listed here were used in preparing this study.

Armstrong, Hamilton Fish. *Tito and Goliath.* New York: Macmillan, 1951.

Barker, Elisabeth. *Macedonia: Its Place in Balkan Power Politics.* London: Royal Institute of International Affairs, 1950.

———. *Truce in the Balkans.* London: Royal Institute of International Affairs, 1948.

Betts, R. R., ed. *Central and South East Europe, 1945–1948.* London: Royal Institute of International Affairs, 1950.

Black, C. E., ed. *Challenge in Eastern Europe.* New Brunswick, Rutgers University Press, 1954.

———. *The Establishment of Constitutional Government in Bulgaria.* Princeton: Princeton University Press, 1944.

BROWN, ALAN A., and NEUBERGER, EGON, eds. *International Trade and Central Planning: An Analysis of Economic Interactions.* Berkeley: University of California Press, 1968.
BROWN, J. F. *The New Eastern Europe: The Khrushchev Era and After.* New York: Frederick A. Praeger, 1966.
BRZEZINSKI, ZBIGNIEW K. *The Soviet Bloc: Unity and Conflict.* Rev. ed. Cambridge: Harvard University Press, 1967.
DEDIJER, VLADIMIR. *Tito.* New York: Simon and Schuster, 1953.
DELLIN, L. A. D., ed. *Bulgaria.* New York: Frederick A. Praeger, 1956.
DEWAR, HUGO. *The Modern Inquisition.* London: Allan Wingate, 1953.
————. *Soviet Trade with Eastern Europe, 1945–1949.* London: Royal Institute of International Affairs, 1951.
FISCHER-GALATI, STEPHEN. *The New Rumania: From People's Democracy to Socialist Republic.* Cambridge: MIT Press, 1967.
————, ed. *Eastern Europe in the Sixties.* New York: Frederick A. Praeger, 1963.
GOLDMAN, MARSHALL I. *Soviet Foreign Aid.* New York: Frederick A. Praeger, 1967.
GRIFFITH, WILLIAM E. *Albania and the Sino-Soviet Rift.* Cambridge: MIT Press, 1963.
GYORGY, ANDREW. *Governments of Danubian Europe.* New York: Holt, Rinehart and Winston, 1949.
IONESCU, GHITA. *The Politics of the European Communist States.* New York: Frederick A. Praeger, 1967.
————. *Communism in Rumania, 1944–1962.* London: Oxford University Press, 1964.
JELAVICH, BARBARA, and JELAVICH, CHARLES, eds. *The Balkans in Transition.* Berkeley: University of California Press, 1963.
KANAPA, JEAN. *Bulgarie d'hier et d'aujourd'hui: le pays de Dimitrov.* Paris: Éditions Sociales, 1953.
LEHRMAN, HAL. *Russia's Europe.* New York: Appleton-Century-Crofts, 1947.
LONDON, KURT, ed. *Eastern Europe in Transition.* Baltimore: Johns Hopkins University Press, 1966.
MEYER, PETER, et al. *The Jews in the Soviet Satellites.* Syracuse: Syracuse University Press, 1953.
MITRANY, DAVID. *Marx Against the Peasant: A Study in Social Dogmatism.* Chapel Hill: University of North Carolina Press, 1951.
NENOFF, DRAGOMIR. *The Bulgarian Communist Party.* New York: National Committee for a Free Europe, 1951.
OREN, NISSAN. *The Bulgarian Communist Party, 1934–1944.* Unpublished Ph. D. dissertation, Columbia University, 1960.
PADEV, MICHAEL. *Dimitrov Wastes No Bullets, Nikola Petkov: The Test Case.* London: Eyre and Spottiswoode, 1948.

PRYOR, FREDERICK L. *The Communist Foreign Trade System*. Cambridge: Harvard University Press, 1963.

ROTHSCHILD, JOSEPH. *The Communist Party of Bulgaria: Origins and Development, 1883–1936*. New York: Columbia University Press, 1959.

ROUCEK, JOSEPH S. *Balkan Politics*. Stanford: Stanford University Press, 1948.

———, and LOTTICH, KENNETH V. *Behind the Iron Curtain: The Soviet Satellite States—East European Nationalism and Education*. Caldwell, Idaho: Caxton Printers, 1964.

SAXENA, H. L. *Bulgaria Under the Red Star*. Delhi: S. Chand, 1957.

SETON-WATSON, HUGH. *The East European Revolution*. London: Methuen, 1956.

SINGLETON, FREDERICK B. *Background to Eastern Europe*. Oxford: Pergamon Press, 1965.

SIPKOV, IVAN. *Legal Sources and Bibliography of Bulgaria*. New York: Frederick A. Praeger, 1956.

SKILLING, HAROLD G. *The Governments of Communist East Europe*. New York: T. Y. Crowell, 1966.

———. *Communism, National and International: Eastern Europe After Stalin*. Toronto: University of Toronto Press, 1964.

STAAR, RICHARD F. *The Communist Regimes in Eastern Europe: An Introduction*. Stanford: Hoover Institute, 1967.

STAVRIANOS, LEFTEN S. *Balkan Federation: A History of the Movement Toward Balkan Unity in Modern Times*. Studies in History, Vol. XXVII, Nos. 1–4, Smith College, Northampton, Mass.: 1944.

TODOROV, KOSTA. *Balkan Firebrand*. New York: Ziff-Davis, 1943.

ULAM, ADAM. *Titoism and the Cominform*. Cambridge: Harvard University Press, 1952.

WARRINER, DOREEN. *Revolution in Eastern Europe*. London: Turnstile Press, 1950.

WILKINSON, HENRY R. *Maps and Politics*. Liverpool: The University Press, 1952.

WOLFF, ROBERT LEE. *The Balkans in Our Time*. Cambridge: Harvard University Press, 1956. (Also New York: W. W. Norton, 1967.)

Index of Names